Essential Psychotherapy

Foundations and Practice

Wolfgang Erhardt
Tilmann Lhündrup Borghardt

Essential Psychotherapy

Foundations and Practice

Based on Buddhist Mind Training

With an introduction to Focusing by Astrid Schillings

NORBU VERLAG
(Norbu Editions)

Publication Information
Title: Essential Psychotherapy – Foundations and Practice, Based on Buddhist Mind Training
Authors: Wolfgang Erhardt, Tilmann Borghardt

Publisher: Norbu editions (Norbu Verlag in der Ekayana gGmbH)
Raitenbucher Str. 17, 79853 Lenzkirch, Germany
www.norbu-verlag.de
info@norbu-verlag.de

Edition and Copyright
First Edition: 2025
ISBN: 978-3-944885-47-6 (Paperback)
ISBN: 978-3-944885-46-9 (Hardcover)
ISBN: 978-3-944885-48-3 (eBook)

Distribution
This book is distributed internationally through Amazon and other retailers.

Credits
Translation from the German original (2016) "Buddhistische Psychologie – Grundlagen und Praxis" (Random House/Arkana Verlag): Kathrin Rehders
Proof reading: Rachel Goody (Vijayamala)
Proof reading and editing: Tilmann Borghardt
Cover design, interior layout and graphics: Friederike Schütt

Abstain from everything harmful,
Cultivate the wholesome,
And free your mind.

THE BUDDHA

Contents

Part Two – Psychotherapy based on Buddhist mind training

Preparing the Ground

Working with the inner dynamics of the Personality

Initial Overview

This book introduces you to the foundations of 'Essential Psychotherapy' (EPT) – a psychotherapeutic approach that combines the wealth of experience of the buddhist tradition with western psychotherapy. It addresses the essential concerns of being human: giving life deep meaning, freeing ourselves from limiting emotional patterns, and awakening to our own potential.

As a widely accessible introduction, this book offers many practical pointers for therapeutic work, both with oneself and with others, which also address these essential concerns. Non-professionals are given an initial understanding of buddhist mind training in addition to the proposed therapeutic interventions. The main objective is to be of concrete benefit for individuals on their paths of healing and to place work with emotional patterns in the context of a path of true awakening. Awakening here means to increasingly free ourselves from restrictive emotional and cognitive patterns and to reveal our inherent potential for awakened qualities such as love, compassion, openness, flexibility and wisdom.

This introduction is aimed at various kinds of people: those who are interested in pursuing this sort of integrative path independently, those who are looking for appropriate therapeutic help, and those who would like to offer help to others after completing their training in Essential Psychotherapy. Additionally, it addresses psychotherapists who wish to integrate their work with a path of awakening and to rely on buddhist teachings that have been tried and tested for two and a half millennia.

The approach reveals a fresh perspective on buddhist teachings without requiring any previous knowledge. In addition to subtle analyses of mental-emotional processes, there are many practical exercises for use on one's own path. Psychotherapeutic understanding refines and strengthens the path of awakening, and buddhist mind training deepens the therapeutic work.

Buddha Śākyamuni (5th century B.C.) described his teachings as a *path* (Skt. *mārga*) based on experience and exploration. He insisted that his audience should not regard his teachings as a faith, religion or philosophy, but examine them by themselves. We can also call this path a *science* of awakening or, as Jack Kornfield writes in 'The Wise Heart':

> "... a living psychology of one of the oldest and best developed systems of healing and insight in the world. This kind of psychology does not differentiate between worldly and spiritual concerns".[1]

In this spirit, this book is dedicated to our teacher, one of the greatest humanists and psychologists of the twentieth century: Gendun Rinpoche – a Tibetan mahāmudrā master, whose understanding of the mind and kindness of heart continues to nourish many of us to this day. He saw the inseparability of the worldly and the spiritual, of saṃsāra and nirvāṇa, and showed everyone the liberating path of direct insight. Thank you!

1 Jack Kornfield, "The Wise Heart", New York, 2008, page 13

Preface to the English Edition

The translation follows the German original, written during the first two cycles of the three years training in Essential Psychotherapy and published in 2016. A French translation was then made available in 2021, serving the second generation of French trainees. Throughout these years the interest from English speaking readers grew continually, our Danish group had to use rough translations into Danish and English.

We could finalize this project thanks to the combined efforts of Kathrin Rehders, who did the initial translation, Rachel Goody (Vijayamala), who with great care improved the English, Tilmann Borghardt, who compared the translation again with the original and slightly adapted some phrases to fit our present understanding, and finally, Friederike Schütt, who did the type setting and graphic design. Our deep gratitude goes to all of them.

We also wish to thank the members of Norbu Editions within the Ekayana Trust for Contemporary Buddhism, who again offered their support for this publication like for the French one.

Hennef, Germany, July 2025,

Wolfgang Erhardt and the team of EPT teachers

Introduction

Our experience in supporting clients in psychotherapy as well as in guiding practitioners who intensively follow the buddhist path shows how the interaction of buddhist mind training and psychotherapeutic understanding harmoniously nurtures one's inner development. When such integration occurs, one can certainly speak of a 'psychotherapy of awakening.' This means primarily that this form of psychotherapy

- is inspired by the path of awakening,
- fits harmoniously into it,
- and offers its psychotherapeutic methods as support for this path.

In the authors' opinion, it is not possible to realize awakening with conventional psychotherapy – which was anyhow never its intention. In order to awaken fully, daily personal training in deep awareness is needed, addressing the most subtle areas of consciousness. This can however be prepared for and initiated through psychotherapy. Buddhist mind training involves working with one's own mind including the emotions (the "psyche" in the western sense) all the way through. It leads ever deeper into wholesome states of mind with increasing stability. This wholesomeness or fundamental sanity reveals itself as the basic nature of mind, and the habitual patterns separating us from it will gradually be dissolved. Thus, buddhist mind training is basically already a psychotherapy of awakening as long as we actually apply it effectively and in all its depth, which we unfortunately often don't do because of our avoidant tendencies.

Shared concerns of buddhist teachers and psychotherapists

Psychotherapists, like buddhist[2] teachers, work for the overall good of the people who come to them. Both groups work primarily with the mind and psyche or, to put it another way: with cognitive and emotional patterns. They also share a focus on the long-term well-being of the people they are accompanying and do not normally seek short-term relief only. They wish to support all aspects of human development and help to integrate therapeutic work into an overall vision of comprehensive healing of the whole person – physically, emotionally and spiritually.

A first collaboration between psychotherapists and buddhist teachers usually happens in the context of a buddhist centre, where often enough participants seek help in psychological crises. When they first meet with buddhist mind training, many people (including therapists) think it may have the answers to *all* emotional and spiritual questions. They hope that this well tested buddhist approach with its many masters could perhaps provide all the help necessary in life – for their search for meaning, contact disorders, attachment traumas, depressive moods, anxieties, psychoses, couple conflicts, or whatever stress and turbulence they may experience in life. But on closer examination or with experience, it becomes clear that additional psychotherapeutic support is often needed.

Buddhist teachers may initially believe that they can help anyone through training in mindfulness, wisdom and compassion. This may be true in theory. But experience in accompanying people shows that many need additional therapeutic support. Often, they are not able to apply the teachings directly to their emotional challenges and restrictive patterns. They need regular, preferably weekly, competent

2 We prefer to write the words "buddha" and "buddhist" in small letters wherever possible. Only when it refers to a specific person or is used as a title "Buddha" is written in capitals.

guidance in order not to bypass the tricky points and to really focus attention where it is needed.

My own experience has taught me (Tilmann) this: During my medical studies I read a lot of psychotherapeutic literature and did several two-month clinical traineeships in psychiatry, neurology and psychosomatics, but did not complete any substantial training in this field. Later, as a monk in our buddhist monastery with some 200 inhabitants and volunteers, I was often responsible for those who exhibited psychological symptoms, managing as best I could. The other lamas (meditation instructors) asked me, as a doctor, to look after the residents and long-term guests who were going through severe mental crises. Depression, drug withdrawal, pre-psychotic confusion, personality disorders, anxiety syndromes, obsessions, psychoses – I have tried my hand at many a clinical picture, with only a little psychotherapeutic knowledge, but with heartfelt enthusiasm and with an understanding that had grown out of buddhist mind training. Sometimes there were quick, surprising improvements, sometimes lasting ones, but often I reached a point where professional help from experienced psychotherapists and psychiatrists became necessary. In the early days, our teacher Gendun Rinpoche was still alive, and he too, even though he was known for his blessing and healing powers, wanted this professional help to be sought.

Through the years I learned to increasingly appreciate the profound guidance of psychotherapists and psychiatrists. Medication was also occasionally necessary and, when carefully prescribed, turned out to be quite compatible with the path of mind training. Some volunteers, who lived in the monastery for longer periods of time, went out for weekly therapy sessions and made valuable inner progress by combining psychotherapy and buddhist mind training. This was also noticed by the psychotherapists: There seemed to be a synergy between buddhist and therapeutic methods. The consulting psychotherapists were often surprised at the rapid progress their patients were making – perhaps partly due to being immersed in a supportive community, and partly thanks to their buddhist mindset and training.

To explain this synergy, it seems that buddhist mind training adds, in some areas, an extra dimension or quality to psychotherapy. For example, it makes it easier for us to relate to the deep resources that manifest themselves in a trusting mind. It nurtures confidence in one's own intrinsically healthy mind. It furthers the continuous training of mental recollection (mindfulness), insight into spiritual principles and awareness of emotional processes – even without support from therapists. The buddhist approach expands our view of the world with its basic understanding of the inevitability of suffering and at the same time the possibility of experiencing sanity (in the sense of an all-encompassing mental health) at any time. It also fosters an attitude of taking full responsibility for one's own life and happiness and engaging in compassionate activity. At the same time, we train ourselves to look without immediately reacting and to simply be aware. Awareness makes it possible to recognize habitual patterns and emotional imprints with their almost instinctive reactions and not fall right back into their trap.

Buddhist teachings, as we have come to know them, are aimed at people who are emotionally relatively stable and can follow their path with daily personal practice. It is assumed that the individual person is able to manage the transfer from receiving general guidance in a group to practicing independently. It's not easy, though. Actually, close individual guidance would be helpful for many, even if they don't need therapy. Buddhist mind training, however, does not normally provide as close guidance as that offered by psychotherapists, with their more or less weekly therapy sessions. Moreover, buddhist teachers are not trained in psychotherapeutic practice, they are not familiar with the very effective methods used there and usually have little time for intensive individual care. In addition, they are the contact person for too many people to be able to accomplish intensive personal guidance.

For all these reasons it makes sense to have increasingly close cooperation, making use of the synergies: buddhist centres often turn to psychotherapists when someone needs additional help. Some buddhist teachers attend psychotherapeutic training and some psychotherapists practise buddhist mind training. In the meantime, it has also become common for many practitioners on the path of awakening to use additional psychotherapeutic support, since it deepens their understanding of their inner processes and offers specific ways to dissolve restrictive emotional patterns. This book will explore different aspects of these interesting and illuminating synergies.

As an aside: If you want a more detailed overview, you can jump to the connecting chapter between Part One and Part Two (chapter J). There you will find a review and summary of each chapter of the book, bringing out other striking synergies and similarities between buddhist mind training and psychotherapy.

Beginnings of Essential Psychotherapy

Students of Trungpa Rinpoche founded the Naropa Institute[3] in Boulder, Colorado, in 1978 and developed the foundations of 'Contemplative Psychotherapy'.[4] In 1987, at the first international conference on 'Buddhism and Psychotherapy' at the World Trade Centre, the Tibetan master Jamgon Kongtrul Rinpoche concluded the exchange with the following words:

> "There was much discussion at this conference about differences between Buddhism and Western psychotherapy. But these differences are artificial, and they hinder mutual recognition and appreciation. Buddhism is not a belief or custom brought about by a specific culture or environment, but a way for students (everywhere) to realize who they are and what the world of their experiences means. There cannot be

3 Today it is called "Naropa University – Training Centre for Contemplative Psychotherapy"

4 In the years after 1991, I (Tilmann) had a very strong friendship with Edward Podvoll, the long-time director of the Naropa Institute and author of the ground-breaking book on psychosis 'Recovering Sanity'. We spent three years together in retreat and cared for patients together. His knowledge and inspiration have stimulated me to explore buddhist-oriented psychotherapy.

> many different truths about what and who we really are, so it is not appropriate to classify buddhism as an eastern culture and then draw corresponding boundaries. Of course, there are differences between East and West, but these differences are based on ideas that have arisen not least because of language barriers. I think it is important that we work our way through these barriers in order to reach a proper, open appreciation of each other, which will then enable us to work together effectively."[5]

Other buddhist teachers, too, are calling for both approaches to be used, to benefit from their synergies. So, in 2002 Jigme Rinpoche asked me (Tilmann) to establish an institute for buddhist oriented psychotherapy. This seemed like an almost impossible dream, since the exchanges had only just begun. But we continued the annual four- to seven-day meetings. Then, in 2009, thanks to the courageous decision of Wolfgang Erhardt, who had been the driving force of these exchanges from the beginning, and with the support of other psychotherapists and buddhist teachers, the 'Institute for Essential Psychotherapy' (EPT Institute) was founded. It offers three-year further education courses for people without previous therapeutic qualifications, and one-and-a-half year courses for certified psychotherapists.

Initial reservations about an integrated approach

Essential Psychotherapy (EPT) integrates insights from two quite different approaches to exploring the mind. It has been developed through the collaboration of psychotherapists and meditation teachers rooted in the buddhist tradition. But this collaboration was not

5 http://www.dharmadownload.net/pages/english/Natsok/0010_Teaching_English/Teaching_English_0002.htm

a forgone conclusion to start with. We used different terminologies and had needs for differentiation and dyed-in-the-wool claims to sovereignty and we had to overcome many a rift in order to finally come to an understanding of one another. Even today there are still reservations in buddhist as well as in therapeutic circles about the interaction of psychotherapy and buddhist mind training.

Buddhist teachers are sometimes concerned by the following:

- They might be worried about a possible *infiltration with foreign beliefs* and want to see the authentic transmission of the tradition safeguarded. Their concern is that close cooperation with psychotherapists could greatly change the presentation and methods of buddhist mind training and that therapeutic thinking could influence and water down the traditional training in deep awareness.
- They are sceptical as to whether one is really following a *common path* or whether their therapeutic-psychological world view may hinder psychotherapists from actually understanding the path of awakening and getting involved with it on deeper levels. For those buddhist teachers, the path of awakening would be the overarching common framework, into which psychotherapeutic work would be integrated.
- They wonder whether psychotherapeutic and buddhist *approaches* are really compatible. For example, is therapeutic work, which uses conceptual reflection, compatible with deeper meditative mind training, which discards conceptual preoccupations?
- Possibly, the *intentions* of psychotherapy and the buddhist path are actually contrary. For example, while therapy may intend to enhance temporary happiness and ego empowerment, the buddhist path intends to enhance ultimate, non-referential happiness and wishes to dissolve the illusion of a stable self.
- *Priorities* may shift, and students may give up the path of awakening because they prefer psychotherapeutic work. This could delay their work on existential questions and more profound levels of being. An example of such profound work, which needs to be done, is preparing for death by developing awareness of impermanence

and the dependent arising of all phenomena and by realizing the inherently free nature of mind.
- Some buddhist teachers see no *need* for cooperation. They assume that buddhist teachings – as long as they are correctly understood and applied – meet all the challenges of life and do not need to be supplemented by psychotherapy.

Some psychotherapists also express reservations:
- They are concerned about people *by-passing* their emotional issues by adopting a seeming 'spiritual' attitude and appearance – but in reality, cultivating avoidance tendencies. A spiritual path used to avoid difficult issues in this way, could make effective psychotherapeutic work impossible.
- They wonder whether psychotherapists and buddhist teachers talk about the same topics and can *understand each other* in depth. Terms like repression, transference, counter-transference, ego-enhancement, basic trust, personality traits, character, trauma, neurotic patterns, to name but a few, have no directly recognizable equivalent in buddhist terminology. The aim of strengthening the ego in psychotherapy, appears to contradict the dissolving of ego-centredness as the declared goal of the buddhist path.
- Psychotherapists sometimes have the feeling that they are viewed with *scepticism* in buddhist circles, and their competence is not valued. They hear from people, some of whom are inexperienced, that their methods are counterproductive on the path of awakening, – almost as if therapeutic work was wasted time for someone on the buddhist path.

Difficulties on both sides:
- To enable the integration of a wide range of competencies it would be necessary for therapists from different schools to get involved in the exchange with buddhist teachers. However, it is by no means a matter of course that psychotherapists of different therapeutic disciplines exchange information with each other. There are still *rifts between schools* such as behaviour therapy, psychoanalysis, gestalt

therapy, Jungian depth psychology, humanistic approaches like focusing and others. The distance to which the long-standing struggle for demarcation of the individual psychotherapy training courses has led is not easy to dissolve, even (or especially) between related forms of therapy.
- The same problem can also be observed among buddhist teachers: It is quite unusual to see representatives of different schools exchanging meaningfully with each other, for example teachers of the Tibetan tradition exchanging with teachers of the Burmese, Thai or Japanese tradition. Many consider their own tradition with a certain *claim to absoluteness* to be the best and there are also personal, methodological, philosophical and historical reasons for not collaborating with another tradition. In the wake of the spreading of buddhism in Asia there were many deep divisions, which have mostly persisted for centuries.

Essential Psychotherapy has been developed by asking the above questions and gradually finding concrete answers to the concerns and difficulties expressed. Preconceived opinions have been softened, exclusive identification with one's own method has been dropped, and bridges of understanding have been built. Such bridges are easy to find as there are many parallels between the insights of buddhist mind training and western psychology and psychotherapy. The systematized descriptions of buddhist teachings (Skt. *abhidharma*), often called Buddhist Psychology, are based on the careful introspection of many generations of practitioners in different countries upon experiencing and liberating the vast variety of human states of mind – always with the question: 'How can the person find healing and freedom amidst ever-present challenges?'

It was particularly helpful during exchanges between representatives of psychotherapy and buddhist mind training to always refer to actual experience, in order to overcome conceptual differences. The point is to focus tirelessly on the essence:

From personal experience, what helps me and others to develop into a deeply integrated human being who follows a path of inner liberation, healing and awakening, which can then be of great benefit to myself and others?

How can we all – not only psychotherapists and buddhist teachers – work hand in hand and learn from each other for the benefit of those we accompany and who accompany us?

Basic Principles of Essential Psychotherapy

Essential Psychotherapy is a buddhist oriented psychotherapy. But only *essential* buddhist teachings are included; cultural and religious aspects of buddhist practice are deliberately not part of the training, in order to make the approach accessible to all. We work in a process-oriented way and support individually diverse ways of healing with means that support direct experience in the present. We use everything that helps to dissolve suffering and harmonizes with a path of awakening as methods. In addition to therapeutic work accompanied by a professional, great emphasis is placed on the personal practice of mindfulness, awareness, opening the heart, and the development of deep understanding. Wherever possible, daily exercises are carried out to familiarise us – therapists and clients alike – with healing perspectives and states of mind. Thanks to these exercises, which connect us with the wisdom and freedom inherent in us, therapeutic progress can be stabilized and used to proceed further on the path. Everyone chooses their own exercises. Some 'classics' are described in this book: Awareness practice with opening of the six senses, breath-based cultivation of awareness, breathing from the heart (exchanging self and other), the contemplation of one's own priorities, natural resting free from grasping or rejecting, and the practice of the Medicine Buddha.

In this therapeutic work, like in buddhist mind training, we adopt a transpersonal and in-depth psychological approach. This means that our therapeutic work supports a true path of liberation, which frees us from emotional, reactive patterns and leads beyond the 'persona' into authentic being, free of veils. This experience is the same for everyone in essence, and therefore it is transpersonal. For this, it is important to focus on each persons' innate qualities, rather than relating to their problems first.

This is primarily about strengthening qualities, encouraging helpful perspectives and establishing new patterns of behaviour. The analysis of dysfunctional patterns comes second, only *after* encouraging the qualities. This sort of analysis has a greater liberating impact when it can rely on the resources of a newly found confidence in one's own inherent qualities and of new possibilities in relating to situations.

The Tibetan teacher Jamgon Kongtrul stressed at the previously mentioned conference that

> "In the heart mind of awakening (bodhicitta) lies the power to work with the mind of another."

By bodhicitta he meant the motivation to work with compassion and wisdom for the good of all living beings and to uncover awakened qualities in everyone. This motivation is the driving force of the collaboration between western psychotherapy and buddhism. The following traditional prayer is often used to strengthen this attitude:

> "May all sentient beings be happy and possess the causes of happiness.
> May we all be free from suffering and its causes.
> May we never be separated from true joy that is free from suffering.
> May we dwell in all situations free from attachment and aversion in great equanimity."

The above lines express the four Immeasurable States of mind: Love, compassion, joy and equanimity. They are of central importance for buddhists but are also deeply appreciated and cultivated in the west. They lead to the altruistic motivation to help all living beings without exception to complete health – that is, to awaken to these exact same qualities of heart mind: Love, compassion and joy, paired with a deep understanding of our being. This is the heart of buddhist mind training and at the same time the heart of buddhist-oriented psychotherapy: an awareness permeated by love.

Therapists, in this context, are people in healing professions who are themselves on a path of healing and share this path with others within the scope of their personal expertise. They have directed their lives towards the development of an alert, all-inclusive, loving awareness and train their mind in many ways, especially through contemplation and meditation. They are dedicated to the development of love, compassion and wisdom. For their own path, but especially for their work as psychotherapists, they develop a basic understanding of the buddhist doctrine with the help of teachers.

Essential Psychotherapy is a buddhist-oriented psychotherapy which continues to develop and from which further expressions will certainly emerge. It touches all areas of human existence, including the different levels of personality, psychodynamics, relationships, and behaviour, as well as the fundamental level of timeless open awareness, also known as the nature of being. Central methods of buddhist mind training and healing are integrated into psychotherapeutic work. Methods that belong to the essence of buddhist teaching and are common to several traditions, are given special emphasis. This is done in the spirit of the One Vehicle or One Path (*Ekayāna*), which Buddha Śākyamuni formulated in the teaching on the four aspects of cultivating awareness (Pali: *satipaṭṭhāna-sutta*):

> "There is only *one* path to awakening – the cultivation of awareness."

The therapeutic basis of Essential Psychotherapy is to be found in the methods of psychosynthesis, focusing, the visualisation techniques of Phyllis Krystal, and behavioural therapy. In all this, an awareness of health is developed, with a view of what it is to be healthy or whole. In therapeutic terms, it is a resource-oriented approach, with Essential Psychotherapy including additional levels of experience that are more spiritual – especially the transpersonal level of awareness that activates the potential for deeper healing.

The process of healing is characterized by increasing inner freedom. Such freedom is only possible on the basis of an increasing awareness of the processes of perceiving, considering, deciding and acting. Our own process as well as our work with clients, will be much more effective, if we personally dedicate ourselves to daily mind training in study and practice, because this will enable the necessary developments in mental calm, motivation and self-knowledge. Meditation methods must be practiced patiently and regularly over a long period of time. They contribute significantly to the personal development of the therapist and have a great influence on the therapy. But their direct application to clients is limited to simple forms. A deeper application of the methods of buddhist mind training is always reserved for one's own personal path of awakening.

Essential Psychotherapy draws inspiration from buddhist teachings. In doing so, it adheres to the *essence* of its wealth of experience but keeps its distance from the *forms (cultural expressions)* of buddhist practice that have developed in its various countries of origin. In the training, reference is made to buddhist texts without having to become a buddhist oneself. It is about taking the challenging path of being connected to the liberating truths themselves, without having to set oneself apart: "Now I am *this*, not *that*. I'm a buddhist now, not a Christian anymore." To draw boundaries in this way hurts the heart, because it leads to further tension. We polarise, and distinguish ourselves from people who describe themselves differently, even though they may want the same thing and pursue the same search. The gate of the heart should always remain open.

Within the buddhist tradition there are two equally important vehicles, both of which are considered within Essential Psychotherapy. Practitioners of southern buddhism in the School of the Older Ones (*Theravāda*) strive – even though they help others in many ways – to completely step out of the cycle of existence at their death. They want the cycle of rebirths to end as soon as possible. The second school includes the practitioners of the

Great Vehicle (*Mahāyāna*), sometimes called northern buddhism, who – on the basis of an awakened understanding of the process of becoming – are prepared to accept birth again until all living beings are freed from suffering. They prepare for a repeated, freely chosen re-entry into the cycle of existence. What is important for both vehicles is that we engage compassionately with the suffering in ourselves and in others, as it manifests now, and walk the path of healing or liberation.

PART ONE

Buddhist mind training in Psychotherapy

Introduction

Emotional veils and stressful emotions

We are probably all familiar with the circling thoughts that we become aware of as soon as we rest or meditate, our 'hamster wheel.' A stimulus leads to a thought, and this triggers a chain of associations, thoughts spin on. Thoughts can arise from a feeling and can also trigger feelings. All of this usually happens automatically.

If we become aware of the thoughts, feelings and associations, we can influence the process. But how does that work – especially when it comes to thoughts and feelings that are particularly entangling? How can we deal with our own impulses and emotions better? We want them to be less of a burden on ourselves and others, and we seek greater inner freedom – especially when we encounter persistent patterns.

It seems that we need three things to clear our emotional patterns:

- To explore the emotional patterns, their triggers, deep causes, effects and true nature.
- To find and strengthen the motivation to give them up as completely as possible.
- To learn and adopt effective approaches that enhance emotional freedom and self-determination. This requires emotionally satisfying solutions for our basic tendencies.

Buddhist teachers usually approach this subject from the principal, elemental, or universal perspective. Personal experience provides the necessary 'material' for an understanding of the basic mechanisms, which are the same for everyone. Psychotherapy, on the other hand, is about understanding the specific mechanisms at play in each individual; the approach is more oriented towards the experience of the individual person. But here as well, a picture of general principles is gradually emerging that can be observed in people with similar tendencies.

Broadly, we can make a rough distinction between stressful and helpful emotions. In this book, we will focus first on the more stressful afflicting emotions, such as fear, anger, pride, jealousy and desire, to name the most important ones. Beneficial emotions that open the heart, such as joy, gratitude, compassion and the like, belong to the opposite category of healing mental forces and antidotes. They play a key role as resources that we can activate, to stop habitual patterns of stressful emotions – but these wholesome mental states are not usually what we refer to when we speak of 'emotions' in this book.

Actually, behind every stressful emotion is a healthy need, such as for peace or protection. The desire to be loved and to feel love combined with the need for intimacy, warmth, communication, and integration, are also central to our striving. We long for vitality and flow.

An urgent task in relation to persistent emotional patterns, is to identify the real needs behind our emotions and to find real answers and solutions. In fact, the needs can always be traced back to basic human themes of freedom, love and joy, we are looking for real peace, for wholeness, harmony and safety. All this can also be described as the striving for authentic being or awakening.

Behind every stressful emotion and need there is an accompanying fear – and it too wants to be seen and accepted. If we relate to these fears in an appropriate, helpful way and take care of them, they can unwind. Buddhist mind training focuses completely on dissolving stressful emotions. Awakening is defined as the liberation from *kleśa* – the Sanskrit term for stressful emotions also called unskilful states of mind. Kleśa is defined as 'affliction.' We are hindered by stressful emotions, so we are not free in how we act and express ourselves. They restrict the expression of our awakened potential. For as long as it has not been brought on to the path, an afflictive emotion reduces our happiness, freedom and ability to love. Thoroughly awakened beings have freed themselves from these limitations. A buddha (Tib. *sangs rgyas*) is defined in the Tibetan tradition as one who has purified all veils (*sangs*) and developed all qualities (*rgyas*).

There are two types of veils: emotional veils and cognitive veils. The emotional veils are states of mind based on lack of awareness, attachment and aversion. Cognitive veils are further subtle consequences of lacking awareness, which lead to a distortion of reality. All veils are *kleśa* – obstacles to fully living out our potential. To free ourselves from all delusion is the central concern of the buddhist path – together with the simultaneous unfolding of the qualities of awakening.

Veils obscure the mind, cause emotional confusion, create narrow states of mind and prevent the unfolding of our inherent qualities. This does not apply to emotions such as joy, gratitude, love, compassion and the like, which on the contrary clarify and expand the mind, reduce emotional confusion and bring out our inherent potential. They lead to awakening and cause the well-being of all living beings.

The term stressful emotion or affliction (*kleśa*) refers to the unclear, agitated, narrow states of mind that arise from dualistic attachment, the root of all emotions. It includes everything which darkens or agitates the mind and thus blocks the understanding of reality.

The term 'emotion' derives from the root meaning 'to get moving' or 'to be agitated'[6] – it is an agitating movement of our mind. In buddhism emotions are understood as mental movements, experienced as separate from an observer, creating turbulence. They are grasped at and given importance in relation to a so called 'I'. The initial mental movement, the first stimulus, is followed by evaluations, hopes and fears that prolong and churn this movement and turn it into an emotional wave. Stressful emotions are therefore mental movements that obscure awareness and create suffering.

Emotions in the *broadest* sense are all mental movements that shape our experience of the world. Buddhist teaching distinguishes between happiness-inducing mental movements and those which produces suffering. Joy, gratitude, authentic love, trust and other such 'wholesome actions of mind' do not cause blockages and suffering.

---

6 The word *emotion* for feeling, emotional movement or mental excitement comes from the French *émotion* with the verb *émouvoir* (to move, to excite) and the Latin *emovere* (to come out, to rummage up). Emotions that are expressed linguistically as exclamations, desires or commands were called *emotives* by Anton Marty (lat. *e-motus*), in English: moved out, shaken.

They are beneficial resources which promote flow, freedom from fixation, an open heart and broad mind.

It seems important to learn to distinguish what is beneficial from what is not. This is not judgemental bias, but simple observation: Unwholesome emotions cause suffering while wholesome emotions bring happiness. Different emotions vary in their effects, but they all have the same basic nature, and all have a distinct emotional function.

Emotions are only a burden if they are accompanied by increased inner tension. Emotional tension can be traced back to a mechanism at work in the depths of our being: the splitting of experience into an experiencing 'I' and an experienced 'other', in other words: subject and object. That's where the sense of an 'I' experiencing a 'thing' comes from – the subject experiences itself in relation to an object. This is what is meant by duality or dualistic fixation. It already contains a certain amount of tension, which is absent in the experience of wholeness.

This dualistic attitude quickly turns into 'I want this' or 'I don't want this', depending on whether the experience is pleasant or unpleasant. According to the buddhist view, this basic dualistic tendency, with the subsequent grasping or rejection, is the source of all stressful emotions. We are actually dealing with only one emotion: the attachment to a subject that is supposed to exist separately from the object, often abbreviated as 'ego clinging'. This underlying dualistic tendency is variously called ignorance, delusion, or better, lack of awareness. A stressful emotion arises when there is a feeling of an 'I' and the feeling of 'something else' being experienced as separate from the 'I'. A supposed centre of experience, the so-called 'subject', focuses on a supposedly separate 'object' and thus anger, pride, desire, jealousy and all the other emotions arise from lack of awareness, depending on the type of attachment and aversion.

Many people assume that emotions arise from contact with an external object. For example, because I see the cup of tea standing here in front of me, I may or may not feel like drinking tea – out of the seeing of this cup, attachment, aversion or indifference, might arise. We believe that emotions arise from situations. But even if we sit here completely calm and undisturbed, many emotions appear, although we do nothing and nothing happens around us: Anger emerges, desire emerges, pride, jealousy, and the impulses of not wanting to be aware. There is no *need* for external triggers for the emergence of an agitating emotion, although these triggers can naturally have a stimulating effect.

When meditating we notice how emotions appear even without recognizable causes and triggers. Buddhist experts explain this process through the workings of emotional patterns (Tib: *bag chags*, Skt: *vāsanā*). These patterns arise from previous actions, thoughts and emotions which have a subconscious after-effect and influence our experience. These unconscious forces, which create a predisposition to feel in similar ways, are also called karmic forces in the buddhist tradition. They are like the seeds of plants that begin to germinate and break through to the earth's surface as soon as the conditions are favourable. These karmic forces are subconsciously active in our mind, usually without us being aware of them, and colour our perception of situations. They will only be consciously perceived when we are not busy with other things and can direct our attention inwards.

Emotional reactions leave traces in our mind which encourage similar reactions in the future, and out of this a pattern will emerge over time. Such patterns have been deeply imprinted and are constantly active – some are like internal motorways or railroad tracks. This becomes particularly clear in meditation when we give space to the mind but remain present without distraction. Karmic tendencies activate themselves – with no order or inner logic being apparent at first. As soon as we create some space, unresolved karmic forces appear in the form of all kinds of thoughts, images or emotional swings, which can rise up suddenly. They reveal themselves by themselves, for example during meditation or when resting, but they are actually incessantly active at all times, colouring our perception.

You could say that an emotion is a mental movement charged with strong energy because of attachment or aversion. We are like an energy field in which emotional and many other forces have an effect. The emotional patterns and habits discernible in it are precisely what is meant by karmic tendencies. Past experiences have created tendencies and patterns in our mind stream. These generate our present associations, interpretations, images and thoughts. What we formerly felt, did, said or thought influences what we feel and think now and how we react to situations – and consequently: Who we are now, our character and personality. 'Personality' is the result of past experiences combined with developed qualities: How we think, what we are attracted to, what is repelling to us, what opinions we have, and what we remember. In short, our view of the world is an expression of karmic tendencies. Karmic view shapes the personality.

Our karmic view reflects whether we have performed many ego-related or many compassionate actions in the past. It reflects how we have felt, thought and acted in the past. The past is not limited to this life. If we were concerned with the welfare of others in the past, then we will find the traces of this in our attitude today. If, on the other hand, we were strongly self-centred, our present personality will show the traces of this self-centredness. The way we are today is a mirror of our previous ways of relating to the world. Given our emotional patterns, we can surmise our past.

This description shouldn't really surprise someone who is familiar with the deep imprints of biographically distant events. The only difference to modern psychology is the timespan under consideration, because the buddhist view also considers the continued effect of experiences from previous lives. Karmic imprinting begins long before this life and goes far beyond this life.

The process of clearing emotional veils

When we relax and just leave mental movements as they are, then one thought after another arises and gives way to the next experience. If we remain aware of this arising and vanishing and do not react emotionally, it becomes a process of karmic purification. Karmic patterns and imprints lead to mental movements, which are exhausted, if they are no longer nourished, thanks to an alert awareness. In relaxed meditation we learn not to react to thoughts and emotions, but to be aware and create inner space in which they can evaporate. With non-attachment, karma can dissolve as it arises, and the karmic tendency to produce thoughts and emotions repeatedly is weakened.

Mental movements are emotionally charged due to the intensity with which we interpret them as being pleasant or unpleasant. Thoughts, images, sensory impressions, etc. that we do not take seriously will not have the same emotional significance for us. Because we interpret them differently, they do not create emotional chain reactions. Applying this understanding, we learn in meditation to let mental movements continue to flow without judgement – even emotions are accepted without interpretation, and experience flows on. To distinguish between mental movements as desirable and undesirable is like pressing down an accelerator pedal of an emotional carousel. This 'clinging' (evaluating, holding as important) is the driving power behind all emotions.

The emotional attachment to certain mental movements leads to chains of thought in which there is increasing emotional involvement. At first there is just a thought, to which a second thought is now attached, which leads to a third – they all comment on, evaluate etc. the previous one. What was initially a single thought, becomes a chain of thoughts which in addition triggers memories, fears, desires and the like – and the whole thing becomes more and more entangled, condensed and knotted. If we look into one such tangle, jealousy for example, we discover that many mental movements (comparative, evaluative, fearful thoughts, as well as associations, memories, images) are part of this tangle.

If we can leave thoughts as they are and let go – even if we are already in the middle of the full entanglement – then a free space develops, the chain breaks. We don't get involved in reaction, we don't identify, but remain conscious and make conscious decisions, such as: 'I want to draw a line' or 'I want to act compassionately and be generous.' There is a freedom of choice.

Our conscious decisions are more appropriate to the situation than emotional reactions, which are an expression of ego clinging. With emotional reactions, we have little freedom of choice. When we remain aware without clinging, we have room for manoeuvre and can use it freely. Those who fixate have no room for manoeuvre – like a monkey that can be caught, if it does not let go of the banana behind the bars. If we are yelled at, we react in either an intimidated or aggressive manner, depending on our character. Emotional reactions are easily predictable! In order to free oneself from predictable reactions and to effect conscious, free action, one needs sustained practice in non-identified flowing with everything that arises.

We have several options here: First, we can stop harmful acts and thus create less entangling turmoil. We can also notice the initial emotional impulse, accept it and let it go. If we are already caught up in emotional confusion, we can resort to methods that calm the mind and apply antidotes. We can also look into the nature of thoughts. If none of this is possible, we could at least draw a line and say, 'So far, but no further.' There are many ways of interrupting emotional chain reactions. Compassion is one of the best, because it leads straight out of the ego centredness.

To most people it seems perfectly normal to be self-centred. In the past, we would have had no problem with the split between 'me' and 'not me.' We would have thought the observer, who checks and judges everything, was reasonable. What is the problem? Well, the problem is that our continuous dualistic separating out of experience, without us noticing it, is the source of constant tension in our mind, the breeding ground of all stressful emotions.

This basic tension is always the same: I and my thoughts, I and what I can have or what I cannot have; I, who cannot stop naming and evaluating. We call this state of tension, even where it seems completely normal and perhaps even pleasant, *saṃsāra*, the cycle of suffering. Saṃsāra describes this dualistic way of experiencing and *nirvāṇa* describes a nondual experience free of this ego-centredness, free of this subtle tension. Nirvāṇa is the dimension of simple being in complete openness, without artificial separation between I and my experience. Contrary to that, tension and clinging undermine joy and happiness. For example, as soon as I am happy, the fear creeps in that it will soon be over, or that something is coming that will destroy my happiness – and with that, it is already gone.

Now how do we find our way out of being full of clinging into being happy, free, full of openness and love? Admittedly, this is the work of a lifetime, or perhaps more than one. We have probably already started this work, and it is now a matter of understanding emotions better and using our mind with greater skill, so that every situation becomes a means of awakening.

The basic emotions

From a buddhist perspective, there is one single basic emotion from which all others arise: the impulse to not want to be aware, i.e. to look away, avoiding having to feel. This is also called 'ignorance' or 'lack of awareness' – not being aware of the true nature of the experience. It includes superficial, unstable perception – a basic characteristic of ego-centredness, and ignorance of the free, nondual nature of mind.

We can also speak of two other basic emotions: Attachment and aversion or in other words, wanting to have and not wanting to have. This is the case with any emotion. One holds on to something and rejects something else.

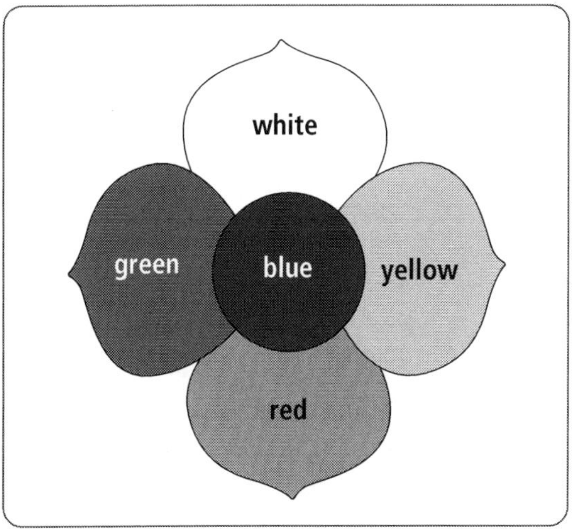

So, all together, we can speak of three basic emotions: not wanting to be aware, attachment and aversion. The *Abhidharma*, the structured summary of buddhist teachings, also names these three – ignorance, desire and anger – followed by pride (identification), neurotic doubts and views. Holding on to any point of view, emotional or not, obstructs direct perception and insight. According to the Buddha, these six basic non-beneficial states of mind prevent awakening or recognizing truth.

However, we will use a representation of five basic emotions as found in tantric buddhism, the *Vajrayāna*. Lack of awareness is in the centre (blue) and the consequences of this lack of awareness – anger, pride, desire and jealousy, white, yellow, red and green – are arranged in a circle around it.[7] They form a *maṇḍala* or energy field of emotional obscuration.

Realizing the nature of mind frees us from lack of awareness. As a consequence, these emotions reveal themselves as an awakened maṇḍala of the five aspects of timeless awareness, pure awareness, which is the true nature of all emotions. What currently forms a maṇḍala of ego-clinging or saṃsāra will manifest as a maṇḍala of awakened awareness: awareness of the space of all phenomena (instead of ignorance) in the centre surrounded by its four main aspects: mirror-like awareness (instead of anger), awareness of the equality of all phenomena (instead of pride), all-distinguishing awareness (instead of desire) and all-perfecting awareness (instead of jealousy).

We will deal with these five basic emotions and also take a closer look at fear and guilt. Fear is not an emotion in its own right, in the Abhidharma, but it is connected with every other emotion and is virtually omnipresent, just like the lack of awareness of which it is the emotional expression.

Just as lack of awareness is seen as the source of all emotions, full awareness, which is also called timeless, nondual awareness, is de-

7 Neurotic doubts and views belong to the lack of awareness. Jealousy is added as an additional basic emotion in this system; it originally belonged to the secondary afflictive emotions according to the Buddha.

scribed as encompassing all forms of awakened awareness. There is only one awakened awareness which, like a diamond, has many facets. When one aspect of timeless awareness is realized, all are realized. And just as there is no awakened awareness without its various facets, so there is no emotion without the subtle presence of the others. Where there is a lack of awareness (ignorance) all others can be found and this applies equally to pride, anger and so on. At the same time, once we have completely dissolved one emotion, all the others are also purified. We cannot dissolve one emotion in all its profundity without necessarily working with all the others as well. The emotion which we work with at any given time is always the one that's here right now; we always work in the present.

Three layers of emotional experience

Two millennia ago, buddhist masters described three levels of emotional experience. Of those, we are usually only aware of the first two:

A. The currently active *disturbing emotion* (Skt. *kleśa*, literally 'affliction'): an obstructive, narrowing state of mind through which our qualities no longer flow freely; also called emotional veils (Skt. *kleśa-avaraṇa*) because they obscure mental clarity.

B. *Habitual patterns* (Skt. *vāsanā*): the latent tendency to react emotionally, in a particular way, over and over again, as well as the cognitive patterns which form a veil and impair clear awareness (Skt. *jñeya-avaraṇa*).

C. *Basic drives* (Skt. *āsrava*), undercurrents: unconscious driving forces constantly influencing us with the wish (1) to confirm our own existence (wanting to exist) or (2) denying it (not wanting to exist) as well as (3) the all-pervading desire to feel sensory experiences and (4) the wish not to be aware, the fundamental tendency to avoid the full clarity of understanding.

These three layers can be briefly explained using the example of a depressive crisis:

(A) The experiences of feeling almost dead, completely dull, or inwardly agitated and anxious correspond to the level of the immediately disturbing emotion.

(B) The tendency to experience oneself as unloved, useless, weak, incapable, overwhelmed, etc., and to interpret external experiences in the light of this, corresponds to the activity of habitual patterns.

(C) The existential themes that become apparent – not wanting to live anymore, longing for pleasant experiences, wanting to be someone, not wanting to feel anymore, etc. – show the usually unconscious basic drives of affirming or avoiding existence, clinging to sensory impressions and avoiding clear understanding.

Awareness practice in working with emotions

Accordingly, the practice of awareness is about detecting these three layers of emotional experience and allowing the vital energy blocked in them to flow again. For this, we
- perceive the current afflictive emotion (tension),
- explore the underlying habitual patterns,
- detect the existential dimension of the experience,

and thereby accept, understand and imbue with awareness all aspects of experience until we are back into the flow. All three aspects of working with emotions are practiced with a loving attitude. There is only one practice: loving awareness!

This includes the other three aspects of mind training:
- Mindfulness, a practice of undistracted presence and calm mind,
- Awareness, to gain insight into the nature of experience and to understand the laws in operation, and
- Love and compassion, to be filled with an accepting, resonant and supportive state of mind in everything.

A. Five steps of Working with Stressful Emotions

A particularly helpful model to illustrate typical buddhist methodology with emotions is the five-step model of the Tibetan master Karma Chakme (18th century) Chakme named his text "The Great Peacock"[8] because of the legendary ability of the peacock to transform even poison into food – hence to turn stressful emotions into awakened awareness. He is answering the question of a meditator: 'How can I work with stressful emotions, to bring them on the path of awakening and to free myself from emotional patterns?'

The answer according to buddhist mind training, as summarized by Chakme is immediately apparent: We can (1) use our awareness by pausing and stopping the emotional reaction. Then we (2) can work with helpful means (remedies) on the emotionally stressful experience. This is further supported (3) by transforming our view of the emotion and (4) by realizing the true nature of emotion. If this is successful, we can (5) use emotional challenges as a path of awakening.

Gendun Rinpoche, a Tibetan master under whose guidance I (Tilmann) meditated in France, taught Karma Chakme's text in public teachings to give an overview of this inner path. The step-by-step approach starts with basic exercises and gradually introduces us to more demanding practices. The five steps in dealing with stressful emotions are:

---

8 See Gendun Rinpoche "The Great Peacock – The Transformation of Emotions in Tibetan Buddhism". A Tibetan lama wrote to the author Karma Chakme Rinpoche that he was not yet able to bring the mental poisons on the path. Chakme answered with the "Great Peacock". However, he only touched upon the first steps briefly and only became more detailed from step three onwards. Knowledge of the first steps, especially the Lodjong mind training, was required. Explanations can be found in the Lodjong anthology "The Great Path of Awakening".

1. Pause mindful in the emotion.
2. Apply suitable remedies to the emotion.
3. Develop a different view of the emotion.
4. Recognize the true nature of the emotion.
5. Use stressful emotions as a path.

In psychotherapeutic work we mainly practice the first three steps: (1) pause, examine, and do not act out; (2) apply remedies that open the heart and mind; and (3) expand your perception, view and understanding of the emotional triggers.

For example, in a situation that causes strong aggressive impulses to arise: (1) I pause, do not to act out, but stay with the breath, and feel what actually makes me angry. (2) A further step could be to practice the compassionate heart-breath (*tonglen*) with the angry part of myself and thereby (3) arrive at a new view of the situation. In this way I might realize how much my own imprints (from childhood, etc.) contribute to an excess of anger and I may also see what a wonderful situation this is for practicing self-compassion and other qualities that are important to me in life.

It is also possible to (4) bring our understanding of the true nature of emotions into our work with clients and encourage them to look at the ungraspable nature of all mental movements and trust that all mental states will dissolve themselves. (5) The fifth step would involve consciously stimulating stressful emotions in order to see through them freshly each time. But to do this, the realization of the true nature of the emotions must be deeply rooted in us, and usually our daily dose of emotions without any extra stimulation is enough.

The origins in the teachings of the Buddha

The aforementioned five steps which summarize the path of buddhist mind training in working with emotions probably have their origin in corresponding statements of the Buddha (5th century BC). In a central teaching on the essence of mind training, the *Sabbasava Sutta*, the Buddha describes how emotional influences can be overcome in seven ways:

(1) *Realizing* the nature of emotions, thus dissolving them, which corresponds to Chakme's step four "recognizing the nature of the emotion".
(2) *Applying restraint* externally and internally, which corresponds to Chakme's step one "pausing mindfully".
(3) *Dealing properly* with the things of this world,
(4) *Patiently enduring* difficulties,
(5) *avoiding* dangerous situations and
(6) *dispelling* emotions by applying remedies, – (3) to (6) are aspects of Chakme's step two "applying remedies".
(7) *Unfolding* mindfulness, exploring reality, energy, joy, calm, concentration and equanimity which corresponds to Chakme's steps two and three, the unfolding of resources through 'applying remedies' and 'changing the attitude or view'.

Chakme's step five "taking emotions as a path" is not found in the Buddha's account.[9] It probably originates from practicing with emotions in a tantric context and from a Tibetan perspective; it represents the natural consequence of the insight developed in step four.

---

9 Original text, Majjhima Nikaya 2:4-21: "For the knowing and the seeing, I say, there is a drying up of all basic drives [Skt: āsrava, Pali: āsava, Tib: zag-pa], but not for the ignorant and those who do not see. Which knowledge and seeing leads to the drying up or increase of the basic drives? Wise attention and unwise attention. Through unwise attention, new currents come up and those that have already come up increase. Through wise attention no new currents arise and those that have already arisen are overcome. Monks, there are basic drives that can be overcome by *realization*. There are basic drives that can be overcome by *restraint*. There are basic drives that can be overcome by proper *handling*. There are basic drives that can be overcome by *patient endurance*. There are basic drives that can be overcome by *avoidance*. There are basic drives that can be overcome by *expulsion*. There are basic drives to be crossed by *unfolding*."

Step 1: Pause

The first step is to pause and to control the emotion in question, since any further reaction would inevitably lead to more suffering. This pausing can be subtle – a barely noticeable shift of our attention – or it can be an energetic, quite visible slowing down of a violent emotional reaction, which requires all our willpower.

Pausing means not being carried away when an emotional reaction starts up, e.g., not perpetuating an emotional reaction that is already active. The important point here is not to allow oneself or others to be harmed. We can do this, for example, by exhaling consciously three times, keeping silent for a short time, bringing mindfulness into the body, or using other methods that allow us to gain some time and distance to weigh up any further response. This includes a measured withdrawal from the situation. What we try to do is to get a foot in the door before the patterns take us any further.

For example, I am about to yell at someone, but at that very moment I say to myself: "Wait, stop! Don't go any further. It will only lead to suffering!" Or if I'm tempted to slip into addictive behaviour, to say, "Stop! It'll bring chaos and suffering!"

It is a matter of pausing and of vigorously countering the excesses of emotions by taming them (i.e. ourselves) with willpower: "No, that's enough, I won't do this. I will not hurt anybody (lie, cheat, drug myself, etc.)" For this we need a clearly established framework of action, which we adhere to with all our strength and always respect – to the best of our ability – to avoid suffering. We decide not to hit anyone, keep our promises, etc. We set ourselves self-imposed limits in our work with emotions, so that we have nothing to regret. Within this framework of not wanting to harm anyone all further work with the emotions can take place.

The boundaries are drawn differently by different people; everyone has to define these boundaries for themselves. In dharma, we avoid the following ten unwholesome actions. (1–3) As far as physical behaviour is concerned, killing, stealing and being unfaithful are listed – these are a 'no-go'. (4–7) As a basis for wholesome communication we give up hurtful speech, as well as lies, meaningless gossip and defamation. They are of no use and create suffering. (8 – 10) In relation to thinking, the point is to pause and not to pursue emotionally driven thoughts of greed, malice and clinging to unwholesome beliefs. Giving into them would only mean further entanglement. Instead, we look into the respective impulses and try to understand them more deeply.

The rule is always to pause as soon as we become aware of such an impulse. If we are in the process of slandering someone, we can say to ourselves: "Stop, it stirs up emotions, brings problems and destroys trust. Find a better way to express yourself!" We limit harmful, thoughtless talk. So, the first step is not to indulge in the unbridled acting out of emotions. Remember: We do not give up the emotions themselves, but the non-beneficial actions that arise from them.

A helpful preliminary exercise is to practice the necessary basic mindfulness in short sequences that last from one to a maximum of five minutes. In this way we practice (as described on the next page) the touch-and-go principle: Briefly perceive the present experience (touch) and immediately turn to the next experience (go). Becoming aware – accepting – letting things flow. We stay with an experience only as long as it takes to perceive and accept it.

From a psychological point of view, this first step of pausing is the start of a healthy strengthening of self-awareness. Conscious pausing stabilizes the observer, leads to an initial disidentification with the emotion, strengthens our self-direction, the so-called 'inner pilot' and helps us to feel what our real concern is in each situation. Using free self-determination, we pause and create distance from the usual automatic responses. In doing this, we stop unhealthy reactive patterns, prevent suffering, find our way into a different inner space, and are no longer the plaything of emotions. A pause is not enough to resolve the underlying emotional patterns but gives us a time-out for reflection. It serves as a basis for further exploration, for the application of methods and for a change of attitude, as described in steps two and three, where a large part of the therapeutic work takes place.

Guided meditation: Making a pause (exercise A.1)

Also suitable as an attunement for a therapy session.

The setup is quite simple: The exercise can be performed in any posture – sitting, standing, lying down, even with slight movement. The sentences are formulated as they would be spoken by a therapist or meditation teacher. We can also record them as audios and practice with them. It can be practiced by anyone. It is about becoming aware on all levels of our being, the 'opening of the six senses.' This sort of short warm-up exercise can be offered at the beginning of a therapy session, or it can be used to relax during a break, or for a period of regeneration, between two sessions with clients. Pausing after each line:

> Whatever is going on right now, give it your full attention.
> What are you experiencing right now?
> You don't need to do anything. Leave everything as it is...
> Feeling all the sensations of the body, what is it like to be in this body?
> Hearing the variety of sounds, how is that?
> Look. Look, what can you see? How is it to see?
> What can you taste?
> Smell?
> What's on your mind?
> How do you feel?
> Notice the mental movements.
> Be aware of thinking, emotional movements, images, sounds, ideas, and so on –
> without getting involved with them.
> What moods can you notice right now?
> Look at how everything is changing!
> Can you see the small changes in your experience?
> Notice the change, the stream of experience.
> Relax into it; into open, non-grasping being, fully conscious.
> After a while, focus your attention on what will come next.

Letting go of what has gone, allow yourself to move on to the next experience.
Awareness. Free from attachment…

The structure of the meditation is as follows: First we intensify our awareness of the sensations in the body, then we include hearing, seeing, smelling and tasting. Then, we expand our attention and add mental movements – thoughts, feelings, images, etc. – and finally we direct them to the mental/emotional mood that can be perceived in the background. All the time practicing the same thing: *notice – accept – let be.* This is the basic attitude of meditation: a non-interfering, loving, accepting awareness that leads to a deeper understanding.

It becomes clear that our experience is not solid and has no substance; it is in constant flux, a continuous stream. This natural flow of experience is temporarily blocked by fixed ideas or overly tense concentration. One way to flow more freely again is to perceive the many small signs of change, the subtle nuances of experience that let us experience how alive we are.

With this we realize what we were previously caught up in and can return to a state of flux – our perceptiveness grows; it now once again encompasses all areas of our being. This experience of renewed flow brings into perspective what we have been preoccupied with. It helps us leave the previous experiences behind and unhook completely from them. Preoccupied with our previous concerns, we may have forgotten to notice the body, left out our surroundings and focused only on this one aspect of our life. This little meditation helps us to come back. We pause, feel, sense – and become the flow again. Awake awareness. It can be very refreshing. With relaxed practice, we soon gain access to an inner freshness. This freshness becomes all the more apparent the more consistently we orientate ourselves in meditation towards the immediate sensual experiences of being alive, such as the sensations of breathing or hearing sounds in the room, without commenting on them and without straying into conceptual thinking.

At the end of this short meditation focusing on pausing, we turn to whatever situation is about to happen, perhaps the therapy session.

We refresh our motivation and become aware of essential issues, such as the ones we are about to address.

Being able to hold an emotion

Step one – pause – does not always include a meditation such as the one described above. But it always concerned with looking inside. When a strong mental movement arises, we do not deny it, but pause, notice it mindfully, accept it, and dwell in the experience without acting out the emotion. Psychotherapists call this the ability to 'hold an emotion.' This requires a certain courage to remain with a mostly unpleasant experience without expressing it outwardly and without acting on it. From a dharmic point of view, the primary concern is not to be carried away by the emotion or its effect. This is the case with the stronger manifestations of attachment and aversion, such as greed, anger, jealousy, fury, pride, fear and their various combinations. These obscure our mind, the clarity of our perception, and cloud our judgement. If we don't stop there and ensure more clarity, we will probably say or do things and make decisions that we may regret when our mind is clear again.

Just think of a strong emotion like anger: Before I let myself be carried away, before I scream, insult, strike out, or curse inwardly or outwardly, it is necessary to say "Stop!" and to pause. We must interrupt the process, which will inevitably lead to even more suffering. We want to somehow find a more relaxed perspective and reclaim the lost 'space'.

For example, it may be difficult to pause in the middle of an encounter with our partner. But when we get carried away by an outburst of anger, we say things that hurt the other person for which we immediately feel sorry. The angry words have a destructive effect, and we have to sort out even more problems afterwards, than were originally there. There are helpful ways of expressing anger that are not destructive, but they require a high degree of presence and practice.[10]

Usually, anger leads to destructive thinking and behaviour and narrow states of mind. This is true for all afflictive emotions, and we will take anger, greed, pride, jealousy and fear, and deal with them as specific examples. All such afflictive emotions lead to a closing down of the heart and a narrowing of the mind. If we simply let them out unchecked, we often end up 'infecting' others with them or causing strong emotional reactions in others. They will be drawn along into the emotional confusion. If others react prudently, the damage will be limited, but emotions can be quite contagious generally.

If our opposite number can deal well with emotionality, we can project more of our emotions on them. This is the situation with the therapist, where we are sometimes encouraged to express emotions externally. In personal practice, it is crucial to become fully aware of them and to explore them inwardly. If we suppress them, that could potentially be self-destructive; if we give them external expression, unthinkingly, they could be destructive to others and to our relationships. It is all about a skilful handling of emotions.

To give a concrete example from my life that illustrates 'pausing': I began meditating at the age of eighteen, and my greatest challenge during these years was meeting my father. Almost every time we dined together, we started to argue. I tried to use my mindfulness training, and I said to myself: "If he annoys you again, remember to take three deep breaths. Pause and find sufficient inner distance before you answer. Make a reasonably clear decision about how you want to respond, using your capacity and don't react automatically." It was about finding the inner space. It took about two years, with many attempts and blunders, before I could control myself reasonably reliably, and determine my own responses. This pausing and reorientation made it possible for us to come into a harmonious relationship in later years: a great gift.

A classic way of stabilizing is to direct mindfulness to the sensations of breathing or to other bodily sensations. This brings us into

10 More detailed explanations on the topic of anger can be found in chapter B.2.

contact with physical experience and away from the contents of the conversation, which triggers our emotions. At the time, I found it difficult to put this into practice in the actual situation. Therapists and dharma teachers can play a supporting role in such cases by practicing helpful pausing with us and accompanying our process. It is possible to pause here and there in therapeutic exchange and to feel the breath, or body when more intense feelings arise – clients as well as therapists. This creates a wholesome template for similar situations in everyday life. It is not subtle psychology, but a necessary first step in self-regulation and tension reduction.

Before we can practice this first step, however, we need to be aware of when and why we want to pause. In some areas of life, we are at an even earlier stage than step one, at *Step Zero*, because we have not yet noticed that we are in an automatic reaction pattern. Many things are still unconscious and repressed. Not only anger and rage, but also fear, pride and competitive impulses – actually the entire range of, as yet, unconscious emotions with their patterns. These need to be brought into the light of consciousness, they need space in the therapeutic process and – to a certain extent – need to be lived out and expressed. An example would be an inhibition on feeling aggression, which leads to depression due to repressed anger. This would not be the time to pause, but to actually feel and allow anger in many small steps of becoming aware. The emotion needs to become conscious, otherwise it can lead to physical illness or spill out in other areas.

In buddhist mind training, it is usually assumed that the necessary awareness of one's own emotions comes from daily mindfulness practice. However, this is by no means always the case, as many have not yet developed the ability to pay attention and allow feelings to arise without acting out or repressing them. That is why a little 'tutoring' from friends, teachers or therapists makes sense and is often necessary – because it is not yet possible on one's own. Mindfulness training usually needs repeated instruction until our inner pilot knows how to find its own way and how to keep on course even when distracted. External supporters encourage us to feel what emotional issues are emerging on the edge of consciousness. They help us to feel, name and express them – just as they are. It is precisely this that is the common task of meditation teachers and psychotherapists, and where strong cooperation becomes effective. Inner observation and exploration are guided from the outside, they are stabilized, and we are 'taken by the hand' until our inner ability has matured.

Strengthening the healthy self (Ego) while dissolving self-centredness

Through pausing, the work of strengthening the ego begins, it is then continued in the following four steps. In this way, a healthy self (ego) is strengthened, gains increasing inner freedom, and correspondingly, neurotic ego-centredness decreases. Here I am addressing a supposed paradox. What is described in buddhist terms as the 'dissolving of ego-centredness' corresponds in psychological terminology to the healthy process of ego-strengthening. This can also be described as 'rediscovering the inner freedom', i.e., experiencing the stability of not being trapped in reactive patterns of behaviour. To find this stability is part of the path of liberation.

For buddhists, the term 'I' or 'self' (Skt. *atman*) stands for the mistaken assumption of having a stable, individual essential core. Finding a way out of this fixating erroneous assumption into a flowing awareness, aware of the process nature of all existence, is the way to awaken. In contrast, in psychology, 'I' or 'self' stands for something healthy, for a dynamically integrative function of our mind. A strong 'I' is up to the challenges of life, while a weak 'I' is trapped in reactive patterns – a plaything of external influences and inner habitual patterns.[11]

Ego-strengthening or strengthening of the observer means perceiving what is going on and consciously deciding to follow an impulse or not. It can be quite helpful to demonstrate and live out a stressful emotion – especially if we have suppressed it before. But if

11 More detailed explanations can be found in chapter G.

this is the case, it happens consciously and in a sort of 'controlled' way, i.e., we avoid harming others or ourselves with it. So, we might hit a sandbag, go into the woods to scream, or cry ourselves out, with sobs expressing emotions that we have previously held back. This is a healthy intermediate step to get back into flow. 'Pausing' allows us to find such skilful ways of expressing our emotions.

A further step, after the conscious living out of a previously suppressed emotion, is to then 'hold' the emotion, as mentioned previously: experiencing and exploring it without acting it out. What does a response of fear feel like, for example? It takes courage to pause and explore it. Many people are so afraid of certain feelings that they need an encouraging helpmate to support them to allow and feel this experience. All these are steps in strengthening a healthy ego that can withstand emotions.

The so-called ego-strength continues to increase until level four and five. Here, the illusion of having a stable core of being is further dissolved – the realization of non-self arises, which gives an extraordinary inner flexibility and includes the ability to respond appropriately to situations. The qualities of awakening are beginning to manifest. We could say that a buddha has the most stable 'I' of all. Completely awakened people are free from reactive patterns and can use all their capacities without blockages because they are no longer attached to a supposed 'I' and are no longer identified with the traces of their lives.

This sounds like a paradox: The most stable I from a psychological point of view is created by not identifying with an I. But it is not really a paradox, because psychologists don't actually mean a concretely existing 'I', but rather certain capacities that together form what we call 'I'. This is dealt with in a separate chapter on 'I and non-self'.

A pause is the beginning of ego-strengthening. We learn to create a healing distance to our own reactive patterns. Distance is something beneficial here. To not react in the habitual ways, such as wanting to be right, reacting with feelings of guilt, fending off unpleasant feelings through aggression, asserting ourselves by belittling the other person, etc. – we have to create a certain distance and not be so identified with our feelings, that a reaction seems necessary. We find that we can survive without playing out the usual habit patterns; we discover new inner spaces of autonomy.

When emotional buttons are pressed and the corresponding identification arises, we react like robots, completely predictable and unfree. We march straight into suffering. So, when we speak of distance here, it is as if a space is created behind the triggering button. The trigger no longer starts off an automatic reaction; the provocation goes nowhere. The usual predictable and manipulable reaction no longer occurs. We discover new freedom.

These are first steps in developing equanimity – comparable to the efforts of an addict not reaching for the bottle, syringe, or cigarette. Here, equanimity is to be understood in its first level of meaning: Our inner mental state becomes independent of external circumstances – neither overconfident nor downcast – not susceptible to external triggers in a reactive way and this with a full, alert awareness! It takes a great inner determination to practice this mindful pause. With strong habitual patterns, pausing is an internal ordeal, which can only be achieved with the utmost determination. However, if the awareness no longer dwells on the trigger, but on the emotional experience itself, then there is usually a reduction in tension after a short while, because the basic emotional impulses finally receive attention. The shadow becomes conscious, and a new space opens up. We can reflect and will have more opportunities for self-determination, i.e., the possibility of making our own decisions and choices. We get a piece of our life back in our own hands.

Step 2: Applying helpful methods

After pausing, we stimulate qualities (resources) in ourselves, which have a beneficial and balancing effect, this is the second stage. So, I might feel angry but would like to face the situation with compassion. Accordingly, I direct the mind to a compassionate understanding of myself and others, which not only helps me out of the anger, but also strengthens my resources. This mitigates the wave of emotion or even dissolves it. I find harmony again. A 'helpful method' moves us away from the emotional blockage back into a flowing experience. It can also be called an antidote or remedy. The second stage involves applying a method that helps to weaken or dissolve the current emotion as well as the underlying habit pattern behind it, at the same time as stimulating the inner qualities.

For example, if I am caught in desire, I can contemplate the transience of the desired object (a classic buddhist method) and draw my attention to the fact that the desired object (or the desired person) cannot be a lasting source of joy because it is ephemeral. As a result, this moderates my desire; I realize that no lasting happiness can be found there, and I become a little more composed. Such contemplation is helpful when there is an unconscious belief in the possibility of finding deep, lasting satisfaction through attaining what we desire. This contemplation of impermanence is often underestimated; it leaves space to pay attention to more reliable sources of joy and happiness.

The first step (the pause) puts into practice the decision not to let oneself be carried away by emotions, out of concern for the welfare of others and oneself. The second step uses that freedom to further reduce the emotional tension through skilful means.

To take another example: I am annoyed because the children's game is interfering 'yet again' with my well-earned nap. But instead of grumbling, I take a deep breath and pause. (Step one: pause). I remember how good it would be to share in their joy and zest for life. That's exactly what I'm going to do: I can empathize with their joy. (Step two: applying wholesome methods). The 'method' I have chosen, realizes my wish, to open myself up to joy wherever possible. Even if I actually want to sleep.

It could also be my wish to want to understand others. In that case, I would briefly think about how difficult it is for children to play quietly – and how hard it was for me when my father punished me when he felt disturbed. The remedy here is to empathize with others, a wonderful way to put one's own reactions into perspective. I imagine walking a few miles in another's shoes. Maybe then I can understand them a bit better.

I could also bring myself to my senses by telling myself that every additional second of anger, further undermines my chances of getting any sleep at all... By the way, many remedies for emotional reactions are actually methods that promote a different attitude and perspective – which is practiced more intensively in step three. There is no sharp division between the steps.

Depending on the emotion, we can use various contemplations, some of which have specific effects on particular manifestations of emotions. We can also practice 'taking and giving' (*tonglen*) as explained later, with the exchange of oneself and others, also called 'heart breathing', whenever we cannot think of anything specific to do. This method is a kind of universal remedy and almost always helpful. Another universal remedy is to simply be aware – everything else then follows naturally.

Antidotes work because our mind cannot fully experience two different types of experience at the same time. Where there is compassion, there can be no anger. A joyful mind cannot be envious at the same time. In generosity there is no greed. Hate cannot exist simultaneously to love. As emotional opposites, they exclude each other at that precise moment when they are experienced – they may follow each other, even relatively closely, but they are never absolutely simultaneously present.

We often experience 'mixed emotions', where there are other feelings underneath a dominant emotion, for example the dominant feeling of hatred combined with underlying fear and hurt self-esteem – and underneath this again, the need for love can be experienced. We notice all this when we let thoughts and images appear that are connected to the initial emotion – an important approach in meditation as well as in psychotherapy. Here we clearly experience how some states of mind can accompany each other, while others are mutually exclusive.

But we must look carefully, otherwise we might think, to give an example, that hate and love could be felt at the same time. One even speaks of love-hate relationships. But in the moments of hate there is no love to be found, only *disappointed* love, *turning away* from love despite all the longing for it. Where there is pride there is no sense of equality in relation to others, only a feeling of superiority or inferiority, even though there may be a feeling of equality in a group of proud people, because their pride is in relation to others outside the group. Where there is jealousy, there can be no feeling of real contentment. Fear knows no confidence and inner peace. Such opposites of their respective stressful emotions are potent antidotes if we stabilize the mind in them.

When using these methods, there is the danger of not really accepting our emotions because they are uncomfortable, and we want to get rid of them as quickly as possible. For example, when we are angry, we are tempted to reach for compassion, or forgiveness, too quickly. We are not really able to cultivate them, because basically we just want to get rid of the anger and do not take the time to look at where it actually originates from, and what healthy function it might have. Anger must not be judged negatively. This judgement often indicates that we are afraid to feel and afraid to empathize. Actually, we are afraid we wouldn't be able to bear feeling it all. So, we have to be careful not to use antidotes to repress our emotions!

To start with, we accept ourselves and our anger and try to understand it. And only then do we engage in empathic understanding of another – and we let this mature and take effect slowly, until it becomes fully apparent. In the same way, it is unhealthy to forgive too quickly, when we feel anger towards someone who has wronged us. Or, with jealousy, we take care not to force ourselves to adopt the attitude of sharing others joy and approving of their behaviour. The application of helpful methods must not become contrived; it is an organic process of activating and applying our resources in accordance with our heart's deepest wishes. This should be underlined three times!

Pausing and Finding Remedies (exercise A.2)

Steps one (pause), two (find a remedy) and three (change perspective) can be done in pairs or in a group, as a playful exercise with a partner. It is a little similar to a therapy session and develops skills of listening, empathizing, understanding the different steps of pausing, and the role of motivation. If you do this exercise alone, you can alternate rolls.

Pairs are formed to deal with an emotion together. The partners sit opposite each other. If we form five such couples, they can even spread themselves around the room as in the fivefold mandala, described later: lack of awareness in the centre, anger in front, pride on the right, desire at the back, jealousy on the left. Each couple devotes themselves to one of these five basic emotions.

Step One: Pause

One person takes on the task of recounting a typical situation where their chosen emotion has carried or could carry them away. The other listens from the heart and asks questions, until they have fully understood the situation.

In the second phase, an attentive dialogue ensues, with both people developing strategies together about how it could be possible, in the emotional situation described, to pause before habitual tendencies carry you away. They pay particular attention to what would motivate them to actually pause. Then they swap roles, and the other person shares a typical situation for them, using the same emotion. Two times ten minutes.

Step Two: Find a remedy

The roll play can be continued in a further exercise the same, or in different pairings. The partners reflect on the question: "What remedies would work for me in this situation?" Again, the partners listen attentively, ask questions, help each other to think it through and compare their experiences.

Step Three: Changing the view of the emotion

The third step, which will be explained in the following section, can also be practiced in the same way. The question would then be: "What view of the emotional challenge would help me deal better with the situation described?"

Example: Someone accuses me angrily. I am hurt, and anger arises. But I pause, just before the outburst. I take a deep breath and create space. This space allows something new: an unusual way of reacting that is not common for me. I don‘t fall into semi-automatic defensiveness, and I don't start a counter-attack, but perhaps say: "What do you actually mean by that?" Or "Did I hurt you?" The other person takes the opportunity to tell me what's bothering them and perhaps how I hurt them. I take care to clear the inner space and listen with the heart. The other person's message reaches me. I am affected and feel why and how I have hurt the person. Maybe I can express my regret. This in turn reaches and touches the other person...

How is this possible? While pausing, we remember that we actually want to understand what annoys others about us, and that it helps to ask before reacting. Pausing opens the space in which we can remember our real motivations. This recollection leads to the choice of an appropriate method, or state of mind, which can activate inner qualities – as in the above example: patience, courage and empathetic questioning. The remedy leads to the experience of the corresponding quality. In this way, as in this example, we find a path from anger to compassion.

Those who do not react automatically can act freely. It would be a classic approach of buddhist mind training, to remember what is most important in our life, our inner orientation (refuge, bodhicitta) in this space of pausing. Remembering one's own priorities is the key point in transitioning from pause to remedy.

When in open states, the difficulty is usually to avoid being drawn back into the story which triggered the emotions in the first place. The other person may continue their hurtful remarks and behaviour that triggers our emotions, we therefore have to stabilize the spaciousness and not pay attention to the triggers. This demonstrates the power of appropriate methods: It connects us in the middle of challenging situations with a powerful inner quality – and this power is stronger than the power of the emotion. Of course, we have to apply the method with the necessary inner strength, and it has to fit the situation.

Step 3: Transforming the view of the emotion

In the third step, we change our view of the emotion. It is not about transforming the emotion itself – poison remains poison, as in nature. But poisons are potential remedies – if one handles them skilfully. Traditionally, this step is called 'transforming' and many people think that it's about transforming the stressful emotions themselves, a kind of alchemy. Not at all. Nor is it about transforming other peoples' attitudes but about transforming one's own perspective and attitude. Here are some examples of helpful views that change our attitudes to challenging emotions:

- Difficulties help me to remain mindful and conscious.
- Difficulties and problems are my best teachers.
- The more difficult feelings, the better! They wake me up to what is essential.
- Emotions are a mirror for my inner development – I can thank them!
- Difficulties bring me back into the flow of compassionate awareness.
- Only through difficulties do I grow. Only through difficulties I can awaken.

Gendun Rinpoche describes it this way in '*The Great Peacock*.'[12]
- No development of generosity without encountering lack.
- No development of endurance without challenging situations.

12 Summary of the explanations in "The Great Peacock" on pp. 73-75 (German edition).

- No development of patience without annoying experiences.
- No development of compassion without encountering suffering.

This culminates in familiar sayings like:
- Problematic people are more helpful than the Buddha because they help to dissolve ego-centredness.
- My emotions are welcome mirrors of my habitual patterns.
- My enemies are my best friends – they strengthen the power of my heart.

To become sincere warriors of the heart is the basic approach of buddhist mind training. We can take steps towards such new perspectives ourselves, as well as with others. Those who see the positive in difficulties can deal with them creatively.

Taking my emotion as a teacher

Tibetans say: Emotion is the Lama coming to visit – it is trying to teach us something. Instead of rejecting it, cultivate an attitude of turning towards it with interest: "Well, well, well, what can I learn from this?" Stressful emotions usually arise when something goes wrong from our point of view. If we accept the challenge, we learn a lot from the situation and gain a deeper understanding of ourselves and others in no time. This is also the basic approach in psychotherapeutic work:

> Learn as much as you can from the challenges of your life.

What makes difficulties difficult are the emotional reactions – and they stimulate wisdom and compassion. They are our spiritual teachers.[13]

Actually, steps two, three and four simply describe the different possibilities that we have once we stop (step one). After we pause, we

13 Explanations of this kind of view can be found in the Lodjong anthology "The Great Path of Awakening".

go on to one of the three following steps – whichever is most appropriate. The most important thing is to create the space first. At this stage, we don't need to know how to proceed after that.

We can remind ourselves of the new perspective with sentences like:
- No fear of emotions. They can't kill you.
- They'll help you get to know yourself.
- Every emotion will pass. The less you hold on, the faster it will pass
- Relaxed mindfulness will teach you everything.
- The less grasping, the less suffering.
- Everything is welcome and dissolves into awareness.

Understanding the nature of the mind shapes our view even when we do not understand the nature of the emotional irruption. We know fundamentally:
- Emotions are in my own mind; they do not come from outside.
- Emotions have no substance; they are movements in mind itself.
- Emotions arise in the mind and dissolve back into it by themselves.

We meet emotional challenges with the view that all mental movements are of the same nature in their very essence. They appear without being tangible. They are an expression of the dynamic nature of mind, they can be clearly experienced and at the same time are 'empty', without a core, without substance. If they are not held on to, they dissolve without a trace. Emotions have no substance. They show us the nature of the mind. Every emotional 'film' teaches us the nature of mental phenomena, regardless of their content. The more the better! The more challenges mastered, the more stable the insight.

Transforming the view in Vajrayāna

Up to this point, the teachings belong to what could be called "mainstream buddhism". The contents are relatively well-known and publicly taught. There are, however, additional methods of working with emotions that have spread in India since about the fourth century.

This is the approach of Vajrayāna or Tantric buddhism, which uses emotions to discover the true nature of our being.

This approach is not entirely unknown in psychotherapy and a similar process is found especially in procedures that use active imagination to bring about a deep change in perspective. With such techniques, inherent resources are used to see emotional challenges in a completely new 'awakened' light.

In Vajrayāna we practice seeing with the heart or eyes of a buddha; we change our view. If we are able to fully immerse ourselves in the vastness of the mind, we do not see arising emotions as enemies to be fought with, but as spontaneous expressions of the mind, which give us the opportunity to recognize its true nature, let go more deeply and enter into real freedom. All movements of the mind are welcome; we do not need to fight them. They simply challenge us to let go more deeply into the open awareness of awakened compassion. When this happens, they dissolve into it immediately.

In this deeply positive, relaxed state of mind, emotions are experienced as having no duration. They appear briefly, dressed up as desire, anger and the like, but dissolve immediately in the vastness. Anger immediately collapses, the open mind is irresistible – compassion wins and becomes even stronger than before the stressful emotion arose. Desire may show itself, but dissolves in an instant – love wins out and is even stronger than before, because it has assimilated the energy of desire.

Energies that are locked up in stressful emotions are released through letting go. They reveal themselves in the inherent qualities of our mind, which come out increasingly. It is as if we are 'transformed.' But it is more accurate to say that what was hidden is uncovered. What sounds so simple is a profound work of transforming deep-rooted views, and it is not possible – however much we might want to – to skip the first two steps.

To make friends with emotions presupposes that they can no longer be a danger to us. And this is only guaranteed if we are no longer driven by them (step one) and can dissolve them with antidotes if necessary (step two). Otherwise, anger, for example, will rise within us and our compassion is suddenly nowhere to be found. The anger will spread and bury everything beneath it. In order to avoid this, first we create space and freedom of choice by applying helpful methods; and only then do we use the emotions to broaden our awareness.

Step 4: Liberating the emotion in its true nature

In order to recognize the true nature of mind, and therefore also of every single emotion, which all arise in mind, we proceed step by step: First, we examine the calm mind without conceptual thought. Later, we dedicate ourselves to the investigation of the moving mind with its many emotional and conceptual movements. In doing so, we direct our inner 'gaze' away from the *contents* of the experience – the trigger of the emotions – towards the *quality* of the experience, its true nature. We are not concerned with *what* happens to us, instead we direct our intuitive antennae at *how* experience itself feels, awareness itself.

In doing so we understand that emotions have no substance, no power of their own and, like all other mental movements are dynamic through and through. This brings the certainty that there is nothing to correct about them, only something to recognize. With this direct seeing, emotions are seen as 'empty', without a core of being, without inherent power. They are seen through and when this vision is active, there is no more fear and fighting, even with strong emotions. Everything that appears in the mind has the same nature: it dissolves by itself, in the very moment that we stop feeding the solidifying emotional processes. Everything is understood in its intangible nature. Even the worst blockages have no substance, nothing solid. This is what is meant by 'empty'. They only have a seeming stability as long as we believe them to be solid. When the grasping is released, the emotional tension is released in that same moment.

With this approach we have three options:

a) We investigate the emotional experience and discover that it is intangible and has no substance.
b) We examine ourselves, the experiencer 'me', the supposed subject, the feeling of an 'I' and discover that this 'me' cannot be found and has no substance, no essence.
c) We examine the 'other', the supposed object, the trigger or subject of our emotion, here it is crucial to really direct our gaze to its essence and not to get caught in describable characteristics. In this way we discover equally as well that nothing is tangible, that it has no substance, it is simply pure process.

Investigation does not refer to an analytical procedure, but a direct gaze that does not require a conceptual answer and goes directly to the centre of the experience. We 'look into' the true essence of our experience, be it the moving mind with feelings, thoughts, images and perceptions, or the silent mind without any special content. It does not matter what kind of experience it is – the basic nature is always the same, just as with the different manifestations of water: whether stormy waves, light splashes, or a calm sea – the essential nature of it is always water.

This recognition of the very nature of an emotion corresponds to entering into nondual awareness. In principle, it is possible, at any time, to experience the direct seeing of the ungraspable nature of being. However, it is usually beyond the scope of the therapeutic setting to practice this in that context. Step four is the realization of the nature of mind at the very moment an emotion is experienced. This insight is then used in step five to specifically seek out emotional challenges and to expand that realization into all areas. Experienced meditation teachers are usually needed as guides to learn these steps.[14]

This 'looking' is most likely to succeed when there is a strong movement in the mind, for example sudden anger. Anger is a strong,

14 Additional explanations can be found in section B.1.

clear feeling. When it appears, we look directly inward: Where is it? Where is the anger to be found? Here, attention leaves the angry 'story' and turns to the nature of experience itself: what is it like to be angry? Who is angry? Where is the anger? Is it to be found in the thumping heart? In the hot face? In the churning stomach? The mounting thoughts?

Emotions are simply expressions of the dynamic nature of mind

We might think that a calm mind is particularly good and preferable to an agitated mind. But emotional movements are essential, and no different in nature from a calm mind or calm awareness. Whether slow or fast, diffuse or clear, emotionally charged or calm – all mental movements are of the same nature: we can't hold on to an angry thought any more than to a clear one. They appear, but they are not tangible. We call this the inseparability of clearly perceivable appearance and ungraspable essence – clarity and empty nature. Like in an ocean whose waves can be perceived without being tangible. Waves of emotion are as much an expression of the dynamic nature of mind as any other mental movement – whether based in insight or confusion.

The more mental movements are recognized as natural dynamic expression, the less of an irritant their appearance will be for us; free of any clinging they can flow unhindered. What has just been heard, read, or experienced in no way hinders the next hearing, reading or experiencing. There is no congestion. Mental movements need not be cleared away, for they have no substance and do not hinder each other.

Emotions show us the nature of all mental movements: dynamic and yet without substance. When this is recognized, they show us the nature of the mind. An awakened and a confused mind have the same nature – only the contents of the experience are different. Whether a beautiful film or a horrible film, whether violent scenes, or the life of a buddha, whether delusion or awareness – every film 'teaches' the nature of the mind and all phenomena equally.

This basic nature manifests in nondual realization, which is called 'timeless awareness' – *jñāna* in Sanskrit, *yeshe* or *rigpa* in Tibetan. It is beyond words – but to indicate it, it is said to be vast like space, without centre or boundaries, clear and unobstructed, aware in every situation of the same, ungraspable nature of all experience, finely differentiated and aware of the inherent perfection of all experience.

Step 5: Taking emotions as the path of awakening

Step four provides the certainty that emotions are insubstantial and have no power. They cannot remain of their own accord. They are only as powerful as the meaning we attribute to them. To take emotions as the path involves stimulating them in order to see their true nature repeatedly, and thus to dissolve all remaining emotional and cognitive veils. The message of step five is: the more emotions are seen through, the more we understand them and the more stable the realization of the nature of the mind becomes. But beware: The previous steps cannot be skipped over. Step five is explained here primarily for the sake of completeness, to give a complete overview of the path.

Emotions now serve practitioners as food for realization. They are stimulated in a variety of ways, in order for us to see again and again, the basic nature of mind into which they dissolve. In this way, resilience is created with complete lack of identification; even the most violent provocations no longer trigger any grasping.[15]

To practice step five, emotions must be mastered through the first four steps to the point where we can (1) pause at any time and (2) use various remedies. (3) Our view of emotions should have changed so

15 In step 5 in the "Great Peacock", Gendun Rinpoche devotes a long time to the yoga of deep sleep for dissolving lack of awareness and only briefly touches on the other emotions. In this passage the Tibetan commentary contains detailed instructions on the practice of Vajrayana and the Six Dharmas of Naropa, which can only be realized in the life of a yogi.

radically that we no longer act them out or run away from them but rather see them as an opportunity and when they come into awareness always (4) recognize their true nature. When these foundations are in place, which is not normally the case, we can (5) 'play with fire' and take the stimulation of emotions as the path of awakening. In doing so we practice step four again and again: seeing through the nature of the emotions. It is like playing with fire, when you stimulate emotions, you need to be sure that you are not going to get caught up in them or even reinforce the emotional patterns.

We can, for example, fuel desire by looking for concrete situations or by imagining situations that stimulate strong desire. But before we get carried away by the desire and react again, i.e. before we fall for it, we look into its true nature to free ourselves completely from its spell. We must sit very firmly in the saddle and not nourish any subconscious fascination with the energy of desire and pretend, for example, that ordinary sexual passion is a spiritual practice.

The same applies to anger and rage. We put ourselves in actual situations, or imagine as vividly as possible, situations that makes us really angry. Before our own mind gets caught up in them, i.e. without letting ourself get carried away by angry chains of thought, speech or activity, we look into the emotion. Again, the point is not to feed a subtle identification with anger and rage.

In addition, there is the practice of provoking situations that evoke strong feelings in us. Any kind of unconventional behaviour can serve this purpose: wearing unusual clothes, sitting on the floor in the supermarket and the like. We then dissolve the feelings that arise by observing them directly.

Pride arises in situations where self-centredness is stimulated, for example through praise, compliments, or criticism. Here, too, we look at what the essential nature of our self-satisfaction, or hurt is, and whether the supposed centre that everything revolves around, this 'I' that feels so great, insignificant or hurt, really exists. This can also be practiced with feelings of loneliness.

To work with jealousy and envy, we imagine situations which give rise to feelings of competitiveness, rivalry, envy and jealousy, where others have more than us, or can do something better, or we expose ourselves to actual situations of this sort, always looking into the essential nature of the experience.

Ignorance and sleep can also be used to realize the nature of mind. We can purposefully seek out states of lack of awareness, they are like banks of fog: diffuse, unclear, tired, sleepy, dull states of mind. We immerse ourselves in the fog and maintain a subtle awareness that recognizes the true nature of these states of mind. When this happens, the mental fog immediately disappears and the open, clear nature of mind is revealed.

Resilience through complete detachment

In his explanations of step five, Chakme refers to buddhist practices known since the 11th century as the 'Six Teachings (Yogas) of Naropa'. They are a specialty of Tibetan buddhism and cannot be found in this form in other traditions, although the experiences associated with them may be quite well known. These methods are practiced in solitude with special attention paid to the ability to actually take emotional experience as a path: Of these six Yogas, the first four are relevant here and will therefore be briefly explained.

The practice of Inner Heat works primarily with the realization of the true nature of joy. Visualizations stimulate the energy of desire and the blessing of the open, joyful nature of mind is invited into this fiery experience. Through this, the energy bound up in attachment to joy and happiness freed from identification and reveals itself as the experience of the four immeasurable qualities – love, compassion, joy and equanimity.

The practice of the Illusory Body takes place between meditation sessions where one practices with all emotions, but especially with pride, anger and jealousy – i.e., with the mental poisons based on comparing oneself with others. The exercises, if done repeatedly in a pair, include consciously provoking each other. For example, by praising ourselves or our partner. Then we criticize ourselves or the other person over the smallest mistakes – an alternating bath of true praise and condemnation. This exercise works with our sore points and can become very dynamic. In order to practice like this, in his first retreat, Gendun Rinpoche went into the room of another practitioner and 'stole' all his offering bowls. He set them up in his own room and waited until his fellow practitioner discovered them – snorting with rage – a good opportunity for both of them to see the essential nature of anger! To practice illusory body means to thoroughly experience the true nature of one's being, *at all times* – no matter what happens.

The practice of Luminosity, also called 'Clear Light' happens in deep sleep. Here one realizes that sleep, as the extreme of mental dullness and lack of awareness, where we normally experience ourselves as unconscious, is also permeated by a subtle bright awareness, a clear, calm mind without any activity.

Finally, the practice of Dream Yoga consists in a series of exercises beginning with lucid dreaming, awareness of the nature of the moving mind in sleep, until the mind active at night, also fully reveals itself as awakened, nondual awareness. These are the four great yogas.

The other two yogas are not relevant to the explanation of the five steps of working with the emotions in this life. They concern transferring consciousness that is released from the body at the time of death into an awakened dimension of mind (Tib. *phowa*) and using the illusory phenomena that appear in the post-death transitional phase (Tib. *bardo*) for awakening. These two practices help to prepare for the moment of dying and the transition to the next life.

Yogins practice Inner Heat on the meditation cushion during the day and Illusory Body between meditation sessions. In deep sleep they practice Luminosity and in the dream phase, Dream Yoga.

They are occupied with this around the clock and use every situation to bring all states of mind onto the path of awakening.[16]

These last explanations are of little direct relevance to psychotherapeutic practice. However, they can serve as an inspiration. The central message is: Everything, without exception, can be used for the practice of awareness! When life gets tough, it stimulates our practice of awareness and is not an emergency, which needs to be responded to in survival mode. We can look into the experience, into these mental 'films', which are created with incredible precision and intensity, but have no substance. It is about practicing in the spirit of a heart full of love, compassion and wisdom in all these situations. Keeping alive the penetrating vision of the nature of existence, makes the loving awareness truly 'storm-proof'. Even violent provocations will then no longer trigger grasping. This is why step five works directly with actual provocations in order to be helpful even in intense situations. It serves to stimulate and free emotional material that has not yet come to the surface.

These five steps allow us to become more flexible, more agile and at the same time more sensitive, without fear of emotions. Basically, we feel more than we did when we were still wearing our protective armour – at least we notice many more feelings, both in ourselves and others – but we have learned how to deal with them and know their true nature. The heart becomes sensitive, very delicate, it resonates with ease, and at the same time there is a great inner permeability, a flow that does not resist this experience and does not hold on to it.

---

16 The "Great Peacock", basis of these explanations, mentions the practice of the Four Mudrās (seals), of which *karmamudrā*, the sexual union with a partner as a practice of awareness, serves to dissolve desire. This requires a high degree of relaxedness and awareness in order not to become entangled in ego-centredness. *Samayamudrā*, the practice of Inner Heat (Tib. *tummo*), stimulates this energy internally without a partner. In *jñānamudrā* (awareness mudrā) one visualizes oneself as a buddha in sexual union: the perfect integration of the inherent male and female qualities. In *mahāmudrā* all phenomena are recognized in their basic unity of manifestation, clarity, and empty nature. Here, manifestation, compassion, joy and clarity stand for the masculine aspect – and empty nature, wisdom, openness stand for the feminine.

B. Inner Work with the five Basic Emotional Patterns

In the previous section, the first few pages gave an overview of the field of forces generated by the five basic emotional patterns and their corresponding five aspects of awakened awareness. The following chapters described these respective patterns individually in their essential features and characteristics. Three *keys* for personal practice with the respective emotion were given to work on each of the basic patterns. Now, as a practical summary, it will be explained how the five steps discussed in chapters A.1–5 (Pause – Apply Remedies – Change of the View – Recognize the Nature of the Emotion – Take the Emotion as a Path) can be applied to the most basic emotional patterns.

In order to describe working with stressful emotions in more detail, we limit ourselves to *five basic emotional patterns*, based on buddhist mind training:

1. Lack of awareness (ignorance, fear)
2. Desire (attachment, craving, dependency)
3. Pride (arrogance, condescension)
4. Anger (aversion, rage, aggression)
5. Jealousy (envy, competitiveness)

The identification of these five basic patterns serves as a kind of basic diagnostic scheme for practitioners of buddhist mind training and replaces the more differentiated diagnoses of psychotherapy for the layperson. So, without having to know these subtler diagnoses, the ordinary person can see which of these basic patterns are currently active and also what remedies are possible. This assumes that these emotional obscurations can be dissolved to such an extent that the timeless awareness of awakening is revealed – an experience that many practitioners have had.

In Tibetan buddhism these five disturbing emotional patterns, like the five buddha families and the five aspects of timeless, awakened awareness, are presented as a maṇḍala in the form of a five-coloured lotus flower. In the buddhist tradition the lotus represents awakening for it grows in muddy waters, but the bud rises above the water and unfolds its flower in pristine purity – symbolizing our mind, which in awakening shows itself in complete purity without having been affected in any way by previous emotional obscurations.

With a more subtle symbolic contemplation of the lotus, the five disturbing emotions are divided between the centre and the four petals, which – as a whole – stands for the world of our emotionally confused perception. The blue centre, where the fruit would come from, symbolizes lack of awareness, the cause of all other patterns of entanglement. On the four petals, seen from the centre, are anger as a white petal in front, pride as a yellow petal on the right, desire as a red petal behind, and jealousy as a green petal on the left.

The colours of the elementary basic energies of our world are assigned to these basic patterns – in close correspondence to the *five elements* that can be found in nature:

- The blue colour stands for the sky and limitless *space* in which everything can take place. It is symbolic of vastness and infinity.
- The white colour stands for flowing, occasionally foaming *water*, a symbol of cohesion and continuity.
- The yellow colour stands for the *earth* that bears everything and produces everything, symbol of stability and reliability.
- The red colour stands for the all-illuminating but also all-consuming *fire*, symbol of warmth and vitality.
- The green colour stands for the *wind* which brings rain, makes everything grow and moves the leaves, symbol of dynamism and power.

Our mind has the same natural characteristics: vastness, continuity, reliability, vitality and dynamism. When they are restricted by emotional obscurations, our perception is coloured as if we were looking through emotional lenses. Of course, this does not mean that we see red when we experience desire. The colours are only symbolic references to the basic qualities of mind and the corresponding buddha families.

Five aspects of timeless awareness

Once they are free from basic emotional patterns, the qualities of mind appear as the *five aspects of timeless awareness*, also called wisdom. These are (in the same order):

1. Space-like awareness: without centre and borders, as vast as a space that allows for all movement.
2. Mirror-like awareness: unobstructed, clear and continuous like appearances in a mirror.
3. Awareness of equality: all experiences are equally 'empty', intangible, without substance.
4. Finely discriminating awareness: vivid, differentiated, unique, subtly distinguishing.
5. All-perfecting awareness: free-flowing, dynamic being is perfect and complete in itself.

These five aspects of awareness, or nature of mind, are present simultaneously, like colours seen in the different facets of a jewel.

Other emotions can be understood as combinations of the five basic patterns. They are secondary emotional distress. There are countless combinations. Impatience for example, has aspects of anger (rage), desire (craving) and lack of awareness (fear, worry). But there is also proud impatience and jealous impatience.

When supporting people, it is usually enough to uncover the basic emotional patterns and their deeper motives. Addressing psychopathological diagnoses can contribute to an over emphasis on the clinical picture. For example, descriptive words such as 'protective reactivity', 'feeling of abandonment', 'lack of self-confidence' and 'protective self-inflation' give rise to more understanding than the expression 'underlying narcissistic personality disorder'. The descriptive formulations remain closer to the experience and suggest that these emotional patterns can be dissolved through work on oneself.

As the energy locked in these patterns is released, the inherent qualities of basic mind, the qualities of natural awareness become apparent. As long as we are aware of the ultimately unstable nature of emotional patterns, it is relatively easy to remain connected to the awakened potential behind all the emotional forces at work, that lead to these symptoms. It is as if the potential buddha is already visible behind the emotional experience. Each of us is such a potential buddha and the path of healing uncovers the buddha potential within us. The Mahāyāna tradition assumes a multitude of buddhas and describes the liberation from obscured to awakened experience symbolically as the maṇḍala of the five archetypal buddhas (in the same order as the lotus above):

1. Buddha Vairocana, representing space-like timeless awareness, is revealed in the dissolution of anxious experiences due to lack of awareness.
2. Buddha Akṣobhya, representing mirror-like timeless awareness, is revealed in the dissolution of angry experiences due to aversion and defensive or aggressive reactions.
3. Buddha Ratnasambhava, representing the timeless awareness of equality, is revealed in the dissolution of proud experiences due to comparing oneself with others.
4. Buddha Amitābha, representing finely discriminating timeless awareness, is revealed in the dissolution of desirous experiences due to attachment and clinging.
5. Buddha Amoghasiddhi, representing all-perfecting timeless awareness, is revealed in the dissolution of jealous experiences due to comparison, competition and rivalry.

The names of the buddhas, their classification and the associated iconography are not relevant in the context of Essential Psychotherapy. The main message is: We all have the entire maṇḍala of emotions and buddhas within us and so all aspects of timeless, nondual awareness are also always present in us – even if we are unaware of it.

On our own path of healing, as well as in a process of supporting others, we are guided by the vision of how we and others could be when our inherent potential is revealed, when all experience is permeated by awareness and the buddha within reveals himself. This is the real meaning of talking of a *buddha nature* in each of us: We express the deep confidence that everyone can heal completely and awaken. We know how tenacious emotional patterns can be, especially those with roots in infancy – and how powerfully these forces can shape our character. However, the more severe the disorder the more important it is to stay connected to the potential for healing.

All psychological pathologies and disorders can be understood as the interplay of the five basic emotions, which lead to an infinite number of individual expressions of the same basic *saṃsāric* issue[17]: an unnecessary, emotionally charged circling around 'myself', which creates suffering, called *ego clinging* or *ego centricity* in buddhist circles. Since getting to know these basic emotional patterns is at the centre of buddhist self-exploration and the mind training that builds on it, special attention is paid to the five basic emotions here.

The maṇḍala principle: opposing poles such as anger/aversion (in front) and desire/craving (behind) are connected to one another via lack of awareness (at the centre). They can easily merge or change into each other. When desire is frustrated, it often turns into aversion, lust turns into anger or hatred. Jealousy and pride are also linked via their common lack of awareness: When the prideful person loses out, jealousy surfaces, when the jealous rival, the one who always comes second, finally prevails, he often becomes as proud and abusive as

17 *Saṃsāra* is the Sanskrit word for continuously cycling in a world of suffering, which is the result of afflictions arising due to the dualistic patterns of seeing the world in terms of subject and object, self and others.

his tormentor. This principle of cross-relationships between pairs of emotions makes the maṇḍala model interesting. It becomes clear how opposing emotions can flip into each other through a lack of awareness. As the maṇḍala of the five emotions, the lotus with four petals and a centre symbolizes the world of entanglement, bondage and self-centredness *(saṃsāra)*. When these energies are liberated, the same life experiences reveal themselves as the world of awakening, freedom and peace *(nirvāṇa)*.

We will now look at the five steps for dealing with each of these five emotions: to pause, to apply helpful methods, to change the view, to recognize one's true nature and to use the emotion as a path of awakening.

1. Lack of awareness

The main forms of lack of awareness are dullness, indifference, doubt, and misconception – the basis of all this is ego-clinging, the basic ignorance characterized by a sense of insecurity or fear.

Basic ignorance

Lack of awareness is a veil that prevents the direct, immediate realization that leads to buddhahood. This refers to two things: (a) not being aware of what the true nature of all phenomena is, and (b) not being aware of how these phenomena manifest on a relative level. A person with complete understanding understands the true nature of all phenomena as dynamic, ungraspable, without substance and empty of an essence. At the same time, they understand exactly how phenomena manifest themselves in a clearly perceptible way thanks to their empty, ungraspable nature and the play of mutual conditionality. Such a person understands the co-dependent relationship of the ultimate and conditioned aspects of reality and in this way is free from basic ignorance. There is the deep understanding that these two aspects of reality are inseparably linked.

Ignorance also means to believe the '*I*' to be real. This basic feeling of a self, based on lack of awareness means that the '*other*' is also taken as real. And from this all the stressful emotions arise: 'I' here, with my emotions, different and separate from everything that is perceived as *other*. This splitting of experience into subject and object prevents liberation. This is what is meant by duality: the belief in the separation of the one who experiences and what is experienced.

Tension arises out of clinging to a self, perceived as separate; all conflicts come from this. Due to lack of awareness, there is no understanding that this supposed "me" is actually dynamic awareness. There is no permanent self to be found in the feeling of me, it is only a mental movement without substance. Out of ignorance, we defend and cherish this me that doesn't really exist. We are so caught up in our self-centredness that it is almost impossible to see anything beyond that.

If we examine the sense of a me, we find nothing that can be identified as an 'I', or a soul. Externally, however, the feeling of self and others is easily confirmed; we just need to touch something. Through physical contact we feel the limits of our body and where the *other* begins: "I am here, and the other is there." But how is it actually experienced? Isn't *the other* also our own perception? No awakened person has yet found a self, and neither has science.

The French philosopher René Descartes famously said: "I think, therefore I am." He wanted to solve the dilemma of not being able to determine with certainty whether there is an I. But no stable I can be derived from the existence of thought. Thinking is dynamic and constantly changes. The real question is whether there is *anyone* who thinks. Thoughts are momentary movements of the mind. Where are yesterday's thoughts? Everything changes, nothing stays. Where in this change is the supposedly permanent I?

In addition, there is the experience of meditators being completely free from conceptual and non-conceptual thinking, just awareness.

Where is the me to be found at this point? Perhaps it is found in observing this experience? But this observation is also a process and also falls away when we become more deeply relaxed. Where is the I then?

I is simply a useful term to communicate with. I and other are neither one nor separate, they are dynamic experience. There is no enduring core in experience, which would define us as a separate, constant individual and provide a sufficient basis for permanent identification and clear separation from the world. *I* is a process, in mutual dependency with everything that surrounds us, dynamic awareness – a living, intangible stream of experience without a solid core, without a *someone.*

What we believe to be an individual core of being, is only an open, dynamic space of awareness that is not different from other people. There is no need to defend this dynamic space of awareness because it cannot be violated – it is simply open space. The territory of the supposed self is in reality an ownerless field of karmic forces. To identify with it is lack of awareness. To understand that there is nothing to defend is wisdom.

My body, *my* family, *my* friends, *my* team, *my* country – ego clinging is endless. It absorbs everything which it wants to identify with and rejects everything that is experienced as threatening and unpleasant. In order to become free, all these identifications have to be dissolved. The entire play of emotions is created by our identifications, clinging to the pleasant and pushing away the unpleasant. The question is always: "What do I want, and what do I want to get rid of?" This is the dual movement of ego-clinging: pulling towards and pushing away, based on the assumption of a truly existing *me.*

Identification creates the basis for suffering. The more we think of *my* cereal bowl as *my* personal bowl the harder it becomes to make it available to others. If *I* consider something mine and someone else wants to use it as well, conflict arises because it is then less *mine.* We don't share our private car as easily as we do our car-sharing scheme or a public bus. This also applies if we identify something as *not mine* and want to keep it away from us, because we don't like it. If someone comes along who doesn't want it either and tries to pass it on to us a conflict arises: we are pushing the unloved thing back and forth between us. This is how all problems arise *I want; I don't want.*

We use the words *I, me* and *mine* to express possession. However, we shouldn't let the terms fool us. They are abstract, static terms that describe a dynamic, living process. The *I* is, just like the *you*, a little different every moment. Fixed identifications are not appropriate, because nothing stable can be found. We can use the terms *I*, *you* and *we*, as well as *my*, *your* and *ours*, aware that they describe dynamic processes, without identification. So, someone can drive *my* car without a conflict arising.

Another example: When looking for a shirt, we find a nice one in a shop. But the first one we try has a stain. We think, "this is not my problem" and buy an identical, though unstained shirt. However, at home, our child stains that new shirt. And now our reaction is: "Oh, *my* shirt!" And a strong emotional reaction may follow. The stain is similar to the one on the first shirt in the shop, but a completely different reaction emerges now that we consider it as *mine*. Strong identification causes strong reactions.

We can live nondually in duality – being aware of the ultimate dimension without *me* and *others* in a relative world where there certainly is me and others. We use the words *I* and *you* without creating a separation.

Another example: In a dream we see our home burning down and experience real panic which we can still feel in all our cells when we wake up. But as soon as we realize that it was a dream, the emotions dissolve. We can translate this into everyday life: If we are aware that our experience is of a dreamlike nature, dynamic, and influenced by countless conditions, there are no longer any lasting problems – they can all be resolved. Insight into the dynamic, ungraspable nature of emotions and all experiences cuts through our deep-rooted belief in a substantial reality, from where all reactions of attachment and aversion arise. Having "cut through the root" grasping to substantial reality will allow us to adopt the most flexible perspective possible, without or with only minimal clinging to this supposed self. Then we also learn to deal really skilfully with the various forces which could either lead to problems or to joy, openness and love. Everything arises in the dynamic interaction of different forces – the more flexible and wiser we act in this field of forces, the better.

Dullness, indifference, neurotic doubts and mistaken beliefs

We have many mechanisms for avoiding unpleasant things. Amongst the most important of them is the avoidance reflex, looking away, and not wanting to see. This applies both to external situations and inner patterns. As an expression of this mainly unconscious wish to be unaware of inner experience, we experience heaviness, absence, apathy, dullness, and clouding of the mind. The lack of clarity and lightness prevents us from seeing and recognizing things clearly, in line with our unconscious desire. We are *tight.* Unfortunately, these avoidance strategies are also at work in people who want to be aware and even in those who teach mindfulness and awareness.

Neglect, indifference, disinterest, and lack of curiosity are also expressions of this avoidance. We exclude areas of life because they become too much for us. We do not want to have anything to do with certain topics, challenges or threatening insights. This is perfectly valid, especially if it is a conscious decision. But we have to accept that in the areas that we avoid, no understanding can develop; it withers away, and the unconscious patterns continue to work with unchecked force.

A third form of lack of awareness is *unhealthy* doubt. *Healthy* doubt is a sign of intelligence and of sufficient emotional freedom not to be fooled or believe blindly. Healthy doubts motivate us to clarify confusion. This healthy doubt is not what is meant here. When lack of awareness leads to doubts, it becomes difficult to think clearly because each thought is immediately challenged by another. No sooner have we made up our mind to take a step than we see a thousand reasons not to act. Neurotic doubts undermine confidence in one's own perception and thinking, and block action. We need a minimum of trust to attempt something. The tense intellect finds innumerable excuses not to get involved. We are afraid of painful experiences, and this unfortunately also prevents liberating experiences.

A fourth aspect of lack of awareness is *beliefs* – an emotional attachment to assumptions about reality that we do not want to test. Traditional examples of beliefs that hinder awakening, when dogmatically held, are beliefs such as that a stable, individual self really exists; or that awakening is impossible or that actions have no consequences. If we question our own assumptions and openly consider other points of view, even mistaken views are not serious – they can be clarified.

However, without openness there is no curiosity and enquiry, and no room for further development. Holding on to views means cementing one's own partial knowledge or ignorance. It becomes almost impossible to correct mistakes in our interpretation. Even correct views can become dogma and be misused for personal gain. Only true flexibility of mind beyond viewpoints protects against this: the 'right view' of the awakened does not adopt positions.

Extract from an EPT group discussion on lack of awareness

This passage is included here as a bit of inspiration on how to exchange ideas with friends about such fundamental topics as basic emotions and to develop an exploratory interest in them. The exchange was preceded by an exercise in which each participant engaged in the experience of ignorance and lack of awareness through memories. Afterwards the participants reported:

> *Participant 1:* I experienced ignorance as lifeless, dull, with little feeling, a routine. Like in a dark bubble, where I can't figure out why I feel this way. This cosy bubble protects me from change. I don't want to be disturbed in the comforting bubble of unawareness. When my wife pricks the bubble, I fight back until I can't stand it anymore. What helps me get out is trust in the reason for her interference and in

her compassion. Then I can embrace the change a little bit. Otherwise, I would fight back constantly so that I continue to remain ignorant. Of course, I can also tell myself that it is full of suffering because it makes me lifeless.

Participant 2: When an impulse for change comes, I immediately react emotionally.

Tilmann: There is a fear behind the reaction: "Leave me alone" – that is the fear of change, of the unknown. Occasionally, this also leads to a kind of playing dead reflex. What gets us out of this? What can motivate us here?

Participant 3: The longing for life. Trust. If I don't have trust and I assume the other person wants to harm me, I continue to resist. The way has to be paved so that my fears don't manifest too quickly.

Participant 4: I reflect on the painful aspect of the emotion to dissolve this ignorance. I want to understand what is behind it and how to escape. I suffer, and I want to understand.

Participant 5: It strikes me that belief in identity is very much born out of this ignorance. I need confidence and trust that it is possible to step out of ignorance. There is such a longing for freedom. You know the saying 'knowledge sets you free.'

Participant 6: Knowledge is power.

Tilmann: And ignorance is powerlessness and fear. Awareness brings clarity. It is difficult to address one's tendency to seek unawareness. This lulling of oneself into it is incredibly seductive – a state of semi-lucidity where nothing is recognized, but time passes in a pleasant manner. This is where we must resolve to look.

Stepping out from the prison of fear

Fear is always present where there is a lack of awareness, and we are unfamiliar with the situation. This also applies to basic human fear or existential fear. It builds up when we are not aware of the nature of existence, i.e., when we do not know who we really are without external reference points, and when we are faced with the unknown, e.g. at death. Neurotic doubts, dogmatic clinging to opinions and stubbornness are all essentially expressions of fear.

Like all other emotions, fear has a purpose: it alerts us to the fact that we do not know, are uninformed and that danger may be imminent. It is an invitation to be more conscious, to feel and to 'pay attention' in the broadest sense of the word, to be aware. Unfortunately, like other emotions fear tends to take on a life of its own and keeps popping up, even when it is not appropriate. Fear becomes a habitual response to the unknown, even a reaction to life itself with all its imponderables.

If it gets to the point where fear constantly kicks in, it is no longer a benevolent aide for our awareness but blocks our willingness to be fully alive. We become walled in by fear and need enormous trust to open the prison door and take the necessary steps into the unknown. Most of the time, suffering has to become unbearable before any real interest arises in opening the door and boldly setting off into the unknown. We have to almost suffocate. Only at that point do we tell ourselves that it can't get any worse. Then we let go of control and learn to trust the opening more than the restrictive barriers built out of fear. Tightness is familiar to us; on the other hand, we experience openness as a risk. Fortunately, however, openness does not happen all at once, but gradually. Openness is the *refuge* of buddhists – this sounds like a paradox, but in fact this is how it is. To enter into awakening with body, speech and mind, into complete openness and flow is the true protection and also helps with dying.

Awakening is fully opening – and this openness becomes our new home. Awakened ones embody open, flowing existence and complete sanity of mind. Teachers support us through their example and their teachings – this enables our heart/mind to blossom like a lotus flower. The petals of timeless awareness unfold. Fortunately, there are many supporters who encourage us to take further steps on the path of opening and to allow love and compassion enter our heart. Teachers guide us by example – and if we look around, we might even find someone in our immediate environment who inspires us in this way.

What prevents us from opening up more is fear: fear of being hurt, fear of suffering, fear of not existing, fear of being nobody, fear of not being loved... There are no stressful emotions without fear. Many emotional responses can be understood as defences against a perceived threat. Fear of thirst, hunger, exhaustion, criticism, loss, rejection, the unpleasant – fear is everywhere. The need for protection builds a ring of defensiveness which becomes a prison.

Deep down are the existential fears, sometimes felt as fear of the unknown and of death. Fear is experienced as a threat to the *I* and somatically, as trembling, tightness, sweating, heart palpitations, diarrhoea, rigidity, over-excitement, heat or cold. We are familiar with the fear of the dissolving of familiar structures, the fear of losing control or autonomy, of our vitality being impaired and much more. Anxiety is a state of tension of body and mind. It is often accompanied by a feeling of a heightened alertness on many levels.

When we approach the door of the metaphorical prison, we are afraid that it will not open, and when we step across the threshold, we are afraid that we will not find our way back in. There is fear everywhere, because whenever we take a step, we encounter something new. The unknown triggers fear. Since change is always accompanied by something new, we are simply afraid of change. Desire is afraid of not getting what is pleasant. Anger is afraid of experiencing something unpleasant. Pride is afraid of being belittled. Jealousy is afraid of losing loved ones or of not being good enough. All stressful emotions have in common that there is fear, because lack of awareness plays a role in all of them. This is why in the abhidharma it is not described as a separate emotion. The assumption that there is *someone* who needs to protect themselves is the root cause of fear.

Fear hinders us more than it benefits us. In the case of imaginary dangers, it is counterproductive anyway, and wisdom would also be a better guide when it comes to real dangers. We don't need fear in order to achieve top physical or mental performances – we rather need keen interest, trust, love, compassion, wisdom... Yes, fear can wake us up, but – more often than not – if it persists, it paralyses us. Therapeutically, we could say, we should address fear because that is where the blockages are. Fear is a signal that something is wrong, but what exactly is going on is unclear. Fear often masks an underlying feeling, as it often causes us to not to take a closer look or to really feel. Of course, fear can also stabilize social interaction but how much more beneficial would it be, if it were stabilized by compassion and mutual care! Fear hinders communication, because it reflects a lack of trust in ourselves and others.

Increased awareness inevitably makes unpleasant things conscious – like all these underlying fears. Therefore, it takes determination to cultivate awareness. When we become aware of what is difficult internally and in others, an inner search for solutions begins. In the process we initially have to endure feelings of incapacity and helplessness. Although we see things more clearly, we don't yet have the capacity to fully integrate this into the path. In reality, lack of awareness has very little going for it, except that it can be resolved. It tangles us up in painful reactions, and its most devastating effect is that we hardly notice the suffering or feel any impulse to do anything about it. Lack of awareness causes an inability to distinguish between what leads to happiness and what leads to suffering.

Three keys: study, contemplation, meditation (exercise B.1)

Preliminary note: For each of the five basic emotions "three keys" for working with these emotional patterns are discussed. No specific exercises are offered beyond that, just these three keys that are to be practiced – as much as possible.

How can we free ourselves from lack of awareness? Since we are dealing with several types, it requires action on various levels. One type of lack of awareness is the lack of knowledge, learnable understanding that others can impart to us through texts or teaching. Studies, discussions and further training can help with that. However, the basic ignorance of believing oneself and others to be truly existent, the fundamental problem of dualistic perception, can only be resolved through personal introspection (contemplation and meditation). Studying is not enough. Buddhist mind training therefore works on several levels. First of all, there are the three trainings: beneficial behaviour, deep mental calm and wisdom:

(1) The basis is beneficial behaviour – *śīla* in Sanskrit, a skilful, beneficial way of thinking, speaking, and acting physically.
(2) On this basis, the mind settles down and experiences deep mental stillness – *samādhi.*
(3) This is the prerequisite for deep understanding, realization of the nature of existence or wisdom – *prajñā.*

These three are the essence of the buddhist path as taught in all traditions. To support them, the Buddha taught three forms of practice, the three sources of wisdom: study, contemplation and meditation.

- *Study:* We hear teachings, share them with others and study texts to gain intellectual understanding.
- *Contemplation*: Then we connect what we have heard and read with our own experiences by reflecting deeply on the content until a deeper understanding emerges from within. This process is called contemplation.
- *Meditation*: The understanding that arises in contemplation takes us beyond questions and answers into a process of spontaneous suchness. Not wanting to change things anymore, that is meditation.

Study

Studying the wisdom teachings gives us an intellectual understanding. It is especially important to understand which actions and attitudes are helpful and which aren't. If we want to free ourselves from suffering, we should not harm others – this is the basis of the entire path. The teachings have many examples of what kind of behaviour makes sense in relation to the aim of becoming free from suffering. Studying them trains our common sense: we learn to distinguish what leads to happiness from what leads to suffering.

Studying changes our views, actions and reactions. Listening to and reading teachings is a necessary part of spiritual practice. Traditional teachings for dissolving lack of awareness cover the Four noble truths (see ch. D), the Four basic thoughts that turn the mind to the Dharma (see ch. C.1), the effects of actions *(karma)*, the twelve links of dependent arising of suffering and liberation, interdependence, our potential to awaken, the six liberating qualities *(pāramitā)* and clarifications on the nature of mind.

In order for study to really clarify and change our nature, we need interest. Interest not only in the teaching, but also in our neighbour, other people, in what is happening in the world and in the arts and sciences. Interest in everything that could be helpful in understanding ourselves and others. It is about having an interest in the world. We have to be curious. This lively interest is open to new things. It causes us to be open and receptive down to the last cell. Interest is the fundamental remedy for ignorance and lack of awareness.

Contemplation

In addition to listening and studying, we need to relate the teachings personally to our situation: "What does this have to do with the me?" Contemplation is a deep concern with these issues. Contemplation changes us more than just absorbing conceptually what we hear. In contemplation, while questioning, initial answers emerge, then there is usually a short pause, the question deepens, we come to feel more, new answers arise, then there is calm again, then perhaps another answer forms, etc. Whoever contemplates in this way understands more deeply. Just contemplating a single instruction like impermanence can change one's whole life. Priorities are adjusted, some things become more important, others less urgent. Dharma teachings are meant to change us.

Meditation

Contemplation, which is still largely conceptual, leads to non-conceptual, simple being – meditation. We learn to be in the present moment, conscious and aware. Meditation begins with the wish to find relaxation. However, we don't only meditate just to relax, but also to release an inner, non-conceptual understanding. This deep understanding of the way things are may later be expressed in concepts, but initially it is non-conceptual. This understanding liberates us from unnecessary suffering and leads to a completely relaxed existence without self-centredness. At first meditation is about mental stability. And we can use classic methods of mindfulness, such as breathing or walking meditation. We learn to be mindful of every movement, every word, every thought. Meditation helps us to be more mindful without judging or suppressing. The more relaxed we are, the more careful and precise our mindfulness becomes.

My first mindfulness exercise (see exercise A.1) may be driving a car: I turn off the radio, feel my posture and other sensations, notice what is going on inside and around me, and otherwise just drive. I bring the otherwise automatic actions of driving, into the centre of my mindfulness and enjoy the clarity of perception that comes with it. I notice how my body leans slightly into the turn together with the car, how thoughts come, and I am no longer connected to what is happening. Joie de vivre lies in the attentive experience of details. I can also choose to practice washing dishes, mowing the lawn and other routine chores and then extend this to other areas.

Gendun Rinpoche often spoke of developing the *wisdom eye*. This eye perceives one's own emotions and state of mind. The most direct way of understanding better and becoming wiser is to become aware of one's own mistakes and shortcomings. We should engage in life-long practice. Awareness is not practiced only to let it go again – over time it will stop being an exercise and become more enjoyable.

In summary, then, there are three methods for developing awareness, *study, contemplation* and *meditation* which release three essential qualities: *beneficial behaviour*, *mental calm* and *wisdom.* They belong together: three methods and three qualities.

Five steps in cultivating awareness

First step: Pause and step into awareness

We say 'stop', we pause and refrain from reacting automatically. We give ourselves time, and remind ourselves how to behave better, stopping the projections, not believing them, considering other points of view, not letting indifference lull us, not taking any further negative actions. We limit the damage, ask for help, and step back in order to learn new ways of behaving.

Second step: Apply helpful methods to support awareness

By pausing, we can apply antidotes: study and contemplate helpful texts, strengthen our focus on what is essential, remember inspiring examples, practice mindfulness, empathize with others, perform beneficial actions, seek help, test novel approaches, share with others, stimulate the mind and arouse interest.

Third step: Transform your perspective of life

The third step is about maintaining an inquiring mindset, even with dull states of mind. Cultivating an open, interested attitude and taking the leap into a radically different view of ourselves: contemplating ourselves as an expression of awakened awareness, as a *buddha in the making*, allowing us to glimpse the vast mind of the buddhas. We no longer regard veiled states of mind as enemies, but as aids to a deeper understanding. Ignorance, dullness and doubt are welcome challenges, asking us to let go more deeply and approach life more intensely. We can deepen inner relaxation and move further into awakened consciousness. By recognizing – relaxing – flowing in openness, understanding and love, our life becomes more energetic and gradually emotions become our friends.

Instead of being so convinced that the world is attacking us, and we are a victim, we discover how we are constantly shaping the world, and we deal with situations differently as a result. We take the initiative, participate, and take responsibility. We can also see ourselves and others, as potential buddhas, and so come into contact with inherent qualities more easily. Maybe we will see with our inner eye that the aggressor has something wonderful in them. This gives us the opportunity to relate to their deeper layers and not to react to the surface. We feed our emotions less – because our attention remains on the essential: the healthiest aspects of ourselves and others.

Fourth step: Liberate lack of awareness in its true nature

This is about seeing the true nature of our clouded states of mind and discovering that they have no concrete existence. Dullness frees itself in the moment of recognition, just like the notions of subject and object. The 'method' consists of looking directly at the feeling of the self, that is, at the one who thinks they are real (the subject), or to sense directly into the trigger of the emotion (the supposed object). This direct looking or sensing dissolves the illusion of both self and other and we experience an amazing inner openness. Experiences of lack of awareness reveal themselves as the awake and open nature of the mind.

Our trust in simple suchness grows. We can forget ourselves and learn that there is actually nothing to defend. Certainty concerning the nature of the mind frees one from fear. We experience openness without control. Mahāmudrā meditation is total release, like falling asleep, but with complete clarity. When we fully let go with awareness, we discover that there is no one, no self.

Presence, familiarity, awareness, and wisdom replace fear. Fear reveals a problem, but not the solution; the solution is only found when the fearful awareness relaxes. Unblocking it leads to panoramic awareness, deeper understanding, and meaningful action. But fearlessness per se is not evidence of wisdom! There is also a sound fear, for example of creating suffering. But the usual fears are rather an expression of lack of awareness, lack of empathy, naivety, numbness and misjudgement of oneself and others.

Fifth step: Take lack of awareness as a path

Everyone who is familiar with looking into cloudy, foggy states of mind can actively seek them out repeatedly to re-experience the illuminating clarity of the nature of mind as a way of dissolving the veil of awareness. In directly experiencing dull states of mind, the timeless awareness of the sphere of all phenomena is revealed. The practice consists of sleeping and dreaming as much as we want, consciously letting ourselves slide into sluggish, dull states, and each time looking at the nature of this experience. In doing so, we rediscover the nature of mind each time. As more moments of ignorance are experienced in this way, realization grows, until there is complete certainty that ignorance never existed and that all veils were just illusory manifestations of mind and have always had the nature of timeless awareness.

2. Anger and resentment

Initial thoughts on the subject of anger and resentment have already been discussed in the context of applying the five steps in Chapter A.1. We will now delve more deeply into it.

All emotions of aversion, like anger, rage, wrath and hatred, actually reflect our desire. Behind the expressed "wanting not to have" there is a strong "wanting to have" and vice versa. Attachment and aversion always go together. When desire is frustrated and we have to experience the undesirable, then aversion, anger and rage all arise. Powerful desire easily leads to strong outbursts of anger, because both desire and anger are nourished by inflexible ideas about how something should be.

Anger and resentment demonstrate that something is important to us and that we feel attacked – it is about *me*. It can simply be that we do not want to expose ourselves to a painful, unpleasant experience. Anger attempts to get rid of the unpleasant. It is trying to prevent suffering from being experienced by *me*. When we become angry, we are indignant that things are not the way we want them to be. When we are *personally* identified with the world views at stake, any deviation from the desired norm is taken as a personal affront. Anger is a rebellion against how the world is. But instead of improving the situation, it usually makes it worse: aggression leads to defence and counter-attack – and the situation becomes entrenched. No one backs down, everyone is right and is fighting for what is best for the world.

From unpleasant sensations to aggression

Everything begins with an unpleasant feeling or thought. It can be an external perception – feeling, seeing, hearing, smelling, tasting – or an idea. This experience is registered as unpleasant. But instead of simply letting the impression pass by, we engage with it, which causes further discomfort. The longer we engage with it, the more impatient and angrier we become. Resentment against the unpleasant grows and can escalate to hostility and eventually to hatred. An imperative desire to eliminate the unpleasant arises. It would be best if it could disappear immediately – if not, then we become aggressive! We increasingly choose an aggressive response, in the belief that it will change things, or at least bring relief.

Anger darkens the mind and does not shy away from harsh words and harmful actions. If the unpleasant occurs repeatedly, it does not stop at a single outburst of anger. We get triggered faster and faster, and the triggers get smaller and smaller. Our character changes. We live in anger, become bitter and experience the world as hostile and aggressive. We attack others constantly as a means of defending ourselves. It begins to give joy to hit others. We become snappy and malicious. Filled with grief, pain, bitterness and hatred we indulge in malicious thoughts. We are increasingly contaminated by this mental poison of anger. Peace is impossible to find. We are like a taut string – overly sensitive, ready to snap. Anyone who touches our sore points must expect violent reactions. Entire groups, and even nations, can become so tense that a small provocation is enough to start a war.

We experience ourselves as *me here* with a territory that needs to be defended against intrusion by *others*. Firmly convinced that aggression comes from outside, we are less and less willing to compromise. We increasingly see every day unpleasant situations as targeted attacks on our well-being. Everything and everyone attack us. We struggle to convince others of our point of view. In the process, we experience an aversion to those closest to us. In our anger we now experience those we love as a constant annoyance. All their actions are inappropriate, and everything is experienced as a provocation. This may lead to increased withdrawal: "Let them do it! They don't understand me anyway. I only care about myself now. I will ignore their questions." Angry denial and disappointment can lead to depression – just as it is well known that the way out of depression is often preceded by experiencing repressed anger.

Anger is often not as crude and clear as described above, but mixed with other emotions, such as guilt. We are aware that something is wrong when we get angry. We feel that we are no longer thinking clearly and that we are not really acting in a rational way. We try to disguise this feeling of being on the wrong track with all sorts of arguments about why we *have to* feel and act like this. When we have a keen sense of how misplaced the anger is, we will try to divert and hide it.

Angry people are often afraid. When we see their fear, compassion awakens, and we can act in a different way. Perhaps we can find empathetic words, which show that their fears are being heard. We no longer relate to the other person's anger, but to their need for protection. We then behave in such a way that allows them to relax.

An angry mood can also arise without an obvious trigger. It searches for and finds a suitable object that brings the latent anger to the surface. The unpleasant perception finds the breeding ground of a mind that is inclined to react angrily. The emotional perspective or inclination is the decisive factor.

To illustrate this: we may have to confess something to a person that we think is guaranteed to make them angry. However, they may react calmly because their view of the situation is different from what we imagined. It depends on the mind-set and perspective of the person themselves, whether anger and aversion arise. The perspective colours the perception. Anger finds no support from a well-meaning, understanding and relaxed perspective.

How we assess a situation depends on the emotional patterns active now. These are the result of past experiences and the emotional tendencies that we have cultivated. They are *karma* – the effects of our past thoughts, feelings, and actions. To make something previously viewed with suspicion more trustworthy, requires positive mental impressions that make our view of the world more open and relaxed.

Beneficial thought and action support an open, positive perspective. Affirmations like "someone who criticizes me gives me a gift" work, if we have the *karmic cushion* for it, i.e. a firmly anchored goodwill. Without this anchoring, our positive perspective will quickly collapse. In order to maintain it, we need the inner strength that flows to us from beneficial experiences. We strengthen this source of power through tireless beneficial actions and a way of thinking that changes our perspective over the long term. That takes patience. Many ways of addressing stressful emotions work on developing a new attitude towards ourselves and the world, which allow us to respond differently. The root cause of anger is the tendency to think of ourselves as more important than others.

Other aspects of anger

A rejection of the unacceptable releases an emotional force which usually manages to change the situation – unfortunately not always for the better. If, however, we channel the energy intent on change more efficiently, it can be helpful. Anger is an attempt to feel less helpless or exposed. It bestows a feeling of strength and vitality – and actually there is a wish to shape the situation. Anger contains a potentially uplifting and clarifying energy as long as we stay mindful and do no harm. We mistakenly think that things can be moved on by doubling or tripling the verbal or aggressive tension. If we are trusted by our friends, short lived bursts of anger won't seriously damage anything, because everyone is aware of our basic positive intention. But anger eats up a great deal of goodwill and love when we allow ourselves to be carried away by it. So, it should be expressed as constructively as possible. As soon as the anger has been expressed, we turn to a constructive way of moving on. There are usually more skilful ways to draw attention to grievances than letting them explode and then picking up the pieces...

There is a particular type of skilful wrath that comes from wise compassion and shows no mercy for wrongdoing. It grabs the demons by the throat and lets them struggle until they give in. This anger is not ego based but directed fully towards the harm done rather than the one who is doing it. We grow beyond ourselves because we feel it is the right thing to do. Anger can also trigger honest communication. We're suddenly expressing something we didn't dare say before – preferably in a manner which gives no offence. Expressing criticism by talking about our own reactions.

Anger and rage also have boundary setting functions, as they protect the vulnerable ego. Intermediate steps are needed to develop healthy ego boundaries, especially in cases of trauma through assault or abuse. This includes feeling the anger in the first place and allowing it to simply be there. Anger that cannot be expressed is usually directed inwards and produces paralysis and sadness. When anger that has been swallowed re-emerges, it is a sign of healing process.

Those who refrain from projecting their anger will inevitably not protect themselves as much as before. They open their heart to their own feelings and will also listen better to the feelings of others. When we engage and show understanding, it may appear as weakness, because the emotional force of anger decreases. But so much more strength lies in admitting our own weaknesses, in opening the heart, in being able to give in at the right time! When we are firmly anchored in ourselves, we do not need anger to ward off assaults, attempted manipulation and mistaken views. It is enough to be anchored in the truth. If there is enough awareness, we do not need anger, only a compassionate, wise perspective.

Before addressing the issue of resolving anger, it is important to point out that the first step is to accept our own anger and our potential for aggression. Under no circumstances should we repress anger and become a *do-gooder*. It is better to express anger and rage in a moderate form than to swallow it. Once we have learned to appropriately express them, we can learn to do so in increasingly constructive and less hurtful ways. But if the first step of self-acceptance of the anger inside has not yet been taken, all the further steps cannot follow.

Three keys: Patience, understanding and compassion (exercise B.2)

When working with anger and rage, the first things that come to mind in buddhist mind training are: patience, understanding and compassion.

Patience

Patience is not just the equanimity of accepting the difficult and waiting until it passes. Real patience gives rise to relaxation and leads to an understanding that helps us breathe easy. Practicing patience is consciously cultivating the ability to relax when things are unpleasant, and especially in relation to the so-called "little" things: when something is bothering us, when traffic is slow, when things take longer than expected, when things go wrong, or when someone makes the same mistake, which we pointed out to them several times before.

The means of developing patience are the same as those for dealing with anger in traditional presentations. A good overview of buddhist mind training techniques is given in the chapter on patience in the

"Jewel Ornament of Liberation", where Gampopa lists nine reflections and five contemplations.[18] They are summarized here:

(1) When we contemplate the lack of freedom of those who causes us harm, we realize that they are trapped in their own emotions and are not as free to act differently as we might assume they are. (2) We consider our own contribution to this difficult situation through our actions (thinking, talking, physical acts) and (3) how our own emotional patterns and perspectives contribute to our experiencing anger. (4) If we had not sought out this situation, difficulties would not have arisen in the first place. We moved towards this person or into this situation. We are responsible for this ourselves and we accept it lovingly.

In addition, (5) part of the responsibility for our anger lies in our elevated level of sensitivity, which makes it difficult to remain calm. (6) With a certain sense of humour, we can ask ourselves: Who is actually more foolish? The one who says or does something annoying out of delusion, or the one who gets upset about it? (7) We can add: Does it actually make sense to get angry? What's the point?

We can also consider (8) how useful is the annoyance? "If nothing or no one challenges me, how would I know where my attachments lie and what I have to work on?" (9) The provocative, challenging situation is a gift, as if it came from our teacher, as a mirror to look in.

(10) Without such challenges, how could we become aware of our negativity and resolve demanding patterns? To free ourselves from old patterns, we need such situations! (11) Those

---

18 Jetsun Gampopa in "The Jewel Ornament of Liberation", chapter 14 on Patience, "Nine reflections to develop patience" and "Training in patience by becoming aware of five things".

who cause us the most problems are actually our best friends on the road to liberation, and we learn to appreciate them in new ways.

(12) It can be helpful to remember that those who cause us difficulties, as well as the situation itself, and all the emotions that arise in the process, are a *sequence of transitory phenomena* – that is, *this too will pass* because everything is change. (13) Finally, having been well prepared by all this, we develop compassion for our adversary by becoming aware of the other person's suffering and putting ourselves in their place. We make ourselves aware that this person, wants to be happy just like us. This creates warm, empathic feelings within us. Awareness is thus established (14), that the only solution to a conflict is to deeply permeate it with awareness and work constructively with the difficult parts in ourselves and others. The complete acceptance of others, as well as ourselves is essential.

These 14 contemplations radically change our view of anger-triggering situations. This corresponds to Step Three – *Changing the View of the Emotion* – of the five steps discussed in Chapter A. As a basis for these contemplations to motivate us to cultivate patience, we contemplate the many benefits of patience until we see deeply how patience makes life easier for everyone.

Understanding

Anger requires a multidimensional understanding of ourselves, the other person, the workings of emotional imprints (karmic forces) and the dreamlike nature of the emotion:

- Understanding ourselves involves knowing our motives and patterns and thus also lovingly accepting ourselves.
- Understanding others means being able to empathize with their

experiences, their perspectives, their motivations and patterns and accepting them lovingly.
- Understanding the workings of karmic forces involves a sense that distant causes and conditions are shaping the emotional experience now.
- Understanding the dreamlike nature of the emotion involves realizing its intangible, insubstantial nature.

The last two of these will be briefly discussed below. The karmic causes and conditions that now lead to anger arising in ourselves or others lie far in the past and can no longer be influenced retrospectively. Our opportunity lies with what is newly created, making a difference *now*. Perhaps this can be illustrated with an example: Something well-meant is completely misunderstood. The other person becomes furious. They don't want to listen and are convinced that they have understood exactly what is meant. Now that makes us angry... Let us say that the situation occurred decades ago so it's hardly possible to clarify the events. If we act intelligently, we can try to plant seeds for a new kind of relationship between the two of us in the present. We give up trying to deal with the other persons old dislike. Instead, we simply do what has a positive impact on the current situation. We turn to what is really constructive and do not continue to try to dissolve the other persons reservations.

It is similar with *karma*: we don't really understand why some people treat us with caution and others with open arms – it seems to have something to do with us and maybe the result of our own patterns and charisma. But instead of struggling with difficult reactions or resting on our laurels, we shape the current situation in such a way that many positive forces arise from it for the future. That is the only thing that makes sense.

Anger dissolves when we recognize our own emotional movies. Reality checking lets us recognize our own distorted perception. We can also investigate *who* is feeling upset – where is this 'I'? Nothing concrete to be found. If we deeply understand that the self does not exist as a concrete person who has to assert themself, defend or attack, the anger collapses. It goes up in smoke as soon as it is no longer nourished – what makes it seem so solid anyway? And what fears and needs lie behind the anger? How can we do justice to those fears in a better way?

An important aid to leaving anger behind is also to think about the possibility of death coming at any time. Do we really want to give this anger so much space, if there is a possibility that we will not see each other again tomorrow? Thinking about the possibility of death at any point, highlights what is really important. Every day, every goodbye, could be the last...

Compassion

Compassion here is the ability to empathize with others, to see through their eyes and then to respond with a warm heart. We exchange places with the other in imagination. Conversely, pity confuses and identifies one's own painful experiences with the experiences of others, and we often remain trapped in our own experience. With compassion, however, we resonate with others and out of compassion we then spontaneously take action to reduce the suffering they feel. Compassion is defined in buddhist mind training as the desire to reduce the suffering of others, followed by action.

In addition, when we think about how caught up in emotions we are, we become softer, and more compassionate towards others who are also caught up. As long as we assume in our anger that someone could behave differently, if they only wanted to do so, nothing would ever change in the situation. Others are by no means as free as we unconsciously assume or wish – they are as trapped in their emotional patterns as we are. They cannot change as easily as we would like them to. We may only have a little emotional leeway ourselves, – but that is exactly what we are using now to find a new perspective through compassionate understanding. A compassionate perspective allows us to perceive and process any irritations that may arise in a completely new way.

We learn not to judge ourselves, but to be forgiving when we get emotional. We allow our own feelings, work patiently on ourselves and with our fears. There will be setbacks, we become realistic and moderate our demands on ourselves. It is best to practice the heart-breath *(tonglen)* explained in chapter F with ourselves, accepting ourselves with our mistakes and our neediness (exercise F.1). We don't need to become anyone else – but we can deal with our feelings more skilfully. I remember a young father of four saying sadly, "I can't contain my anger. To take three breaths before I say anything seems impossible!" But he patiently continued to practice controlling his impulses. After two years he reported beaming: "Now I almost always manage it. When I get angry, I take deep breaths and take refuge. Then everything is not so bad!" From then on, he got his foot in the door in time more often. That's the type of patience it takes – keep on working.

Five steps in resolving anger

First step: Pause and set boundaries around anger

The initial step is to say "stop", "time out, I need some space!" We pause, because we do not want to be carried away by anger. We do not allow ourselves to inflict physical or emotional injuries on others from which they may have great difficulty in recovering. We realize how aggressive behaviour fuels the spiral of aggression and we draw a line: *Only express anger in a way that doesn't hurt anyone.* This is how we make the decision to prevent ourselves from being drawn in certain reactions, e.g. "I will not hurt anyone, I will not kill anybody, I will avoid words that hurt others etc." So, we first draw the line in the form of an inner agreement and then stick to this agreement in actual situations.

The work on ourselves begins within these boundaries. We can try out more appropriate ways of dealing with anger: We can direct our attention to bodily sensations, count breaths, or even change the situation by changing posture or moving to another room. We can internally scale the intensity of the experience (0 – 10) to distance ourselves. In all this, we practice self-acceptance and take loving care of ourselves, giving ourselves space and time. We might even use this space to ask for help. Take a deep breath, use I-messages (e.g. talk about yourself not accusing the other), stay calm, name your own needs, listen to the other person. It can help to say to yourself, "There is anger," or to say, "I am angry, but I am more than anger."

There are other de-escalating measures: If someone – for example in the context of a romantic relationship – feels unseen and overwhelmed, there are behavioural therapy interventions such as showing a *yellow card* as a warning, and – if needed – a *red card* as an imperative stop sign, just like in European football. There are even couples who act it out with a certain sense of humour by climbing onto a stable kitchen table to fight up there or who consciously go into the guest bathroom to continue arguing there. All this with the knowledge that it is difficult to keep a quarrel going in a small space. We can also just go for a walk or sit on our meditation cushion. These methods help to free us from identification with the emotion.

Second step: Apply helpful methods to dissolve anger

Among the tools available are the 14 contemplations mentioned previously as a means to develop patience. In addition, it helps to do lots of small positive things, because they create a benevolent attitude in our mind. We also practice anything that will help develop a deeper understanding of ourselves and others, as well as equanimity and compassion (see discussion in chapter F).

In order for methods such as breathing from the heart to be effective even when we are emotionally stressed, we need to practice them repeatedly – especially when we are doing reasonably well – until we have integrated them. With frequent, relaxed practice, these methods flow into our lives almost unnoticed and are then available to us in stressful situations. The objective of all these remedies is to find our way into that open and warm state of mind where others are as important as we are – and we are as important as them. The unity of love, compassion and wisdom, also called the mind of awakening *(bodhicitta)* is the universal remedy.

It is all about regaining inner flexibility. The world will not stop irritating us. To help others, we need to learn how to deal with these irritations and make sure that we do not constantly fall victim to our reactions. We strengthen our own capacity to act by reminding ourselves: "I can do something." Even if these are simply *valve activities* that have no more than a discharging effect: sports, dance, listening to or making music, hiking, gardening, visiting friends... positive things do help reduce the basic tension. Joy and happiness do not depend on *what* we do, but *how* we do it. Initially, we need activities that help us relax, then we can learn to relax the mind directly, without having to do anything: quiet contemplation, meditation, doing nothing...

Furthermore, we can work with the feelings retrospectively by turning towards the associated emotions, such as feelings of helplessness, desperation and having excessive demands. We infuse them all with loving awareness (see exercises F.1 – 4). On an emotional level there is often a wounded child – we experience ourselves transported back to our childhood: not being seen, not taken seriously, or understood. The adult is angry at authority, but underneath the three-year-old struggles with their father or mother.

It is easier for everyone, if we let go of fixed ideas, free ourselves from expectations, step out of roles, do not overwhelm ourselves and others, and do not let ourselves be aggravated by feelings of being rejected. We give up looking for culprits – it is usually too complex anyway. Instead, we focus on reconciliation, forgiving and asking for forgiveness. We can seek open dialogue to understand each other better. Perhaps we can put the subject of the dispute aside for a while. Rarely is a point so important that it is worth the controversy it sparks. And even with important points, it depends very much on *how* we argue. It is usually far more intelligent to prioritize face to face encounters, especially when dealing with people with diametrically opposed views. Once the human connection has been re-established, and everyone feels respected and heard, we can talk about matters which were previously difficult to discuss. In doing so, fresh solutions can often be found without the old endless unproductive arguments.

We create the basis for a life with less aggression by focusing on true happiness and actively promoting inner contentment. Instead of trying to change the world, we work on ourselves. We open ourselves to the care and love of others, cultivating relaxation and allowing feelings of connectedness to arise. We practice renouncing the unnecessary, helping each other and giving small gifts.

Third step: Transform your perspective of anger

The third step is about taking a new, helpful perspective: We can see the annoyance as a welcome lesson and even rejoice in it. It teaches us mindfulness, compassion and wisdom – everything a noble warrior needs. It promotes the qualities we need in order to help others. All situations are aids and pointers on the way, welcome challenges that help us let go even more deeply and enable us to turn to the true sources of happiness. This invigorates the practice, because anger becomes an ally.

In a way, the longer it marinates, the more exciting it becomes – and the clearer the mind becomes. The exciting part is to find out how we can relax with these challenges. Is it still possible to remain anchored in love and compassion, even now? Can we remain flexible, open and modest when arrows are fired at us? Difficult situations are difficult because we reach our limits and resistances are triggered. Showing us where we are stuck and have become identified.

For example, when we have to spend time with someone who has a lot of aggression, we can see them as our teacher in patience, compassion and understanding. If we fail to stay calm, we realize where our practice can go deeper. From that point of view, the other person's annoyance is welcome, it's how we know where we are still stuck.

In situations that makes us angry, there are at least two alternative approaches – realizing this helps enormously. For example, assuming that the other person has the best of intentions, that they are acting out of love or care, or simply assuming that there is a misunderstanding, or that we haven't hit the right note, etc.

The heart-breath (chapter F) is also a wonderful method for changing our perspective, because we connect benevolently with ourselves and the other person. In fact, all the classic methods of buddhist mind training open up new perspectives. Even a simple recollection of our *refuge* (chapter C: Clarifying the meaning of our life) brings the essentials back into consciousness and changes our inner orientation. We can also contemplate the positive sides of the person who we find difficult or imagine that they are our best friend. We consciously practice seeing things from the perspective of the other person, even the adversary: placing ourselves as the adversary and them as ourselves, until a complete exchange of inner experience has taken place. It helps to give victory to others and to accept defeat, to be considerate and forgiving of ourselves, instead of expecting this from others and to reach out to others instead of rejecting them.

We can contemplate how great the suffering of all living beings is and how they long for happiness as much as we do. As a result, we increasingly focus on the well-being of all and take an expansive perspective in which we do not regard others as rivals in happiness but deeply wish them freedom from suffering and complete well-being.

We can also meditate on ourselves as the buddha of the vajra family, Akṣobhya, symbolic of complete freedom from anger and the unimpeded, unblocked, mirror-like awareness of the awakened ones. There is also the better-known meditation on ourselves and all living beings as Buddha Avalokiteśvara, which is the same in essence. In this practice we enter into the expanse of the awakened compassion of all buddhas and regard all arising mind movements as aids to understanding the spontaneous activity of buddha-mind more deeply. Emerging anger is no longer seen as *my* anger, but as a dynamic expression of awareness. Anger is incorporated in this essential view of things. We look at its true nature and its strong but previously blocked energy is released and brings new insight and compassion. So, we apply the view of a buddha for whom anger is not a problem. Anger is simply energy or process.

Fourth step: Liberate anger in its true nature

The point here is to recognize the nature of mind in anger. To accomplish this, we look directly into the angry states of mind and discover that they have no concrete existence. They are *empty*, without a core of being, an essence. Aversion frees itself in the moment of recognition. Anger consists of thoughts that have no substance. Completely independent of the content of the anger, we make the process of attachment and rejection itself the object of practice.

Technically speaking, there are two ways of looking (or feeling into it): looking directly at the self, i.e., at the person who is angry (the supposed subject), or looking directly into the anger itself (the object). In fact, it is the same experience that is taken as the object of intuitive looking in slightly different ways: Sometimes we look more into the sense of self, sometimes more into the sense of otherness, into that which is perceived as not-me. In doing so, we let go directly into the centre of anger and experience that the observer and the observed are inseparable. In this moment of merging with the anger, the nature of the mind is revealed. This is even easier when the anger is strong, because with weaker emotions it is more difficult to let go of the observing distance. The best training grounds are angry feelings that arise in meditation. Where we may have the presence of mind to let go into them. In realization only clear, free mind remains. The inner turmoil is over immediately; there is no more anger to be found. An amazing discovery: anger is illusory.

Fifth step: Take anger as a path

The key here is to use anger as the path to awaken. We expose ourselves to provocations or consciously stimulate anger by thinking about things that make us angry. Each time the emotion is clearly felt, we look inside to re-discover its true nature and see through the deception. Stimulating the habitual patterns of aversion makes them conscious and direct seeing dissolves them. All angry states of mind have the same nature of mind – their dissolution reveals the mirror-like, completely unobstructed, free-flowing quality of awareness. The principle is the same for all emotions: stimulate the emotion and recognize its true nature. Śāntideva writes in *Entry to the Bodhisattva Path.*

> "Those who care nothing for their own suffering,
> conquer hate and all other mental poisons.
> Whoever achieves such victory is a true hero –
> the others are just killing corpses."[19]

3. Pride

Due to lack of awareness (in other words, due to fear and belief in a self) the desire to be special and the dislike of not being special transforms into pride. Pride is not fundamentally different from lack of awareness and desire and inevitably involves a tendency toward anger and jealousy. Proud people inevitably experience resentment when their own importance and their qualities are questioned. If they let this "insult" get to them, they become angry. But they often repress this unpleasant feeling. When someone says: "You're stupid," if they identify with it, they get angry. Without pride, the comment would not be a problem. Ego clinging is the starting point of pride.

Pride identifies itself with supposed or actual qualities that do not necessarily have to be our own. We can also identify with the qualities of *others*, e.g., with the supposed qualities of someone in our family: "*My* son is really good, the best in his class!" With pride it doesn't matter whether a quality is really there or not. It's enough for us to believe that it is. It may even be a mistake of which we are proud. A thief, for example, can be proud that they are really good at breaking in, no house has proved too much for them. A confidence trickster may be proud of how well they can lie to everyone and get anything they want. This is pride about supposed qualities, that in reality are character flaws. Pride also identifies itself with the mistakes of others,

19 Śāntideva, in Bodhicaryāvatāra, "The Bodhisattva's Way to Awakening", chapter 6, verse 20.

for example: "My son beats up everyone who gets in his way, no one can hurt him!"

Pride always finds something to latch on to, even if it is the total absence of any qualities, for example: "I'm the worst off of everyone. I have the worst disease. No one suffers like I do. I am the most depressed." It's all pride – it's all about being someone special and getting special attention. When this proud, twisted identification is questioned, for example, when we are told that there may be someone with a more serious illnesses, anger immediately rises up, a sure sign of hidden pride. This identification with one's own illness is a variant of the "completely misguided pride" described below (point 6).

Seven kinds of pride

As we can already see from this brief introduction, pride has an enormous range of different manifestations. Buddhist mind training distinguishes between seven such forms:

Arrogance

The first form of pride is arrogance or haughtiness, defined as *the belief that one is greatly superior to one's peers.* So, it's about the relationship to peers who have as many qualities as we do in a given area. We believe that we are vastly superior to them, even though we are in fact equally qualified. This is called arrogance and is often accompanied by a tendency to disparaging or aggressive impertinence when pushing away our equals. We try to undermine them with small biting remarks.

Condescension

The second form of pride is condescension, a *feeling of superiority over anyone deemed inferior.* This refers to our relationship with people who are less competent than we are and who we look down on. This form of complacent condescension or feigned affection is characterized by the attitude: "I have to lower myself to their level." We are so convinced we are superior that it is a great courtesy to respond to the other person at all. Condescension is characteristic of this feeling of superiority, which is often mixed with contempt for those less capable than us.

Presumptuousness

The third form of pride is presumptuousness – feeling *superior to those who are actually superior to us.* This severe form of pride looks down on others who have more qualities, abilities and skills than we do. We see neither our own faults nor the qualities of others. We do not notice that they are superior to us, and think, for example, that we can surpass them in competence in their specialist area. In a group, someone new may feel like they know better. Without taking in the skills of those present, they take the lead, and with great articulateness, put the whole thing down. If specialists are not particularly articulate, we may feel that they are not competent and that we could do better. A feeling of superiority arises in us, even though they know a lot more about the matter. Presumptuousness blocks our receptiveness and thus all further learning. There is no way to show the path to someone who is presumptuous.

Pretension

Undervaluing or pretension is a variant of presumptuousness. It is taking *oneself to be only slightly inferior to someone who is vastly superior to us.* We encounter a person who is far superior to us in competence, ability, insight, understanding and experience, and we think, "I'm not lacking much here. I'm almost like them. They're still superior to me, but only by a little. Soon I'll be better than them." We may notice the other's qualities, but we completely underestimate how great the difference is between us. The only reason we do not slide into complete presumptuousness and claim that we are better than them, is because the superior qualities of the person in question are unmistakably great and simply undeniable.

Conceit

Conceit, the fifth variation of pride, consists of *imagining that we have greater qualities than we actually have.* This describes the fundamental lack of objectivity that is present in all forms of pride. Unlike previous forms, it is not a matter of comparison with others but concerns only our own view of ourselves. We can be proud even without others. We can live alone on an island or in complete seclusion, and feel that we possess enormous qualities, such as being particularly brave, compassionate, or patient, an excellent swimmer, or whatever. There are no limits to conceit. As long as our imagined qualities are not put to the test by concrete situations, we can continue to believe in them unchallenged.

Completely misplaced pride

The next form of pride really takes this to the extreme. Completely misplaced pride can be defined as the thought that *one has abilities in a field where one has none at all, even to the extent that one takes pride in faults or defects.*

There is no actual basis for pride. We believe we are generous, but never actually give anything away. We think we are compassionate, but don't actually care about others. We think we have a certain quality without any evidence. This is a complete error. So, we may live in the belief that we are open to criticism but never take criticism seriously and choke it off immediately when it is expressed. We think it's easy to talk to us, but in truth we never listen.

The second variant of this completely misplaced pride is being proud of something that is actually a mistake or fault, such as being proud of how we fought our way to the top, elbowing others out of the way. This is the pride of ambitious people, who do not care about the well-being of others. They are selfish, but consider it a quality, to the extent that someone who is without any scruples in their social interactions pretends to be an example of compassion. They may even view their rude behaviour as compassionate, as a means of toughening others up. Unfortunately, such an attitude may even be used to justify killing, as an act of compassion. At the same time, there are militant pacifists whose whole behaviour is actually warlike. Such people are convinced that they are peaceful, but are filled with intolerance, constantly at war with the other people's beliefs. Such excesses of pride do not immediately manifest themselves as consistent character traits. There can be short-lived spurts of them. Who doesn't have moments of pride, for example by enjoying a victory at the expense of others, by having outwitted or tricked someone, even if it is just the parking attendant?

Complacency

Finally, we come to a particularly fundamental form of pride, complacency or vanity. It is defined as *self-satisfaction in connection with the assumption that these aggregates, of which our life experience is composed, make up a self.*[20] We identify, for example, with our outer, physical appearance, or with our mental abilities. This is something we all do. Complacency arises when we take self-satisfied pleasure in this body, composed of organs, bones, muscles and skin and look at ourselves in the mirror thinking how good we look. We can also identify with our own mental abilities, or the wonderful sound of our own voice and are happy to show off our qualities. We mistake beauty, strength and mental acuity for personal achievement, identify with them and feed of them with vanity. It then becomes particularly difficult when our voice becomes fragile, our skin wrinkled and our memory weak! We struggle in vain to stop the wheel of time. These long-established patterns of identification keep us locked in.

If we understand this, we will be careful not to identify with qualities that are ephemeral. It is absolutely essential that we seek to access the inherent, true qualities of being human, and to build our sense

20 The so-called *aggregates* (Skt. *skandhas*) refer to five basic processes, which together build up our experience of the world: (1) *perceiving forms* through our various senses, (2) *experiencing feeling tones* of an agreeable, disagreeable or neither-nor nature, (3) *distinguishing the various experiences from each other*, (4) *generating mental impulses*, which shape our experience in wholesome or unwholesome ways, and (5) *experiencing different states of consciousness* as a result of the interaction of all these factors. These five aspects of mental functioning are the building blocks of our believe in a personal self.

of self on them, without pride. Since these qualities don't belong to anyone and are common to all, they are also a good remedy for pride.

Other aspects of pride

Pride protects us, because the 'trivial things of this world' no longer upset us as much. From our ivory tower, the world seems far away: we aren't really affected by the suffering and problems around us. Pride offers a certain stability, as proud people are completely focused on themselves and find self-confidence in that. This makes them feel deceptively secure in dealing with others. When pride falters, so does this apparent self-confidence. But as long as it is maintained, one is barely affected by negative comments. Really proud people don't care about the opinions of others – all that counts is their own opinion. Pride is an emotional corset that supports and restricts at the same time – and if it is removed, the person collapses.

Pride gives us a sense of richness and abundance. But self-doubt can suddenly appear: "What do I really have to give? Who loves me anyway? I don't really have these qualities." Such doubts are experienced as a failure and quickly pushed aside. Pride resists inner work. It does not accept help. Only our own ideas can be any good! It is difficult to speak to a proud person. They live in an ivory tower, surrounded by servants. There is no willingness to question themselves. They sit in their fortress of self-assertion and do not question themselves on principle. A few qualities are enough to build an edifice of pride upon. They don't want to look any deeper, because self-doubt lurks in the depths – that's scary. A proud person is not capable of looking inward at their own weaknesses with the *eye of wisdom*. If they notice a flaw in themselves, they would be extremely embarrassed if others noticed it too. Self-criticism is diametrically opposed to pride. Pride collapses when we see our mistakes. This is also the greatest antidote to pride. Recognizing and admitting our own mistakes is exactly what dissolves pride.

For a proud person, contact with others means only that they are an audience. They're really just there to clap and say how great the proud person is. When they stop doing that, they no longer belong to the inner circle. The ivory tower keeps getting higher. Contacts are divided into potential admirers who might be useful and potential enemies who could undermine one's position.

The only things at stake for a proud person are to avoid defeat, criticism and humiliation, and to attain victory, praise and fame. These concerns dominate their life. Of course, a proud person is not always at the top of the social ladder. They have their superiors and people who can actually do things better. The proud person is obsessed with the question: "Is this someone I must show respect to because they are above me, or can I put them in the category of people who are below me?" Proud people will try to see how they can match up to their superiors and then surpass them. First, they have to become like them and then outdo them when the opportunity arises.

A proud person may call others 'friends' but does not really open up to them. They are used for specific ends. As soon as friends have served their purpose, they are left behind, so they don't get in the way of ambition. Well-meaning friends become a hinderance because they may not be as nimble at climbing the social ladder. Someone for whom pride is the defining characteristic has no peer friendships. Equal relationships with flowing interchange are unknown to a proud person. So, one of its characteristics is loneliness. Somebody who has no friends, should ask if the problem is pride.

There will be moments when, despite the desire for admiration, there will also be the desire for equal exchange. But because of their aloofness and tendency to humiliate others and point out their mistakes, no one will want to stay connected.

Pride includes exaggeration. Our own small achievements are inflated, and the contributions of others are forgotten. Narratives always have the same flavour. They are about how wonderful we are. We demand admiration and exaggerate our qualities, athletic achievements, travel experiences, victories, romantic adventures, all to make ourselves seem more interesting. Gross exaggeration can be used as an antidote to pride. Pride's attempt to advertise itself in the most dazzling colours dissolves into shared laughter. We exaggerate until it becomes obviously absurd and harmless.

Pride may be the most significant obstacle on the spiritual path. It closes the gates to blessings, help from teachers and the community. The door to compassion and connection with other living beings is closed. Pride is initially a pleasant feeling. We feel comfortable and self-satisfied, but we are stuck. It may take a long time for pride to become unpleasant enough that we want to get rid of it. Working on pride means descending from relative well-being into the uncomfortable world of our own inadequacy and neediness. Pride, at least at first, is not painful – it lulls and blinds us.

When pride collapses, there is a painful awakening: We see our mistakes and must admit to ourselves that we are quite ordinary, just like everyone else, perhaps even worse off than they are. We fall from a seemingly divine experience down to earth, to normality – and that usually hurts. But there is no other way. Later we will feel more comfortable, a lot lighter than when we carried the burden of our pride. We'll find it easier to relate to others. They will say "You are suddenly so human!". We make friends and somehow everything becomes easier, more carefree. Joy and exuberance arise because we no longer need to protect our self-image.

Pride, as buddhist texts describe it, is the last emotion that dissolves on the path of awakening. The reason for this is that the remaining ego-centred tendencies will continue to try to feed on the newly emerging and ever-increasing qualities for a long time. It's difficult enough to dissolve pride when we don't have many qualities – and when real qualities appear its doesn't get any easier, because now we seem to have a real reason to be proud. We can become proud of how deeply we meditate, how fearlessly we handle situations, how well we overcome emotional difficulties, in short: any qualities that appear. All *progress* along the way can again be used as fuel for pride and complacency. Our ego-clinging reclaims these qualities in retrospect. What really helps is to surrender completely to the blessing and to practicing devotion. We also need to realize that these qualities are not based on our self-centred actions, but are the spontaneous expression of natural being, when "I" finally is not in the way.

Three keys: Simplicity, devotion, friendship (exercise B.3)

Dissolving pride increases the joy of life. When genuine qualities take its place, something entirely new emerges which cures the deep-seated weakness of self-esteem. These qualities are summarized by three keywords: simplicity, devotion and friendship.

Simplicity

Simplicity here means the courage to just be who we are and not hide. As long as we strive to be the best, things get very complicated. It's not just about doing the best we can. We also want to succeed, to have an excellent position or to protect our position. We fend off criticism without listening. It's hard to teach us anything – even well-meaning advice is rejected. We find it easy to see faults in others. Being simple means giving up this complicated defensiveness and having the courage not to be special, just ordinary – with natural qualities. Simplicity makes us flexible. Because we don't want to be anyone special, we can make room for others. We become more flexible, both serving and leading, whatever the situation requires. We used to be as cluttered and ridged as a wardrobe, but thanks to increasing flexibility we can flow with situations – there are no longer any fundamental obstacles to getting involved with others.

Devotion

Devotion is a way of opening the heart. Entrusting oneself to the advice and guidance of someone who knows the way better, is a cure for pride. When we admit we need help, we don't feel so proud. With the acceptance of being guided and receiving help, comes the ability to see the qualities of others. We can take others as role models. When pride dissolves, we don't stop developing qualities, but we realize that they are not born out of ego clinging. We discover that these qualities ultimately come from buddha nature, and we are grateful that outer guides have shown us the way to the buddha within. This no longer has anything to do with inflated self-esteem. There is something very liberating in the discovery that the less identified we are, the more qualities flow. We do not need to create anything. To the extent that ego-clinging actually dissolves, to that extent all qualities will emerge. They are the natural expression of the nature of mind, and we don't need to do anything to create them – we only need to allow them, to surrender to them!

Devotion involves the modesty not to stand in the way of what is good. We are what is needed right now. A bodhisattva prayer says, "May I be the earth that bears them. May I be the bridge that leads them across. I will be to living beings exactly what they need right now." This is modesty. Without fixed ideas we serve and help where we can and don't need to be anyone special. Humility is a sign that simplicity is achieved. When we are simple and natural, we are also modest and humble in the best sense of the word. When we listen to the needs of the situation and follow the spirit of awakening, pride doesn't stand a chance.

Friendship

This means friends who respect each other as equals, who communicate and meet each other in their simplicity and ordinariness. Meeting each other on the natural human level, where we are all equal, is a cure for pride. This includes showing our weaknesses and the realization that we do not excel in everything. We climb down from our tower to where all people meet, and we are just someone among others. Gendun Rinpoche was an example of someone who was completely natural – it is not possible to be more human. He was so normal, there was no distance. There were times when people would come and lay their heads on his knees, in his lap. He took them, he stroked them, there was no distance. He was a friend to everyone. Time didn't matter. He didn't send people away and tell them their time was up. He was open, accepting and completely natural – fully human.

Five steps in resolving pride

First step: Pause and do not be fooled by pride

The first step is to pause and to refuse to cooperate with pride. We curb and relax the tendencies to inflate ourselves. We do not fall for the lure of pride.

In order for this to be possible, we first have to notice that pride spreads throughout our thinking, feeling and acting. It often feels seductively pleasant. Our face shines with self-confidence and well-being. We come alive, the conversation begins to flow, and we start to put ourselves in the limelight. We feel comfortable with it. Be careful! Pause, don't take pride's bait. Immediately refrain from any further proud behaviour. No need to exaggerate, tell stories, or emphasize our own qualities. We make an inner resolve not to encourage pride anymore but *just be ordinary.* That is what we cultivate now.

This deep determination not to let pride get the better of us is preceded by an awareness of the devastating effects of pride. Pausing gives us the opportunity to act differently in the future. There may be an awkward gap as a result, but we can continue talking normally and naturally, laughing at ourselves. This is made possible through finding joy in not being anyone special: "Enough of pride – now ordinariness is celebrated!"

To leave pride behind, we need to notice when we become artificial. There's something unnatural about pride. It is an expression of the need to show others how great or special we are. We play a role. So, it's a question of relaxing and dropping the mask. Usually painful feelings of loneliness, insecurity, wilful ignorance, fear and neediness lie behind this, which we do not want others to see. But that is exactly what is needed. We will learn to reveal ourselves with all these normal feelings, without much drama. The exercises that are described in the book will help. When we show ourselves, there can be real human connection. Superman and Superwoman are fictions. We can become real people with feelings, just like everyone else. Only then can we reach out to others with compassion and experience true joy and ease. With compassion and love as the energy of our encounters, everything flows.

Proud people are stuck in their habit patterns; they can be wonderful entertainers and make everyone laugh. But this is not real flexibility, which shows in the ability to switch from joy to seriousness and to deep compassion for someone who is currently experiencing something quite different; and then switch back again to lightness – not being fixed in any role, that's really natural being.

Second step: Apply helpful methods to reduce pride

In this second step anything is welcome which can help us to find a connected, sensitive, compassionate way of being. A long list of tools could be made, but only the most important ones will be listed here. *Taking refuge* is particularly helpful. By this is meant praying inwardly for guidance from the Awakened Ones, acknowledging that we need help. If we find ourselves getting lost in pride, recognizing that we need help, and managing to take refuge, then pride is no longer a real problem.

We can practice the *heart-breath* (chapter F), when we are open to help, we also notice how others need support, and then a real exchange can take place with an open heart. Heart breathing is never practiced out of pride, it develops its power through connected, simple being. With heart breathing we are not a great bodhisattva who frees the world from suffering, but a person with difficulties and weaknesses, who is aware that others also experience such challenges, and who is now ready to share their difficulties and support them with joy and love.

It is not so much about applying methods as it is about discovery, noticing the hidden pride that lurks behind other emotions, such as false modesty or feelings of inferiority, fear of failure or step fright. We notice our divisive attitude, how we emotionally dissociate and how strongly self-referential we are, and other uncomfortable aspects inherent in pride. We acknowledge pride to ourselves and others, stop hiding it and try to understand what lies behind it. We train ourselves – one could almost say out of self-interest, because we want to recover from pride – to serve others, doing small favours for them or giving them gifts, gestures of attention. We learn to genuinely appreciate others.

In the middle of a *fit of pride* it really helps to develop an awareness of one's own limitations. We see that we have no reason to be proud. This is revealed by the simple question: "If I really am as great as I think I am, why aren't I enlightened yet?" On closer inspection, our supposed qualities are of a purely worldly nature. We are not able to free ourselves (let alone others) from saṃsāra.

We can also recall the transience of the qualities we are so proud of – are any of them helpful in a breakup, or with illness, old age or death? Genuine qualities, whenever they actually appear, are not of our own making, but expressions of the nature of the mind itself and therefore nothing to be proud of. These true qualities manifest through letting go and not through self-centredness. It also helps to see how insignificant and interchangeable we actually are, for all our uniqueness. What will our friends truly remember with gratitude when we die – our worldly achievements or our humanity? It is good to contemplate our own weakness and to become aware of our own mistakes. As proud people we need the "thorn" of healthy shame in order to cultivate a new, open attitude. If vanity is an issue, it helps to meditate on the true nature of one's body to dissolve the exaggerated sense of one's own attractiveness.

We will develop the courage and confidence to show our feelings, fears and weaknesses. We will acknowledge our desire for love and attention and our dependence on others, learn to appreciate constructive criticism, stop avoiding difficult situations and build up a healthy self-esteem with confidence in actual abilities.

We will feel the need to cultivate peer friendships and to open ourselves to the care and love of others. We practice dealing with ourselves in a playful way and fulfil our roles flexibly, sometimes helping others and sometimes letting others help us. There is a joy in taking others as more important than ourselves, letting them take centre stage and holding back, until a satisfying sense of 'us' emerges. It helps to consciously cultivate an awareness of the qualities of others – to appreciate the qualities of our parents, teachers, relatives, friends and colleagues, with a special emphasis on contemplating the essential equality of ourselves and others in our true being (buddha nature).

We can also use specific methods as part of buddhist mind training, such as prostrations, refuge prayers, praise, bodhicitta contemplations, meditations on the heart-breath *(tonglen)*, guru yoga and the practice of cutting through *(chod)*, to name but a few. In fact, all sincerely applied dharma methods contribute to the dissolution of pride.

Third step: Transform a proud worldview into an experience of equality

The process just described develops into an ever more expansive, benevolent state of mind, in which all people and other living beings are equally important and equally valuable. They are recognized in their fundamental similarity: We all seek happiness and want to avoid suffering – and our minds all function in the same way. We share the same emotions and experience similar challenges and joys with only slight individual differences when we look at ourselves independently of culture, role, gender, age and possessions.

We assess our own mistakes and qualities more realistically. This in itself is a change in perspective. We do not need to deny our qualities, only place them in the service of others. Instead of considering how this situation can serve us, we ask ourselves how we can serve the situation? A radical change. Truly serving the wider situation, deeply committed to the greater good, and humbly, without attracting attention, contributing to the world, is a cure for pride. But pride likes to sneak in through the back door: we are not here to become the world's most famous and humble servant. We simply do our best.

Pride cannot be eliminated just by changing our behaviour – but practicing new ways of behaving is an essential part of the process.

Again and again, we call up the spirit of sincere service, devotion and compassion, again and again we distance ourselves from proud thoughts until we can smile about them. The change in perspective becomes clear when we no longer take ourselves so seriously and can laugh at ourselves. As pride fades, we will naturally share simple being more and more with others, just because what more is there to give to others than a few moments in naturally connected being?

Gendun Rinpoche's humorous "Notes for the proud" are a great help in this respect: "If I really were as great as I think I am, I should have been enlightened long ago! Why am I still wandering around in the cycle of existence? Why am I still trapped in emotional confusion? This proves that I am not as smart and wise as I think. It shows that I lacked the positive force to meet buddhas in the past and really follow the awakened masters. Otherwise, I would have been enlightened long ago! Fortunately, someone is now taking me by the hand and showing me the way. Without the blessing of the lama, I would be lost. The guru shows me my faults and how I can free myself from them. It's only thanks to the blessings of buddha, dharma and saṅgha that can I find out how to do this. I must be on the wrong track, because I have been wandering around saṃsāra since beginningless time, so no reason for pride. Millions upon millions of living beings have already found enlightenment and I'm still stuck."[21] By reasoning like this, pride gives way.

Perhaps we are familiar with thoughts like: "They should be happy that I am joining them now! It's a real boost to this project when someone like me shows up! The leader should be glad to have me here." Anyone who thinks like this is blind to how much help we have been given through the patience of our parents, teachers, trainers, friends, siblings, bosses, peers and employees, enabling us to find our way in the world. They have all taken care of us and shown us how this and that works. Reflecting on this, gratitude arises for all the support that others and of course nature give us. We begin to live with an

---

21 Notes from personal instructions from Gendun Rinpoche to the author (T. Borghardt), 1992.

awareness of interdependence – how deeply we all depend on each other and on nature.

The third step in the *Great Peacock* with each emotion involves entering into the expanded awareness of the buddhas, for example, the awareness that we ourselves, like everyone else are actually buddhas, like Tārā, Avalokiteśvara, the Medicine Buddha and so on. Entering into this awareness is called cultivating *vajra pride.* This is the 'pride' of the buddhas, an unshakable sense of self-worth based on the inherent qualities of the mind, completely free from attachment to an imagined self. Vajra pride is indestructible and is not subject to emotional influences – it is living in the awareness of all awakened qualities. There is no hesitation, no procrastination; there is complete self-confidence, free from belief in a personal, permanent, separately existing self. We could say it is an unshakable trust in our "true self" – that dimension of being that is common to all of us, a wealth of qualities, without centre, without owner, and completely free-flowing. There is no place for fear, awakened beings are unwavering. The *centre*, if we can speak of one at all, is bodhicitta, there is no splitting of reality into self and others. This is what vajra pride is: unwavering bodhicitta that expresses itself in spontaneous action for the good of the whole situation.

Fourth step: Liberate pride in its true nature

The fourth step, liberating pride in its true nature, is the same as for the other emotions: Looking into the proud impulse or thought, and looking directly into proud, egocentric states of mind. But how do we actually look into an emotion? We need mindfulness to notice the emotion, in this case pride. In the experience of pride, there is a sense of a core to the emotion where the energy is most dense. This is where we look, this is where we turn our attention, with a quick about-turn. This *feeling of density* may be physically located, in the stomach, in the heart or in the head, or it may seem like it is 'in the space of the mind', or the centre of thoughts which cannot be localized. We go where we feel the greatest intensity and see what happens.

Fifth step: Take pride as a path

The fifth step, taking pride as a path, is only possible if we have already recognized the true nature of pride. We then consciously place ourselves in situations where pride is stimulated – maybe when we get a lot of attention for something we have done well, the kind of situation that makes us forget our own shortcomings and that feeds pride. Once we have a clear sense of pride, we immediately look into that feeling. We will probably be doing this for the rest of our lives. There is no use running away from pride and avoiding situations where pride is triggered. Such as not teaching, because the ego might feed on it. If we do that pride will never dissolve. We just avoid it – but it continues in the background, like it always has. It is better to expose it and take it on directly. Working directly instead of avoiding it – this applies to all emotions.

We consciously allow pride to arise, to see its empty, ungraspable, dreamlike nature, each time, and in this way dissolve ego-centredness; the more moments of pride, the more opportunities to see the nature of the mind – and all of them equally ungraspable. We call the resulting realization the awareness of the equality of all phenomena.

What pulls pride up from the roots, is recognizing the nature of the one who is proud, the subject, the I. When we directly experience that this I does not really exist, that this observer is *empty,* that it has no innermost core that could be called an I, then we realize that all the qualities with which pride identifies itself, belong to no one. They are spontaneously present and active, and also without a core of being, without a centre. This realization cuts pride at the root.

Several teachers have explained to us that pride is difficult to dissolve and subtly accompanies practitioners up to the high bodhisattva levels. Therefore, we should not let go of our practice, or rather: let go especially here and systematically uproot the proud identifications until ego-clinging is no longer nourished and is finally completely dissolved.

Gendun Rinpoche says in his *Heart Advice:*[22]

> "When Dharma practitioners become narrow-minded and dogmatic and begin to believe that they belong to an elite that has a monopoly on wisdom, then their practice has become clouded by pride and jealousy and no longer has anything to do with real Dharma. If we want to correct such a grave aberration, we must become aware of our own pride and attempt to develop openness. Every day and in every situation, we should try hard to cultivate this openness and presence of mind. That constitutes true discipline, and through it our practice will deepen day by day. If we do not notice our pride, we will become more and more tense and prone to feelings of anger in our interactions with others. This anger may even be directed against our own teacher and against the practice of Dharma. That would be of the greatest danger for a practitioner."

4. Desire

In buddhist mind training, the word desire is used in an extremely broad sense, not only for sexual desire, strong craving, or addiction. Desire (craving) begins with the fact that we find an experience pleasant and want more of it. The evaluation *pleasant* (pleasant for *me*) is followed by a clinging that wants this experience to continue. This often goes unnoticed. The craving begins with wanting to have the beautiful flower from the garden in the living room. Desire in the sense of a *kleśa*, i.e. a stressful emotion, means wanting to possess an object that is seen as really existing. This can be a concrete object, a person, or even a concept, like reputation, fame, happiness etc.

22 Gendun Rinpoche in "Heart Advice from a Mahamudra Master" (Norbu Editions), page 190, in the chapter on "How to deal with Emotions in Meditation and Everyday Life".

For example, let's take a cup. We notice its distinctive features and think, "I like it!" Intrigued, we take a closer look. The attraction intensifies and we want to possess it: "Oh, how nice to have it at home!" This desire may lead to concrete actions: We buy it and take it home. Over time, we get used to it and develop a real attachment to it. If someone else wants a cup of tea, we prefer to offer them a different cup. It's hard to part with *our* cup. We always want to drink from it. There may even be a dependency and, to take the example to the extreme, we can't drink from any other cup!

The cup can be replaced by any other object of desire – everything that has been said applies equally to people who attract us. We can interrupt the process described at any time, even when we first have the desire to possess. We remember, for example, that ephemeral objects like the cup are not a source of lasting happiness. It becomes difficult when we are dependent. Then we have to decide to undergo a withdrawal treatment to regain inner freedom. The process is similar for every object of attachment, whether it is a cigarette, girlfriend, child or car. The attachment becomes deeply engrained, becomes a habit and sometimes escalates to the point of dependency. It makes us feel trapped and tense and leads to unfortunate acts of greed and possessiveness.

We do many things to keep the object or person of our attachment firmly within our sphere of influence. We try to establish a relationship between ourselves and the object or person that we want, to act as glue. We consider anything that could disrupt this relationship as an enemy. We even get into rages, become aggressive and destructive when there is a slight threat. Simply because we want to protect something we're attached to. We are afraid of separation, afraid of losing our privileged relationship with the object or person, afraid of finding ourselves alone, with a feeling of emptiness and dissatisfaction. We are on the run from inner emptiness and get involved in all sorts of attachments and distractions to avoid confrontation with reality.

Attachment as the basis of all emotions

Craving and attachment can be found in every stressful emotion. There is no emotional surge without clinging to something we desire or rejecting something we dislike. Attachment and desire fixate on something pleasant; anger, rage and fury fixate on something unpleasant and behind it all is the clinging to an imagined "I." In all stressful, burdening emotions there is a corresponding desire. We want to be left alone and that's why we get annoyed if someone disturbs our peace. We cling proudly to what we think we are or want to be. Likewise, without attachment to what we desire, there would be no envy or jealousy. We only get involved if someone has something that we want for ourselves or has more of it than we do. Because attachment is so omnipresent and always leads to tension, we practice its direct opposite – letting experiences flow on and remaining relaxed – as a basic healing approach.

Of course, the ability to grasp and fixate are absolutely necessary mental capacities. We need them every time we want to delve deeper into something. But unfortunately, this holding on and fixating develops into a strong habit and takes on a life of its own; it leads to us not being able to let go even when we want to! Unconsciously, we feel we can't let go or are not allowed to. Clinging and holding on have become quasi-automatic mechanisms that keep the internal hamster wheel turning – we cannot stop thinking due to clinging and are afraid of giving up control. What actually happens when we decide to let go more of sense perceptions, thoughts and emotions? Are we less happy?

Can happiness be found through holding on? No. Clinging cannot bring true happiness. Ignorantly, we become addicted through attachment and lose our freedom. We don't realize that happiness is found in a free, flowing mind, independent of all these coveted objects and people. Perhaps we have already had the experience of being simply happy with the way things are. These moments are not very spectacular and often don't get much attention. Just sitting at ease on the sofa and looking at the vastness of the sky or sitting relaxed on a park bench and just feeling how it is to be alive – or just breathing easily, nothing special. Joy cannot be held on to – it disappears as soon as we cling. But unaware of these simple basic facts of life, looking for happiness, we cling again and again to pleasant, joyful, happy experiences and it seems inconceivable that we could be happy any other way. This is ignorance, the opposite of wisdom: We consider what causes suffering to be happiness and indispensable, and what causes happiness we consider to be suffering and dangerous.

Clinging is recognizable by the fact that we get angry when we lose something, and we suffer from the loss or separation. Possessing or not possessing things is not an indication of how attached we are. Someone may own a great deal and be completely unattached and generous at the same time. It all depends on the state of mind.

Actually, what we cling to is the experience of happiness, and we think it is an attribute of the person or object experienced as pleasant. This is confused. Opening our mind makes us happy – the pleasant situation is only the trigger. Even unpleasant experiences or lack can generate happiness, if our mind opens. If our actions are directed towards making others happy – and we act in terms of *we* not *I* – then our own pursuit of happiness is catered for within that. We take on inconveniences of a personal nature in order to create a better situation overall. We feel happier when we can be of help. In this way, we develop the ability to bear suffering, and this makes us happy. We recognize that suffering and joy depend on personal priorities and views. In the end, everything depends on our state of mind.

As far as other people are concerned it is about turning attachment into support, into real love that allows space. Attachment suffocates love. A relationship is harmonious when we open up to fresh experience and let go of the old so that love can show itself. Then we are free to express our love in many different ways. Love is devotion and giving – and out of this happiness arises. Suffering comes from clinging and controlling. The challenge in relationships is to move from grasping to giving.

Attachment is based on fear – the fear of not having something or someone, and so we constantly take precautions to be ready for all eventualities, in order to pacify feelings of emptiness, restlessness, loneliness and desire. We do not want to experience lack, so we acquire always more possessions. If we are still able to share with others, desire and fear have not completely taken over. In our fear of experiencing lack, we keep anything that might come in handy one day, even a piece of string for example. And we might get upset if our partner wants to throw it away. In this way, we keep so many little things, just in case. This makes sense within reason – but a fear of coming into contact with unpleasant experiences underlies this: "I won't have what I need." If we learn not only to endure such experiences, but also to be able to continue to be happy during them, our inner freedom greatly expands.

If we observe ourselves over time, we will find two different unpleasant experiences associated with lack: The first is *boredom*: Time feels like it's standing still. We want distraction. Something to stimulate us, and end this feeling of being stuck. We desperately seek distraction from our hunger and thirst, anything to fill the hole. This is desire: the inability to deal with feelings of inner emptiness. If we can open into it, it disappears. Boredom is the sign of a tense, searching mind. We can relax through these feelings until we come out *on the other side*, deeply relaxed, at ease and fresh. Those who have had experience of this are no longer afraid of boredom. The fear of being terribly bored keeps many from meditating. But if we relax, boredom is short-lived. If we are still bored, we are not yet relaxed.

The second major difficulty is *loneliness*: feeling alone and cut off. We want to get out of this prison, where we are completely on our own. We need communication, exchange, openness. When we really open up to others, we don't feel lonely. People who meet openly, resonate with each other and their edges soften. This is perhaps the main drive behind sexual desire: to merge, to dissolve, and to forget ourselves. But if we keep the desire going, we keep up the tension, the distance, and due to this we continue to feel lonely and separated, even though we are not alone. It may be that we feel unspeakably alone at a big party because we cannot find a way of being open. Many people think it takes contact with others to open up. But even if we simply open internally, we feel connected, not separate, and a great inner freedom arises. We don't have to depend on others to escape loneliness. Like boredom, loneliness is a tension arising from searching, from want-ing. It dissolves when we relax.

The desire to find true contentment could motivate us to work on transforming the energy of desire. Satisfying desire superficially brings no real contentment; as soon as it is fulfilled a little, the next one comes up. It is like drinking salt water; it does not quench our thirst. Desire is not a basic need – it cannot be satisfied. Thirst or hunger are primary, basic needs – they can be appeased; they are not insatiable. In fact, desire is based on the need for satisfaction, peace and quiet. This is what we have to take care – of inner fulfilment. This is probably what sexual desire is all about: peace, fulfilment, connecting, flowing, opening and love – it is about qualities of being, more than about the sexual act. The following description from a participant illustrates this:

> "Once I was full of sexual desire, very aroused, but then I went to a storytelling evening where Sufi tales were recited. The arousal suddenly went away; it was very calming. The evening was more fulfilling and subtler, lighter than the sexual arousal. This wasn't a simple replacement; it was on a different plane. Fulfilment on the heart level. I realized how transient desire is. You experience something new and then jump at it. But I don't think an intellectual lecture would have had the same effect. There was real love in the stories, my heart was touched and that dissolved the tension and sexual desire."

Other aspects of craving and desire

There is a great wealth hidden in craving and desire. They, like everything else, only become a problem when attachment arises. The rise of desire itself does no harm to anyone. It quickly dissolves again, if it does not lead to identification. The problem is clinging to the emotion, not the emotion itself, which can even be used as fuel on the path. Everyone experiences how stressful clinging is. So why do we keep preferencing it to relaxation? Because it has benefits:

Desire is interested and brings us into connection, into communication with the world – and this creates joy! This is how the feeling arises that desire is a prerequisite for joy and connection. When we hear about dissolving attachment, we automatically fear losing joy, connection, losing our partners and friends. We mistake desire and attachment for the glue that holds our relationships together – what a fundamental confusion! We can also be interested in others out of love and come into connection through simple joie de vivre. The less attachment we have, the more capable of love we become. The true glue of our relationships is love, responsibility and care. This frees relationships from the whirlwinds of wanting and not wanting. We can desire without attachment – relaxed desire.

Desire affirms the world: The affirmation: "I am here and want precisely this" resonates with a positive basic attitude towards life. This is a basic affirmation of oneself, others and the many beautiful things in this world. But we can affirm and enjoy our being here without wanting to capture the beautiful experiences. This becomes possible once we combine the joy of the unique momentary experience with an awareness of its constant change – relaxed enjoyment.

Desire develops the ability to distinguish precisely: Desire for the greatest possible fulfilment sharpens our awareness of the subtle distinctions between similar objects or people. The search for the best vintage wine, the most beautiful piece of music, the top model, the best of whatever it is, refines the differentiation. But a relaxed interest develops this ability, without the stress of not being able to enjoy sub-optimal, normal sound experiences, tastes, relationships, etc. Love and compassion could also develop this ability, but differently.

Desire generates a high intensity of affection: The best example is that of lovers whose thoughts revolve constantly around the loved one. Everything is thought of. Lovers try to read each other's minds: What might give her pleasure? Being in love involves an intensity of affection which is hard to beat. And this affection does not disappear when the desire and associated fears diminish. Qualities of stress-free, joyful care can appear free of the high degree of attachment – a keen sense of what the other person enjoys and the pleasure of giving exactly that.

Those who cling to pleasure will develop an aversion to situations that do not offer this gratification. Desire is not satisfied with what we have now. When we are content, there is no desire. Let us cultivate contentment, simplicity, and even frugality – we are the first to benefit from this happiness

Three keys: Relaxation, giving, and loving (exercise B.4)

Relaxation

Relaxation means staying in the flow of both pleasant and unpleasant experiences. Being relaxed makes us happy, but it also requires the willingness to give things up and to let things be. We renounce to manipulate things in our favour; we let go and find our way into a relaxed state. This attitude of being prepared to let go of what is tempting, is needed to be free of the merry go round of desires. It is a question of no longer looking for external happiness but finding it within. Relaxing craving is not always easy. But if we manage to let go, we will experience the relaxed freedom and joy associated with it. The joy of being relaxed then itself becomes an incentive to pay less attention to desires that arise.

Generosity

Giving creates freedom. It dissolves craving and attachment. Wanting is healed by giving. We practice giving *and* receiving – giving *and* accepting help. In the therapeutic setting we practice generously giving our wholehearted attention to others. There is the saying: 'to lend an ear.' Through deep listening we gift people our interest in their lives. Giving frees us from the grip of desire. Wanting to possess becomes comparatively uninteresting, because giving and communicating are more satisfying.

Love

To love means to be deeply interested in the well-being of the other. Love gives what is good. It's not calculating. The more in love we are, the less attached, desirous and manipulating. Love gets rid of hidden motives for giving, and so, the recipient can freely enjoy the gift. They are free to simply be happy and feed on love with no obligation to give anything back. They are also free to then pass on this gift of joy and love to others – this is the natural progression. There are methods of developing love, kindness and goodwill, the most important of which is the heart-breath *(tonglen)* – which we will discuss later. But nothing is more effective than simply loving, that is showing deep kindness and compassionate interest to everyone we meet. We can engage with love in every situation.

Five steps in resolving desire

First step: Pause, set limits and keep a distance

The first step is to say "stop" and to refrain from acting out the impulses of craving, because acting out these impulses leads to entanglement and suffering. So, we do not insist on having satisfaction. Out of respect for ourselves and others, we pause in the midst of the emotional surge and put a stop to the projections that inflate the qualities of the desired object or person in our mind. We do our best not to be tempted to do harm in order to obtain what we desire. Maybe we have to make clear agreements with ourselves and others to break free from an addiction – we do whatever helps not to fall for the fantasies and delusions of desire.

Second step: Apply helpful methods to be less influenced by desire

The second step consists in employing antidotes, such as contemplations on impermanence and the true nature of the desired object. By pausing, we can give ourselves the possibility of acting differently. It also enables us to ask for help, to clarify priorities, to take positive action, to develop generosity and true kindness.

a) Dissolving desire through contemplation

- We can contemplate the impermanence of the desired person or object.
- We can contemplate the transience of the joy we derive from the fulfilment of that desire.
- We can contemplate the less attractive aspects of the desired person.[23] We can simply focus our attention on the many signs of change (fatigue, aging, illness, defecation, flatulence, sweat, odour...), aspects of the person we don't normally want to see. It is not about feeling aversion but about taking off the glasses of desire and adopting a balanced, sober view.
- A particularly sobering contemplation, recommended by the Buddha specifically against sensual desire, is to imagine what the body of the desired person looks like under the surface of the skin, layer by layer, organ by organ. Do we still experience them as desirable?
- Or we imagine what the desired person looks like at 60, 80 or 100 years of age. Will we still love them when they are old, frail or sick? We can apply this with slight modifications to objects and projects. This contemplation is not only sobering, but it also clarifies what we really love and value in the other person or what fundamentally motivates us in the relationship.
- We can also contemplate our own possible death: "If I were to die tonight, would I still want to follow the impulses of my de-

---

23 See, for example, the five meditations in Karma Chakme's Letter of Advice called "The Great Peacock", published in a teaching by Gendun Rinpoche "Working with the Emotions" (Editions Dzambala, 1992).

sire, or is something else more important? How would I use the time I have left, if I were to die in three years?" Thinking about death clarifies our priorities for life and dying alike. It can help free us from desire. We often realize how unimportant the fulfilment of our desires is in the light of possible imminent death.

- We can also contemplate what a prison the cycles of desire are. Attachment leads to craving, which leads to tension and to actions that bring only temporary relief, which leads to renewed craving, which in turn leads to disappointed desire with frustrated craving and renewed desire. Reflecting on and understanding this hamster wheel of craving, disappointment, hope and fear can also help let go of desires in concrete situations, when their fulfilment is not really important. It is about breaking free from all addictive behaviour.

b) Promoting relaxation and practicing letting go

- We can consider the dreamlike quality of the desired experience; how it is without substance, ungraspable, and how it melts away in an instant, with recurring dreams of hope, we can remember that 'I' and the object of 'my desire' are impermanent and not a constant source of joy.
- When meditating, we can practice not clinging to thoughts that arise, and the same for any other sensation. Sounds are perceived and we simply let them pass. Later we can practice this with emotionally coloured thoughts. The more we practice letting go, the easier it becomes to have the attitude, "That's interesting, but I won't dwell on it, because it leads to unnecessary complications." We become wiser and develop the ability to act on that wisdom, cultivating a relaxed attitude wherever possible.
- We can particularly practice developing satisfaction with our current circumstances and renunciation instead of over-involvement.
- We can also look directly into desire or dissatisfaction, into their basic nature. These feelings are nowhere to be found – desire is

an attitude, not a thing. Experiencing that there is nothing to be found saps the force of desire. All we really need to do is let the wave of desire rush by – just wait for it to pass – it has no substance and doesn't last. In this way, we can think of desire as a teacher that shows us how to let go.

c) Promoting true happiness

- We could also take care of being genuinely happy by allowing ourselves to relax in everyday life, allowing ourselves to open and experience the qualities we have always wanted. We actively ensure inner satisfaction and fulfilment. To do this, however, we must overcome moments of listlessness and discover the joys of disciplined action. This makes us less hungry and less dependent on the objects of our attachment. We are relaxed and freer as a result.
- We enjoy genuine quality of life by focusing on reliable sources of happiness that give inner peace. Exchanging the evening beer in front of the TV for the happiness of connecting with others. Opening up to care and love. We nurture and allow ourselves to be nurtured. We go from superficial satisfaction to more deeply fulfilling ways of being. The point is to actually make the connection we long for. Closeness and connectedness come about when we allow these feelings. Then attachments will have less power.
- We can adopt an attitude of sharing freely. This involves putting ourselves in others' shoes and making them happy, either through actions or in imagination, even when this might not be easy. Keeping the well-being of all in mind and taking a wide perspective makes us particularly happy. When we do this, we don't regard others as rivals in happiness, but as beloved friends to whom we wish the fulfilment of their heart's desires.

d) Special methods

- With stubborn habit patterns, it is helpful to make clear agreements with ourselves to resolve specific harmful behaviour.

- To get used to giving, we can give regularly or make symbolic offerings.
- The heart-breath meditation (tonglen) with giving and receiving especially helps to develop love and other heart qualities.

The sūtra requested by the lay practitioner *Ugra* states:

> "What we give is ours,
> what we keep at home is not ours.
> What we give away has value,
> what we keep at home is worthless.
> What we give away, we do not need to protect,
> what we keep at home, we must protect.
> What we give away, we don't need to worry about,
> what we keep at home is troubling.
> What we give away leads directly to awakening,
> what we keep at home leads to the next harmful act.
> What we give away brings great prosperity,
> what we keep at home does not bring prosperity.
> What we give away becomes an inexhaustible treasure,
> what we keep at home will run out..."[24]

Third step: Transform your perspective of desire

Sometimes desire is seen as an enemy. But this is not a helpful view. Rather, we can explore it to understand it more deeply. Then we discover its inherent qualities of interest, attention and openness to others. As we focus on the deeper emotional meaning of desire, external attachments fall away. We experience its clear energy, aimed at connection and fulfilment, with the possibility of love. Desire shows that something is needed – but it is often unclear at first what that is. We welcome attachment and craving as challenges that help us let

24 Quoted after Gampopa in "The Jewel Ornament of Liberation", chapter 12 on generosity.

go more deeply and turn to true sources of happiness. The practice is energized by making friends with desire. Particularly helpful are meditations in which we see ourselves as an aspect of the Buddha (e.g. Avalokiteśvara or Tārā) and get immersed in vast love and generosity without attachment. In insightful meditation we experience rising projections of desire as an expression of our deep appreciation of life. This is the present of the third step.

Fourth step: Liberate desire in its true nature

The fourth step is to look directly into the nature of the attached, ego-centred states of mind and perceive their "emptiness," the absence of solid existence. Clinging frees itself in the moment of realization. To experience the true nature of desire is to see the nature of mind. In that moment we realize simultaneously that there is no one who desires or loves, and that the desiring mind is basically just openness. We recognize that desire is illusory (insubstantial and changing), without an essence. There is nothing permanent in these movements of desire and craving.

Fifth step: Take desire as a path

When we have experience of seeing the empty, insubstantial nature of desire, it is possible to stimulate it to boiling point and completely dissolve the patterns of attachment. We stimulate it by consciously thinking of objects or persons we desire, and each time the desire is strong enough, we look into its true nature and experience again that it has no substance and no power. The all-distinguishing timeless awareness opens up – without anyone who desires.

5. Jealousy and Envy

Jealousy is a combination of anger, pride, desire, and lack of awareness. It is a feeling of anger, resentment or hostility when faced with others' good fortune. Jealousy is the desire to have what the other person has, be it a thing or a person.[25] It occurs when someone else is enjoying something *I* consider as *mine* or would like to be *mine*. Jealousy also includes envy and rivalry, where the rivalry can relate to all kinds of desirable objects, people and qualities.

Jealousy fears having to share an advantage or losing it to someone else. It is afraid of being excluded from happiness. So, jealousy exists *before* the loss, through just anticipating it. The mere idea of our partner cheating on us is enough to create jealousy.

Jealousy appears when what is desired is in danger of slipping away or seems unattainable. We knot up internally and can no longer enjoy the beauty or good fortune of others. As soon as we notice something desirable in others, comparisons set in: "Do I have that too? Am I as good?" If the answer is, "Okay, I have this too," we can relax; if not, we tense up.

In addition to envy and constriction there is often a feeling of being left out. It may seem that two of our friends get along better with each other than they do with us – and we can't rejoice because we want to be in that position. We might want to be the best friends of these people ourselves and not share them with others. Behind this is the fear of having to live without enjoying something, an agonizing feeling of lack, or emptiness. If we feel rich and complete, there is no jealousy.

Nobody wants to be jealous. Unlike pride, jealousy is never a comfortable feeling. It eats us up inside, but it is hard to get rid of. The feeling of not being as happy or fortunate as others is too strong. We want so much to be as happy as they are that we just can't let go. We are in prison. A way-out could be compassion or rejoicing in others, but that is exactly what is unattainable.

---

25 The First Mipham Rinpoche (Jamgon Ju Mipham Gyatso) defines jealousy in his "Introduction to the Procedure of Experts" (Mipham Kejug): "Jealousy belongs to the category of anger and includes not being able to bear the welfare of others due to clinging to profit, honour etc. as much as being mentally deeply troubled. It supports unhappiness and the mistake of not being able to let the mind rest naturally" (translation from Tibetan).

The jealous mindset: Looking with the eyes of jealousy

Jealous people devalue the joy of others in order to not suffer from their own sense of lack. An extreme would be if our partner loved someone else deeply and has never been happier than they are at the present. The more we become aware of the happiness of others, or the greater we think it is, the more we experience it as a threat. We feel the desire to destroy their happiness. This can go so far that jealous rage is even directed at the person or object of desire itself, following the logic: "If I can't enjoy it (her or him), then no one else will either!"

This destructive energy can also turn against us, if it can't find other outlets. Melancholy is often jealousy turned inward. Since we can't be happy, we are depressed, we can't allow ourselves to be happy, can't share others' joy and we close down. If we admitted that living in this world could be fun, we would have to ask ourselves why we were always so grumpy. We prefer to see the world in a gloomy light: "The world is nothing but suffering." This is a melancholic, jealous view of the world which ignores everything that constitutes a real path of awakening. When these distressing patterns dissolve, pure joy remains!

Jealousy is often accompanied by the suspicion that others might think badly of us. We can also accuse them of being jealous of us and that their real concern is to be better than us. When we do something good, we feel that everyone else is jealous of us. Through the lens of jealousy, we see jealousy everywhere – without seeing our own. We think that others are constantly evaluating other people's actions and comparing them to their own, when actually this is what we are doing, without realizing it. It doesn't strike us that we are jealous ourselves. We constantly think, perhaps unconsciously, that we aren't good enough and don't have enough.

Jealousy begrudges others their easy communication, their little pleasures, their parties together, whatever. After a party where two friends talked without us, we look suspiciously: Are they treating us differently? We are constantly prepared for the worst, because something may have been said or done against us. Always being on the alert is the burden of chronic jealousy. Ideally, we would even like to control our partner's wandering gaze.

Absence of jealousy can be a sign of pride, because we don't see any reason to be jealous: "Others are no match for me anyway. Why should *I* envy anyone?" But once the proud self-image collapses and doubts about one's own qualities arise, jealousy will immediately reveal itself.

Another form of jealousy is rivalry, which – unfortunately – is the usual driving force behind competing with others. Rarely are there truly "sporting" competitions where we are happy when others are better than us. This rivalry happens in all areas of society, even in friendships – a constant comparison with others. We want more recognition than others, more money, more influence, more knowledge, more friends, etc.

If that is our goal, we can roll up our sleeves and say to ourselves: "Get to work! I will show them." Ambition, jealousy, envy and rivalry release enormous amounts of energy; restless, dissatisfied energy that is bent on constant improvement, be it sporting achievements, personal successes, company sales or successes in the social or spiritual field. Unfortunately, ambitious, competitive striving can be highly effective. With this motivation we can do a lot for our own well-being, our own family, our own group, we can set a lot in motion. This energy in itself is wonderful, because it can achieve so much, but there is this compulsiveness to everything, an inability to sit still and simply enjoy. We are not exactly relaxed and happy. Gendun Rinpoche once said,

> "If only you would walk the spiritual path with as much energy as you muster for worldly goals! How much you take on when you play football! But when it comes to inner work, which is actually much more important, you despair all too easily!"

To overcome this competitive attitude, buddhist mind training encourages us to cultivate the opposite attitude: giving victory to others, taking defeat to ourselves.[26] Such an attitude is *really* courageous: wanting less for ourselves and being happy on top of that! Instead, what our society considers courageous, is often simply stupidity. Competitiveness and profit-seeking put ourselves, others, and the entire world at risk – a harrowing lack of wisdom and compassion. If we really have the well-being of all concerned at heart, we will rejoice wherever we see it arising. Heartfelt interest in the well-being of others dissolves jealousy, envy and competitiveness.

Three keys: Honest communication, equanimity and joy (exercise B.5)

Honest communication

Direct, honest communication seems to be particularly important in dissolving jealousy and envy, in addition to equanimity, joy and compassion. Frank communication, open and direct, keeps us from falling into jealousy. It creates a high degree of transparency without scheming. If we are jealous and envious of someone, it is best to seek direct communication, otherwise difficulties are inevitable. In face-to-face encounters, we probably can't hide the fact that we find it difficult to seek resolution and have inhibitions. But we will discover that the other person is a human being like us, with weaknesses and qualities. There is no point in harbouring aversion, because this person is also only human. Through direct communication we discover the other person as a human being – and usually that is enough.

If direct contact is not possible, we can practice the heart-breath exchange. For this, imagine the person sitting in front of you as if you were talking with each other. Breathe in and out, feeling them. Ask them inwardly how they are and listen attentively to your intuitive re-

---

26 Jamgon Kongtrul Lodrö Thaye, in his commentary on the 13th verse of Seven-Point Mind Training "The Main Road to Enlightenment", quotes the Kadampa master Langri Tangpa: "However much profound Dharma I consult, there is nothing more to understand than this: all faults are yours, all qualities belong to respected living beings, and because of this vital point, give profit and victory to others, take loss and defeat upon yourself."

sponse. Try to empathize, while breathing in and out, and share with the person in front how you feel inside. To declare yourself ready for "a benevolent coexistence" of the two of you, could be a good start. We ask them what they want – and listen to the intuitive answer as if it were real. Maybe we wish them luck and imagine support flowing to them, while breathing out. This imagined exchange is a way of preparing for a face-to-face conversation later.

Equanimity

Equanimity is primarily a matter of not judging so strongly out of attachment and aversion. Jealousy does not continue without judging – it is left without support. We can train equanimity in meditation by learning to observe our experiences, thoughts and feelings without judging them as desirable or undesirable. And in everyday life we practice accepting ourselves and others just as we are. We stop criticizing ourselves or others in this unconstructive way. A jealous mind is a fault-finding mind – never satisfied.

Equanimity involves a deep acceptance that sometimes we are less strong than others, less high up, less skilled, less intelligent, less loved, less whatever. This is what life teaches us – we can't always be better off or even as well off as others, especially not when we grow old and maybe nobody cares about us anymore. Embrace and accept it as it is. Being normal – even when we are still young and have life ahead of us. We can save ourselves the stress of wanting to have things we don't have and be who we aren't! The solution lies in acceptance of simple being. If we are not trying to be someone special, we don't get jealous of others – the comparison stops abruptly when we accept ourselves for who we are. As long as we try to convince others of our importance and special qualities we are out of balance.

Trungpa Rinpoche once described his feeling of being a grain of sand on the beach, as open, wide and free as the sky above the beach, a feeling of simply being a grain of sand among countless other grains of sand – nobody distinguishes between us and the grain of sand next to us. Just being this unknown grain of sand among countless others opens the mind to become as vast as the sky. Such a person no longer feels separate from the other grains of sand; neither do they feel separate from the sky above. The mind is free because there is no longer any striving for self-importance and for giving special meaning to this self.

Joy

With jealousy, developing the joy inherent in the relaxed mind plus the joy that comes from compassion are especially important. There is a way of doing this, which nowadays is often neglected: making sincere wishes for the well-being of all – aspiration prayers that all beings may be happy, that they may be joyful and experience the supreme joy of awakening. Prayers that they all may attain enlightenment even before us! Such prayers, if done sincerely, anchor the mind in the wholesome, as do mantras. We can make wishes to be able to contribute in all possible ways to everyone's joy and be of help to them.

Prayers have to feel right and be sincere, otherwise they are experienced as contrived. As soon as we notice jealousy, we can formulate a corresponding wish – something that expresses good will for the person who is the source of the jealousy; even if it is only: "I wish you no headaches today! May my jealousy stay with me and not harm you." If this creates more space internally, we can wish more such happiness to others – always in harmony with our inner feelings, in full integrity.

The prayers of the great awakened ones can inspire us, serve as an example, and help us to find our own words. We stop and feel into the words which are suggested: Do they resonate with us? Which prayer opens our heart? Only that will work for us. We can also formulate our own prayers. When we pray, we make wishes for all living beings, and we are included with them: May we all be spared from suffering. May we all find true happiness. May well-being and qualities increase. May everyone attain enlightenment as soon as possible! We dedicate this to the awakening of all. We are careful to always stay in the 'We-mode.'

If we use the inspiration of traditional prayers while formulating our own, then prayer will free up and become spontaneous. This spontaneous prayer for the good of all then no longer needs pre-formulated words. It may then be enough to always say the same heart prayer or mantra (prayer formula) like Om Mani Padme Hum.[27] Its sound will contain all the prayers we have already said and will be an expression of all the positive thoughts we have connected to it. But nothing beats the joy that humour releases. That's why it would be a gift for everyone, if we wrote the following note in our hearts and never forgot it:

> "Finally, I cannot stress enough the importance of having fun and not taking ourselves or life too seriously. One of the major flaws of many traditional spiritual systems is that they often make us take life so terribly seriously... if I had to lay out a set of principles for a spiritual path for healing, top of the list would be to laugh as often as possible every single day – and preferably at ourselves. This would come before any form of prayer, meditation, chanting or changing our eating habits. Everyday problems seem less and less important if they are viewed with humour and love."[28]

Five steps in resolving jealousy

First step: Pause and don't follow the jealousy

Noticing jealousy, we say with conviction: "No, I won't let you fool me. I will not speak disparagingly of others or harm them in any other way." We pause, realign ourselves inwardly (for example by connecting with our refuge), practice the heart-breath, make wishing prayers – whatever feels right. We put a stop to the jealous tendencies, distance ourselves, and relax. Behind this is the deep determination not to be taken in by jealousy. The motivation to really get rid

---

27 The mantra of the Buddha of Awakened Compassion (Avalokiteśvara) means, to put it simply: "Through the blessings of the Awakened Ones may the qualities of awakened compassion be experienced everywhere."

28 Anita Moorjani, "Dying to be me – My Journey from Cancer to Near Death to True Healing", Hay House Inc., 2014.

of it arises when we see its painful consequences and strive for real freedom and self-determination, when we want to find compassion, joy and inner peace and learn to really love.

Second step: Apply helpful methods to reduce jealousy

Pausing opens up the possibility of applying antidotes, such as sorting out our inner orientation, reconnecting through the heart-breath or through wishes. We use the situations where others are happy to join in with their joy. We develop genuine joy in the well-being and abilities of all. Instead of competing, we think, "it's great they are so good." We stop comparing and accept the situation as it is: Everyone experiences what they have sown, there is no alternative anyway. We are rich because we have found the dharma – why nurture the illusion that having more would make us happier? Wealthy people are not necessarily happier. We all possess fundamentally the same qualities; all have the same potential for happiness. Therefore, we focus on gaining access to our own buddha nature. We let go of thinking in terms of performance and competition. Life is too short for that; we will devote it to more essential things.

We boldly seek direct communication with potential rivals, address difficult situations and share recurring jealous thoughts. We speak out. We face the feeling of lack, show our weaknesses and reveal our desire for love and attention. We build up healthy self-esteem, trust ourselves and others, and immediately restore trust when it has been shaken. We rejoice in the success, well-being and beneficial actions of others as if they were our own. We offer to others more than they hope for and learn not to bind friends and loved ones to us. We are committed to ensuring that others have it better than we do. We take as our role model those who work joyfully and unstintingly for the good of all and work together with them wherever possible.

Third step: Transform the perspective of jealousy

The start of a new perspective could be that we regard jealousy as a teacher that makes us aware: "Look, you are comparing yourself to others and are taking yourself a little too seriously right now!" We see jealousy as an opportunity to keep working on ourselves. This new attitude involves always staying alive to joy – even when it happens in a context of competitiveness. Becoming familiar with this joyful attitude, the contrast to jealousy is immense. Jealousy won't be able to take roots anymore, because our groundedness in a positive attitude makes it easy to find our way back into an open mind.

Vajrayāna buddhism invites us to exchange the view of self-centredness for the view of awakening, where there are no more comparisons. Everything is the manifestation of buddha-mind. Even emotional tendencies are the dynamic manifestation of that very mind. What we make of it depends on our perspective: Perhaps, we remember the feeling of being one of those countless grains of sand under the vast sky – a perspective where everything is perfect as it is. When our self-centred view gives way to the view of awakening, then there is no one left to identify with jealous thoughts, and the blocked energy is available for the benefit of all. Jealousy as a friend says, "Oops, remember awakened awareness!" Thanks to this reminder, we can quickly open up to the new perspective again. The energy of jealousy is released, and we can do a lot for others – full of energy and relaxed at the same time.

Fourth step: Liberate jealousy in its true nature

To see the true nature of jealousy, let's look into the jealous experience. There is no centre to be found, no one who possesses this jealousy. We realize that the whole jealous drama is without substance, a dreamlike manifestation of the mind without inherent force, which we can deal with as we please – or just let it be. We can discover a centreless openness where we thought the centre of the jealousy was. Our energy flows freely again and it is impossible to engage with the jealous identification again.

Step five: Take jealousy as a path

Once the nature of jealousy is recognized, we can seek out situations which stimulate our tendencies to compare and to feel a short-coming or lack, such as when a competition is taking place. Repeatedly, when comparison, jealousy or rivalry arise, we look directly into the seeming centre of the emotion, and in this way, we take jealousy as a path to awakening. We stimulate jealousy to see the empty nature of the emotional experience each time. In doing so, the all-accomplishing, timeless awareness is revealed. It realizes that the situation as it is – as flawed as it may be – is complete and perfect in itself. Jealousy is never satisfied. All-accomplishing awareness on the other hand, realizes that the nature of any experience is perfect and complete in itself. This different view of existence, full of benevolence and free from jealousy, is described by Gendun Rinpoche:[29]

> "Bodhisattvas are keenly interested in others and are deeply affected when others suffer. From the depths of their hearts, they wish others to be full of happiness and free of suffering. When others experience happiness, they too are deeply happy, as others' happiness is their sole concern. Wherever such benevolence is found, any kind of jealousy, competition, pride, anger, and envy simply disappear.
>
> Bodhisattvas have no desire to be better or happier than others. In their hearts there is no place left for jealousy, and so they experience true inner peace, lasting joy, and a deep mental stability. Free of personal interests, they no longer cling to objects that they formerly chased after. Recognizing these objects as projections of the mind, they find inner peace. This peace springs from their concern for others – this is what we call mental calmness. Being free from attachment, a deep happiness arises in them, and their minds turn toward other beings, with the sole wish that others may be happy and free themselves from all suffering."

29 Gendun Rinpoche in "Heart Advice from a Mahamudra Master" (Norbu Editions, 2010) at the end of the chapter "How to deal with Emotions in Meditation and Everyday Life" (p. 192).

Summary: A new beginning on the stage of our life

These five basic emotional patterns describe the kind of drama we engage in each day. So far, the entire performance has been scripted by the emotions. Perhaps we now have a sense that this performance is a projection of our own views. We may think it a tragedy. A look behind the scenes also suggests a comedy. And: On the stage of our projections, we can change roles. If we dislike the old role, we can change it. How about an entirely new production, "The Path of Liberation" for example? We use our freedom of choice to give the play a new twist. The way is open in front of us; any role is possible. We can even make angels out of demons, but of course that takes practice. We have to empathize with them. We practice dealing with our projections in new ways, so that more lightness and liberation really arises. There are challenges, but no problems.

The drama will change as we let go. We discover new freedoms and new ways to behave. When we develop mindfulness, we can pause and act differently. We can pay attention to other feelings; compassion is much more pleasant than anger. We discover the play of love, joy, generosity, etc. and discover that they too are simply movements of our own mind. But this new production does not cause suffering; it even helps to ease others' tragedies. We become aware that everything is a manifestation of the mind, without substance, the illusory play of the moving mind. Thinking, speaking, acting take place – and nobody is identified with it. We are free in this play.

To escape the current drama, we can imagine the curtain going down. We have a short interval to collect ourselves and we have an idea of what our new role might look like. The curtain rises and the next act begins. So far, the play has been completely improvised; we have had no idea where it was going and who the director was. Now we anticipate that we can have a say in any number of decisions – we are going to try it out. We'd like a more joyful scene. We practice being more relaxed, more playful with ourselves, without making everything into a problem.

We give ourselves a little shove to step out on stage in the new second act and slip into our role. It is only a play. We soon get used to the new role. And then the curtain falls again. We have learned something new and plunge enthusiastically into the next act. In this way our lives develop from one act to the next.

At some point we die, that's the last act in this life. Our attitude when dying is the fruit of our life: How brave we have become! But there is still no end to the drama in sight – the curtain rises again, and our after-death performance begins... The more determined we are as we take on this new role, the easier the new beginnings will be – we are given a new life.

C. Clarifying the Meaning of One's Own Life

To bring about this *renewal* that we have just been exploring on the stage of our lives, we need to be clear about the direction we want our life to take. What is really important to us? This concerns the meaning of our personal lives – an absolutely essential issue underlaying many emotional crises, which are often *crises of meaning* in an emotional guise. We want to give our lives deeper meaning – but we have to find out for ourselves exactly what that meaning is. Our purpose isn't predetermined by any external authority – by God or by nature – but is found by contacting our deepest heart's desires.

Others cannot know what qualities inspire us most, and how we can best access our innate nature, our *buddha nature*. Only we can define our own goals in life in such a way that it becomes a lasting inspiration, a deeply motivating force that guides us through challenges and problems and helps us to create each *act* on the stage of life. In order to release this power, we need to clarify the meaning of our own life by personally exploring what the motivation is for engaging in life, accepting it and finding joy in it.

Many people, including some who seek psychotherapeutic support, are unsure about the true direction of their lives. Psychotherapy which focuses on essentials and is therefore *essential* will by its very nature help to clarify this meaning. This happens without any manipulation, just by inner sensing into qualities that inspire us – a process that continues throughout our lives, so that our sense of what we actually live for becomes ever more attuned.

Anyone who is connected to their purpose in life, their personal, unique motivation, gains an extraordinary inner stability and strength. Letting ourselves be guided by these meaningful qualities and aligning ourselves to them, serves as a compass in demanding situations.

In this way, the qualities become our *refuge* – a buddhist term that describes the central focus of our life on awakening; a focus that protects us from uncertainty and gives us safety and trust. If we keep the focus on these qualities alive, it gives us clarity and an unwavering understanding of the way – just like a compass. Clarifying the meaning of life is therefore an important additional tool when working with ourselves or with clients.[30]

Clarifying our priorities through contemplation (exercise C.1)

The exercise consists of seven steps and each step can be contemplated individually. Once we have become familiar with the individual steps, these reflections as a whole can form part of our daily practice; they are particularly helpful as a way into morning meditation. The later exercises in this chapter all build on this first one.

1. Before we even get to our own priorities, we lay a foundation of gratitude and appreciation for our human existence. Central questions we can ask ourselves are:
   – What can I be thankful for, here and now, today?
   – What do I appreciate most in my current life circumstances?
   The answers are personal, and we may initially have trouble finding them. But don't be discouraged, even if the only answer is: "I'm grateful to be able to breathe." We continue until we have a list of small and large things in our life to be grateful for despite all the difficulties. For example, we can be grateful that there are people who explore such issues and share their experience – and

30 These basic contemplations are found in many standard works of Tibetan buddhist mind training, for example: (1) "The Jewel Ornament of Liberation" by Jetsun Gampopa, (2) "Mahāmudrā – The Torch of True Meaning" by Jamgon Kongtrul Lodrö Thaye, (3) "Mahāmudrā – The Ocean of True Meaning" by Karmapa Wangchug Dorje, and (4) "Heart Advice of a Mahāmudrā Master" by Gendun Rinpoche.

have done so for centuries. We can appreciate how the wisdom of humanity is passed on from one generation to the next, and how we benefit from it. A feeling arises of how precious our lives actually are.

2. Then we contemplate our own mortality and the impermanence of all existence. "Yes, I too will die – and it is completely uncertain when that will be. I don't know when, it could be much earlier than statistics would suggest – quite unexpectedly." We become aware of how everything in nature changes and how our own experience is in constant flux. We contemplate the process nature of all being – all is change. This means that even our current life circumstances may only continue for a brief time. We get in touch with a sense of urgency, a desire to really use this precious situation for what is most important to us. An awareness develops that there is no time to lose.
3. Then we ask ourselves further questions:
   - What is really important to me now?
   - What is or would be my top priority in the face of impending death?
   - What specifically do I want to do now; how do I address my concerns?
   - How do I want to use this precious situation?
   - What do I want to do – and not do?
4. To further refine priorities, we can ask:
   - Where can I find true happiness in life, in death and beyond?
   - Where can I find what I am looking for in the depths of my heart? What emotional and spiritual qualities are especially important to me? How do I want to live so that I regret nothing at the time of death? Is it love, simplicity, natural being, wisdom, playful ease? What exactly is it? Which inner qualities inspire me and should be part of the realisation of my true, awakened self? (Exercises C.2 and C.3 will help with this.)
5. Then we inwardly focus on these qualities – on what is most important to us – and feel them with every cell of our being (see

exercise C.4). We then anchor the alignment with these qualities (e.g. with my personal *refuge*), by making an agreement with ourselves to use every opportunity and all circumstances to awaken and practice these essential qualities within us.

6. This is the beginning of the practice of releasing the qualities within our own mind stream. In this respect awareness of the breath in connection with the heart qualities ("heart-breath" or *tonglen*) is especially helpful.
7. Then all that remains for us is to practice this awakening mind under all circumstances of our daily lives. Out of this, straightforward signs of being familiar with the awakened qualities will appear.

Contemplating the qualities that particularly inspire me (exercise C.2)

To take the first exercise further, I would like to invite you, the reader, to try out the following sequence of exercises on yourself. We will focus on the following questions:

- What are the qualities in life I care about?
- Which one is *most* important, the true meaning of my life?
- What do I want to focus my healing process on?

You can record the following exercise (and any of the others, of course) and then listen back to it, pausing it every so often, to give yourself time, or you can just read it extremely slowly, taking care of each step until it feels complete:

Finding a place where I feel comfortable, I adopt any relaxed posture.

I feel the many different sensations of the body directly.

Among other sensations, I can feel the breath flowing, feel the contact with the floor and with the seat.

Gradually I feel the sensations in the soles of my feet, toes, insteps, ankles, lower legs, thighs, buttocks and pelvis, all the sensations throughout my lower body.

Then one by one the different sensations arising in the upper body.

I continue by opening up to the space surrounding the body, sensations of spaciousness and mobility.

Wherever I feel tension in the body – whether in the shoulder, the neck, or the stomach – I allow it to loosen up a little and allow movement to enter.

I let go especially in the abdomen, – since there is nothing to defend. The stomach can relax and soften. The breath flows, and I experience the movements of the abdominal wall.

Breathing in and breathing out I become aware of the whole body. Inhaling and exhaling I allow the body to relax. The mind also relaxes. Breathing in. Breathing out.

While inhaling and exhaling I connect with the flow of life, the vital sensations in body and mind. I notice how alive it is everywhere.

In this relaxed awareness, well connected with the body, I ask myself: What is most important to me in this life (and maybe even beyond this life)? Which qualities are most important to me?

Breathing in and out, I give myself all the space to feel the quality of being that I want to experience, to live by. What quality do I think life is worth living for?

To make it more conscious, and to anchor it, I name the quality with a single word or phrase or find an image for it – and then let go and continue to breathe.

Again, I can ask myself the same question: What qualities are most important to me? And listen to the inner responses – a feeling for the quality I want to manifest.

Several such intuitive images, feelings and beliefs may arise – accompanied by joy and inspiration: Yes, this is how I want to be, this is how I want to live! I name each quality or find an image which expresses it and keep coming back to the breath, feeling the quality within the body too.

And again I ask myself: What qualities do I want to encourage in my stream of being? Which ones do I want to give more space to, so they unfold fully? What qualities do I want to absorb myself in?

Finally, I ask myself: Are these all the qualities that inspire me, or is there something else left that needs attention and is particularly important to me now?

Then I connect these qualities with the contemplation of my own death and ask myself: Are these the qualities with which I want to breathe my last breath? Or are there other qualities that become particularly important in the dying process? What qualities do I want to guide my mind stream during the 'great transition'?

Do these qualities inspire me to the depths of my being, or would it take something else to release the forces of deep inspiration?

When assisting others in this work, we try to sense each of their personally significant qualities to find out what they really mean. If it is not obvious, we ask questions or ask for some examples from personal experience.

All these inspiring qualities together actually describe how we imagine our own awakening. If these qualities are active in us without any self-centredness, then they are awakened qualities. They first weaken and then dissolve ego centredness. Even if someone named only three qualities, it would be enough, because they are all connected. The quality of love is linked to the desire to be motivated by love when we encounter others, and to be lovingly devoted to them, without being self-concerned. It includes equanimity and serenity and much more. If we *tug* a little at the quality we identified, others will gradually emerge as well – the entire range of qualities emerge because they are all connected to each other.

For example, there is no generosity without love and compassion – we want to understand how best to support people, and ourselves, with love and compassion. This gives rise to wisdom – which arises in the wake of generosity, love and compassion. They are all connected. The same open attitude runs like a thread through all these qualities of mind – they are inseparable, one is a condition for the other.

When our inner inspiration becomes clear, we also know where our lifeblood comes from and why it sometimes dries up. We can then begin to actively shape our own process of awakening. This process depends on recollecting the qualities that provide us with lifeblood, as often as possible. This inner alignment is the essential aspect of the healing process.

Writing down particularly inspiring qualities (exercise C.3)

After contemplating the qualities that particularly inspire us, it's helpful to write down the most important ones. There may be many qualities involved, so it's worth identifying the most significant ones and underlining them, so that we can focus our energies on those.

We can do this on our own, or with a group of friends – it takes willingness to share our heart wishes, as well as paper and pens, and the time to listen and talk to one another. When a group pools the qualities that inspire them, it becomes clear how individual and yet connected our hearts concerns are.

For example, the following qualities were identified in a group which was training in Essential Psychotherapy: Generosity, liveliness, love, simplicity, a good heart, lightness, dancing dynamic being, inner freedom, wisdom, understanding, courage, freedom from fear, creativity, patience, loving awareness, compassion, kindness, warmth of heart, honesty, sincerity, forgiveness, gentleness, trust, clarity, presence, gratitude, generosity, acceptance, receiving, understanding, competence, gratitude, agility, contentment, naturalness, enjoyment of life, self-love, openness, joy, healthy ability to stand up for values and needs, determination, respect, dignity, ability to bond, vitality, humour, skill, energy, an absence of prejudice, equanimity, serenity, balance, authenticity, being in the flow, flexibility, ease, suppleness, stability, groundedness, being centred, strength, security, connectedness, friendship, modesty, self-confidence...

In buddhist practice, inner focus on qualities that particularly inspire us corresponds to the focus on awakening, which is also called *refuge.* This is a bit of an unfortunate translation, because going for refuge has nothing to do with *fleeing* or running away. It's true meaning is to "align oneself" with the real source of stability, clarity, purpose, and protection.

Awakening is a translation of *bodhi* in Sanskrit; accordingly, a *buddha* is an *awakened one.* Awakening to unveiled inner freedom is the very purpose of buddhist mind training. The qualities of awakening become outwardly manifest in awakened beings and can be experienced internally in our own mind. They are called the liberating qualities (pāramitā) that *lead to the other shore* or simply the qualities of our *buddha nature.* By this is meant that there are inherent qualities in each of us that naturally manifest when the obscuring blocks or veils dissolve. These qualities are the real driving force on the path of awakening. We can sense these qualities, because they are already at work within in us.

One prayer that expresses these thoughts and experiences is Śāntideva's eighth century refuge prayer which is often used in the Tibetan tradition:

> "Until enlightenment I take refuge in
> The buddha, the dharma, and the supreme community (saṅgha).
> Through the positive power of liberating qualities like generosity etc.
> May I realize perfect awakening, for the benefit of all living beings."

To put this in a less buddhist way:

> "In order to realize the real purpose of my life,
> I align myself with the inspiring qualities of awakening (buddha).
> In doing so I rely on a liberating understanding of the nature of life (dharma)
> and on authentic spiritual friends and companions (saṅgha).
> May I, by practicing liberating qualities like generosity, love, simplicity, etc., realize full awakening for the benefit of all."

Finding the qualities that are most important to us personally, provides a vision of how and for what we want to live. By implementing this vision, as best we can, it evolves and becomes clearer, incorporating new experiences and gaining strength. For further clarification, we can compare them to traditional descriptions of the qualities of awakening, which express the experiences and life goals of previous generations. By comparing our own inspiration with these traditional ideals, our personal vision of the meaning of life can be refined until we reach an inner vision that is coherent and right for us. Then all that remains is to put it into practice.

Buddha, dharma and saṅgha correspond to the goal, the way and the support. Even though these Sanskrit words may mean little to us, we all need clarity with regard to our goal or purpose in life, the path to follow in order to realize it, and all the resources and support we need.

Practicing the significant qualities that give us meaning, is our path, our *dharma*. It is based on the qualities which we want to live for; so, our therapeutic work also needs to be based on these qualities.

Just like us, many psychotherapeutic clients want to find a clear orientation and way of making decisions in the countless situations of their lives: what are their goals in life? Where does their life force want to go? How can we help our clients find this out? And how can we enable them to make it happen? How can we support the activation of these qualities in them? As therapists we want to support these qualities, their life goals.

By doing the two exercises outlined above, it becomes clear that simply contemplating these qualities already has a beneficial effect. With repeated, regular contemplation the effect is even more lasting, especially if we feel the qualities in every cell of our body (see exercise C.3). This strengthens the positive forces in us – the *healing mental factors*. Positive pathways emerge, and the drives that are neither beneficial for us nor others (the so-called "unwholesome mental factors") are no longer given energy. Similar to the buddhist practice of going for refuge, Essential Psychotherapy focuses intensively on strengthening the healing qualities that are at the centre of the clients' meaning of life.

In a crisis, the need to clarify our own purpose in life is particularly strong. Only when we have a strong heartfelt connection with the meaning of our life, do we find the strength to rediscover the path to awakening. In addition, we need to be clear about who can help us. The path of awakening and the path of healing are easier with the support of competent friends, helpers, companions and role models – this is our *saṅgha* – the community of those who are aligned to same qualities. First are those who know the way and are willing to guide and support us. In addition, our own inherent qualities, inspiring people, texts, audio, videos – and last but not least, nature – are among the resources available. We contact these resources in a purposeful manner, because they stimulate our innermost orientation.

The deepest resource is our ground of being (our *buddha nature*), from which all qualities arise. Our *refuge* is our guiding star; the inspiration we experience through the qualities we hold dear. This guiding star directs our thoughts, words and actions – it motivates us to realize these qualities. So, we experience ourselves in continuous motion towards the source of inspiration. The central inspiration is awakening itself, the entry into authentic, true being. How can we stay connected to these qualities in everyday life? What causes us to find our way into these qualities? The answer is: remembering them repeatedly with our whole body!

Experiencing the qualities in every cell of our body (exercise C.4)

The following exercise can become part of our daily practice:

Everything that happened today, just now, what you have just experienced – let all that fall away, as if dissolving into the ground...

Exhaling fully helps to let go completely. No need to worry about the future, it will happen by itself...

Then ask yourself: What do I care about? Which state of mind do I want to influence my next breath? My next inbreath, my next outbreath?

Take ten conscious breaths...

Breathing in, breathing out, with the quality you care about...

Now open all six senses, experiencing all the bodily sensations without preference...

See, without looking at anything...

Listen, without listening to anything...

Smell, without following the smell...

Taste without getting caught up in anything...

Feel what it's like to be aware...

...alert, open mind, open senses, open eyes...

At ease, not wanting anything...

Bring to mind an essential quality that is close to your heart. Feel it inside. Breathe with it...

Feel it with every cell. Let the breath become one with that quality...

Stay for at least three breaths in the direct experience of this quality, how it completely fills you and inspires you freshly...

If you want, you can add another quality. Stay with it, breathing, until it takes root deep inside you...

When the time comes, move into activity, with this essential quality.

Further considerations: With each transition from one situation to the next, we can recall the essential qualities. Whether we leave our house, get on a bus, have time between two clients, meet someone... Whenever something new happens, we "go for refuge." That means we remember what is essential, the source of our strength to deal with the new situation. We use every gap between two situations to adjust our compass: What is essential now? It helps to first feel the body and to relax, then to align the heart with the qualities, feeling them throughout the whole body as we breathe. This would be a three minute exercise during your counselling.

The outbreath can help us to relax more deeply – as if we were letting everything go with the flow of breath. Cutting our links to what went before. This can feel like a refreshing shower, a tingling fresh feeling that travels down through the body, with no need to think about who or what comes next. It's about opening into this uncontrived space – as if we were a blank sheet of paper. Simply being in the unformed now. In this openness we connect with the natural qualities of the mind and allow ourselves to breathe it in. Then we move on to the next situation. We bring in the next client, turn to a person, the files or emails.

This adjustment of the compass at the beginning of an event can also be supported by a prayer, by reading an inspiring text, a mantra, or the visualization of a buddha. We take refuge in the inherent awakened qualities.

These inherent qualities are not personal achievements; they are found in everyone. Initially, we may experience them as *my* qualities, but on closer inspection we notice that the less *I* there is, the more clearly these qualities appear. These are not created, conditioned qualities, but intrinsic qualities of the mind. They are the real refuge, the deepest resource. In the therapeutic process we remain intimately connected to them, while we bring difficulties and challenges to mind to be worked on. In doing so, we make sure that we are not overwhelmed by the difficulties but remain connected to the experience of the unadulterated now, with all its qualities, as continuously as possible. Awakening means: being awake, conscious, aware, without feelings of centre or separation, fluid, creative, connected, spontaneously active for the benefit of the situation as a whole.

Ten practical steps to cope with having lost the meaning of life (exercise C.5)

The question of the meaning of life can be addressed from yet another perspective. What is the point of our lives when everything falls apart? There may be a serious crisis, which will be deliberately exaggerated in what follows (but unfortunately it is also a real example).

Let's assume: We cannot find work despite having qualifications, cannot support ourselves or our family through having a job, and we feel completely worthless. We have so little money; we never go out. We are dissatisfied with ourselves and fight with our partner. It can get so difficult that we spend most of our time in front of the TV, surfing the internet or just staying in bed, because there is no reason to get up. However, it may be that we can give ourselves a nudge every day and struggle through our lives, taking care of our children, but without any prospects. Maybe we start drinking to forget everything. We probably blame others initially – the government, the banks, society and the well off – but we end up blaming ourselves for being so useless. The feeling of guilt and failure weighs heavily on us. What is the point of life in such a situation?

To take it to the extreme, we can imagine that we live in a country which is in crisis, we are unemployed and are paralyzed from a bad accident. What is it that stops us from taking our own life? What gives life meaning in such a situation?

To find the way through, we have to proceed step by step, with the smallest possible increments. The ten steps outlined below are spread over several days or even weeks. We only go as far as feels helpful and we start again the next day until each step feels integrated. It may be helpful to record our thoughts and feelings, and to adapt these reflections to the reality we face.

Step 1: Making a clear assessment of the situation

We reflect that many causes and conditions are responsible for our present circumstances – some may well be the result of how our country and society function today. Perhaps evil-minded, selfishly motivated people are also partly responsible, this even includes the materialistic attitude of normal people. Maybe we were too naive, too unaware, and certain personal deficits may have played a role in things turning out like this. All this is true. We see how everywhere, be it unemployment, divorce, accident or illness, there are causes and conditions at work that we can lament with reason – but then what? Complaining does not really help.

What helps is a clear, blunt assessment of the situation: it is catastrophic and there is no outside help on the horizon for the time being, if at all. What is more, waiting for outside help keeps us stuck in a dead end – and makes it difficult to mobilize our own energies. We are stuck in the most demanding situation we have ever experienced – it feels hopeless, and we now finally admit this to ourself. It is not easy, but necessary. So, what is the point of seeing the situation so clearly?

Step 2: Arriving at an acceptance of the situation

Seeing the situation clearly and realistically makes it possible to work with it. Hard as it is, we accept that this is how things are at the moment: there is a crisis, of unemployment, poverty, disability, loneliness and so on – all the things we never wanted to happen. By facing the facts, we stop the denial and can grasp the situation more deeply. Acceptance loosens the obstacles; resentment dissolves and a new attitude establishes itself. Now we can look at whether anything in the situation can change?

Step 3: Seeing that change is possible in principle

It's important to find out whether the situation can be changed. We may get caught up in how society, the economy or other external conditions need to change and how impossible it is to fully recover. But such outer conditions as these are difficult to influence. They are the result of many factors, most of which are beyond our control.

Nevertheless, there is change everywhere – in society, in the family, in one's own body. Everything changes, life is a process, an expression of dynamic forces. We feel different all the time, different moods appear – sometimes we are completely desperate and then a glimmer of hope appears; sometimes we feel deeply tired and exhausted and then we feel fresh energy in the body. On closer inspection, nothing stays the same. Experience changes, even if sometimes only subtly. Change is the law of life. So, in principle, change is not only possible but certain!

Step 4: Realizing that the consciousness of the individual is where things change

The actions, words and thoughts of countless individuals have an influence on our life. In addition to the forces of nature, our world is formed by the sum of the effects of our thoughts and actions, a gigantic network of mutual influence. What others think, say and do based on their respective consciousness influences, shapes, and changes our experience, family and relationships. But all too often we feel like a victim of changing conditions and circumstances. How can we influence and use this constant change to find a way into more helpful states of consciousness – even if we are stuck in a wheelchair?

Step 5: Insight – Starting with ourselves

We can't directly influence what others think, say and do – we can only influence this in ourselves. This is where we can start at any time, as difficult as it may seem. We can learn to control our thoughts and direct the mind. By working with our own mind, gradually, we can bring about quite surprising changes in direction. We can consciously direct our mind towards something beneficial; engage with something that interests us, turn towards someone with an open mind, letting goodwill flow. This can even stimulate others to go in the same direction. That's why we focus on where we can immediately (!) bring about beneficial change: our own attitude.

Step 6: Clarifying the direction to take

But which direction should we take when working with our own mind? Where exactly do we want to go? The decisive factor here is which qualities are most important to us in life. We could write down which qualities inspire us most – qualities like love, friendship, understanding – maybe simplicity, or creativity. Making a list, as long as we like, of all the qualities worth living for. Then underline the ones that are most important to us. These qualities have the power to give meaning to our life. For example, they describe how it would feel to be happy inside, even as an unemployed wheelchair user. What inspires us deep down, which heart qualities give us the strength to make the best out of life?

Step 7: Consciously placing these qualities at the centre of our life

Once we realize which qualities really inspire and give us strength, we can use them as an orientation. It's like recalibrating our compass and then wholeheartedly living out this inner vision. Going through life can be compared to crossing uncharted territory. We need to be well orientated – and a finely tuned compass will help, especially when we inevitably meet inconvenient situations, feel hopeless and want to give up. We orientate ourselves towards the qualities we want to bring into being, and we always find our way back to them. With them we give our life a very personal meaning – we focus on what is most important to us. However, it takes real determination to take life into our own hands and direct the mind in this way, right now, repeatedly.

Step 8: Regularly checking the direction

To develop consistency in our inner work, we must keep reminding ourselves of our direction with sufficient intensity. This will allow these qualities to develop in our mind so that they inspire our thoughts, words and actions. Someone who has to cope with a heavy blow of fate and – as in our example, has to live with a disability – can hardly lead a happy, meaningful life just because of a one-off decision. It takes continuous work, and it will be important to look for these qualities regularly and anchor them deep within (see exercise C.3). For this we need breaks, to pause and use our inner compass to see whether we are still going in the desired direction – these breaks are moments of contemplation. Perhaps we could set up a small place at home whose design and contents remind us of these qualities: a flower, a painting, a candle.

Step 9: Nourishing the qualities until we are naturally immersed in them

In the hustle and bustle of everyday life, we may be struck by how quickly we forget the qualities we have consciously placed in the centre of our lives. It takes daily practice over a prolonged period of time to nourish and anchor them until, with years of practice, they become completely natural, the free, natural expression of our being. The entire buddhist path is about this and presumably this is also true for other spiritual traditions. And: We can also awaken in a wheelchair!

Step 10: Inspire others to do the same

And of course, while still on the path, we share all this with everyone we meet or think of. We put them in touch with the qualities of simple being through our thoughts, words and actions. In this way, we stimulate meaningful change around us – within the ever-changing context of countless interdependent factors.

Life is about these qualities that give it a meaning and motivate us to shape our lives accordingly – healing creative forces. If someone shares their personal "heart wishes" in a group, we find ourselves resonating with almost all the qualities that are described. There is a feeling that we are one person, the qualities that are important to others could also be part of our own purpose in life:

Respect, compassion, love, generosity, kindness, benevolence, wisdom, understanding, awareness, vision, clarity, trust, stability, wholesomeness, reliability, pure motivation. Freshness, joy, presence, openness, gentleness, connection, compassion, warmth of heart, skill, freedom, freedom from desire, peace of mind, understanding, purity of heart, beneficial activity, gratitude, equanimity, sincerity, honesty, directness, authenticity, wholeness, patience, perseverance, simplicity, naturalness, energy, courage, fearlessness, serenity, ease, balance.

These qualities have been inspiring people for thousands of years; there is nothing specifically personal about them – the only personal thing is our choice of current priorities. The qualities that inspire us deeply connect us to almost everyone's chosen qualities. It seems that they are inherent qualities whose beneficial effects are known by the heart of humanity.

Seven steps to anchor the meaning of life deep in ourselves (exercise C.6)

As a summary of the above exercises, the following seven steps emerged:

1. First, we feel the body and ground ourselves, especially with the help of the sensations in the feet and the buttocks. Then we cultivate an awareness of the sensations of breathing, in order to settle.
2. Then we become aware (as in exercises C.2 and C.3) of the qualities that are essential to us by naming them and feeling them in the body at the same time.
3. For the "as-if" step we ask ourselves: "How does it feel when I imagine myself becoming completely one with these qualities?" We experience them with our whole being as if they had already unfolded completely within us.
4. We allow this experience to expand and feel into its centre.
5. Then we respectfully ask our deepest intuition to show us a symbol for these qualities.
6. Afterwards, we turn our attention to: "What is the next step to

start living out these qualities? What would it take to make this happen now?"

7. Finally, we embed the symbol (from step 5) deeply by imagining it inspiring us in different situations and then round off the exercise with a few moments of sitting quietly.

The exercises in this chapter help us become aware of our source of inspiration, our personal refuge. Going for refuge is a movement of inner alignment with the key qualities that we wish to live out. We are moving towards what is a clear inspiration for us – where we have the certainty: "This is the way! This is what I trust without any fear." Our refuge is where we want to go. We are quite different individual beings – and the description of our qualities of refuge as well as the symbols we use for them must fit us exactly.

One participant of the EPT training had never worked on this issue before. Here is a short excerpt from our dialogue that illustrates working with the symbol.

Tilmann: Where do you really want to go? What is your inner direction?

Participant: I can't even name it, but there is an image of a tree.

Tilmann: A tree? What do you think or feel when the tree appears?

Participant: Its roots.

Tilmann: What do the roots stand for?

Participant: For being connected to the essence, what is essential.

Tilmann: What else comes up when you imagine the tree?

Participant: Its branches and twigs go to infinity; they cover the whole of space.

Tilmann: Is it as if they were all-encompassing, all-pervading in space?

Participant: Yes, it is. That which is fed by the essential can pervade the whole of space. That is what I feel as my refuge.

This woman was able to experience her heart quality in the symbol of the all-pervading tree. The image then continued to accompany her as a source of inspiration. It was imbued with the fullness of her experience and a sense of what she is drawn to deep down in her being, which direction her inner development should go. Remembering the image from time to time was sufficient to strengthen her inner orientation, no more words were needed for the time being.

Everyone has their own symbols – these have special power, because they have more impact on the unconscious than concepts. Classic buddhist symbols representing the qualities of awakening include the Buddha's footprint, the lotus flower and the eight-spoked dharma wheel. Images of the Buddha were only used as a symbol of awakening from the third century BC onwards, due to the influence of Greek sculptors in the Gandhara empire. Before that the refuge was not represented as a person (but for example by an empty throne in the Ajanta caves).

Breathing consciously with these qualities in the heart (exercise C.7)

We practice the heart-breath (see chapter F) by breathing in and out while experiencing the qualities of the heart. This is first established in meditation and then extended to all activities.

- With these qualities in the heart ... breathe in and breathe out.
- With these qualities in the heart ... feel the whole body.
- With these qualities ... hear and listen.
- With these qualities ... see whatever your eyes perceive.
- With these qualities ... smell and taste.
- Perceive everything with these qualities in the heart.
- With these qualities ... lie, sit, stand, walk and dance.
- With these qualities ... talk and sing.
- Simply be, wherever you are, with these qualities in the heart.

Practising this allows for a conscious, heartfelt presence at all times in constant connection with our actual heart's qualities and wishes.

Meeting each other through heart-breath, without anything to do (exercise C.8)

For this little exercise we sit down in pairs opposite each other (we can also do this in imagination), as if we wanted to meditate. But the difference is that we look at each other without doing anything and just stay inwardly connected to the heart qualities. We give each other space and take care not to get caught up in thoughts about the other person. Continue until we have found complete peace and warm relaxation.

The exercise helps us to carry the loving awareness developed in individual practice over into communication with another person. It develops our capacity to simply be without doing anything while maintaining a heartfelt connection. This is needed to support each other on our paths.

D. Four Insights – Four Steps – Four Truths

Usually doctors and therapists have a four steps process when patients come to them with symptoms of an illness:

1. They investigate the problem.
2. They analyse the causes of the problem.
3. They consider the extent to which healing is possible and define the therapy goals.
4. They explain the therapy and encourage patients to carry it out.

These four steps occur more or less explicitly in every therapy, and this is how the Buddha proceeded 2500 years ago. He explained them in his first teaching in Sarnath near Benares, where he presented four insights that correspond to the classic therapeutic approach – but which, in contrast to individual therapy, can be applied universally. They became known as the "four noble truths" and serve as a guide for a psychotherapy of awakening. They describe four insights, common to all those who deeply look at the nature of existence:

1. *There is an experience of a quasi-omnipresent tension* – (a) the suffering and tension due to unpleasant experiences, (b) the subtle tension stimulated by pleasant experiences, and (c) the very subtle tension in all experiences involving the sense of a self as the centre of perception.
2. *There are identifiable causes of this tension* – firstly emotional tendencies of identification that trigger grasping, and secondly cognitive tendencies which separate a perceiving "self" (a subject) from a perceived "other".

3. *It is possible to experience a state completely free of any tension* – a completely open, flowing awareness, called "awakening". So, healing is possible! We experience the challenges of life without reacting to them with tendencies that cause tension.
4. *There is a viable, reliable way to find a way into that freedom and out of unnecessary tension* – and thus to become free from all reactive suffering. So, the therapy promises success.

These four truths or insights involve an in-depth analysis of existence with regard to four fundamental questions:

1. First, what are we suffering from? What oppresses us, what do we want to be free of?
2. What are the deeper, real causes of both gross and subtle forms of suffering? What do we have to free ourselves from so that it reduces?
3. To what extent is it possible to free oneself from suffering? What forms of suffering can be dissolved? Is awakening possible? What potential for healing do we experience?
4. What does a path to awakening look like? What are the next steps? What is particularly important? How can therapeutic work support awakening?

The inner logic of these four steps is obvious – one follows from the other. *First step:* We start from our own immediate experience. Alongside all that is beautiful and wonderful, there is always a certain amount of suffering, tension, stress, dissatisfaction and at the same time the desire to be less stressed, to suffer less and to happier. Acknowledging and accepting this, is the first step.

Second step: Instead of simply accepting the unsatisfactory situation with resignation, we look more closely: Where in our emotional patterns and ways of seeing things are there forces at work that lead to this specific manifestation of suffering? Investigating like this, we gradually become aware of the causes of suffering and dissatisfaction. For a therapeutically relevant analysis this would also include aspects of our personal history which has conditioned us, like childhood traumata, attachment disorders, deprivation and much more. Consciously investigating and accepting the underlying causes is the necessary second step.

Third step: Then we ask ourselves, if there is an alternative to continuing to function with the usual habit patterns and predisposing ourselves to continue to suffer and be unsatisfied. The bottom line is: Is there real happiness? Is there an end to suffering, as buddhist teachings put it, or is there at least the possibility of dissolving certain forms of suffering? Is there awakening? How much freedom, joy and happiness are actually possible for us humans? Or, to put it bluntly, "Doctor, can I be cured? Do I have to accept this forever, or is there a way out?"

We instinctively look around to see, if we can spot inspiring role models, people who have managed to largely free themselves or "awaken." Here the testimony of the Buddha is not quite enough, because his awakening was a long time ago. But fortunately, there are living examples of such awakening in our time. We can guess our realistic chances of healing based on examples alive today – assuming that we are basically structured in a comparable way (we "tick" similarly) and have similar opportunities as those who inspire us. Finding role models of healing and awakening and being inspired by the possibility of complete healing, leads to the next step.

Fourth step: When we meet or hear about such examples of inner healing, it makes sense to ask them and ourselves: "How can I set out on a similar path? What do I need to work on? For what do I need to look out?" We learn from the experiences of those who have travelled the path and connect this understanding with our own experiences and concerns. Setting out on the path is the decisive step or process.

To summarize the similarity between the Buddha's four insights or truths and psychotherapy:

The 1st truth corresponds to the diagnosis of the problem – we grasp the problem the patients come with, their specific form of suffering.

The 2nd truth is the diagnosis of the cause – we explore the actual cause of the suffering. What habit patterns are present, where do we have to start?

The 3rd truth corresponds to the therapeutic objective – healing or recovery.

The 4th truth is the therapy – the path that eliminates the causes of suffering, the way of liberation, healing or awakening.

The four truths as daily practice (exercise D.1)

We can apply the understanding of these four essential insights to our daily contemplative practice – and use them throughout our whole life:

1. To deepen our insight into the presence of suffering we explore to what extent tightness, stress, tension, dissatisfaction, and entanglement are present in me.
2. To deepen our insight into the causes of suffering we explore the underlying mental attitudes, thoughts, emotional habits and forces that create unnecessary tension.
3. To deepen our insight into the possibility of freedom from suffering we explore states of deep relaxation where the mind is completely free from any stress, open, at peace, joyful.
4. To deepen our insight into the path to freedom from suffering (healing) we apply the necessary methods to recognize and relax all those mental habits that cause suffering.

These four steps are the daily practice of every practitioner of buddhist mind training. They are the direct expression of the four core insights that became known as the Four Truths. As we practice them and explore our minds in this way, the insights become progressively deeper. We also understand their connection to therapeutic work:

1. When we take stock of our own behaviour and thus establish our personal "diagnosis of illness," we cannot help noticing that stress, tension and suffering are omnipresent in experience, in three forms:

- We experience tension due to obviously *unpleasant* experiences. This gives rise to feelings such as "I don't like this", "this is not good", "I have a problem" and perhaps "I would like to sort it out" or "I need help" – we notice the many feelings of dissatisfaction.
- We experience tension caused by our resistance to change in *pleasant* experiences. Easy-going life situations, romantic relationships, friendships, cherished family ties, reliable professional contacts, our own health and of course good weather – everything changes, and we have difficulties accepting that. When the pleasant turns unpleasant, we are forced to cope with loss, parting and separation. We might get tense well in advance, wanting to hold on to nice experiences. Such grasping leads to constant grieving, not accepting unavoidable change.
- Deep down there is another layer of suffering: the tension caused by dualistic perception due to separating a subject from an object of experience. This dualistic split creates an almost continuous, unconscious subtle tension with feelings of separateness. The signs are wanting to be in control and a longing for unity, deep peace and merging.

2. Through continued observation the causes of this suffering become apparent, and we establish our "diagnosis of the causes". These include emotional veils, the reactive emotional habits, our personal historic ruts, i.e. patterns of inflexible personality structures, fixations and identifications which have emerged from past experiences. These are ultimately based on a lack of awareness creating cognitive veils which constantly distort our perception. We experience situations with resistance or with desire and attachment.

3. Recognizing the causes also makes the "objective of the therapy" clearer: it seems possible to put an end to this suffering. Exemplars of such inner freedom give the necessary certainty that it

is possible in principle to attain full mental and spiritual health; healing is indeed possible! Peace (*nirvāṇa*), real happiness, deep harmony, attunement and contentment through dissolving the causes of suffering. Awakening is fluidity of mind, with a completely open heart. It is free from emotional and cognitive veils, completely unencumbered and spontaneous; compassion combined with insight into the non-self; timeless, nondual awareness in which the inherent qualities are free to manifest in all their fullness and without blockages.

4. The "therapy" – the path of liberation or healing is now obvious. We set to work and follow the so-called Eightfold Path. In doing so, we work on (1) our understanding, (2) motivation, (3) communication, (4) ethical behaviour, (5) engagement in wholesome livelihood, (6) developing a deep striving for authentic being (7) anchoring in mindfulness, (8) finding inner composure through deepening awareness.

First truth: What is suffering and what is happiness?

An example from therapeutic work: A client comes with "burn out": having had complete exhaustion for many months with long-term emotional overload. Finding a way out of the burn out is their immediate concern and thus the task of the therapy. Our task is of course to help the client to cope better with the obvious suffering in situations which they experience as highly unpleasant and to work on the emotional causes (over-identification, fear of failure, high expectations) for such tension. However, a psychotherapy of awakening also envisages a fundamental long term stress reduction, which includes all three levels of suffering and is basically the same for everyone:

(1) First of all, we need to develop the ability to accept unpleasant situations (mental, emotional and physical stress), to work on

them and not to reinforce them through rejection, but to deal with them in a most relaxed way.

(2) At the same time, we learn to stay relaxed in happy situations as well, not bringing stress into them by fearing and fighting their inevitable change but using them for deep relaxation and the experience of real joy.

(3) We also begin to work with the underlying tension, a feeling of separateness, a need for control, an inner restlessness or anxiety that is present almost all the time. This basic tension is already there on waking up in the morning and in the most quiet and simple moments. It accompanies the sense of "me" – always present when a supposed "I" is at the centre of perception. We are talking about the basic dualistic tension that arises whenever a supposed subject splits itself off from a supposed object of perception. From a buddhist point of view, this is the deep cause of all stress – the "existential stress" where an existential separateness is experienced. Feeling separated from one's own experience, from the body, from others, from the environment – a constant, subtle struggle. And deep down there is also a longing for peace, for relaxed being. This peace can only be found when we have clarified all these areas.

Coming back to our example: If we carry the above three points in our hearts, we will not only help the client with burn out to process the emotional triggers of their exhaustion. We will also keep an eye on these deeper layers of stress during the therapy, in order to open up ways of deepening relaxation for the client – if desired. It can be helpful to pass on information about where competent guidance in meditation can be found.

The goal is to forget ourselves with full awareness (!) more and more often. This self-forgetting is an essential quality for being genuinely happy, because it enables us to experience fully and to really flow in experience and action. The therapeutic mandate is to relieve obvious suffering, but we know that there are three more layers underneath: denial of the unpleasant, clinging to the pleasant and deep separation from experience.

Whether divorce, parting, aging or illness – where there was something pleasant previously, which is no longer there: a romantic relationship, a friendship, youthful vigour or health. We don't suffer so much from *what is*, like being without a partner, for example, but are constantly preoccupied with the fact that the familiar comfort *is no longer*. Within the apparent suffering is the suffering caused by change. And in it, in turn, is the suffering caused by dualistic perception, to put it bluntly: this tendency to observe and want to control everything, even within deep meditative calm.

Basically, there is no other way to real happiness than to deal with all these inner causes of stress and unhappiness. Everybody knows that nothing can make us truly happy – the most wonderful partners, the best holidays, the greatest sunsets, the biggest triumphs, the highest reputation and dream living conditions – if we can't relax. Yes, it is as simple as that: Unnecessary mental tension prevents joy and happiness. Mental relaxation, on the other hand, brings joy and happiness, regardless of external conditions. Staying relaxed in any situation without unnecessary tension is the path to awakening and happiness. Yes, it can be summed up in such a simple way. But what is not easy is to actually relax in this way in all situations, free from the reactive patterns of our identifications.

Happiness is to be found in awareness itself – relaxed awareness is joyful by nature. We probably know this experience too; perhaps if we have just received a deeply soothing, relaxing massage. When we open our eyes after the massage, fully aware and at the same time really relaxed, we are filled with a warm joy, a loving, grateful feeling. It is also possible to discover this joyful experience without massage – a relaxed, awake state. The joy, the inner happiness, is always there once the mind is released from all expectations and fears. Relaxed being is an inexhaustible source of happiness. Carrying this in the heart is part of a psychotherapy of awakening.

Second truth: Suffering arises from lack of awareness

A variety of causes provoke suffering, stress and tension in the body and mind. But here, too, the analysis can be condensed to one essential cause: whenever our mind closes down, lack of awareness is at play and with it a certain narrowing of heart or mind. Developing loving awareness dissolves this narrowness; compassion and wisdom free us from suffering. They are the two cornerstones of buddhist mind training – developing them creates a "wise heart," as Jack Kornfield called his wonderful book on this subject.

So where do we lack awareness? In relation to the nature of existence, its essential, unchanging characteristics. For all narrowness of heart and mind arises from not seeing, not experiencing these essential characteristics. This unawareness leads to fixations and blockages that prevent us from living in the natural flow of a wise heart.

We are not fully aware of the change inherent in all things and experiences. This leads to the illusion of permanence, with a fear of impermanence, and also to an exhausting desire to hold on to or not want situations, feelings, thoughts, experiences and things that are passing phenomena.

We need a deeper awareness of ourselves, of what we call the "I" – of our ever-changing process nature. Believing in a stable ego, a fixed person, whether oneself or others, always leads to disappointment, while an awareness of the dynamic nature of our being is a constantly flowing source of joy in life. We need to overcome our belief in stability, where there is no stability, as well as our belief in a concrete soul as an unchangeable, truly existing personal core, where, on closer inspection, there is only dynamic openness.

We lack awareness of the ever-changing process nature of our feelings and sensory experiences. We consider them to be all too concrete, stable and reliable, giving them a great power over us. This also applies to thoughts, memories and sensory impressions – they are all actually of a changeable nature, dynamic creations of our mind. When we are fully aware of this, we can deal with our experiences and thoughts more playfully.

When we do not see clearly, we are not fully aware of why we have certain experiences, why we go through this or that. Life sometimes seems to us as a game of chance or as unfair, because we do not see the subtle effects of our attitudes, thoughts, words and other actions. We fail to see the fine web of cause-effect relationships that weaves through our lives.

Let us become aware of the jewel we carry with us: our own mind. It can be so fluid, open and loving when we relax completely! We need to see that the freedom of heart we long for is already there – just around the corner, so to speak, in experience just as it is, in the "ordinary mind" of complete ease. An abundance of qualities is to be discovered in our relaxed heart mind. The sum total of our inherent qualities is called our "buddha nature". When we are not aware of our potential, trapped in emotional veils, we even doubt our own ability to love and to be open. But on closer inspection, these veils turn out to be ungraspable, without any substance. They have no power of their own, and they only conceal our true nature when we nourish them.

Every moment of lack of awareness leads to narrow states of mind full of solidification, wanting and grasping, combined with suffering, stress and tension. When we see through the mechanisms, we become highly motivated to stop grasping and clinging. And thanks to the flowing awareness which then arises, we will experience awake, free and happy states.

Even when we have already addressed some individual areas of lack of awareness, we may still not really see the direct connections between being aware and experiencing freedom and happiness, on the one hand, and lack of awareness with experiences of narrowness and suffering on the other. A precise sensing and deeper awareness will clarify that until direct experiences arise how every bit of increasing awareness bestows a deeper understanding of how things are and gives more space and new possibilities, bringing relief from oppressive feelings – all the way to freedom from fear and suffering.

This connection between lack of awareness and suffering is described by many experienced meditators: when the nature of life and mind is not understood, this unavoidably leads to suffering. Key insights into life and mind according to buddhism are as follows:[31]

- Complete stability is nowhere to be found. Life is change, transience. Impermanence *(anitya)* is a universal characteristic of existence.
- A fixed personal self, a stable essence of a person or an unchanging individual soul cannot be found anywhere, either by scientific research or by introspection. From that perspective it is correct to speak of "no stable self" *(anātman).*
- However, there is a dynamic occurrence of life experiences that is subjectively felt as personal and continuous, which develops and changes under the influence of creative *(karmic)* forces – a dynamic self.
- Thoughts, feelings and other states of mind don't show any lasting stability either; if they are not held on to, they vanish of their own accord in no time and our experience reveals itself as a constant play of mental formations *(saṁskāra).*
- Our life is not just determined by external forces or predestined according to a pre-existing plan, nor is it a mere series of coincidences. The world we personally experience is the result of countless interwoven mental, verbal and physical actions *(karma)*, which colour our perception of the world.
- We discover that there is not only an unfree, painful experience of life with manifold fixations, entanglements and fears *(saṃsāra)*, but also a completely free, awake, unencumbered and relaxed experience of life *(nirvāṇa).*
- Furthermore, it turns out that the emotional and cognitive veils, which colour our perception and create so much suffering, have no inherent power to bind us. They dissolve without remainder as soon as they are no longer fed, revealing the inherent poten-

31 The Sanskrit terms for the classical buddhist teachings are given in brackets.

tial of our mind, our inherent qualities called buddha nature *(tathāgatagarbha)*.

- Due to lack of awareness solid reality is attributed to external things and one identifies with the body, sensory perceptions, feelings, thoughts and all other mental processes as "I" and "mine." The erroneous assumption of a self as the centre or owner of these processes automatically leads to emotional reactions of grasping (attachment and aversion), which result in entanglement and suffering. At the same time, non-identification and non-grasping equally automatically lead to relaxation, open mind and liberation. This is called the two-fold dependent arising *(pratītyasamutpāda)* of suffering or freedom.

Each such discovery deepens our awareness and inner freedom. Love and compassion arise naturally, but they manifest in relatively unsentimental ways. We simply recognize that despite a lot of personal differences we are really all in the same boat. We are fundamentally trapped in the same delusions, experience remarkably similar suffering and carry within us the same desire for happiness and freedom of heart. These insights, summarized as the second truth, enable us to examine the root causes of psychological problems in depth.

Third truth: Awakening is possible, and suffering can have an end!

In a therapeutic context we might define full awakening *(buddha)* as "total spiritual healing". A fully awakened person would then be a fully healed person. And complete awakening – the final goal of the spiritual path – would correspond to perfect sanity of mind. There are many points which support this analogy.

The mahāyāna buddhist tradition defines the great awakening of a buddha as complete purification of all restrictive states of mind *(kleśa)* including freedom from all emotional and cognitive veils *(āvaraṇa)* and accompanied by the complete unfolding of all inherent qualities *(pāramitā),* all originating from compassion, and including continuous insightful awareness *(jñāna)* of the relative and ultimate aspects of reality.

According to this definition, buddhahood – or in our context perfect healing or complete sanity – is not a state of physical health or prowess nor does it mean to achieve some kind of eternal health overriding the laws of birth, age, sickness and death that apply to every human body. Rather, the path to complete liberation is about a completely sane mind, an unobstructed, loving and fully aware mind without self-concern. When the Buddha experienced awakening, he was initially not at all sure whether this could be communicated. But he convinced himself to try and point to this awakening in words. This is his teaching on the truth of the cessation of all suffering, which describes the potential within us: liberation from suffering through wisdom and compassion, entering timeless awareness with ensuing enlightened activity for the benefit of all. This vision of complete healing of the mind gives us an inkling of the ultimate goal of therapeutic endeavour.

The possible cessation of suffering was a crucial point in the Buddha's conversation with his first five disciples. His awe-inspiring presence inspired them to believe in his awakening. When he said, "You have the same possibility to awaken," they asked, "Who can testify to that?"

He said, "No one can bear witness to my awakening except perhaps the Earth", and he touched the ground with the fingertips of his right hand. It is said that the earth trembled in response. We don't have to believe in the earthquake; what is meant is that his way of being itself testified to awakening. Being in harmony with nature and with all that is, bears witness to the truth of the cessation of suffering, which is called *nirvāṇa*, peace.

Is it naïve to believe that we can actually become "healed" in the broadest sense – someone emotionally whole, balanced, happy and resilient – with a sound capacity to enjoy life? Without taking anything personally? Without ever losing our equilibrium? Without getting upset about unpleasant and provocative things, and at the same time without repressing and ignoring them? Is such a stable state achievable for us?

The enlightenment of the great teachers is described as just such a definitive healing: they continue to experience both the pleasant and the unpleasant, but rest in a stable inner equilibrium, as they no longer identify, in a healthy way, with what they have experienced or the person experiencing. For the rest of us, reactive, emotional patterns are constantly kicking in – and cognitive veils cloud our view of reality. So, we are all "on the path" and our state of health is reflected in how quickly we regain our inner balance. From this perspective, healing is a dynamic process, which is constantly taking place, a constant path of healing and recovery amidst multiple destabilizing forces. Seen in this light, we are all on our paths to healing, a continuous path of awakening. This might be meant when buddhist teachings say: "Awakening takes place in the now".

How I envision a completely healthy person (exercise D.2)

This simple exercise helps us to get a clearer sense of our own vision of health (and perhaps of awakening) – and to define: What is my own therapeutic goal? What do I think possible with regard to health and awakening?

All we need for the exercise is time, a piece of paper, and a pen – and then we reflect:

What is a healthy person like? How far can I awaken? What is it like when I really put my insights into practice with the full force of heart and mind?

Then we let our mind play with a realistic vision of complete healing and jot down some bullet points. As a second part of the exercise, we can share our ideas with someone else who, if possible, has also done this exercise. In the conversation that unfolds, we will probably come to a clearer sense of what our heart's wish in terms of healing is.

We are talking about the experience of awakening and healing – the heart mind of awakening, *bodhicitta* – an open, wise, loving heart. *Citta* in Sanskrit means heart or mind and *bodhi* means awakening. Awakening is complete openness, being completely unobstructed; it is a centreless awareness, free from all ego-centredness, free from the illusion that there is a 'someone', a core of being. It is a spontaneous awareness that needs no centre – an abundance of qualities that no one possesses. Healing or awakening means living in the abundance of natural qualities, being completely in flow – unhindered manifestation of all inherent qualities and abilities.

Therapy and awareness training bring these natural, inherent qualities to the fore. We support people in allowing space for these qualities. This has the best long-term results because creating space is not based on effort. We do not create qualities, we allow them. The curtains are opened. An experience of awakening is reliable when it is not based on effort – then it can manifest again and again. True therapy, similar to the path of awakening, consists of bringing this effortlessness into all areas of life. Rigid personality patterns bind energy. When this energy is released, the inherent qualities are revealed.

Fourth truth: Treading the path of awakening and healing

In order to follow the path, we need to first clearly assess the challenges which we find ourselves in (1st truth) and to identify the causes of our difficulties (2nd truth). Then we need to know where we actually want to go (3rd truth) and how we can get there (4th truth). The instructions and methods for following the path of awakening are the direct result of our understanding of the first three truths and many of these methods can also be used in therapeutic practice. Here we will mention only some of the most important exercises of buddhist mind training:

- Basically, all attempts at healing and awakening involve practicing the eightfold path of the noble ones: developing a helpful understanding (view), a beneficial inner attitude, beneficial speech, beneficial action, a helpful way of life, right effort, right mindfulness, and deep meditation (chapter A – I, exercise D.3).
- Treading the path involves practicing liberating qualities like generosity, wholesome conduct, patience, joyful perseverance, meditative stability, wisdom, skilful means, aspiration, strength, and timeless awareness (ch. A, B, G).
- As a foundation we contemplate four basic thoughts in order to identify our own priorities: We consider the preciousness of this life, its impermanence, the effects of our actions and the true sources of happiness and suffering (ex. C.1).
- This makes our own inner orientation clear, and it then becomes crucial not to lose sight of this focus on the real meaning of our life: our focus on refuge (ex. C.5, C.6).
- All along the path we practice wholesome activity, avoid harming ourselves or others, support each other to be skilful and cultivate positivity and awareness.
- In particular, we set free compassion, love and wisdom within ourselves and practice this in all areas (ch. F).
- In support of this, we immediately apply the remedies for disturbing emotions as soon as they appear (ch. A and B).
- We also support this process by examining our own mind and developing a reality-based view of the nature of existence, ultimately leaving all views behind and rooting ourselves entirely in direct experience (ch. E and G).
- The main method is to cultivate loving awareness in all areas of experience (body, sensations, mind, dharmas), to bring about mental calm and insight and to find one's way into natural being (ch. E).

The path of awakening is described in five paths, thirteen stages and four yogas, providing a kind of map which gives an idea of what experiences can emerge and must be lived through. Buddhist mind training is neither a religion nor a philosophy, but a path *(mārga)* that is followed through inner practice. The Buddha always spoke of a *path* of liberation and awakening, of a path of inner transformation and understanding – a path that unfolds through personal experience.

Faith can be an obstacle on such a path, because simply believing what is taught all too easily prevents personal enquiry and practice and ultimately limits personal understanding. But what is definitely needed for the path is trust, at least enough trust to try it out. Follow the instructions of our predecessors we quickly learn from our personal experience and come to an understanding of the nature of life, an inner knowledge that gradually condenses into certainty.

In this sense, the buddhist path can also be described as a science of liberation, or a science of the mind. Over the centuries, the original teachings have been increasingly laid out and supplemented, resulting in a wide variety of buddhist traditions, methods and exercises. Here, we are using only a few out of all of these instructions. We selected those which are directly relevant to supporting patients and limit ourselves – in the true spirit of Essential Psychotherapy – to the essentials.

The Eightfold Path as a process of healing and personal practice (exercise D.3)

The four truths described above correspond to the basic principles of therapeutic activity: anamnesis (case taking) – diagnosis of causes – perspective of healing – therapy. The Buddha also saw it this way: He considered himself as a doctor, the dharma as a medicine, the practitioner as patient and personal practice as therapy. As in medicine, the best therapy consists of eliminating the causes of suffering, i.e. the disease. The buddhist path of awakening or self-healing became famous as the Eightfold Path of the Noble Ones *(ārya-mārga)*. It gives an overview of the "therapy plan" and consists of practicing eight factors, all geared towards healing and awakening:

1. Right understanding, a helpful view or vision, deep wisdom
2. Wholesome attitude, compassionate motivation
3. Beneficial, true speech, authentic communication
4. Respectful, beneficial activity
5. Helpful, healthy way of life, unharmful profession
6. Energy in pursuit of the truth, interest in the essential
7. Comprehensive awareness, stable mindfulness, focused on the essential
8. Undistracted presence, deep meditation, abiding in the wholesome

Taken together these eight factors describe a healing process that leads to awakening. They mutually reinforce each other as in a large circular motion or in a positively augmentative, interactive network: the eighth link strengthens the first and second as well as all the others; all the factors strengthen each other. We can imagine the description of the eight links as a conversation with the Buddha as a physician. He would say to the patient:

> "First of all, clarify your own *view*, your understanding of the present situation, because you need to know why the therapy is necessary and where it is supposed to lead.
>
> When you see this more clearly, you will then need to develop the *motivation* to really heal. This motivation needs to be kept alive all the time in order to resolve three areas in your life: to develop wholesome ways of communicating, authentic *speech*, helpful *action* and a considerate *lifestyle.*
>
> To put it simply: When you speak and write, make sure that you don't create any further causes of suffering, but set healing forces in motion. When you act physically, make sure that you do not hurt anyone, but contribute to the well-being of others. Act with care and respect. See to it that you have a wholesome occupation and put the way you live on a healthy

footing so that your livelihood does not depend on harmful activity and your income does not come from unwholesome sources.

This will create a good foundation for your efforts to heal and will allow you to progress in your inner work with mind itself. You will naturally take an interest in mind training. By applying yourself to it, your mindfulness and *awareness* will deepen and expand without many obstacles until you easily find your way into undistracted, relaxed presence and *deep meditation.*

If you energetically devote yourself to these eight aspects of your therapy plan, your naturally healthy being will emerge ever more clearly; you will experience the interconnections between these eight links and realize awakening."

To sum it up with slightly different words:

1. Refine, clarify and realign the view.
2. Cultivate an open heart.
3. Communicate in a wholesome way.
4. Act in wholesome ways.
5. Engage in the world in wholesome ways with the right profession.
6. Focus on the essential in every situation.
7. Stay undistracted in wholesome mind states.
8. Continue until the wholesome completely permeates you.

In Essential Psychotherapy we work with these eight aspects of the healing path. Ethics also plays a key role here. We do not need to talk much about ethical principles, but if we want the client, the person we are supporting, to be truly well, we must encourage them to live life on a good ethical basis.

A legitimate question arises: What happens when the treatment goal is achieved, i.e. when the therapeutic task has been fulfilled? The client may present with panic attacks or anxiety disorder and the therapy at some point satisfactorily relieves or eliminates the symptoms. But it may, under certain circumstances, also raise existential questions that require answers. What to do? Surely, we can't go through the whole eightfold path in therapy!? Certainly not, not even in Essential Psychotherapy.

A helpful attitude is to stick to the official guidelines in the context of approving therapies for health insurance, for example. Once the treatment goal is achieved, the treatment is over for the time being. We don't talk about meditation on our own initiative. However, there may be small hints in the therapy room that invite further reflection, for example a buddha statue, the image of the famous egg of psychosynthesis, a Zen calligraphy, an icon of Mary and Christ and such like. If – and only if – clients ask questions about them, we can respond. It is different when someone comes expressly for individual sessions in Essential Psychotherapy and has a curiosity about these deeper dimensions: Then we can expand on this in our consultation with the client.

E. Cultivating Awareness

Developing deeper awareness is the crucial factor in any emotional healing process, just as on the path to awakening. There is great deal of research and writing on the subject. The entire movement of mindfulness-based programs and therapies is rightly based on this. Since we have already made quite a few texts available on the theme of developing awareness[32], the following be limited to the material relevant to training in EPT.

The original words for mindfulness or awareness – in Pali *sati*, in Sanskrit *smṛti* and in Tibetan *dran pa* – all mean: to keep reminding ourselves of the essential – of that which we want to keep the mind on. It allows us to hold the thread and keep attention on what we have chosen to prioritise. The best translation for *sati* seems to be "awareness of the essential."

If we feel it is important to observe the sensations of breathing, then *sati* stays aware of breathing by continuously maintaining our attention on it. If at other times it seems more important to remember our heartfelt motivation, then *sati* will focus on that. *Sati* can have any focus, but it can also remind us to be without focus, to just stay open and relaxed, and can bring us back to this openness of mind continuously. So, this capacity of "recollection" (another good translation) takes on different tasks depending on the situation – but its function is always to stay aware of what is essential right now (for example reading these lines). It remembers what is essential to us in a given situation and ensures that we don't get distracted from it.

---

32 See the free access media library of the Ekayana Institute [https://ekayana-institut.de/en/] for texts, audios and videos on meditation, cultivating awareness, introduction to mahāmudrā, satipaṭṭhāna, ānāpānasati and related topics.

Mindfulness is receiving increased attention as a therapeutic supplement and even as a therapeutic method, for example Mindfulness Based Stress Reduction (MBSR) or Mindfulness Based Cognitive Therapy (MBCT), which are recognized as being remarkably effective and rely principally on developing mindfulness. However, these approaches are not only about maintaining mindfulness, but about developing an awareness that "stays undistractedly in what is wholesome."[33] This is the definition of what buddhist mindfulness training is about. Wholesomeness, or beneficence, are qualities of mind that support liberation and awakening. They contribute to deeper healing and make the heart-mind free, supple and awake. Mindful awareness perceives what is truly wholesome in increasingly subtle ways.

Sati – awareness of the essential – continuously supports our internal navigator. It perceives whether we are still on track or, for example, if there are early signs of emotional entanglement. It reminds us of healing and self-care. Awareness guides us with confidence and trust out of emotionally dangerous trigger zones and ensures skilful handling of challenges. Awareness helps us to implement the decision to take loving care of ourselves and others. It gives stability. It helps us to settle in wholesome states of mind and releases joy. It gives direction to our thinking.

Awareness of omnipresent change, the process nature of existence, has also proven particularly helpful in therapy: Experiences are constantly arising and changing into something else. Nothing remains, everything changes, everything is in process. Through being aware of the process nature of life we get less caught up in trying to hold on to things that pass. Awareness also shows us that we can influence the process at any time. It makes us less attached to the idea of a permanent self when used to carefully examine this supposed 'I'. How does the feeling of a 'self' arise? How do self-centred thoughts arise? What actually is personality? Awareness can develop from being attentive to the breath, into an awakened awareness of simple being – being

33 Definition by the great Mahāyāna master Asaṅga in his work Bodhisattvabhūmi, quoted after Gampopa, ch. 16, Ornament of Liberation.

aware without an object, just as it is, one with the basic truths of life. We can describe the whole path to complete awakening as a process of increasing, expanding, and deepening awareness.

Let's take the classic therapeutic situation: We become aware of an issue and attentively direct our inner gaze towards it, while at the same time remaining connected to the body's sensations. We follow a path of mindful exploration. The Buddha's teaching is all about exploring and understanding life. We explore the feelings that arise and their causes as well as helpful new attitudes. We are mindful researchers – and the subtler our awareness, the more successful our research. The more continuously we are mindful and aware, the more material we have to deepen our understanding. Mindfulness is being in the moment – present. As it moves between physical sensation, sense impressions, thoughts, feelings, impulses, intuitions, motivations and moods it becomes aware of deeper and deeper layers of experience and sees more and more connections.

We are not evenly aware of everything but chose to focus on what is most pertinent to our tasks. The rest of our many impressions, perceptions, thoughts and emotional movements do not receive the same attention. Right now, when reading – we privilege visual perception, understanding the text, and perhaps perceiving inner reactions to the contents. Once we stop reading, our hearing will probably become stronger again or we will become more aware of our body. In all this, there is always a deliberate choice about what we direct the mind to.

When exploring the mind, we use this capacity to focus our attention and increase awareness in specific areas. On the path of awakening as well as on the therapeutic path we chose wholesome, helpful contents of awareness to focus on. After exploring our emotional state, we consciously turn to the qualities (resources) that we want to strengthen. This process of "becoming familiar with the wholesome" is called meditation in the buddhist tradition (*bhavana* in Sanskrit, *sgom pa* in Tibetan). To meditate thus means to cultivate a wholesome awareness, to enhance beneficial states of mind that contribute to and are an expression of heart opening and deeper understanding. This is exactly what we do in the therapeutic process as well.

In the therapeutic process, the therapist supports the client to explore their emotional issue and work with it in a wholesome, healing way. So, instead of just one person, two people direct their awareness to the issue, which is of immense help. The client would otherwise have to do this alone but usually lacks the strength and experience to keep the attention in these challenging areas in a beneficial way. The therapist acts as a co-pilot and accompanies the client's awareness in the process of feeling, exploring, accepting, understanding, and trying out new attitudes.

A similar process takes place with meditation masters. They dwell in the wholesome, speak out of the wholesome and help the listener to settle in it. Later on, at home, the practitioners have to continue independently – just like clients who continue applying what they have learned for the rest of the week. And for as long as we can't to do it on our own, we ask others for help.

Much of this book can be used on our own, without external guidance. Exercises that need guidance from a therapist are specifically marked, all others can be tried alone. Almost all of us have emotionally difficult areas that are hard to tackle alone. The problem is that we often cleverly avoid them as soon as they 'knock on the door.' Or, if we tackle them alone, we might quickly end up being enmeshed in our usual reactions and judgements – back in our old patterns, old perspectives. In order to explore these areas in a helpful way and find real solutions, we need gentle support and sometimes a fearless, loving mirror. We need help from the outside to look with awareness and develop a new perspective. For this, therapists and clients alike practice mindful awareness; therapeutic processes require awareness on both sides. All such processes of becoming aware require mindfulness.

The therapeutic situation is a kind of meditation session: Our appointment is at ten o'clock and let's say we have 50 minutes. We prepare ourselves, arrive on time and are fully mindful, because we want to use the limited time well for the essentials. The clearly defined outer conditions are a framework that enable heightened mindfulness.

Both, the therapist and the client are particularly careful because of their commitment to a process of healing. Their heightened mindfulness is a good precondition for something helpful to happen.

Life is always in flux, even if sometimes a little bumpy and slow. Therapists help us wherever we feel blocked and encounter difficulties, feel that we are not flowing properly. With their support we discover ways to flow more freely. In addition to using therapeutic know how, the therapeutic process involves adopting a loving, easy attitude which allows for the space to 'dance' with each other – in other words, taking sensitive steps together in mutually open exchange. The dance revolves around looking at where things are stuck and how they could flow. And we repeatedly discover that our supposedly solid problems are not so solid after all.

Releasing blockages and continuing in the flow

Emotional blockages are like barricades built by children to dam up a stream. The dams are never completely watertight; the water always seeps through somewhere – and will also overflow. In an analogous way, somehow life always goes on despite all the problems we might have. Therapeutic work facilitates that natural flow; it opens the dams and makes processes easier. We are dealing with self-made dams, which used to be helpful previously, but now hinder us. Often, we forgot in the interim, that we piled up the stones ourselves. In a therapeutic session, one of those stones then becomes the subject of attention. The stone – our theme – feels really solid at first. But when loving, non-judgemental awareness comes in, that seeming solidity turns out to be a process. This freeing up is a little painful perhaps at first yet relieving in the end.

Sometimes our life seems like a wild foaming brook with many impeding stones. We would prefer to clear them all away. But that's actually not even necessary. Blockages can be transformed through awareness, mindfulness and goodwill – and cease to be blockages.

They are not solid anymore. Through loving acceptance and conscious engagement, we discover an opening and flow; the whole situation becomes more permeable. We can clear out some rocks here and there, but we are not a foaming brook clearing company.

Our river of life needs the eddies just as much as the clear stretches! The "biodynamics" must be preserved – that's the human touch. We learn to flow around the stones, because the flow of life will always bring us new challenges, new so-called stones. We can enjoy the small waterfalls as welcome stimulation along the way. It is enough that it flows. We can never do away with certain challenges anyway, such as the fact that our bodies are a constant challenge – nor can we simply turn our fellow human beings into low-maintenance versions of their species.

Actually, we don't need to clear away rocks at all, but rather our awareness of the situation changes. The image of the dam while helpful, is also limited. It is by no means the case that we can put rocks we have inherited or acquired through our lives to the side. We transform them through loving awareness into a fresh, new healing experience. So, for example, the experience of having been abused as a child can be transformed through love and awareness, but we cannot remove it from our lives.

Basically, therapeutic processes are similar to buddhist mind training: stepping away from everything that causes suffering, seeing through the emotional patterns and erroneous assumptions about reality, dissolving obstructive attitudes, releasing and stabilizing inherent qualities (resources), opening to free being, and developing trust in our own nature. The point is to gain access to our deepest potential and to fully awaken to the possibility of healing within us, to bring about a beneficial flow. It is especially healing when the gap between imagination and direct experience is narrowed through detailed awareness. We repeatedly take care to be clear about our orientation and to be clearly present with what is. We strengthen our motivation to feel what is going on inwardly and to work through our own emotional filters.

The Fourfold Cultivation of Awareness (Satipaṭṭhāna, exercise E.1)

1. First of all, we become aware of the five primary senses: touch, sight, hearing, smell and taste. These five are the *physical formations* or five outer senses spoken of in buddhism. For the sake of the practice, we turn to one sense after the other and notice the intensity of experience that takes place in each sense field.
2. Then we become increasingly aware of the movements of the sixth sense – consciousness, the so-called *mental formations*, i.e. the arising sensations, thoughts, emotions and mental movements of a conceptual *and* non-conceptual nature. These mental movements include perceiving pleasant and unpleasant feelings, noticing details, structuring the experience, comparing, classifying, naming, evaluating, judging and commenting on the sensory experiences in the five primary sensory fields. Inner dialogues take place constantly; we think, consider, plan and remember. Ideas, images, impressions emerge, all kinds of emotional movements and impulses to act.
3. In the third stage of awareness practice, the presence of background moods, deeper states of mind, becomes apparent: emotional tones, changing mental states, the mind sometimes feeling narrow, at other times vast, trapped or free, tense or relaxed. This awareness of mental states and moods is traditionally called awareness of *mind.*
4. These first three – physical formations, mental formations and mind – are not separate areas of perception. Together they provide a wealth of observations where connections and patterns of functioning reveal themselves. Perceiving such *connections and inner laws* of how the mind works is traditionally called awareness of *dharmas.* For example, an understanding can arise of how physical experience, thinking, emotions and deeper states of mind, all influence each other to produce happiness or suffering. Or an understanding of what makes our heart mind narrow

or expansive, what leads to painful experiences and what leads to liberated experience.

To give an overview: in practicing awareness we can direct our attention in two ways: Either we observe *what* is happening or we observe *how* it is experienced. The first is a more factual attention, the second focuses on the qualities of experience. This can easily be illustrated:

Please look around you for a moment and ask yourself: what is there to see? Take the time to look carefully with as little judgement as possible.

Then take a short break and look around again with the inner question: What is it like to see all this? How does the experience *feel*? Take time to experience how it feels to be visually aware right now.

Do you notice the difference? This is what the path of awakening as well as the therapeutic process is all about. Mindfulness should not remain a mere looking at external facts but needs to become an awareness of the qualities of inner experience.

Let's go through the four areas of cultivating awareness again, first of all with a more factual attention, which is basic mindfulness, using the question: *what can be observed?*

1. In the case of the physical formations of feeling the body, seeing, hearing, smelling and tasting, our first guiding questions are: what is going on? What is happening? What is perceived? Thereby, we learn to perceive without reacting immediately, by using naming and evaluating.
2. We then extend this relaxed, non-judgemental attitude to the mental formations and learn to allow thoughts, emotional impulses, images, inner sounds, etc. to arise without getting caught up in them.
3. The awareness then deepens to perceive the inner moods. Whether we feel good or bad, expansive or narrow – whatever our current condition is –, we perceive it without intervening and without identifying ourselves with it.
4. At this point, we perceive increasingly clearly that nothing stays the same, that everything changes. We notice the ubiquitous

change and ascertain clear connections for example between certain thoughts, simultaneous feelings in the body and ensuing moods or inner experiences.

Now let's go through these four steps once again, cultivating a deeper awareness of *how it is experienced*, that is we turn our attention to the quality of the experience itself.

1. In perceiving the five primary sense experiences – touch, sight, hearing, smell and taste – we direct our attention to: how is it to feel, see, hear, smell or taste? This does not mean whether it is pleasant or unpleasant, but how the act of seeing etc. is experienced in itself. What is it like to feel a bodily experience? Is it tangible? How does it arise and how long does it last? Can it be distinguished from the next experience? We focus our attention on the unique, intangible quality of the present experience.
2. We extend this approach to the mental formations: what is it like to think, feel, experience inner images? *How* is it to experience all these inner mind movements? Here too, it is not about whether it is pleasant or unpleasant, but about the way in which thoughts, images, impulses, etc. arise and change, and new things keep coming. If a pleasant or unpleasant experience occurs, then we check: what is it like to experience something pleasant or unpleasant? Do these experiences differ in nature or only in content?
3. The same is true for mind as such and moods: How is it that the mind feels? What is it like to be aware? Or to be unaware? What is the quality of mental experience in each case, same or different? Does awareness always feel the same or are there differences? How is it to 'just be'?
4. When we look at the universal laws *(dharmas)*, such as change and intangible nature, we focus on what it is like to experience change. *How* is it to just experience? Is there someone who experiences all this? How do experiences arise and pass away? How do joy and suffering come about and pass? What is it like to feel compassion, to love? How does it feel to awaken a benev-

olent motivation for everything we do? What effect does it have on the mind? Noticing the effects of different mental attitudes is part of the practice of awareness. Mindfulness of dharmas means directing one's attention to that which liberates and leads to awakening.

When practising the above two sets of four exercises we notice that the second approach builds on the first and deepens our sense of presence. Mindfulness of events becomes an awareness of the nature of life. Actually, the two approaches cannot be separated. The first is very helpful to relax and calm the mind, while the second develops more insight. They belong together, since a clearer and calmer mind will "see" and understand. The questions of the second set help to support the insight process just as the therapist's questions and sensitive comments help the client not only to tell their story, but to arrive at a liberating experience with understanding. It becomes obvious that our inner world is not so much structured by facts, but mostly by how we process and interpret these so-called facts. This world of interpretations – established on the basis of our previous experiences – is more "real" to us, emotionally far more relevant, than objective facts. We believe what we *experience* inside.

Exploration in four steps – an exercise for two (exercise E.2)

For the following exercise, we pair up to accompany each other in the process of mindful exploration. The task is to go through the four areas one after the other – (1) physical formations: the experiences of the five senses, (2) mental formations: sensory perceptions, thinking, images, (3) mind: mental moods and qualities, (4) dharmas: observable connections between areas of experience, inner laws. Taking turns, we guide each other with sensitivity through a process of inquiring meditation. Using questions like the ones below is the main tool of the inquiry:

1. What do you experience in your body and in the body-based senses right now? How does that feel? How do you experience being aware of each part and area of the body?
2. What goes on in the mind when sensing the body, hearing, seeing, smelling, tasting? What kind of mental movements are perceptible right now? How is it to think, to perceive?
3. What mood is the mind in right now? Is it narrow or expansive, joyful or sad? And what does this mood feel like from the inside? How is it to be conscious and aware?
4. Then we pick an inner law, easy to observe, to examine together. It could be the ever-presence of change, or observations on cause-and-effect relationships. Helpful questions are: Is there something stable in your experience? What do you experience more strongly, the coming or the going of experiences? How long does an experience actually last? How is it that the mind gets vaster or narrower? If you think of something or imagine something now – how does it affect your body, your mind?

It is better not to just accompany someone else all the time, but to explore together. One person starts, and then the other one picks up the flow and initiates the next step. So, one person feels and reports on what is happening in their body right now, and the observer helps them to sense into and express this even more precisely. Then they swap and the other person is helped to feel the body, to feel the sensations, to perceive the mental moods and to direct their gaze towards liberating truths. We can consciously insert moments of silence in between, where we have time to tune in to what is going on. But it can also be a flowing conversation, where we take it in turns going through the four areas. If several groups of two do this at the same time, it is advisable to ring a bell or otherwise give a signal at the end of each of the four stages.

In total we can take about half an hour and divide the time accordingly. We sit across from each other and one of us starts: "Okay, I'll start and accompany your exploration. – What do you feel..." After a few minutes we switch, and the other one leads the exploration. The observer helps us to sense in more precisely by asking: "How does that feel?" Until they get a feeling of the other person's experience themselves and can guess what is going on. This need not cover everything that can be experienced. The companion inquires and sometimes also mirrors a little bit. This helps the other person to sense in more precisely and also to formulate the experience more precisely. Change over every few minutes.

In this way we learn to direct our mindfulness into these different areas one after the other. We will get accustomed to always keep in mind these areas in the therapy session as well. "How do I and the other person feel on a physical level – what is noticeable there? What kind of images, associations and thoughts emerge? What is the mental state, is the mind open or narrow? What feelings arise? What patterns, laws and interconnections can be noticed? What might a certain narrative have to do with me feeling open or closed right now?"

At the end, we share openly what felt healing about the exercise and what we found helpful. In this way we reinforce what is beneficial. Being named, it leaves stronger traces. And in that moment, we feel it again with every cell of the body. By re-experiencing the healing, it has more force and leaves a stronger memory trace.

Awareness with Breathing, in sixteen steps (Ānāpānasati, exercise E.3)

The concise, yet time profound presentation of cultivating awareness with breathing provides an excellent basis for awareness training. In his instructions from 2.500 years ago, the Buddha leads us through a complete cycle of calming and insight meditation. The sixteen steps reflect stages of awareness which also take place in therapeutic processes. The main part of the *Ānāpānasati Sutta*, the Buddha's teaching called "Cultivating Awareness with Breathing in and Breathing out" is quoted below *(in italics)*:[34]

> *Dear practitioners of the wholesome! Awareness with breathing, when cultivated and pursued, bears great fruit and brings great benefit, since it perfects the fourfold cultivation of awareness. Awareness completes the seven factors of awakening, and these bring to perfection true awareness and liberation.*

The Buddha considers meditating on the experience of breathing an excellent method for developing the above-mentioned four steps in the cultivation of awareness and thereby realizing awakening. Breathing is a wonderful support for awareness because it is a natural, automatic process that reflects our feelings and connects body and mind. So, we take something completely familiar as a basis for practice. It is obvious that the Buddha was not concerned with concentrating on the breath. The breath simply accompanies the entire process of cultivating deeper awareness and serves as an anchor, so to speak, for undistracted being.
The Buddha said *(quoted in italics):*

> *"How do we practice and cultivate awareness with breathing? Well, we go into the forest, to the foot of a tree or into an empty hut, sit down and cross our legs. Holding the body upright, we establish awareness in front of us. Then, mindfully we breathe in and mindfully we breathe out.*

1. *Breathing in long we know 'I breathe in long.' Breathing out long we know 'I breathe out long.'*
   In a place suitable for the practice of awareness, we sit comforta-

34 Ānāpānasati Sutta, no. 118 in the "Collection of Middle Length Teachings" of the Pali canon. The text presented here is the translation of the author (Tilmann Borghardt). *Ānā* means to inhale, *pāna* means to exhale, *sati* means awareness, and *sutta* means teaching. Detailed teachings on this can be found in the media library of the Ekayana Institute [https://ekayana-institut.de/].

bly, with the upper body as straight as possible, while the body is as relaxed and fluid as possible. Then we direct the mindfulness to the breath and first become aware of what it is like to breathe in and out deeply and long. To allow for long, deep breathing is often a need at the beginning of meditation. We allow for this and follow the breathing sensations as closely as possible.

2. *Breathing in short, we know 'I breathe in short.' Breathing out short we know 'I breathe out short.'*
   We become aware of the depth of the different breaths without controlling them. Shorter breaths soon follow, as body and mind calm down. We are aware of the depth and length of the breaths and begin to notice subtle differences from one breath to another. While we inhale and exhale in this way, we begin to also notice the rest of the body more.

3. *Breathing in I experience the whole breathing body. Breathing out I experience the whole breathing body.*
   We perceive the entire breathing cycle, with all the accompanying sensations in the whole body, down to the most subtle sensations. Breathing in and breathing out we experience the body in its entirety, relaxing into the experience each time without naming the experience or reacting to it.

4. *Breathing in I calm the physical formations. Breathing out I calm the physical formations.*
   We relax, and our physical experience calms with every inhalation and exhalation. We always open to the next experience, without holding on in any way – it is a completely relaxed and at the same time awake experience. Again, and again we return to the relaxed awareness of breathing. It is an uncomplicated way of being, where there is nothing else to do but to be aware. We use the breath to find our way into flowing awareness.

5. *Breathing in I experience joy. Breathing out I experience joy.*
   We practice entering into direct experience, free of thinking and analysis. This simple being and the peace and harmony that come with it, is experienced as greatly beneficial and is experienced in the body as pleasant and joyful. The feeling of well-being can at times become quite intense. It is simply noticed and left as it is.

6. *Breathing in I experience happiness. Breathing out I experience happiness.*
   Simple being deepens, and the mind becomes joyful and light. Happiness here refers to subtle forms of well-being which come about with deeper relaxation. Awareness of the body recedes into the background, but we stay aware of inhaling and exhaling without controlling them; just letting it flow.

7. *Breathing in I experience the mental formations. Breathing out I experience the mental formations.*
   We are now aware, in addition to the breath, of all experiences of the six senses: touch, sight, hearing, smell, taste, the corresponding mental movements and also the many mental movements that don't have a trigger in the outer senses. Now that the body is calm, it becomes clear that all experience is mental – a mass of mental movements. Again, and again we return to inhaling and exhaling without getting caught up in any mental movement.

8. *Breathing in I calm the mental formations. Breathing out I calm the mental formations.*
   That is, we relax all thinking, commenting etc. and always return to the inbreath and outbreath. Being fully aware on the inbreath calms the mental fabrications, being fully aware on the outbreath calms the mental fabrications. What has a calming effect here is again simply being with what is – primarily the breath. We take care not to nourish the mental formations and not to let the mind wander, because it easily gets caught up in attachment and

aversion. Against the backdrop of this basic awareness of breathing we notice fluctuations in our mental state.

9. *Breathing in I experience the mind. Breathing out I experience the mind.*
   We take a closer look at the mind without forgetting to be aware of breathing. What's the mind like right now when breathing in? Is it tired, fresh, expansive or closed? What is it like when breathing out? Tense, relaxed? Light or dark? Breathing in we experience the mind without holding on, breathing out we experience the mind without holding on. We experience how our mood constantly changes, depending on the degree of our inner grasping, wanting, not wanting, and so on. What is the mind like right now?

10. *Breathing in I delight the mind. Breathing out I delight the mind.*
    Breathing in we relax the mind and treat it in a way that brings joy – and breathing out we do the same. We allow it to open into the areas where joy arises all by itself naturally. Breathing in and breathing out we thus gladden and delight the mind through deeper relaxation. There is no struggle, no judging. The mind is as it is – and is simply left as it is. This is especially wholesome – and this wholesome relaxation is exactly where our attention gathers. Awareness begins to rest in itself, to become aware of its own clear, joyful, intangible quality.

11. *Breathing in I steady the mind. Breathing out I steady the mind.*
    We let the mind gather in present experience – in what is, right now. This is no longer a concentration that requires effort. The only thing we have to do is to let ourselves fall back into the present experience of breathing, again, and again. There is a sense of the mind gathering by itself. It no longer wants to get caught up in stressful clinging, discerning and evaluating, but enjoys

resting in direct experience. There is usually a slight attachment to this deeply pleasant experience. That is why the Buddha continues:

12. *Breathing in I free the mind. Breathing out I free the mind.*
In each moment of breathing in and breathing out, we free the mind from ideas about how it should be, from all constraints, and drop all manipulation – especially the subtle clinging to a calm mind. We give the mind full freedom to be, to sense, to feel. Breathing in and breathing out we find a free, open, flowing awareness.

13. *Breathing in I see impermanence. Breathing out I see impermanence.*
Breathing in we notice change, breathing out we notice change. There is an intuitive experience of how everything is process. Nothing stays; everything is always new. We breathe in the flow of experience; we become the flow. Breathing in we are aware of all appearances changing, breathing out we are aware of all appearances changing. This awareness comes from being one with the experience, not from an observing distance. Then it is indeed liberating. Whatever experience arises is experienced as intangible, without centre, without limits – an all-encompassing process of being, perfectly clear, but at the same time intangible.

14. *Breathing in I see the fading away. Breathing out I see the fading away.*
We experience an immediate release of clinging due to this deep experience of the process nature of existence. Where there is nothing to grasp, the desire to grasp diminishes, grasping fades away, we become less entangled – an unencumbered, alert simplicity is revealed. And we continue: Fully aware we breathe in and out – aware of change and of how little grasping is felt.

15. *Breathing in I see cessation. Breathing out I see cessation.*
    This process continues until all entanglement, all grasping, all identification ceases. Due to the deep realization of existence, there are no more impulses of wanting to hold on and solidify. Nobody claims to be someone anymore, a someone who stands out and is different from the process of existence.

16. *Breathing in I see complete release. Breathing out I see complete release.*
    Breathing in we experience fully relaxed being. Breathing out we experience fully relaxed being. Alert, fully aware, natural relaxation. This could be awakening... On our level it is perhaps an awareness of being "more relaxed than ever before" – completely at ease, one with the flow, carefree, knowing, light and clear. Ultimately this is nondual, timeless awareness.

This is how awareness with breathing is cultivated and pursued so that it bears great fruit and brings great benefit."

With this the Buddha ends his guided meditation, which can be used by anyone, whether beginner or advanced. In step 13, the awareness of impermanence can be replaced by other *dharmas*, other subjects of interest, for example the conditionality of all existence, or compassion, wherever the mind dwells in spontaneous understanding.

An important part of the exercise is to experience the connection between understanding and effortless relaxation. This is – to a lesser degree and perhaps in smaller steps – what happens in therapy when there is a deep recognition and seeing through one's own patterns, followed by experiencing a new, relaxed way of being, often accompanied by a certain joy.

The 4x4 steps of awareness practice at a glance

I. Physical Formations

1. Take a long breath and accept everything as it is.
2. Take a short breath and gradually settle.
3. Let awareness spread through the whole body and be fully present in the body.
4. Let the whole body calm down and be open to all physical experience.

II. Mental formations

1. Discover joy with your whole body and feel how pleasant relaxed, non-judgemental presence is.
2. Discover happiness and experience how much joy is released by aware presence.
3. Experience the feeling tone of each mental formation and accept the inner movements of all six senses.
4. Calm the mental formations and relax into the inner movements.

III. Mind

1. Experience the mind and accept the subtle moods without judgement
2. Delight the mind through undirected, flowing awareness in calm presence.
3. Steady the mind through joyful absorption in experience.
4. Free the mind from any remaining holding on to blissful calm.

IV. Dharmas

1. See and understand impermanence and other characteristics of existence.
2. See how the grasping fades and how understanding leads to deeper flow.
3. See how all grasping ceases and let go completely into simple being.
4. See complete release, being awake, completely free and fully at ease.

This practice is the starting point of many different meditations on breathing taught in the buddhist world. As you can see above, there are sixteen instructions in four groups of four, where awareness is successively developed of physical formations (the body), mental formations (all sensations), mind (moods, qualities of mind), and dharmas (inner connections, laws). It is advisable to practice these sixteen steps very precisely for a while, until at some point we feel at ease to improvise with them. This approach has nothing to do with intellectual analysis but is all about refining our direct awareness of how things are. A calm, joyfully open mind sees clearly and can be directed to explore any question.

When awareness lights up the shadows, the dark areas of our being, our unhelpful habit patterns, they can be dissolved. But many of us, and I speak from experience, unconsciously avoid looking at these dark sides. Support from someone else can help with this. To live a free life, all aspects of experience must be penetrated by awareness. Liberation happens by inviting previously repressed aspects of experience into our awareness and understanding them.

The four major steps also describe the procedure of any therapy. They reveal basic therapeutic principles, a fundamental matrix: The point is to permeate the experience (1) of the body, (2) of mental formations and (3) of our moods and mental states with clear awareness to such an extent that (4) a liberating understanding arises of the underlying truths within them. This is the core of dharma practice as well as the core of psychotherapy. Methods of awakening and healing are essentially the same and thus can develop amazing synergies.

In a psychotherapeutic session, someone may come with palpitations, breathing difficulties, restlessness and trembling – so we are dealing with "physical formations." When clients come with interpersonal problems, suffer from obsessive thoughts, or want to address their emotional issues, we are dealing with "mental formations". If they just feel bad, blocked, maybe sad or annoyed, then we are dealing with underlying states of "mind". Or if certain connections are unclear: someone or something is bothering them and they want to understand how and why – here we are in the realm of "dharmas", exploring the causes of suffering and its resolution.

Actually, these four levels always go together. An emotional issue has effects in the body, in thinking, in our mood, and usually the inner connections are unclear. Deepening our awareness in itself will already have a healing effect and will make a decisive contribution to a cure.

As part of the Advanced training course in Essential Psychotherapy, participants are encouraged to become so familiar with these four steps of cultivating awareness through personal practice that they can, where needed, guide others in them. In summary, we pursue the following goals:

1. We learn to lead ourselves and others to a relaxed experience of the body without identification. We practice a non-judgemental attitude towards physical sensations, find increased physical presence and stability and learn to step out of superfluous, compulsive thought patterns concerning our physical experiences until a healing calm arises.
2. When this is reasonably stable, we expand our awareness to include all six senses. In doing so, we become aware of the inner processes and practice again to accept the experience without reacting emotionally to it, without identifying ourselves with it. Awareness becomes a friend.
3. Then we practice perceiving the background moods and underlying mental states, relaxing them and opening doors to joyful experiences. The objective is to become familiar with flowing, relaxed, undirected being. We free the mind from grasping and goal orientation.
4. In all this we explore the inner laws and connections and develop insight, becoming familiar with a knowing awareness that leads to ever-deepening, wide-awake relaxation. We discover what it feels like to stop struggling and become one with the experience.
5. We develop our own ability to stay mindful and aware, to relax and to perceive with fewer filters. The ability to handle our own

mind in this way enables us to help others to follow the path of awareness.

There is another important piece of heart advice: The mere recognition of an emotion or emotional pattern is not enough to free ourselves from it completely. This awareness and the resultant initial understanding are 'only' a first, but crucial step. It then requires further steps to integrate this new awareness into experience until it really changes our way of seeing the world and our behaviour. Let us take an example. Not only must we recognize hurt pride, but we also need to accept it lovingly. We have to track it down repeatedly, see through it, recognize its consequences and develop the motivation to free ourselves from pride and the deeper layers of experience that make us so insecure.

When applying this practically, it is a matter of no longer being enslaved by the habit patterns of pride and of cultivating alternative attitudes as often as possible. So, when we notice pride in our attitude, we internally withdraw from its influence and cultivate an open, empathetic attitude in which we can open-heartedly experience ourselves and others as equals – "fully human" – as authentic and natural as possible. We practice this constantly until the patterns of pride hardly arise.

Dissolving pride deeply, then requires having repeated experiences of the non-existence of a solid self. This deeply motivates us to quit the delusion of pride every time it surfaces. Unfortunately, mere mindfulness meditation does not eliminate pride – it only creates a superficial equanimity. The deep equanimity of those who have become totally free of pride seems only to be found through a penetrating realization of the true nature of "non-self" – in other words, the fact that there is no one to be proud of.

Until recently, many meditation teachers taught mindfulness according to the touch-and-go principle: touch and move on, this means becoming aware of the experience, letting it go and opening up to the next experience. These days, it is clear that we need a few intermediate steps, especially in the case of negatively charged experiences: awareness is followed by acceptance, which means not letting go right away. Especially with difficult experiences, a loving and accepting approach is needed: let it be as it is. Followed by a deeply accepting abiding *in* this shifting, uncomfortable experience.

To stay with it, right in it, without modifying it, allows for a full awareness of its nature to mature. With this accepting awareness, the painful experience changes, and a new experience will arise all by itself – and the previous experience is no longer there. Actually, we don't have to let it go in the sense of letting it go somewhere else. It's enough not to hold on to it as it is there, and to be open for a new, fresh experience. So, in short: perceive – accept – stay without grasping or pushing away – fill it with awareness – and flow on.

To let go is an essential instruction for pleasurable experiences, while accepting is more important for unpleasant ones. This is how we avoid repression in meditation. This intermediate step of remaining without holding on or pushing away corresponds in psychotherapy to being able to "hold" an emotion, to stay with it while getting to know it, instead of covering it up, running away from it, or acting it out.

The instructions on cultivating awareness, already so many years ago, point to an awareness that connects physical and mental experiences with the exploration of liberating truths like the constant change of all experience or the absence of a self in the experience. It encourages us to allow for a moving, dynamic awareness.

Developing mindfulness or awareness is not about just walking when we walk, just seeing when we see. We learned that as a child. Now we can walk, feel, think, speak, see, hear all at the same time. The teaching "just walk" means to walk without unnecessary baggage, without an "I," without all the unnecessary thinking. It is good to do things simply and to be fully involved in them, because otherwise we never learn to simply walk with awareness. To learn we must occasionally focus on one thing exclusively.

However, the actual object of any training in awareness is the complexity of human experience. Sometimes we zoom in on one area and focus exclusively on it, then move to another area, and then widen out to a more panoramic awareness. This continues until we become very fluid, and our mind is totally flexible, able to be aware of all six senses at once. This is what the Buddha teaches in the Ānāpānasati Sutta: being aware with all senses open, developing an understanding of the deeper characteristics of life. Always connected to both body and mind, integrating all experiences of life. To limit mindfulness to single things or activities helps us to become open. However, the goal is a flowing activity in the midst of this rather difficult world, which requires the integration of all our mental capacities. Wherever we are, in any situation in life – whether sitting crooked or straight, lying on our belly or back, running about or doing a headstand – we practice awareness, being fully present, fully alive.

Conceptual and non-conceptual thinking

When practicing awareness, it is vital to befriend thinking rather than seeing it as an enemy, and to imbue it with awareness. Buddhist teachings distinguish between conceptual and non-conceptual thinking – this is an essential key. Many believe that thinking is always conceptual, but far from it, its conceptual aspect is actually just like the tip of an iceberg. We can all imagine, for example, a lake in detail, without naming those details. This is non-conceptual thinking. We can also look around us now, scanning our visual field from the left to the right, and take in a wealth of visual impressions, which we can store as an overall impression at least for a short time. This too is thinking – and we have hardly labelled anything conceptually. Such visual impressions are in fact non-conceptual mental movements, which leave a non-conceptual memory that can even be connected with emotions. All this is thinking, not in words, but in images and other forms of subtle mental activity. Many people believe that they only think when they think conceptually. But the bulk of our thinking consists of non-conceptual thinking and understanding. We then express what we have already experienced (seen, felt, recognized) in concepts. Words are used to communicate and also to stabilize our experience – and they slow down the thinking and feeling processes mostly in a helpful way.

Non-conceptual thinking includes imagining, thinking in visual images, memories, sights, sounds, smells, body sensations, tastes, and abstract feelings. It is very agile, dynamic, fast, non-material, subjective, and always unique.

Conceptual thinking is verbal, linguistic. It names or labels what is experienced and thought non-conceptually. Thinking by means of commonly used language is usually more abstract than non-conceptual thinking, although it can be connected to personal experience. It has a slowing down, structuring and clarifying function and is a necessary prerequisite for verbal communication. Emotionally driven thinking is initially non-conceptual, as is associative thinking.

With these mostly non-conceptual mental movements we *shape* our world: sensing, fearing, hoping, evaluating, feeling, believing, planning, making sense, getting involved, shutting down, repeating, resisting, fixing, holding on, defending, influencing, wanting to change, intending, trying, deciding, testing, checking, imagining... All this can be or become conscious. Imagine, if there were mindfulness and awareness in all these areas! We could experience, understand and shape our world more consciously.

This is what is meant by "mental formations" in buddhist mind training (point two of the fourfold cultivation of awareness): conceptual and non-conceptual thinking taken together – all these mental processes that shape ("form") our experience of the world.

Cultivating awareness in the therapeutic process

When someone talks about their fears, I (Tilmann) become attentive and ask: "Describe it in more detail, how does it feel?" In doing so, I connect with the place inside of myself that really wants to get the feeling and understand. I show my deep interest and resonance.

I want to be able to feel internally what is going on for others. Then I can support them in their process. The other person senses my empathic interest, takes courage and opens up further. I carefully articulate a little of what I feel and think I understand. The person I am working with compares this with their own experience, maybe nods: "Yes, exactly" or describes it more precisely. In this manner, we go on step by step – connected in mindful sensing. There is a flow that is nurtured by loving awareness. I remain aware of the qualities of my partner – a form of mindfulness that stimulates healing in the other person. They notice that I can bear it when they talk about their fear and they become calmer, even though there may still be massive tensions inside.

Actually, awareness becomes a new way of being. Once we get used to it, we can't just turn it off. Ultimately it permeates all aspects of our being, even dreams and deep sleep. Are we ready to be fully aware and loving? This sincere willingness will lead to the loving awareness penetrating even into the furthest recesses of our being. And then we will embody it in such a way that it is contagious in a positive sense. Mindfulness, awareness, and presence are constantly in demand everywhere – even when the therapist or dharma teacher comes home tired. There is no break – therefore it is crucial that it is a relaxed awareness. In psychotherapeutic methods such as free association or in awareness exercises such as opening the six senses this relaxed and aware quality of being is used and trained in.

In cases of strong emotional stress, it is especially helpful to ground mindfulness in the body. For example, we can observe the rise and fall of the breath at the abdomen and also count the breaths. On the one hand, this brings us into relation with the basic quality of being alive – mindful presence, and on the other hand it is an effective method of reducing tension, which works very quickly.

A woman panicked heavily when she tried to get into a car. The driver, a participant on a training course, told her: "Breathe slowly, and look at me while you breathe." They breathed together for a few minutes and kept eye contact. Soon she was able to get into the car. Sometimes mindfulness can reduce stress this quickly. But for the woman it did take a combination of eye contact, feeling emotionally connected and safe, plus a good grounding in the sensations of the body (breath in this case) to free herself from panicky experience and thought patterns. Mindfulness slows down experience. We breathe, stand, look, feel consciously. This creates more space, the fear is no longer everything, it can be experienced within a space which includes other perceptions.

Behind our emotions are strategies to prevent just being. This is where mindfulness and awareness come in. To some extent they are exposing and uncomfortable. As we notice more, feel more, the unconscious, the repressed comes up... and we also discover the fundamental joy of being, which shows in just being, in simple, relaxed suchness. But it is precisely this simple suchness which is initially experienced as unsettling and may trigger fear. Awareness leads beyond that fear into the inherent joy of being aware – to experience, be, without being anyone, without a core, just process. To be able to relax deeply, we need to feel protected and secure. Only when the space is felt as safe do we dare to venture into unknown areas. Therefore, it is a priority for therapists and meditation teachers to provide just such a protected space.

All practice is about being aware and understanding the four noble truths already described: Where is tension, suffering, stress? Where does this narrow state of mind come from? Is there a solution? And how do we get there? This is the basic function of a liberating awareness: the ability to realize the roots of suffering and to take the necessary steps towards their dissolution. Mindfulness is the necessary starting point, but it has nothing inherently liberating to it! Burglars, liars, artists and athletes also have to be very mindful, but this by itself will not lead them into deeper understanding and waking up. Mindfulness *(sati)* must be directed to the essential questions of our life – how can I really be free and happy?

Mahāmudrā, natural being

The awakening the buddhist teachers speak of is basically an amazingly simple, relaxed state of mind, so unspectacular that in the Mahāmudrā tradition it is also called "ordinary mind" – so it is actually, a deeply normal consciousness completely free of unnecessary tension. An example of this is the moment of falling asleep, when we let go of all worries, of all identifications. Being as relaxed while wide awake, with all senses active, yet without a centre, is called awakening or ordinary mind. We all carry this inside of us, and thus intuitively feel of how easy it could be. It happens when there is a deep enough confidence in forgetting oneself, similar to falling asleep.

Many Mahāmudrā masters describe the reality we experience as a combination of three aspects. This description originates with the Yogacara school of India (4th to 8th century):[35]

- the imagined aspect of reality
- the conditioned aspect of reality
- the ultimate aspect of reality

The imagined aspect comprises our thoughts, emotions, ideas and inner images of experience. For example, ideas of happiness and suffering, our view of the world, and our ideas about ourselves and others – all of which are not part of direct experience.

The conditioned aspect comprises all the experiences of the six senses that are actually perceived, present experience without interpretations: changing experience under the influence of changing conditions.

The ultimate or "perfect" aspect refers to the fact that experience has no substance, no stable essence and does not exist independently, of its own accord. So-called reality is ultimately an ungraspable dynamic, free of subject and object, creative and lively, spacious awareness.

---

35 See the Third Karmapa Rangjung Dorje in "Luminous Heart", translated and introduced by Karl Brunnhölzl, pp. 35-53.

The three aspects are inseparable – always present together:

- All imagination arises conditionally and is ultimately ungraspable and without substance.
- Conditioned experience is further elaborated on in imaginary mental processes while being ungraspable and insubstantial.
- This ultimately ungraspable mind, awareness as such, is by nature dynamic and constantly gives rise to new conditioned experiences which are processed in imagination.

The three aspects of reality are as inseparable as the light, warmth and movement of a fire. Problems arise when we live only in imagined reality, which to some extent resembles fiction. We could almost call it fictional reality.

By developing intuitive insight, we discover that the reality we experience is ultimately illusory: it arises dependent on conditions and has no permanence. This is why it is called "dream-like" – like the seemingly real images of a dream which arise in dependence on inner processes and have no substance. Constant change manifests in dependence on causes and conditions – and all this takes place in ungraspable mind: conditioned experience without substance.

Psychologically, we might put it like this: A deep process of healing involves experiencing that ideas, emotions and the like have no substance whatsoever, even if they trigger all kinds of energetic, hormonal and neurological processes. Changing imaginary processes (the concepts, views and emotions with which conditioned experience is perceived) continuously influence and change our whole organism energetically. Nothing has substance in this world of experience, not even our supposedly material body – it too is process.

The changing experiences of our life arise in processes which we can influence to some extent. And the more aware we are of their insubstantial, conditioned nature, the freer and more skilful we can be in shaping them. Caught in our patterns, we feel at the mercy of these processes – but in full possession of our inner flexibility we can influence them, and often in a decisive way. To make this possible, we help people in the therapeutic process to find a way from their imagined reality, where problems appear so real and substantial, into a more direct experience and to recognize its process nature.

Ideas have an astonishing tenacity: They are reproduced over and over in the same way – and thus our recurring problem is always the same. But when experiencing the problematic issue directly, an amazing inner dynamic is revealed – everything is in flux after all. This opens up new creative possibilities and we can influence life, direct the flow a little bit, in the awareness of its conditioned process nature. Stepping into the nondual experience of that very process in the midst of direct experience is then the tasting or seeing of its ultimate aspect.

When mindfulness and awareness unfold in this sense, mahāmudrā reveals itself – the natural being of the awakened ones. The idea of *someone* who is sitting here and reading, or speaking and moving, has dissolved. This is personally experienced vastness and release, without any idea of a person. It is free being, in which the needed and helpful is spontaneously done. Vastness (of the mind) and precision (of the action) at the same time. Every hand movement, every gesture is an expression of this natural being. There are no more distracting thoughts, no more inner chatter, where mind and body are not synchronized. It is an integrated being without ego identification. True awareness. Being in the truth – awareness recognizing all aspects of reality. This is the aim which our psychotherapeutic support can also envisage. Because in this natural being there is true happiness, beyond conditions.

The Mahāmudrā prayer of the Third Karmapa (exercise E.4)

As a guideline to present mahāmudrā during the training in Essential Psychotherapy we use a classic prayer (see below) that can serve as a commentary. It introduces the practice of simple being, recognizing the intangible nature of all experiences, and we can use it for daily practice, even if we take only four lines at a time. This famous text gives an overview of the path of mahāmudrā in 25 verses. It would go beyond the scope of this book to include the necessary detailed explanations here.[36] This short, profound prayer is therefore only offered here as an inspiration with some footnotes to clarify the meaning a little bit. May the prayer serve as a support to enter into this wide awake, open awareness of mahāmudrā:[37]

The Path of Aspiration for the Mahāmudrā of Definite Meaning

by the Third Karmapa Rangjung Dorje[38]

NAMO GURU *(Homage to the Teachers)*

Lamas and yidam deities of the mandalas,
Victorious Ones and your heirs in the three times and ten directions,
Please lovingly consider me and grant your blessings
That my aspiration prayers may be realised exactly as intended.

---

36 For detailed instructions consult the book "Mahamudra – The Ocean of True Meaning" of the Ninth Karmapa Wangchug Dorje, translated by Henrik Havlat. This text was thoroughly explained in transmissions in Greece and Brazil of which you can find audio recordings and transcripts in the media library of the Ekayana Institute [https://ekayana-institut.de/en/].

37 The following is the author's own translation from the Tibetan.

38 Karmapa Rangjung Dorje (1284–1339) composed this prayer on the shores of the Chinese Ocean. A path of aspiration is at once prayer, instruction, inner commitment, and practice. True meaning indicates that the instruction is given at the level of ultimate or definitive meaning.

Springing forth from the snow mountain of the pure intentions
Of myself and all the countless sentient beings,
May streams of wholesome activity, undefiled by the threefold sphere,
Flow into the ocean of the four buddha bodies of the Victorious Ones.[39]

For as long as this is not accomplished, however long that may be,
May we, throughout our succession of lives and rebirths,
Not even know the words "harmful deed" or "suffering",
But enjoy the splendour of an ocean of beneficial deeds and happiness.

May we obtain the supreme freedoms and endowments[40], and with trust, energy and wisdom
Follow excellent spiritual guides, receive the nectar of their instructions,
Accomplish them correctly and without any obstacles
Practice the true dharma in all our lives.

Hearing the scriptures and applying reason free us from the veil of not knowing.

---

39 *Pure intentions* refers to the bodhicitta state of mind, which is as flawless as fresh snow. The *threefold sphere* refers to action performed with the erroneous belief (1) in an I as the subject or centre, (2) in objects existing separately, and (3) in concrete actions happening between subject and object. The four *buddha bodies* (Skt. *kāya)* are the bodies of truth, enjoyment, emanation and essential nature as four aspects of awakened being. The body of truth *(dharmakāya)* is the nondual dimension of mind, the body of enjoyment *(saṃbhogakāya)* is its inherent dynamism, the emanation body *(nirmāṇakāya)* is the spontaneous expression of this dynamism in perceptible form, and the body of essential nature *(svabhāvikakāya)* is the inseparable unity of these three.

40 The *freedoms and endowments* are prerequisites for dharma practice: to attain a human body with a receptive mind that can understand at a time and in a place where contact with an authentic lineage is possible.

Contemplating the oral key instructions overcomes the darkness of doubt.
The luminosity arising from meditation clarifies reality as it is –
May the radiance of this threefold wisdom increase.[41]

Through the nature of the ground, the two truths free from the extremes of eternalism and nihilism,
And the supreme path, the two accumulations free from the extremes of assertion and denial,
We attain the fruit, the two benefits free from the extremes of becoming and peace –
May we meet with this dharma free from deviation and error.[42]

The ground of purification is mind itself, the unity of clarity and emptiness.
That which purifies is the great vajra yoga of mahamudra.
What is to be purified are the adventitious stains

41 *Hearing* means to wholeheartedly engage intellectually with the teaching: studying texts and listening to the teachers. *Contemplating* means to relate that the understanding gained from our studies to our personal experience. In *meditation*, we go beyond all reflections into non-conceptual presence. The *wisdom* arising from these three then illuminates our path like a torch.

42 The *two truths* – the recognition of cause and effect as relative truth, and the intangible nature of being as ultimate truth – are the antidotes to belief in *eternalism* (existence) and *nihilism* (non-existence) respectively. The *two accumulations* of positive force and timeless awareness are acquired with an attitude free of expectation, exaggeration, and false assertions, and free of disdain, scepticism, and denial. *Assertion* means taking for true what does not really exist, like a stable self. *Denial* means holding to be untrue what actually has an effect, like actions. Generating positive force (merit) counteracts the error of denying the law of cause and effect, like disregarding wholesome action. Expanding timeless awareness counteracts attachment to subject and object. The *two benefits* – for ourselves and for others – are realized as one in the attainment of buddhahood. The benefit for ourselves is liberation from the sufferings of *becoming* in the cycle of existences, and the benefit for others is spontaneous activity for the benefit of all, which involves renouncing abiding in rapt *peace*.

of confusion,[43]
May the fruit of purification, the stainless dharmakaya, be actualised.

To have cut assertions concerning the ground is certainty of the view.[44]
Sustaining that undistractedly is the key point of meditation.
To exercise proficiency in the meaning of meditation in all situations is supreme action.
May we have certainty in view, meditation and action.

All phenomena are manifestations of mind,
And concerning mind, there is no mind – mind is empty by nature.
Empty and unobstructed it appears in every possible form.
Examining this thoroughly, may we cut the root which is the basis.[45]

Self-arising appearances without any existence are mistaken for objects,
And by the power of ignorance, self-arising awareness is mistaken for a self.[46]
This dualistic fixation has made us wander in the sphere of samsaric existences.

---

43 *Adventitious stains* are the emotional and cognitive veils that – tenacious as they may be – only temporarily cloud the view. They can dissolve at any time, since they are not part of our basic nature.

44 *Assertions* here are false assumptions and doubts regarding the nature of our mind.

45 All the *phenomena* of experience are *empty* of a self-nature, which means they have no unchanging, separate core of being, but are always process. This understanding cuts through the basis of all confusion – the dualistic fixation in subject and object – which is the *root* of all suffering.

46 *Self-arising appearances* are the spontaneously appearing mental movements that manifest without any deliberate intention from anyone, simply through interdependent origination. *Self-arising awareness* is the awareness, which is the ground of our being, always present and spontaneously aware of itself.

May we cut the illusory productions of non-awareness
at the very root.

Mind is not existent, since even the Victorious Ones
do not see it.
It is not non-existent, since it is the basis of the whole
of samsara-nirvana.
It is neither both at once, nor none of them, but the
Middle Way of Unity.
May we realise the true nature of mind, free from
extremes.[47]

There is no way to indicate it and say: "This is it."
There is no way to refute it and say: "This is not it."
The nature of phenomena, beyond conceptual understanding,
is not composed.
May we gain certainty in this authentic, ultimate end.

Not realising this, we circle in the ocean of samsara.
Realising it, Buddha is not somewhere else.
Everything is this; nothing is not this.
May we see the true nature, the hidden dimension of the
all-ground.[48]

Appearance is mind and emptiness is also mind.
Realisation is mind, but confusion is also our mind.

---

47 *True nature* (Sanskrit: *dharmatā*) means how something really is, its suchness.

48 The *all-ground* (Sanskrit: *ālaya*) is the basis of all mental states, all experiences. As the basic consciousness (*ālaya-vijñāna*) it acts like a store house which unconsciously maintains dualistic perception characterized by ego-centredness – it is thus the basis of saṃsāra. When the illusion of a self falls away, the same all-ground shows as nondual, timeless awareness and is thus the basis of nirvāṇa.

Arising is mind and cessation is mind.
May all assertions be severed in mind.[49]

Unspoiled by the efforts of intentional meditation,
And not agitated by the winds of ordinary preoccupations,
May we know how to rest in unfabricated naturalness,
just as it occurs by itself,
And expertly sustain the practice of mind as it truly is.[50]

The waves of coarse and subtle thoughts calm down in
themselves
And the river of undisturbed mind comes to abide naturally.
Free from the silt and mire of torpor and dullness,
May the ocean of mental calm remain unperturbed
and stable.[51]

Looking repeatedly into the mind that cannot be seen,
Clear seeing arises that, as it is, nothing is to be seen,
And severs all doubts about what is or is not.
Free from confusion, may it by itself know its own nature.[52]

---

49 When cutting through *assertions*, fallacies and doubts, there is no one to *sever* anything. They all dissolve by themselves in the experience of the nature of mind.

50 *Ordinary preoccupations* are activities that distract from the essential and important. *Unfabricated naturalness* is a complete letting go, like a bundle of straw that falls apart when the string is cut.

51 A *naturally abiding mind* is the fruit of the practice of mental calm (Sanskrit: *śamatha*), the main obstacles of which are (1) *torpor*: an unclear, foggy, confused mind like a bright, but chaotic room; (2) *dullness*: a dark, dull mind like a room without light; and (3) *agitation*: a perturbed, excited mind like a lake with many *waves*.

52 This describes the practice of *intuitive insight* (Sanskrit: *vipaśyanā*), which means a penetrating, non-conceptual, direct and *clear seeing* which cuts through all *doubts* about being or non-being, the nature of life, the reality which is not actually visible. Direct understanding dissolves all *confusion*, due to which one affirms or denies views.

Looking into the objects, there are no objects – they are seen
to be mind.
Looking into the mind, there is no mind – it is empty by
nature.
Looking into both, dualistic grasping is freed in itself.
May we realise luminous clarity, mind as it really is.

Free from mental fabrication, it is the Great Seal
(mahamudra).
Devoid of extremes, it is the Great Middle Way
(maha-madhyamaka).
Encompassing all these, it is also called Great Completion
(maha-ati).
Knowing one, the meaning of all is realized – may we
attain that confidence.

Free from attachment, great joy is uninterrupted.
Free from clinging to characteristics, luminous clarity is
unobscured.
Beyond the intellect, non-conceptuality is spontaneously
present.
Without effort, may these experiences be unceasing.[53]

Clinging to desired 'good' experiences is liberated in itself
And confusion about 'bad' thoughts is purified in the space
of its own nature:
Ordinary mind is free from abandoning and cultivating and
cannot be obtained.
May we realise freedom from projections, the true nature of
phenomena.

53 The three main experiences of mental calm are *joy, clarity,* and *non-conceptuality*. They manifest here as joy free from any attachment, which becomes nondual *great joy*. Mental clarity frees itself from attachment to perceived characteristics, free from labelling, and shows as the *luminous clarity* of mind's nature. *Spontaneous non-conceptuality* is free from blocking movements; it is centreless being, free from conceptual fixation – mahāmudrā.

The nature of beings has always been buddha,
But not realising this, they wander endlessly in samsara.
For sentient beings, whose suffering knows no bounds,
May unbearable compassion arise in this stream of being!

Since unbearable compassion is strong and has no barriers,
In the moments of such love the meaning of the 'empty nature' nakedly dawns.
May we practise this unerring, supreme path of unity
Day and night, without ever leaving it.[54]

Through the power of meditation may the eyes and higher perceptions appear,
And may we ripen sentient beings, cultivate buddha realms,
And perfect the paths of aspiration for the accomplishment of all buddha dharmas.
By bringing to completion the ripening, cultivation, and perfection may we all awaken to buddhahood.[55]

---

54 When the dualistic patterns of self-centredness are inactivated by overwhelming *love* or *compassion*, the power of naturally compassionate mind can manifest unhindered, and the *empty, intangible nature* of all phenomena becomes apparent. The *path of unity* is to live in the inseparable unity of compassion and wisdom, appearance and emptiness, relative and ultimate truth, saṃsāra and nirvāṇa.

50 The *eyes and higher perceptions* are faculties of heightened perception. They include five eyes of wisdom, like seeing past lives, and six extraordinary faculties, such as perceiving thoughts of others. *Buddha dharmas* refers to the qualities and activities of awakened beings. When accomplished, bodhisattvas are able to lead living beings to maturity through introductions that help to *ripen* their understanding of the nature of mind, *purify* their vision through essential teachings, and thus *cultivate* the mind of every living being as a pure buddha realm.

By the compassion of the buddhas and their offspring in the ten directions
And by the power of everything pure and beneficial,
May the pure paths of aspiration of myself and all sentient beings
be realised just as they are intended.

F. Antennas of the Heart: Living Compassionate Resonance

To feel what an encounter is really about, we extend our antennas of the heart. Then we perceive subtly what the actual feelings, needs and concerns of our counterpart are. When we express them in a resonant way, the other person feels understood and the encounter unfolds further. This compassionate resonance creates a clear feeling in us for what moves this person deeply. To feel into it requires experience and intuition.

It helps us to realize inwardly that the other person has the same qualities as we do: the potential to fully awaken, the so-called buddha nature, many qualities that can mature. We can welcome these qualities in the other inwardly at the beginning of the encounter: "I welcome the buddha in you. One could also say, I greet your deepest qualities, your ground of being, your divine spark." This can also be connected with perceiving oneself and the other person filled with light, or full of light in one's heart and forehead. These are small aids to be able to let oneself in more deeply and to stay connected with the resources. At the same time our whole organism reacts with us.

Breathing from the heart: Giving and Receiving (Tonglen)

The practice of "giving and receiving" (Tib. Tong-len) is well known as an effective breathing meditation that strengthens kindness of heart and compassion. It builds on the awareness of inhaling and exhaling and connects the breath with *bodhicitta*, the mind of awakening. This method can also be used in the therapeutic situation to get into a deep resonance. While someone tells us about burdensome experiences, we open ourselves completely to accept the difficult and painful within us, to become completely open to them. We let it enter our heart with the inhalation, like a big sphere of light, without holding on to the heavy, and so it dissolves again immediately. We connect this with the wish that our counterpart may be free from everything oppressive. With the exhalation we let heartfelt support flow towards him. In doing this, we can visualize a stream of light, but we can also do without it. We share everything that is salutary, all love, all qualities with the other person and imagine that he/she awakens to his/her buddha-qualities.

This is the process of Tonglen: Accepting with the inhalation, giving support with the exhalation. We give support lovingly and accept everything difficult with compassion. Supporting generously and accepting with compassion – with a warm heart. The person does not even need to be present to practice Tonglen; we can simply imagine her presence. As long as she is present to us, we let the heart-breath continue to flow until we feel that the support has arrived. In our own consciousness, there is no longer any resistance to painful experiences and no more holding on to a sense of well-being, to our own qualities, to our life force, in short: to everything that we normally want to keep to ourselves. Everything that we would normally protect, we give away from our heart, and everything that we would normally fend off, we open ourselves to. This is possible when we do not objectify, do not hold on to anything. What's coming dissolves in the open mind, and the same open mind lets everything flow, holds nothing back.

Tonglen was and is the heart practice of many people. It has spread especially in Tibetan buddhism through the Seven-Point Mind Training (Lodjong) but is similar in many ways to the practices of Kindness (Metta) and the Four Immeasurable Qualities (Brahmavihāras) in southern buddhism. Breathing in is compassion and breathing out is love.

Breathing from the heart (Tonglen) with ourselves (exercise F.1)

It is important, especially in our time, when so many of us find it difficult to accept ourselves, to begin the Tonglen process with ourselves. We begin by inviting the awakened awareness, for example in the form of a buddha before us or above us. We can also call this awakened awareness Higher or True Self. Then we take time to feel the inspiring, trustworthy, wholesome presence of the awakened awareness. When this is felt, we ask this wholesome presence to settle in our hearts as a light-figure or to merge with our heart. Then we breathe with the light-filled presence in our heart, as if the breath would flow through the light in the heart and nourish our entire organism with it. We take the loving Buddha-Breath with every cell of our being and anchor the experience deeply in our "cell" memory – so that we can also later find our way back to the feeling of being deeply accepted.

Once we are well anchored in the loving acceptance of ourselves, in warm self-care, we start the second part of the process: working with burdens or strains. In doing so, we make sure that we remain well anchored in the resource, i.e. the loving accepting awareness. Burdensome emotional issues either emerge of their own accord or we bring them specifically to consciousness. It is enough to "touch" them very briefly, to let them light up in our consciousness for a short time and then to switch directly back into awakened awareness, as if the buddha in our heart would accept this burden lovingly and compassionately. In doing so, we change our perspective and experience the burdening emotion (including the situation that triggers it) from the "eyes" or, better said, with the heart of an awakened person. This protects against re-identification (and possible re-traumatization). So, we swing from the awakened awareness with the heart-breath into the awareness of difficulties, challenges and problems. And before we get involved again, we are already back in relaxed awareness. With this swinging between resource (buddha awareness, 80–90%) and challenge (10–20%) we continue to breathe in the heart-breath all the time, feeling and resonating with the inhalation and letting the support flow with the exhalation. Once the problem feels rounded or completed and we have found deep self- acceptance, then we rest in it for a longer time, experience the integrating effect again with each cell and let the experience fade away without any further concepts. If we have visualized a buddha or another awakened presence, it will dissolve into our heart.

Here once again are the seven steps at a glance:

1. Invite the awakened awareness.
2. Feel the inspiring presence of the awakened awareness.
3. Let the awakened presence melt into the heart.
4. Breathe with the luminous presence in the heart.
5. Anchor the healing, loving, and accepting awareness.
6. Swinging between resource and challenge:
   while inhaling, accept and empathize with what arises; while exhaling, support and let it flow.
7. Rest, widen, close.

Breathing from the heart (Tonglen) with another person (exercise F.2)

The same form of practice can then be extended to other people. In doing so, we imagine that the person is present in the room in front of us – in the same sitting position as we are. We breathe with the awakened presence in the heart and feel what moves the other person. This can be done in complete silence or by communicating internally, as if we were conducting a dialogue. In this exchange, we can ask specifically the needs of the other person or address difficult issues. In doing so, our task is to remain anchored in the heart-breath, in deep acceptance, in flowing and empathetically resonating. We continue to pay attention to doing good to ourselves and support the other person to the best of our ability.

With Tonglen, I (Tilmann) allow myself to empathize to the extent that I can inwardly come to an experience of the other person that is very close to their own feelings. It can even lead to the certainty:

If I express this now, it is certainly exactly what corresponds to him. In order for this "heart-antenna" to function reasonably reliably, my own problems need to have dissolved to such an extent that there is no longer any need to take care of myself in the situation.

To fully engage in this practice would mean to fully engage with the other person, to put all my resources at her disposal and to be ready to feel everything the other person feels. I experience this practice as very enriching, because through it, being human opens up to a degree that I have never known before. I am becoming human myself because I feel the humanity of everyone I meet. This *can* also be painful, but that is part of it – being anchored in awakened awareness helps.

There are therapeutic approaches that would recommend maintaining a degree of self-protection: Feel the other, help him, but do not let his problems get inside you, as if you had a little protective barrier. This is where buddhist mind training is a little different: We first learn to become familiar with the non-self, the so-called "ultimate mind of awakening". From feeling this dimension, where there is nothing to protect, it is possible to let go of this self-protection. But this force of wisdom first needs to become awake and active within us. Then it is possible to balance the increasing sensitivity with increasing wisdom, so that painful feelings do not flood us, but are recognized in their true nature as dreamlike experiences.

We open ourselves and deeply accept the suffering of others. Apart from experiencing the qualities we also perceive everything that burdens the other person. We allow this suffering to come completely into our consciousness. There, however, it is not objectified, but dissolves like snowflakes on a hot stone or like darkness dissolving in the light of the buddhaqualities, in the light of the open heart. Our heart opens very wide without assuming that there is a core of being that needs to be protected. But that takes a lot of practice. Until we make the experience that all heaviness actually dissolves on the spot. We simply leave the heaviness where it is. We perceive it and continue to breathe sensitively, without the idea of breathing in the suffering. It is enough if we are touched in the heart and extend the antennas of the heart.

In psychological terms, phenomena of transmission (and counter transmission) also play a role in these processes – especially when we ourselves have not yet found our way into emotional clarification. Example: Someone enters the room, and we suddenly feel anger that we did not notice before. If, assuming good self-knowledge, there is no reason for this annoyance in us, then it can be a transference phenomenon. We resonate with the experience of the other – something is in resonance with us. We feel something that actually has to do with the feeling and sensation of the other. With this interpretation one can work in the therapeutic situation and ask: "Is it possible that there is trouble?" Then we listen carefully to what is really going on in the other person, without insisting on our own experience.

We have to make sure that our experience has something to do with the reality of the other person. We must not cultivate the imagination: "Just because I experience it this way, the other person's reality is really like that." Verifying our interpretations is absolutely necessary, combined with a good knowledge of ourselves. And for this self-knowledge, the daily practice of awareness is so important – until we know ourselves so well that we notice when something occurs that is not part of our ordinary experience.

Something unusual is happening in us because of the encounter with the other. We vibrate like a bell through the "sound" of the other bell entering the room. Mind you: We do not feel the other, but the resonance of our own bell. When one resonating body sounds, other resonating bodies start to vibrate. What sounds within us has to do with ourselves but is triggered by the other. We don't know what is going on with the other person, but based on the vibration that arises in us, we formulate a hypothesis about what the other person might experience.

We work with this phenomenon in the process of transmission, and possibly counter transmission. It also plays a role in Tonglen, especially with those present.

Breathing from the heart (Tonglen) in couple relationship (exercise F.3)

It stands to reason to use the heart-breath also in couple therapy. This has already proven to be successful, even if it does not replace direct communication, but only prepares it. First of all, we support the client in collecting himself. Once he is well rested within himself, we ask him – as described above – to invite the awakened presence into his heart. This is followed by a phase of heart breathing with oneself, in order to come to deep self-acceptance. In a further step, the client imagines the partner in front of him or her in the same sitting position. The first step is to allow and experience a feeling of silent connection. Then the client begins to ask sensitively how the partner is doing and listens inwardly for the answer. He/she lets himself/herself be touched by it in the heart, continues to breathe with all the qualities of the heart, stabilizes in the resource (the awakened awareness) and then lets an answer arise. It can already take the form of loving support (e.g. light from the heart). Then it is felt how the answer is received. The answer is adjusted until it is accepted in the conception as truly supportive. This process of questioning and answering is repeated several times, in all variations and forms of deepening it that seem helpful, until the process is rounded off. The client imagines how her partner is deeply touched in her heart and is internally filled with light.

Afterwards all conceptions dissolve and after a short pause the exercise is completed. Here again the important steps at a glance:

1. Support the client to collect himself.
2. Invite awakened presence into the heart.
3. Support in the heart-breath with yourself.
4. Imagine the partner in front of you.
5. Allow silent, connected presence.
6. Ask sensitive questions, how the partner feels;
   hear the answer inwardly
7. Allow yourself to be touched, possibly heart-breath with yourself to stabilize.

8. Let a heartfelt answer or support flow.
9. Imagine how the support is received. Repeat several times.
10. Rounding off.
11. Dissolve.

Bodhicitta means to live in the We-mode (exercise F.4)

Actually, the practice of the heart-breath (Tonglen) is about deepening our relationship to others and dissolving the unnecessary separation between ourselves and others. Until we feel connected in a way that others are as important to us as we are to ourselves. Bodhicitta – the mind of awakening – is living and acting out of the "we". Thereby egoism as well as altruism (its antidote) dissolve into a spontaneous grasp of the overall situation of which we are a part – with the spontaneous compassionate willingness to do everything that serves the overall situation.

Whether we are alone, in pairs, in a group, or looking after the planet as a whole: we always look beyond the horizon and include those who are not present. This is a daily exercise. This broad mindset is based on the deep experience of how closely we are all interwoven. We breathe the same air, drink the same water, eat from the same earth, have the same desire for happiness, etc. – connectedness in mutual dependence. "We" cannot be separated from each other – it is all about salutary interrelations. The loving, wise understanding practiced in the heart-breath with acceptance and support nourishes the We. Me and you – in relation to the greater We. Everyone has their own desires and fears, which can bring about potentially endless conflicts. Thinking in the We-mode brings solution and flow. "We" is the overall situation, i.e. all those involved and all those affected by our actions. Learning to include the "you" and the "us" leads to a radical change of perspective: first to find out from *ego*-ism – then to find out from *alter*-ism (altruism), which is still based on the experience of "other" and separateness and is often a little artificial, to find out into the panoramic awareness, which perceives and includes everything and everyone – "as far as the sky reaches".

Buddha nature: Everyone can awaken!

Everyone can awaken, since the qualities of awakening are inherent in the mind itself. When our consciousness is free from constricting imaginations and emotional veils, these inherent qualities reveal themselves in all their fullness. Awakening is not a personal achievement. It reveals itself when the mind is completely open and relaxed, and for most people it occurs gradually as a process of increasing clarity as the constricting emotional and cognitive patterns gradually dissolve.

People (parents, friends, Dharma teachers, psychotherapists) who know this process act as catalysts on this path. They inspire us to uncover the treasure in our own mind. Through our inner work we gain a certain freedom that gives us the strength to work with others. We have discovered something that is transforming our lives from the ground up. Our path still has its ups and downs, but a clear experience of possible inner freedom has emerged, and we make this experience available to others.

The Buddha considered everyone capable of attaining the same awakening as himself. Just as Christ suggested to everyone that they too should become sons and daughters of God – and then sit at the right and left of God. Actually, the point is that we all enter into the succession of the awakened ones. In their footsteps, our natural being is revealed – and it is into this very path that truly curative, therapeutic interventions are inserted.

We help each other to develop deep trust in our own ability to heal and awaken fully. We develop a "pure view" of ourselves and others as potential buddhas. A radically different view, which sees the good, the noble, the buddhaqualities in others, combined with respect for ourselves and others. It gives us an inner dignity through the knowledge that the mind is originally good, deeply unaffected by all the difficulties we have gone through. We know: freedom is possible, the first seeds of awakening are already visible.

Behold the noble being in every human (exercise F.5)

Jack Kornfield, in *The Wise Heart,* names as the first principle on the path of awakening:

> "Behold the noble inner being and the beauty in every human."

We can further develop the exercise offered by Kornfield and consciously choose the inner attitude we want to adopt towards others. It is an exercise in a new perspective: pick a person for today's exercise and put her in front of you in your mind. Start with the heart-breath as described above (Tonglen with yourself). Then extend this posture to the other person.

See the other (1) as an innocent, playful child, or else (2) as a dying, vulnerable, open, without hiding anything, or (3) as a person like you, who desires happiness, dignity, and love and wants to avoid suffering. See his qualities, his beauty, show respect and feel his goodness.

Perform this exercise with different people to experience them more deeply with the heart. The starting point of the buddhist teachings is understanding, as well as respect for ourselves and for each individual being with a deep respect for our kinship – in our wishes and fears – with reverence for their inherent buddhaqualities. Developing this respect strengthens the inner goodness in ourselves and in all those we meet.

All will benefit from our basic good will if we see in them their buddha nature. In the same manner, we also see the wounded child who seeks happiness, wants to avoid suffering and often follows clumsy strategies to get its needs met. But we also look deeper and perceive the one who is an awakened being in her potential – and this awakened potential receives unconditional support. The emotional surface movements are not worthy of our trust, they are as unreliable as emotions are, but the innermost part of a person is trustworthy through and through. We perceive the emotional waves and accept them without getting caught up in evaluations and reactions. But our support goes above all into uncovering the inner intact, awakened potential.

Settling in compassionate goodness (exercise F.6)

The following exercise consists of several elements: "gathering downwards", "gathering upwards", "gathering in the middle" and the "heart-breath".

Sit relaxed, as upright as possible...

When you are ready, imagine that with every exhalation you now go a little deeper into relaxation, just like an elevator. As if you were pressing a button sliding down towards the earth. With each exhalation you continue into a well-grounded, relaxed expanse.

Use the exhalation as a symbol to let go deeper and deeper, one "floor" after the other...

With the inhalation open yourself for what is, and how it is; with the exhalation let go deep into exactly this experience. Emphasize the experience of ground contact, the earth element, stability, trust and at the same time deep relaxation.

Deeply let go of everything that concerns you...

As you do, the stomach-area widens. The abdomen and pelvis become wide, and the lower body becomes very supple, nestles up to the floor, the seat...

The back remains straight...

If you want, you can connect inwardly as well as with the centre of the earth...

Enjoy it for a few more breaths...

When you are ready inside, press the button in the elevator, which will take you back to the top: with each inhalation you will go up one floor...

Thereby, stay in this deep relaxation...

Imagine that you get to the top of the roof, where it becomes very wide and bright. Light-flooded, wide-open being...

The mind remains as calm and collected as before, when you collected it downstairs and now, you collect it upstairs in the vastness of the space... very wide, bright and clear...

The lower body is still in the stable, supple width of before; and now the upper body and the head area are widening, as if the space would be felt...

After you have enjoyed this for a while, let the inner elevator go to about your heart level, where you experience the centre of your being, to integrate both aspects of being – stability and expansiveness...

The breath now flows from the heart...

Breathing in open yourself into deep acceptance and letting come; breathing out open yourself into complete free flowing...

Let it come and let it flow...

Breathing in open yourself to being connected with every-thing and feel your connection with everyone around you, feel their presence...

Breathing out, let your simple being flow towards all others – a gift of suchness, inwardly connected...

You can extend this in the imagination through all walls and beyond all boundaries until it reaches all living beings...

Breathing in with compassion – breathing out with loving support...

Breathing in is as if the stream of breath enters you from all directions simultaneously; and breathing out is as if you exhale in all directions simultaneously...

As if light would stream in and out...
Receiving acceptance and giving letting flow...
Enjoy this for a while – if possible, without any effort...
After a while, feel your body again, open your eyes, look around, ready for the next contact.
Feel where you are, take your time. Then perhaps consciously approach someone – in simple being.

Encountering each other in simple being

The following quotation is attributed to Master Eckhart:

> "The most important hour is always the present,
> the most important person is always the one who is facing you,
> and the most necessary thing to do is always love."

This is how we can concretely live *bodhicitta*, the mind of awakening: always now, always with the one we are encountering, and always with love. Then we are not frightened by the prospects of an endless activity for the benefit of all – it is always only about now and about simple, loving being. A person comes to us in the therapeutic practice, or we meet him somewhere – in being. We are in the same boat, because as humans we have similar basic experiences and carry the same potential of awakening within us. At the same time, we have our specific, personal form – like weather beech trees. Among other things, structures have formed which sometimes prevent a healthy flow, a salutary being. If we are aware of all this and have already gained some experience of how to find our way into the flow, then we can support the flow of being of others to find into a more relaxed being.

Through the recognition of what was just a prison, the vision of suchness opens up. The basic attitude in the encounter is the non-judgemental inner readiness to share the being with each other.

"I discover you in your being and share my being with you. You discover me in my being and share your being with me." In case people seek our support to find a way out of their blockages, it is important that we are in a salutary stream. Otherwise, we will disappoint the expectations of those who come to us. A healer appears like contagious in his flow and stimulates this detached being in us, so that the experience of inner flow is established as if by itself. The therapist's humanity cures – that which he or she radiates. The detached, loving being. It is profoundly beneficial to meet someone who flows without worries, is full of love, listens attentively, is with us, communicates in depth and is reliable. Someone who, moreover, does not get stuck on what we express.

In simple being, the mind opens and detaches itself from what is troubling us and what needs to be done – the mountains that sometimes wait for us. Simple, free flowing being connects us and everyone we meet with the salutary, with the healing, with the awakening. This is exactly what we can give to others; this is what nourishes our exchange.

Attunement for the therapy session: There are several ways to get attuned for the therapy session. First of all, there is the cultivation of awareness while breathing in and out (Ānāpānasati Sutta). The 16 steps described therein lead us, even in a shortened form, into a deeply detached being. We can also practice the heart-breath, which emphasizes more love and compassion. Another possibility is to consider oneself and the other person as buddha (e.g. as Medicine Buddha), which strengthens the pure view and the trust in the healing powers. Finally, we can also use the Mahāmudrā practice as an attunement – unconditional, natural being in realizing the true nature of all experience.

These different approaches are equally good gates into detached, flowing being. We use them according to our heart's desire and our current state of mind. Above all, it seems important to practice a kind of "mental hygiene" every day and thereby find our way into the experience of detached being. We can regard this as a promise we make to our fellow human beings (and clients):

> "Yes, every day I take care of my mind, my inner balance.
> I tune in and take care to be in the flow as best I can,
> so that I can help you find your way into the flow."

G. The Self and the Non-self

We form a picture of ourselves that is more stable than the actual experience – which is basically just process. Images, on the other hand, are stable. This is why self-image and reality are constantly diverging. The Buddha said that no "Atman" could be found. Today, *Atman* is translated as self, ego or soul. But the Buddha meant an individual, personal, indivisible core of being that is not dependent on conditions – most likely what we would call the unchangeable individual soul. He pointed out that the ego is pure process and not a constant, unchangeable self that remains the same in all experience and even after death.

We objectify the process-like continuity of experience through concepts such as "I", "self" – which is as true and at the same time inaccurate as giving a constantly changing stream of water from its source to its mouth the same name "Rhine". The name is not the problem, but only the belief that the river is always the same. The river itself is unique in every moment, something completely special – just as we humans are special, unique streams of experience. Unique and at the same time a process through and through. In this process there are personality traits that distinguish us from other streams, but these traits are also subject to change. It is about dissolving a fixed idea of the ego, about recognizing the processual nature of the ego and by no means about dissolving an ego. It is about this being in the flow. How can I help myself to be in the flow, not identified with ideas about myself, but in experiencing?

Fixed ideas of a constant I have a restrictive effect on our experience and limit our inner mobility. Realizing how our experience is constantly changing and how we ourselves are a constant process helps us to adapt flexibly to the constantly new. But at the same time there is the continuity of the familiar and the same. When we wake up in the morning, we pick up the experience of yesterday, the day before yesterday, last month and last year. Continuity in change. We link similar things and create inner structures, images and ideas that help us find our way around. We learn how to link different areas of experience within the change in a meaningful way. All of this makes sense – as long as it remains amenable for a continuous adaptation to the stream of life, which always brings something new. We must not confuse concepts, inner images and imagination with experience, not live in imaginations, otherwise a conflict between imagination and reality will arise. Basically, it is simply a matter of continuous reality check – what is it really like?

A human is not a closed, independent entity, but an open system, in constant exchange with the environment – not only through the body, which absorbs and excretes food, but also through sensory perception and social contacts. Our feelings and thoughts are constantly influenced by a variety of factors – it is a systemic happening. Perception, sensation, differentiation, shaping, consciousness are in constant exchange – "interbeing", as Thich Nhat Hanh calls it. The Buddha spoke of conditioned arising in mutual dependence.

The five aggregates of existence: Is there a self?

To make it clearer how much we are process, the Buddha examined the pillars of our ego-identification in his famous analysis of the five *skandhas* (aggregates or factors of existence):

1. Perceiving sensory forms (forms)
2. Sensing emotional tints (sensations)
3. Making distinctions (distinctions)
4. Forming experiences (mental formations)
5. Experiencing states of consciousness (states of consciousness)

The Buddha was asked whether there was an *atman*, an unchanging soul or stable self. He then pointed to a pile of wood in sight and said that it would be more or less like that pile of wood: the so-called ego is an interaction of many factors and processes. One could roughly distinguish five aggregates (literally: "pile"): forms, sensations, distinctions, shapes and states of consciousness. But if one takes a closer look, one will see that these too are in turn composed, conditional and a constant process.

1. There are the *forms* that are perceived by the eyes, but also the perceptions of the ears, the nose, the tongue and the palate, and the body – all these perceptions of sense forms alternate in a constant flow with each other, arising from contact between sense organs, sense objects and sense consciousness, which in turn are processes. The changing perceptions of form are not a sufficient basis for a stable, unchangeable self.
2. Perception is followed by the *sensation* of pleasant, unpleasant and neutral (irrelevant), in many different emotional tints, which in turn are constantly changing and are conditioned by many factors (individual, cultural, situational, etc.). The same experience can sometimes be pleasant, sometimes unpleasant, sometimes irrelevant, sometimes important, in different intensity. The changing feelings are not a sufficient basis for a stable, unchanging self.
3. *Distinctions*: The perceptions are not only classified in terms of the emotional tints but also distinguished from each other in terms of content. Forms, structures and contents of experience are recorded, compared and named within our conceptual frame of reference. This distinction is influenced by many factors and changes depending on conditions and situations. The changing distinctions are not a sufficient basis for a stable, unchanging self.
4. Perception, sensation, and distinction are followed by further *formations*, working in the outer world and forming inner experience. Our mental powers, emotions and motivations are significantly involved in this, i.e. wanting and not wanting, ego- and we-related attitudes, more or less wholesome intentions. In short: different mental factors that shape our perception of the world and lead to actions with body, speech and mind. All this

is subject to various influences and is constantly changing. The changing formations are not a sufficient basis for a stable, unchangeable self.

5. The product of perception, sensation, distinction and forming are the correspondingly diverse *states of consciousness* of the six senses: sensing (the body), seeing, hearing, smelling, tasting and mental experience (thinking, feeling etc.). There is no stability to be found in these states either. These are conditional processes, depending on many factors. The changing states of consciousness are not a sufficient basis for a stable, unchangeable self.

So much for the Buddha's argumentation. The first three aggregates – perceiving, feeling, distinguishing – give us information about life. A multitude of personal interpretations already contribute to the evaluation of the experiences as pleasant- unpleasant neutral and to the differentiating comparison with earlier experiences. Even in the form perception of the five outer senses, personal differences already play a role: depending on where we direct our attention and how our sense organs are structured, we perceive only partial aspects of life, and these may even be distorted.

Our lives are based on this information. We think, speak and act, take an interest, linger on something, explore it, want something, take hold of it, let go of it, turn to others and experience a lot of feelings, in almost incessant succession. Salutary creative forces cause experiences of joy and happiness; non-salutary creative forces cause tension and suffering. Sometimes we use the abilities of self-reflection and consciously give direction to these creative processes. All this leads to the continuous experience of different states of mind – called consciousness. And in all this there is no centre to be found, these are processes without a central controlling or guiding authority. All this is me – and yet I am not. This ego is not stable – it is a flowing experience without a core of being. But in this experience, also in the awakened experience, formative forces are active like motivation, wisdom, compassion and the like, which we would normally assign to the ego.

Ego-strength on the path of awakening

If we compare the descriptions of the ego in Western psychology with the Buddhist mind training, it becomes obvious that a fully integrated ego is actually the qualities of an awakened person. We encourage the reader to relate the following description of the capabilities of the ego inwardly to how a buddha is described.

The terms "ego strength" and "ego weakness" were introduced by Sigmund Freud.[56] The ego is understood here as the instance that makes a reasonable, realistic decision when faced with challenges and mediates between different requirements. This ability is called ego-strength. The buddhist teachings would call this ability "discriminating wisdom" (prajñā). If the "ego" of psychoanalytical teachings unconsciously and without its own guidance follows the drive impulses of the "it" or allows itself to be dominated by the forces of the "super-ego", then we are dealing with I-weakness – in buddhist terms a "lack of awareness" (avidya) characterized by habitual patterns.

Alfred Adler describes the "ego" as acting independently and with a will or determination. The will is found in the buddhist teachings divided into the three functions "striving" (chanda), "determination" (adhimukti) and "envisioning" (smṛti). According to Freud, the two functions of the ego are the engagement with the environment and the engagement with the intra-psychic instances of the super-ego and the id. The ego has the possibility to control, ward off or satisfy the impulses of the id (also in the imagination) and to check the controlling influences of the super-ego.

The psychoanalytic ego-psychology[57] emphasizes the creative defences of the nascent ego (the ego as a process) against threatening impressions – today we would say: growing in creatively dealing with challenges. The achievement of the ego is to "create a harmony between the id, the superego and the powers of the outside world" –

56 For the following paragraphs, our gratitude goes to the well-researched articles in Wikipedia, which give an excellent insight into the subject of "ego-psychology".

57 Starting with Anna Freud "The ego and the defense mechanisms" (1936).

something that fails in neurosis. Heinz Hartmann uses the term "self" to describe the ability to experience and reflect on oneself. He also emphasized that the healthy ego functions can develop best in a conflict-free environment through innate (!) potentials of the ego. This led to a theory of the development of the ego that takes place free of conflict solely through everyday challenges and through successful, satisfying relationships with the environment. These explanations bring to mind buddhist descriptions of how our inherent potential needs to be freed from veils and blockages and then unfold its full force as it flows with situations.

The assumption that innate ego functions exist, which are already present in infancy, created the basis for the observations on infants by René A. Spitz and Margaret Mahler. With this, the development of the patient's autonomy came to the fore in psychoanalytic treatment. Even after this brief digression we can see important parallels to buddhist teachings: the ego is defined on the basis of functions, as a dynamic, interactive event in the balance of acting forces and conditions. The goal of this natural process is "harmony" and "autonomy" – buddhist teachers would say: inner peace and freedom.

Hartmann considers the ego as a system of functions – a constructed instance that serves to explain the functioning of the psyche. He does not ascribe a core of essence to this system. The most important task of the system is to organize itself, and its functions become more differentiated in the course of the development. The ego functions were described by Heinz Hartmann, Leopold Bellak and Barnett Meyers. They are summarized here:

Functions of the ego are to perceive, to think clearly, to be able to communicate what is thought, to concentrate oneself, to remember and to judge, which includes to foresee consequences, to conclude logically and to recognize cause-effect relations. Then there is the relation to reality: to be able to check reality, i.e. to distinguish between inner and outer sensations and images and to maintain the perception of reality, which includes to be able to constantly match the experience of outer events and bodily sensations and to experience coherence, and to distinguish between subjective and objective aspects of the experience. It is also about aligning one's own needs with social norms, values and customs and developing a keen sense for signs that emotional impulses are becoming too strong and could have negative effects.

Connected to this are the abilities to regulate impulses, moods and affects and to tolerate frustration of one's own needs instead of automatically acting out impulses. Also, the ability to be intensively and constantly related to other people (object constancy) and to perceive them in their good as well as their negative qualities (ambivalence ability) are important functions of the ego. Furthermore, psychoanalysis describes the ability to abandon oneself to imagining and dreaming and then to be able to regain a normal relationship to reality. Further ego functions are to be able to regulate how one reacts to internal and external stimuli in order to avoid being swamped (the so-called stimulus barrier) and to be able to correctly assess one's own abilities and coping skills. In addition, emotional protective functions serve to regulate emotions that are difficult to bear. These functions are found in all people. Many of them run almost automatically, while others are used specifically, such as the ability to integrate experiences witnessed as contradictory in a satisfying way.

In psychoanalytic theory, almost all disorders of the development of the ego are due to disorders in early childhood before reaching object constancy at about one and a half years of age. This should make Dharma practitioners sit up and take notice, since buddhist literature hardly addresses this. The assumption is even obvious that some of the things described as "karmic patterns" can be traced back to early childhood experiences that acted as causes, triggers or reinforcers. Modern research has found that babies have the ability to communicate with their environment at a very early age. He perceives his environment very clearly, even if the terms for this are still missing, and is able to distinguish between his actions and those of others at an early age. He actively contacts reference persons and can regulate them – all indications for the thesis that many ego functions are innate.

Jane Loevinger[58] understands the ego as the totality of integrative processes whose main task is to give meaning to intra- and interpersonal experiences. In the course of ego development, a specific pattern is formed of how a person perceives and interprets herself and the world. In the course of development, this ego structure undergoes constant transformations that lead to ever greater awareness. According to Loevinger, the ego is not a psychological instance (as in psychoanalysis, for example), but a process that organizes a person's thoughts and experiences. This process of selecting and interpreting thoughts and experiences is what constitutes the stability of the reached ego-development level.

In this model we speak of "development" when the thought structures with which we make the world understandable become more and more differentiated and integrated, so that an increasingly adequate picture of reality becomes possible. In the course of this development, qualitative leaps occur, each of which results in a new internal structure that can be described as stages of development. If this happens, one speaks of a "transformation", because a new and more comprehensive way of perceiving oneself and the world has emerged. This corresponds to the development of new, ever more helpful perspectives that take over from each other on the path of awakening. In Loevinger's ego-development model, the following stages with such qualitative leaps are distinguished for adults:

At a very young age we are at the *impulsive* level.

This is followed by the *self-oriented* level. Here the own advantage is in the foreground, other people are seen as a means for the own satisfaction of needs and represent less a value in itself. An opportunistic behaviour towards others shows and the time horizon is rather short. The focus is strongly on concrete things, feedback is usually rejected, the actions are stereotypical with an eye-by-eye mentality and predominantly external blame.

---

58 Loevinger, J. (1966), in "The meaning and measurement of ego development", American Psychologist, 21, 195-206, and Loevinger, J. (1976) in "Ego development. Conception and theories". San Francisco: Jossey-Bass

On the *community-determined* level, thinking and acting is primarily oriented to the rules and norms of the relevant reference group, one's own identity is defined by them, and membership and subordination to their views are predominant. The preservation of one's own face is a central concern, strong feelings of guilt arise when the expectations of others are violated, conflicts are avoided, contacts tend to be superficial, and thinking is predominantly in either-or categories.

On the *rationalist level*, the orientation towards clear standards, rational thinking and causal explanations prevail. The motivation is to distinguish oneself from others, with fixed ideas about how things are and should be. This is where self-awareness, self-criticism and seeing different perspectives as well as the search for motives for one's own behaviour begin. However, the thinking is rather narrow and technical with emphasis on efficiency rather than effectiveness.

At the *self-determined* level, there are fully developed and self-defined values, ideas and goals, a trained identity with strong goal orientation and self-optimization. The complexity of situations is accepted, one has a rich inner life, cultivating mutuality in relationships with respect for individual differences. However, the own shadow of subjectivity is often not seen.

On the *relativizing level*, an awareness of how one's own perception shapes the view of the world begins. This leads to a stronger questioning of one's own views and those of other people and a relativistic view of the world. There is a greater awareness of internal/external conflicts and paradoxes without being able to integrate them, and a very individual, personal way.

At the *systemic level*, the fully developed ability to take on different perspectives while simultaneously focusing on processes and goals, a systemic grasp of relationships (circularity) and the ability to integrate contradictory aspects and opinions is evident. There is a high motivation to develop oneself further. Conflicts are dealt with openness and creativity with a high tolerance for ambiguity. There is a high level of respect for the autonomy of other people and reconciliation with one's own parts that are experienced as negative.

At the *integrated level*, one is no longer bound to an explicit system of values, attitudes, practices, etc. Experiences are constantly reassessed and put into different contexts. One realizes one's own goals and values to a high degree, can integrate paradoxes, develops a high awareness of where one's attention is directed and develops a special sense of symbolism. The need to evaluate things and people is abandoned. It comes to a being one with the world, without holding on, by getting involved in the flow of things.

On the *fluid level*, the ability to playfully alternate between the serious and the trivial becomes apparent; different states of consciousness merge smoothly, thinking becomes panoramic in large time cycles and historical dimensions with a full acceptance of otherness and of people as they are.

It is surprising how similar the description of these developmental levels is to the guiding principles of buddhist mind training. Both are clearly concerned with a systemically related, integrated, flowing being, the perfect expression of which is considered to be a buddha in Asia.

The awakened qualities of a healthy self

What psychology calls ego-strength is the ability to handle situations wisely and skilfully so that we time and again find balance. Inner stability is the successful adaptation to a challenging situation. Fixations have the consequence that new situations cannot be answered adequately because we are blocked. This leads to instability. This ability to go through life in "flowing stability" is described in buddhist psychology as the presence of the liberating qualities (pāramitā).

Dharma practice always leads to the strengthening and not at all to the weakening of the abilities of a healthy ego. Increasing mindfulness leads to a stronger anchoring in the being, to a more awake experience. It is actually a confusion of terms: we work with two different concepts of the ego. What psychology defines as a healthy ego, there is nothing to resolve. This is not the ego, whose existence is questioned in buddhist teachings. The ego, which is spoken of in the Dharma, does not need to be dissolved either – for this delimited, unchangeable, personal ego does not exist at all. What dissolves is an erroneous assumption and not a really existing ego. Only an idea of something that cannot be found is dissolved.

The process of developing the liberating qualities up to buddhahood is identical with the process described as ego-strengthening in psychology. A buddha has the most stable ego of all! A stream of mind on the path of awakening becomes more and more stable, less and less distracted, less and less upset and at the same time more and more adaptable, more and more open and thus shows all the qualities that are attributed to a stable, integrated personality.

So, it is a great misunderstanding to say: Please do not practice the buddhist path too early, so that the ego strengthening can still take place before the ego is dissolved. No ego is dissolved. There is no such thing. There is no ego-dissolution, only the dissolution of erroneous ideas of a solid, eternal, delimited ego.

Actually, no ego is strengthened in ego-strengthening either, but only the dynamic functions, which are all together called "ego". The stream of mind will always remain a stream – in constant change. In such a manner, there is no final health, but only homeostasis, a balance of dynamic forces within the entire system that must be constantly found anew. Health is not a state but a process.

The perfect example of a healthy ego or personality is a buddha. In the following I (Tilmann) will not describe a utopia but have actually met people with such qualities. I am thinking in particular of Gendun Rinpoche[59], who looked after me for eleven years and whose doctor I was allowed to be during the last three years of his life. It was possible for me to personally verify whether these qualities really exist. In fact, with him I experienced neither emotional fixations nor any adherence to ideas. Now the classic description:

59 His biography is available in "Heart Advice of a Mahamudra Master", Norbu editions.

Fully awakened people no longer act impulsively. Their action is based on a flowing being with panoramic awareness, in which they perceive the needs of all participants. They act compassionately without feeling separated from others or the world, spontaneously, free from personal intentions and without pursuing their own interests. They are aware of the interdependence of all being and see through the deceptively real quality of sensory impressions and personal perceptions. They have freed themselves from all fixed ideas and opinions, they do not represent any world view or standpoints. There is no longer any adherence to previous experiences and no rushing ahead into future ones. Moreover, the present is not reified. Their entire being is characterized by complete naturalness and simplicity, free of any complications. Their inner vision, it is said, spans entire world ages. They are described in the traditional representations by means of the awakened qualities: love, compassion, joy, generosity, beneficial behaviour, patience, energetic endurance, meditative stability, wisdom, strength, determination, truthfulness, equanimity and timeless awareness. These are exactly the mental qualities and abilities of a fully integrated healthy personality.

The healthy ego, of which Western psychology speaks, is further strengthened on the path of awakening and freed from all remaining blockages. In the process, the above-described developmental steps are passed through, whereby the last stage of the flowing being undergoes further refinement until the stream of mind has been released from any fixation – emotionally as well as cognitively. This is traditionally described as passing through the ten bodhisattva levels, whose names give some idea of the experience: Supreme Joy, Immaculate, Illuminating, Radiating Light, Extremely Difficult Practice, Becoming Manifest, Far Gone, Unshakeable, Excellent Intelligence and Dharma Clouds.[60]

60 The description of the 10 bodhisattva stages, buddhahood, and of awakened activity is found for example in Gampopa's "Ornament of Liberation", chapters 19 – 21.

H. The Healing Buddha within us

A central inspiration on my personal path was the practice of the Medicine Buddha. I met it during my medical studies, while I was already treating homoeopathically. I was inspired to keep alive in the encounter between practitioner and patient the notion that in the depths of our being we are both completely sound – and that we only have to allow or enable these qualities to manifest themselves. Each one of us is deeply healthy and has the full potential to awaken, just like a seed carries the tree or like a baby carries the adult within itself. Even more apt is the example of the sky: actually, the cloud cover only needs to break open and the blue sky becomes visible. It was only covered. In the same manner, our awakened qualities are also covered by emotional and cognitive veils.

To visualize myself and my respective counterpart in our essence as a Medicine Buddha helps me even today to stay connected almost continuously with the healthy, healing and awakened in us in a conversation, while I am outwardly simply in conversation and do not put anything over the situation. Visualizing serves to activate our antennas for deeper layers of being. Thereby the inner qualities within ourselves are addressed. I am always touched by the deep blue colour, which reminds me of the vastness and infinity of the sky – symbol of the intangible mind.

The light body of the Medicine Buddha has the deep blue of the beryl, a blue jewel which nowadays is almost only found as light blue aquamarine beryl. But there must also have been deep blue beryl – with a colour similar to lapis lazuli, but translucent. A friend, Herbert, painted a beautiful picture of the Medicine Buddha for my wedding, which accompanies me since then. Then, during a week of contemplative silence on the California coast more than 30 years ago, I had the vision of a blue and gold book on healing and awakening that I had to write. It has never left me, and this is book is the expression of it... The Dharma associated with psychotherapy is this medicine where the paths of healing and awakening merge.

The twelve wishes of the Medicine Buddha

From the Tibetan teacher Tenga Rinpoche I (Tilmann) heard for the first time about the inspiring twelve wishes of the Medicine Buddha, which he made for the time of his final enlightenment when he was the Bodhisattva "Master of all remedies" (Skt. Bhaiṣajyaguru).[61] These wishes express a broad view of what healing is. The classical text reads as follows:

61 Further information: Raoul Birnbaum in "The Healing Buddha", 1989 (Shambala)

When I am fully awakened:

1. May the light of my awakened mind spread in all countless worlds and make all living beings like me.
2. May this light illuminate all living beings that are bathed in darkness.
3. May it meet the needs of every living being with equanimity.
4. May it lead those who have gone astray back to the path of the Great Awakening.
5. May it take all who have confidence in me on the path of training.
6. May it heal all those who suffer from physical or mental ailments.
7. May it heal all those who are physically or mentally ill, and provide friends, family and a home for those who have none, and lead them to awakening.
8. May it see to it that until their enlightenment all are reborn under favourable conditions.
9. May it protect the living beings from deception, show them the liberated vision and the bodhisattva path of awakening.
10. May it save those who are tortured, imprisoned or sentenced to death.
11. May it feed the hungry and quench all thirst.
12. May it provide clothing for the unclothed and destitute.

When it is said that the Light of Awakening carries out these activities, then "light" means the spontaneous action of a buddha, free from relating to an ego. In the visualizations of Tibetan buddhism, light is a symbol for the alignment of our mind. Where the light shines, there our attention goes.

For the co-author Wolfgang the encounter with the Medicine Buddha was also very strong. He has been practicing it for almost 30 years now in therapy sessions as a continuous inspiration, combined with a little inner visualization. He is convinced that this strengthens intuition and alertness and supports the therapeutic process in a wholesome way. Through the inner focus on the Medicine Buddha a healing field is created, so that inner healing powers are activated in the client. During intensive inner processes of the client, it is as if the healing energies of the Medicine Buddha flow through the hands to the client and strengthen the healing field.

Both of us have found the Medicine Buddha a central inspiration in the development of Essential Psychotherapy and the founding of the Institute for Essential Psychotherapy.

A simple meditation on the Medicine Buddha (exercise H.1)

This practice, in its simplest form, can be performed by anyone. For example, to speak the mantra of the Medicine Buddha, one does not need to consider oneself a buddhist. The Meditation on the Medicine Buddha is a powerful method and can also illustrate what is meant by Vajrayāna view in the third step, "Transforming the View of Emotion". The mantra of the Medicine Buddha is in Tibetan/Nepali pronunciation:

TEYATHA. OM BHEKADSE BHEKADSE MAHĀ BHEKADSE
RADSA SAMUDGATE SOHA.

ཏདྱ་ཐཱ༔ ཨོཾ་བྷཻ་ཥ་ཛྱེ་བྷཻ་ཥ་ཛྱེ་མ་ཧཱ་བྷཻ་ཥ་ཛྱེ་ར་ཛ་ས་མུདྒ་ཏེ་སྭཱ་ཧཱ༔

The original Sanskrit is transliterated as:

TADYATHĀ OṀ BHAIṢAJYE BHAIṢAJYE MAHĀ BHAIṢAJYE
RĀJA SAMUDGATE SVĀHĀ.

Everyone is invited to recite this mantra; it is not secret. In the detailed visualization, this mantra is in the heart of the Medicine Buddha and surrounds the central seed syllable HUNG. It stands for the awakening mind, for love and compassion and all the natural qualities of timeless awareness. HUNG is the seed syllable of healing activity, a dynamic awareness, free of ego relation. From HUNG emanate rays of light in the five colours of the five buddha- families, predominantly blue, and bring about the well-being of all living beings, free from discrimination – like a sun that sends its light in all directions.

TEYATHA (or TADYAṬHĀ) means "Listen!" and is an invocation to all awakened ones. OM is the wisdom of all awakened ones. BHEKADSE (or BHAIṢAJYE) means *healer*, also sometimes translated as *doctor* or *healing dimension*. MAHĀ means *great*, that is, *great healer*. RADSA (or RĀJA) means *king*. SAMUD roughly means *beyond (all suffering)*. GATE means *to go*. SOHA (or SVĀHĀ) means: "May it be so!" So, the mantra means summarized:

> "Listen you awakened ones! Wisdom of all awakened ones, may we go with the Healer, the Great Healer, the King of all Healers beyond all suffering!"

Or more simply translated:

> "May through the wisdom of all awakened ones
> manifest the deeply healing itself in such a way
> that all living beings go beyond suffering."

The "King of all Healers" is one's own awakened, free-flowing awareness – the blessing of simple, natural nondual being.

When I first learned this practice, I was painfully aware of how deeply involved I was in my ego relation. Then I would sit down and make wishes each time before the patients came in for homeopathic treatment: "May the blessing of the awakened, this awakened dimension, contribute to the very thing that contributes to the well-being of everyone, especially the person who comes in with all his or her surroundings. I ask the healing energy of the buddhas to shape this situation. May they open my heart and mind and give me intuitive access to knowledge of healing."

With such prayers I open my heart as best I can and leave the self-centred attitude behind me. Then I continue the practice with the mantra, which reminds me that the Medicine Buddha is an expression of our inherent healing qualities – the awakened therapist within us. It is in this awareness that I speak this mantra inwardly. I say it quietly or inaudibly in order to awaken the inner therapist.

When I look into the eyes of a client, I welcome the healing dimension, the Medicine Buddha within him or her. This is something of the most beautiful of all: to contact the healing dimension in the other person – it is the knowledge that the actual healing is already there. In this trust the therapist can relax and does not need to be wiser than his counterpart. The point is to create a wakeful, healing situation in which this inner knowledge comes to light. This frees me from the role of the knowledgeable. I let the wisdom and healing powers work in me. This is known in all spiritual healing traditions of the world. Healing never takes place out of the ego, but always out of the opening, out of the dissolved being, some call this a blessing. It is a force of inspiration that is freely available to all. In the same way, we can turn to the Christ nature in others and call upon the Christ nature in ourselves and in the universe. It is about the healing principle, not the words. We are addressing the self-healing forces. Above all, we need to create the space for the mind to find into natural ease; the body will then gradually follow. We act from a deep conviction: Something in you knows better than me what is good for you. You are your own healer; as a therapist I am there to listen to your process and to support it, so that it can come to healing unknotting, development.

This practice on the Buddha probably originated in the 2nd/3rd century AD due to visions.[62] It is said that Buddha Shakyamuni took the form of the Blue Medicine Buddha to teach the four Medicine Tantras on which Tibetan medicine is based. There are always practitioners to whom the Medicine Buddha spontaneously appears as a vision and explains to them how they can help living beings. The healing energy of the buddhas seems to manifest in this way. These spontaneous visions occur again and again, but it remains to be seen whether there is a being of light that exists as a Medicine Buddha, so

62 The first Chinese translation of the sūtra from Sanskrit dates already from the 4th century.

to speak. It can also simply be the blessing of the ultimate dimension in interaction with the devotion of the practitioners and the needs of the living beings.

Through the practice of the Medicine Buddha, I myself find access to the wholesome within myself and others. It is a wonderful bridge into the flowing being. When I experience myself and others as a Medicine Buddha, I am no longer trapped in the normal view. It shows a trust in the awakened dimension of the mind, which knows out of itself what is good for me, a trust in the spontaneously healing nature of the mind.

We may perhaps guess that in our true nature we are completely intact. When all veils, distortions and blockages are removed, the wholesome comes out and to connect with it is already salutary in itself. It connects to deep layers of love and knowledge, free from all fear, beyond all symptoms and diseases. The heart of the teachings in the four Medicine Tantras attributed to the Medicine Buddha is the work with the five mind poisons – which is described in the opening chapter. It says that all diseases that are not caused by outside influences have psychosomatic roots in the basic emotional blockages.

The Medicine Buddha therefore holds in his left hand a bowl of healing nectar, the nectar of awakened awareness, and on the right a myrobalan branch with three fruits. These three fruits stand for the force to neutralize the three inner poisons: ignorance, desire and hatred or in other words: lack of awareness, attachment and aversion. In the approach of Tibetan medicine, which is based on the Medicine Tantras, all physical disturbances are caused by energetic blockages, which in turn are caused by mental-emotional imbalances – in the end: not being aware is associated with fear, holding on to and pushing away life experiences. Life as a struggle instead of a flow. This is seen as the deeper cause of our suffering – and the path of healing is to see through these patterns and the basic deception.

The practice of Medicine Buddha is based on the conviction that there is no step-by-step path, but that awakening can take place at any time, in the present moment. Awakening only exists in the now, like a moment when the sky opens up and we see it – the blue sky of timeless awareness. This is possible at any time. If we believe that it takes a long way, then it takes a long way. Basically, we enshrine it. The assumption of a long way is ultimately an obstacle on the path of healing.

Little moments of freedom from suffering can flash up at any time, in the middle of the most severe depression or psychosis, in a cancerous condition or even in chronic pain. There is always a gap, a break, where for a moment freedom from pain is experienced – a small hint of what is possible when the subtle energies flow more harmoniously. Totally surprising. Part of our approach in Essential Psychotherapy is to always keep the focus on the salutary aspects in order to facilitate such experiences.

An invocation of the Medicine Buddha from around the 4th century AD reads:

> "I bow to the perfect, pure, accomplished
> Medicine Buddha,
> the King of Vaidurya Light,
> the fully purified, accomplished, victorious Buddha,
> the Awakened to suchness, who has subdued all enemies.
> Guru of Medicine, King of Vaidurya Light,
> please, in this moment, purify and free me
> and all living beings from physical and mental diseases, from
> harmful actions, from veils and habitual patterns.",

This invocation has become known as the short form of practice and can be practiced together with the Mantra. When we speak it, we visualize ourselves and all others as immersed in the blue light of the Medicine Buddha, accompanied by the iridescent light of all the colours of the rainbow. At the same time, we trust that our mental movements are deeply healing. Whenever light is spoken of, it symbolizes movements in awareness.

In our heart is the radiant blue seed syllable HŪṂ, surrounded by the blue mantra of the Medicine Buddha. The HŪṂ stands for his awakened qualities and the power of blessings, for boundless love, immeasurable compassion and the wisdom that permeates all realms of existence, bringing help for mental and physical problems and all diseases. From the HŪṂ and from the Mantra circle in the heart, light radiates to all buddhas, predominantly blue, bringing offerings to them. This means that our attention goes to the buddhas, and our mind opens to the healing awareness. Then the light comes back with their blessing and merges into the seed syllable HŪṂ in the heart – that is we experience this awareness in our own mind stream. Afterwards, light radiates again to all living beings and touches them with love, compassion and wisdom, so that they all become Medicine Buddhas. This light as well comes back from this blessed activity into our heart with the HŪṂ – and deeply connected with all awakened ones and with all living beings we stay in the realization of the suchness – just like that.

As soon as we are in the awareness of the Medicine Buddha, our eyes are like light that goes to others and touches them lovingly. All this is meant by the light. Heart and mind go along when we look somewhere or think of someone. Whenever we look like this, healing light shines from our heart, because we are in a healing dimension. This is the healing movement of the mind that flows to all living beings and comes back again. It drenches all living and inanimate things and goes beyond all imagined limits. It imbues everything in healing communication. Healing is communicated. And this is what we underline with the mantra.

This mantra is nothing else than the words use before and after in normal speech. When the mind is in the dimension of healing, speech has mantra quality. It is pure expression of the non-judgemental, open, healing being. To practice this, we speak a mantra. A mantra is always unselfish because there is no purposeful speaking. A Mantra is always an expression of healing truth. It stabilizes our awareness in the healing dimension. *Man* comes from manas, which signifies mind, and *tra* comes from a verb that signifies stabilizing. A mantra stabilizes the mind in awakened awareness. A Mantra does not intend to create conceptual communication. Mantra means to stabilize the mind in a curative, healing awareness.

At the end of the practice, we dedicate all that is wholesome that may have been arisen:

> "Through this wholesome, may quickly realize the sublime Medicine Buddha and lead all living beings without exception into this realization."

The dedication contains a declaration of an intention: to actually realize awakening, and a realization: that it is not possible with the ego. With the dedication we step out of all identification, remain for a moment in completely natural being and then continue our daily activity.

I. Preparing for Dying and Accompanying Others

In Essential Psychotherapy we include all therapeutic methods and focus on the particularly essential questions of existence Therefore, a description of our approach would be incomplete unless we also include the end of this life – the so-called death, the "big move", as Tibetans sometimes call it. What helps in the face of death?

A concise answer can be found in the seven-point mind training of Mahāyāna, which was brought to Tibet by Atisha in the 11th century. The fourth point is called "The Quintessence of Practice for the Whole Life". And the two memory verses for this point are: "What to do in this life" and "What to do when dying". For life it says: "Apply the five forces – that is the essence of the core teachings". And for dying, it says, "The teachings for passing over are the same five forces." Now what are these five forces that summarize all the teachings?

The Five Forces of Mahāyāna Mind Training

First we will read in full what the famous master Jamgon Kongtrul Lodrö Thaye writes about this[63] and then it will be explained briefly:

> "The Five Forces summarize the key points of practice and all the profound core teachings for the application of the noble Dharma.

63 Jamgon Kongtrul Lodrö Thaye "The Great Path of Awakening", his commentary on the Mahāyāna mind training in seven points.

First, the *force of drive*: Give the mind a strong impulse by saying to yourself, 'From now until awakening, but especially until my death, and especially this year and this month, but especially from today to tomorrow, I will never separate from the two aspects of bodhicitta.'[64]

Second, the *force of habituation*: Whatever actions you perform – whether they are beneficial, not beneficial, or neutral – carefully maintain mindfulness and awareness and practice never losing both aspects of bodhicitta. In short, practice in the mind of awakening, the most important of all healing practices.

Third, the *force of the white seed*: In order to bring forth and let grow the mind of awakening, make unceasing efforts with body, speech and spirit in beneficial action, without ever thinking that it is already enough.

Fourth, the *force of rejection*: If self-centred thoughts arise, think, 'You are to blame that I have been wandering around in the cycle of existence since beginningless time, experiencing all kinds of suffering. You are also solely responsible for all the negativity and suffering that I encounter in this life. Even now there is no happiness in your company. Therefore, I must immediately do everything possible to destroy you.' So, reject the thoughts of self-attachment vigorously from you.
Fifth, the *force of wishing prayers*: At the end of every beneficial action, pray: 'May I become capable – even if I am alone – of leading all living beings to buddhahood. Therefore, from now on, until I attain buddhahood, may I not even dream of

64 The two aspects of bodhicitta are the *relative* bodhicitta as active compassion in aspiration and application, and the *ultimate* bodhicitta as insight into the true nature of phenomena, highest wisdom.

forgetting the two aspects of the precious bodhicitta, but may I continue to let them grow. May I be able to turn all difficult situations into allies for my practice of bodhicitta.' Say this sincerely and in this way dedicate everything wholesome to this goal."

1. When we speak of *drive*, we mean the intention to practice compassion and wisdom now. Now and not later: always keep the mind focused on the most important things.
2. By *habituation* is meant the continued practice of bodhicitta, the mind of awakening, until we are completely absorbed in it and experience that compassion, love, wisdom and all the other qualities of detached being flow spontaneously and show themselves in all situations.
3. *White seeding* means to continuously perform many healing actions with body, speech and mind and to nourish bodhicitta even in the smallest actions, so that many positive impressions accompany us, and a great positive force is built up on which we can trust even in difficult situations.
4. By *rejection* is meant the radical departure from ego-centred patterns. We drop them as if we were burning ourselves on them. In this way we protect the practice of the wholesome and dissolve the patterns of suffering-creating ego-relationship. The point is not to get involved in emotional entanglements under any circumstances; not to give space to old patterns.
5. *Wishing prayers* mean the affirmation of the inner alignment – a constant dedication and giving of all the good things in our life, so that we do not identify ourselves, but always re-align ourselves to the completely free, awake, open being without centre and boundaries, which is also called awakening.

Take a moment to contemplate this description with the question: "If I would actually apply these five powers in my life – is there anything missing?"

You probably have to agree with the author: these five forces really do hit the essence. And there is actually nothing to explain, it is the implementation that matters, in every situation.

Before we come to the application of the same five forces in dying, let us mention a few key points regarding the preparation for and accompaniment of dying.

Steps in preparing for dying (exercise I.1)

Preparation for dying concerns us ourselves, today – in our present situation. Supporting others in this process only comes into question after we ourselves have gone through it several times. In total we have named eight steps:

1. We tune in by deeply contemplating our own mortality until we come to the following certainties: "I am mortal" and "It can happen at any time" and "In death nothing and nobody can accompany me."[65]
2. We contemplate on the basis of these irrefutable certainties: "How do I want to live so that I have nothing to regret when I die? What qualities do I want to develop before dying?"

   On the whole, the answer is clear: "I want to have realized the meaning of my life." But that is not enough. It is advisable to name and even write down the meaning of one's life very precisely. It must not remain with generalities but must speak to us so deeply from the heart that it also releases the necessary strength to really align our life to it. Here are some examples from the group work for what participants felt was the meaning of life:
   - To live in connectedness, in harmony with everyone and everything, in true peace.

65 As a support for this reflection, you might want to consult Gampopa in "Ornament of Liberation", ch. 4, where he gives nine contemplations concerning the certainty of our death, the uncertainty concerning its time, and the fact that nothing and nobody will accompany us then.

- No more unspoken things on your heart, fully clarified relationships.
- To use my time well to really practice the Dharma.
- Open my heart, develop compassion for myself and others, live a deeply healing life.
- Living in true simplicity.
- Developing wisdom, a deep understanding of mind and life.
- Finding out of the separation into a unified existence.
- To be in the good.
- Being true to one's own values and living authentic self-determination.
- Living in friendship, living in the "We", strengthening the family, having enough time for relatives
- Rising in love; releasing all the joy of life.
- To develop deep trust in being and in my own mind, so that I can face death without fear.
- To be well prepared for dying; to discard emotional patterns and find inner stability.
- To have actually done something for the world, to have contributed to its salvation.
- To have been a good role model and to have given and exemplified important things to the next generation

3. Then comes another exercise where we ask ourselves the same question several times but with different time periods, and each time we sincerely contemplate the answer: "If I were to die at the following time (tonight, in a week, in a month, in a year, in three years, in ten years, or only at the age of one hundred years), how would I want to live until then? What would be especially important to me? What would be unimportant and would fall away?"
4. It is important to feel the questions and answers in each case in the whole body, with the whole being – as if it were really so.
5. Through these questions a feeling crystallizes, what is really most important to me in the face of death. It is advisable to ask inwardly for a symbol or an image, perhaps to find or create a

characteristic situation that symbolizes exactly these qualities and can serve as a guiding star for the coming months.

6. We deepen this idea by experiencing, feeling, hearing, seeing, smelling, tasting and anchoring it with as many senses as possible, so that it is and remains accessible at all times.
7. Then we dissolve the temporal conceptions, because after all we do not know when we die and ask ourselves: "When do I really want to live what I now experience as important? When do I want to put it into practice?"
8. Then follows the question: "Where does the important get its place in my life? What exactly are the next steps?" We imagine this as clearly and concretely as possible, and it is best to write it down. We make concrete decisions about the implementation and integration of our central heart's desire and consider ways to stay in contact with the representative symbol so that we can draw strength from it.

This concludes the contemplation of the preparation for dying, which we should do at least once a year, if not more often. In short, it can be part of our daily practice with the simple question: "What is particularly important today in the face of a possible death?

Applying the Five Forces in living and dying

After this contemplation to prepare for dying, let us continue with the five forces in life. They appear all the more meaningful and substantial through this process.

1. The *drive*, the motivation is: never forget the essential – always live the essential! In short: always carry compassion and wisdom in their inseparable unity in the heart.
2. It takes *habituation*, especially if I have been focusing on the less important things in life for a long time. It is now a matter

of becoming familiar with the essential, the own heart's desire, through constant practice.

3. *White sowing* means to take one's own life into one's own hands. To do! To create! Not to be distracted. Tirelessly living the essential even in the smallest actions and taking every opportunity.
4. Develop the force of *renunciation:* External influences and inner patterns that keep me from the essential, rejecting them, saying "Stop!" inwardly and pausing when counterforces arise. To make the deep decision not to let myself be controlled by harmful patterns and not to fall for the many distractions. This has to do with will, clarity and determination.
5. I strengthen the force of the *wishing prayers* by always remembering what is essential, possibly with the symbol that stands for my long-term orientation. It also involves dedicating my life to the essential and not making a new "I" project out of it but anchoring myself deeply in the "we".

What is it about? To really live what is my main concern.

Here are a few mods examples from the group work on decisions and questions regarding the implementation in everyday life that arose during this contemplation:

Simple lifestyle, building trust in one's own mind, learning to give up control, letting go, practicing disidentification, reducing fear, creating clear conditions in relationships, in possessions, tidying up all unfinished business on the outside, updating one's will, clearing up internally and spiritually. Transferring responsibility. Clarify: How do I want to die? Who should be present? How do I want to be accompanied further after death? Where do I want to go after death? Clarify: Rebirth, pure realms of existence, God, heaven... open myself, consider different possibilities. Find out: How can I connect with the qualities of the heart that are important to me? Apply effortless techniques that I can also practice while lying down. Wishful prayers as a daily practice. Working with dreams until the realization of their illusory nature has become stable. Deepening refuge. Develop bodhicitta in everything. "Yes" to dying, to vulnerability, to aging. See dying as a chance. Building positive automatisms (waking up and falling asleep with refuge – as if I would die and wake up again).

And now about dying. First of all, the quote from Jamgon Kongtrul Lodrö Thaye in full:

> "When asked how the teachings of this tradition are to be practiced at the time of death, it is said: *'The teachings on transference (Phowa) in Mahāyāna are the same five forces...'*
>
> If we are trained in this practice and we are afflicted with a deadly disease, the first thing we should do is to pass on all possessions. We can generally offer it to the Master and the jewels of refuge, or we can give it to those we think would benefit from it greatly. To do this – without a trace of attachment, clinging or worry – is the force of the white seed.
>
> If you are able to do so, offer prayers in seven parts. Otherwise, pray with a one-pointed mind: 'By the power of all the roots of the wholesome that I have accumulated in the three times, may I never forget the precious mind of awakening in all my lives, and may I let it grow ever stronger through practice. May I meet authentic Lamas who make these teachings. I ask you, Lama and you precious jewels, bless me, so that this happens in the same way.' – This is the *force of wishing prayers.*
>
> 'This clinging to the beloved self has made me suffer in countless lives, and now I also experience the suffering of dying. Since an I or mind ultimately do not exist, there is also no death. I will do my best to destroy you, this self-attachment that thinks *I am sick* and *I am dying.*' – These and similar thoughts are the *force of renunciation.*
>
> To think, 'In everything that comes – death, the intermediate state, and the next life – I will remain uninterruptedly connected with the two kinds of precious bodhicitta' – that is the *force of the drive.*
>
> To keep the two types of bodhicitta practiced before clearly present – that is the *force of habituation.*

Briefly summarized:

1. The *white seed* consists in using all that we possess for healing and distributing it among the people.
2. The *wishing prayers* are now about orienting myself to continue my practice of the essential under the best possible conditions after death. It would be good to have a clear idea of where and how I want to continue after death.
3. *Renunciation* in the process of dying, to turn away from ego-centred thinking with every precious breath, which might be the last.
4. *Drive* here means to cultivate the bodhicitta motivation with every breath, i.e. to use every remaining breath for the essential.
5. *Habituation* means to use the remaining time for the realization and stabilization of the inner attitude, until deep certainty and security occurs when thinking about the soon coming death. In this way we can enter the dying process in complete peace and look death confidently "in the eye". Many people died completely relaxed after such preparation.

There is already a lot of literature on the subject of terminal care for others. The essential points are to help to clean up the previous life, to clarify relationships, to order and distribute possessions (writing a will) and to enable inner relief, by pronouncing difficult experiences and, if possible, to arrange the funeral in advance, i.e. to clarify what kind of celebration is desired, what kind of prayers and the like. The preparation for the great transition also includes a good knowledge of the dying process, a possible preparation for organ donation, so that the person feels joy in case he or she experiences something after death. We should also help the dying person to clarify the frame of mind in which he or she wants to die and where the "journey" after the separation of body and mind should go, so that our prayers can support him or her as much as possible in exactly that. Of course, it is also important to design the environment of the dying person in such a manner that the most favourable conditions possible are created in which the mind of the person can clear, gather and align itself inwardly. We also help the dying person to make good use of all remaining time, to practice in the essential – in complete accordance with his or her own heart's desires.

Guided meditation: Preparing for dying (exercise I.2)

The below exercise can be performed alone or in a group. A good time is in the evening, before going to bed – or even just before falling asleep. In doing so, we make sure that the atmosphere is protected and undisturbed. It takes about 30 minutes. We can also offer it to sick or dying persons. Of course, the words need to be adapted to the situation.

If later we are lucky enough to make a smooth transition into the next life, then this will probably also be when lying down. Therefore, it is recommended that we adopt the most relaxed posture possible during this exercise, for example, half-lying on a relaxing armchair or lying on the floor with a soft carpet pad or lying directly in bed.

At first, we feel the many bodily sensations. We take our time to arrive completely at this complex experience.

In particular, we feel the chest and abdominal wall widening and lifting with the breath, only to sink back again and lower.

The sensations of breathing are an indication of how everything comes and goes, changes, just like an inbreath coming from an outbreath.

I imagine how I might lie in bed one day and prepare myself for the last exhalation in this body.

(1) I invite all the beautiful and precious experiences that I was allowed to experience to rise in my memory. Once again, I honour each of them and then let them go with a conscious exhalation.

With all my memories I practice letting go and giving myself away. I extend this to all my possessions and to everything that was and is important to me in this life. Everything is given away and dedicated: Whatever belonged to me, may it now benefit others. May it continue to work for the benefit of all! This is the power of the White Seed: Whatever I leave behind, may it do good like a good seed.

(2) Again, I focus my attention on the sensations of breathing, this time especially on the inhalation.

With each breathing in I open myself to the unknown that is coming right now – as if I were stepping with my consciousness to the threshold of the new and unknown, to the threshold of the next *Now*.

It will be the same with the great transition, the great move into the after. How do I want to live this transition into the new and unknown, with what state of mind? With love, with wisdom, with joy, what is close to my heart?

With exactly these qualities we breathe at the threshold of the new – in breathing in and out. We breathe with bodhicitta, the heart mind of awakening.

The state of mind with which I live now has an effect on where I am in the next experience. When the mind leaves this body, where do I want to go, how do I want to be there? Breathe with exactly this attitude of mind and heart quality.

This is the power of the wishing prayers with which we align ourselves inwardly at every moment. It is a clear feeling: that is where I want to go – into this mind, into these qualities of the heart!

May I always be connected with my real concern and find the support I need to continue on the path of awakening.

(3) Breathing in and out I use every moment to merge with these qualities and to anchor myself deeply in the mind of awakening. Nothing can stop me from this. I energetically reject the temptations of self- centred thinking and cultivate joy, love and trust.

Now, for the great transition, a flexible, open mind is needed. Nobody asks for the "I" here, it is all about the great openness. In this awareness I breathe and let nothing come in between. I remain mindful of what is essential. That is the force of turning renunciation.

(4) As I breathe like this, I anchor this motivation very firmly in my mind: whatever comes, be it simply the next moment or the great transition with the experiences of the intermediate state or even a next life – I will always remain connected to this state of mind!

I am aware that all emerging experiences are process and that there is nothing solid inherent in them. Breathing in and out I practice dwelling in the detached awareness of the true nature of all being.

I breathe in the unity of love and awareness. I breathe sensitively, open to everything and at the same time I am aware of the true nature of everything.

The alignment, come what may, to always remain in the loving awareness of awakening is the force of the drive. It keeps me unswervingly and relaxed on course – it is the unswerving force of the clear alignment of our heart. With this relaxed, trusting force of the heart we breathe in and breathe out.

(5) In this manner, I use every breath and all my remaining time to stay connected with love and awareness. I practice dwelling in love and awareness until there is deep certainty that the great transition will be easy in this state of mind.

We continue to practice and develop the force of habituation until we are completely familiar with the detached, flowing being in true openness – until we experience it as the most natural and self-evident thing in the world. Nothing stirs us up anymore. I have arrived at the simple, bright being. Simply detached – just like that.

A healing journey to the Land of the Buddha (exercise I.3)

In the traditional teachings we are encouraged to go to the pure "land of joy" (Dewachen, Sukhavati) of Buddha Amitabha after death, i.e. to let the stream of mind cross over into a mental dimension of awakening. We might just as well go to the land of the Medicine Buddha – this practice was often performed in Tibet for the deceased. Without saying too much about it, I (Tilmann) would like to give you a little taste of what it can feel like to enter such a pure realm of consciousness with a guided meditation. This meditation takes about 40 minutes; it is inspired by the descriptions of the practice on the Medicine Buddha and descriptions of his "pure land". It can be used as a healing meditation or for clarifying personal questions or as help in preparation for dying.

First of all, we focus inwardly on what motivates us right now to enter into a contemplative process...

We deepen the awareness of our own refuge and orientation...

Then we feel how it feels to sit...

We let the attention go once through the whole body...

Maybe we can relax here and there even more...

It usually does you good to take one or two deep breaths ...

And then to leave the breath to itself...

We remain slightly connected to the breath as we now move into conscious hearing

See, smell and taste consciously...

And to notice all that what is going on inside of us...

Meanwhile, we allow ourselves to relax again and again into this present experience...

Whatever thoughts, feelings, moods and perceptions may come up – this is exactly where we relax...

Whatever reservations there may be about one's own experience – all this may simply be as it is...

Accept, accept again and again – and relax into it...

By relaxing into it, life flows on...

Let us now go on a little healing journey – a journey to a place where we can recover and experience inner balance. Everything on this journey will be as it suits our needs and would do us good.

Symbolically we enter through a big gate and take our first steps into this land of healing – just take a look around...

Maybe we discover a path we would like to explore. We can follow it a little bit and see what awaits us there...

We allow ourselves to let all the experiences come that are good for us – maybe the path winds its way, maybe it goes straight...

Maybe we perceive pleasant scents. Maybe there are flowers or trees – or even living beings from which this scent emanates...

Groves, clearings... Meadows, brooks ... Hills, valleys...

Maybe a small waterfall... or a lake...

Various places that invite us to stop and rest...

What place attracts you, right now, what kind of place would you like to have? ... Just such a fitting place appears in your imagination...

Feel how you would like to be in this first place of contemplation: walking, standing, sitting, lying...

What temperature would be pleasant? Should the sun shine? If so, where is it? ...

Feel how your body feels in this situation, the contact with the ground...

Everything has an enchanting effect, deeply balancing.

Everything has a soothing effect... There is deep serenity...

And at the same time there are wonderful sounds, noises – of plants and animals...

Everything is permeated by trust... No one is afraid of the other...

All are in confidence... We can relax deeply...

Relax into exactly this experience...

Our breath sweeps in, sweeps out, and the air is so pleasant, so nourishing...

Even the animals invite us to taste the fruits – if we want to do

so at all...
Everything welcomes us...
We look around, in all directions...
In the distance is a light, a healing, soothing light...
It seems to come from over there – that is where the source seems to be...
With great ease our feet set themselves in motion and carry us in this direction. We are very curious and interested ...
The light becomes stronger as we move over meadows, through forests, over hills and through valleys...
All senses are open...
Again and again, there are encounters with others along the way – loving, warm contacts...
We can invite someone to go with us or join others...
Or we can continue to roam alone, curious...
Where does this wonderful light come from? It touches and broadens my heart...
And gives me a strange lightness...
We come to a wide, flowing terrain with soft grass and flowers, a little uphill, with a slope in the distance – from there the light seems to come...
I move towards it and see that it comes from a being of light...
Who could that be? I've never seen anything like it.
People whisper to me: "This is the source of healing in this country". I begin to see the outlines of a being full of light, with a loving expression on my face...
Our eyes meet...
I have the feeling of knowing this person forever, as if we had been waiting for each other...
The arms of this person open: "Come here! Wonderful that you are here, sit with me, we have all the time in the world."
There are countless others around us, but I have the feeling of a unique relationship between me and this being of light. The figure looks like a buddha, as the awakened ones are represented, but it is very much alive, and we can't say for

sure whether it is a man or a woman until this too is clarified...

A dialogue develops between us: through light loops – from mouth to mouth, from heart to heart... I ask inwardly: "Who are you?", and the answer is already there: "I am you". I breathe deeply and can hardly believe what I heard. Already the answer comes: "Yes, believe me, we are not different."

In this way an exchange from heart to heart, from mouth to mouth, the light circles between us, flows through our whole being, all chakras...

I can ask questions... and get answers...

At times I simply let myself be nourished, flooded and be in exchange with the light, without doing anything – in exchange with the awakened being of light opposite and also, if I want to, with all the others around us...

We are connected to each other by coloured light bands; the light floods all areas of the body and brings healing...

It is as if we breathe light...

I perceive that my body has become light, I too shine in the light – maybe in blue, maybe in the colours of the rainbow...

Depending on what I direct the mind to, the colour changes – a play of light...

And there where the thoughts go, there also goes the light.

I look around me and see that everything has become light, even the trees, the stones, the soil, the other people and the animals...

We can ask all questions and get clarifying answers.

It is not clear where these answers come from. They just come...

As if being connected was its own source...

A deep knowledge of what it is like arises – simple being ...

The mind is free...

There is no need to create ideas...

And there is no holding on... Everything can be simple...

(After a while, the singing bowl sounds)

J. The "Bridge" from Part One to Part Two

Review of Part One

It is a great gain for the inner path that today, at the same time as the traditional buddhist methods, so many psychotherapeutic methods and approaches are available to us. The synergies in dissolving the emotional veils cannot be overlooked: Someone who has been trained in mental calmness and insight discovers and grasps surprisingly quickly the emotional and biographical connections that psychotherapeutic work is all about. It is also much easier to apply the dissolving methods (use of guiding principles, inner healing images, mindfulness of triggers, scaling, inner-child work, etc.) because the mind is trained to remember tasks of mind training in everyday life.

Let's make it concrete: of the Five Steps in Working with Emotions (chapter A), the first three are used continuously in psychotherapy – and are therefore not new territory for buddhist practitioners. They will find further interesting ideas for mental exercise in the exercises of the next chapters. They receive special help on their path through personal guidance in uncovering the inner themes and patterns that they otherwise skilfully, albeit unconsciously, hide from their own inner eye. An uncovering therapeutic work will thwart the avoidance of unpleasant insights, which is especially common among spiritual practitioners.

Psychotherapeutic guidance will make aware unconscious biographical connections for our emotions and thus enable their processing and resolution. This goes deeper and is more effective than a general relaxation and a letting go of an emerging stream of mind stuff, as is often practiced in meditation. The therapeutic attention is focused on our difficult experiences and shadows and just as specifically stimulates the corresponding resources.

Psychotherapeutic work, like buddhist practice, is about liberation from suffering, be it fears, depressions, compulsions and addictions or relationship disorders, eating disorders and physical complaints without organically tangible findings (somatoform disorders), in which psychological stress is expressed. With exact feeling it becomes clear how every thought, every emotion has subtle effects on the physical state of mind. If we keep thinking or feeling something similar, traces of it will show up in our bodies. At first, it is only functional effects, later on there may even be organ changes. Open states of mind, for example joy, love and trust, influence the organs and tissues in a wholesome direction. Tight mental states, traumas, neuroses and unconscious basic conflicts influence the organism in a non-wholesome direction.

In therapeutic work, the five main emotions (chapter B) are always at the centre of attention, the dissolution of which is the focus of buddhist practice. Psychotherapy, however, uses a different terminology. It tends to rather speak of needs and fears – and often sees emotions as unconscious attempts to solve problems. It therefore sees emotions as meaningful, albeit often clumsy or even obstructive attempts to overcome the challenges. Thus, fear has actually the "sense" to let us become particularly attentive in order to master a danger well. Seen in this way, fear makes sense. The same applies to other emotions – from the personal point of view of the person concerned, they are reactions that make sense.

If I assume that my emotion has a deeper meaning and do not simply dismiss it, but rather explore it, then I succeed in tracking down the underlying needs. Only if I recognize these can I do justice to them and find new, even more sensible solutions for them. Like this, stress can trigger the desire for food. But what is it really about? The underlying needs are desires for relaxation, peace. We want to forget and have the heart and mind free again. We all know this. The desire for chocolate or for three beers may not be an optimal emotional reaction, but it does make sense.

Primarily the solution for a content life lies within ourselves, in a more skilful handling of our own mind – and secondarily this new mentality shapes our relationships with our fellow humans and the environment.

In this second step – the interaction with our fellow human beings – lies another strength of psychotherapy: it trains in the perception and linguistic expression of feelings and needs and cultivates the inner resonance with our counterpart. In this way, it makes a significant contribution to the realization of an essential basic concern of buddhist mind training: peaceful, respectful communication in mutual giving and taking, with a mind of love, compassion and understanding.

This concern is found among buddhists embedded in the ten virtuous acts, of which the points 4 to 7 concern speaking. Perhaps it is useful to list all ten at this point, because the others also reflect the spirit of buddhist ethics, in which a bridge to the ethical attitude in psychotherapy can also be found. The ten virtuous acts are[66]:

1. Protecting the lives of others
2. Giving generously
3. Maintaining a wholesome sexual behaviour
4. Telling the truth sincerely
5. Reconciling the disputed and enemies
6. Speaking calmly and trustworthy
7. Saying meaningful things
8. Desiring little and being easily satisfied
9. Practicing love and similar qualities
10. Dwelling on what is true and meaningful

All socially engaged people, just like the Buddha, are interested in this wholesome behaviour, at the centre of which is sincere commu-

66 This list is found in many texts, here quoted after Gampopa in "Ornament of Liberation", chapter 6.

nication: true, reconciling, calm, trustworthy and meaningful (see steps 4 to 7). In the psychotherapeutic environment, first and foremost the talking therapy according to Carl Rogers and all humanistic approaches based on it, as well as the non- violent communication according to Marshall B. Rosenberg, should be mentioned. But *every* psychotherapeutic approach cultivates this kind of communication. Communicating in this way is the basis for mutual understanding and for growing insight into what others trigger in us and what we trigger in them – and how we can support each other in growing and becoming freer.

The clarification of the meaning of our life (chapter C) experiences an adjustment to the deeper individual needs through psychotherapeutic work. It does not remain an abstract guideline ("I want to attain enlightenment") but is filled with the qualities that are close to our hearts. In this way, the buddhist "refuge" in Buddha, Dharma and Saṅgha – the symbol of all awakened qualities – can be experienced directly within us. All the more so, because thanks to the therapeutic emphasis on whole-body experience, it can be felt right into every cell. This in turn deepens the buddhist training of the mind, for example through the heart-breath (Tonglen), where we connect with exactly these meaningful qualities of refuge.

The Four Truths of the Noble ones (chapter D), which form the basis of the buddhist teachings, gain in conciseness by comparison with the therapeutic procedure – hence the Buddha's reference to the similar approach of doctors and people seeking liberation. In every psychotherapy session, in every meditation session and in every important moment of our lives, the same four questions are asked again and again: "Where is unnecessary tension? What causes it? Can I dissolve them? How do I do that?" Followed by four deepening insights: "Ah, here I feel tension. Ah, this is where it comes from! Ah, indeed, it can be dissolved! Ah, so that's how it works!" In the following second part, we will deal primarily with answers to question four: how does it work concretely? – and provide corresponding helpful psychotherapeutic exercises.

The practice of continuous awareness (chapter E) is more than just mindfulness. It forms the basis for a real understanding of one's own mind. Awareness practice is the centre and heart of buddhist practice and goes far beyond what is needed or practiced in psychotherapeutic practice. Awareness practice not only serves to cope with emotionally challenging situations but leads to the exploration of the most subtle states of mind until we know "every corner" of our mind, dual as well as nondual states of mind, the nondual active mind, the nondual calm mind without thoughts, awareness in dreams and deep sleep and the like. In short: Awareness practice lets us experience how different free and narrow states of mind are – and this practice takes place in the area that would be classified as "mentally healthy" from a therapeutic point of view.

Being mentally healthy is not yet the awakening or liberation that buddhist practice is ultimately about. However, its prerequisite is the dissolving of the emotional veils – there is no awakening without having dissolved the emotional veils! Ideally, psychotherapy prepares and accompanies the path of awakening – it tills the field of mental health and helps to find one's own strength. It leads out of neurotic suffering with an erroneous view of oneself, which often does not allow to open up, to let go and to experience oneself as intact. In fact, the question arises as to what kind of stable bonding and positive, compassionate bonding experiences are needed in order to be able to let go in depth and experience awakening. A base or field of wholesome relationships and bonding experiences seems to be helpful, if not essential, for a comprehensive awakening

The concern to extend the antennae of our heart and to live more compassionately (chapter F) is an area where buddhist and psychotherapeutic approaches are largely congruent. What are the differences? The buddhist approach often quickly leaves the concrete interpersonal level and lets the heart's mind expand in all directions to embrace all living beings without exception – as in the Metta meditation of loving kindness. The strength of this practice lies in this all-encompassing vastness – for no one is excluded; there is not a single enemy to whom our benevolence would not apply. But what good are the worldwide meditations of kindness if, after getting up, we are irritated again as soon as someone makes us feel uncomfortable! The practice of the seven-point mind training (Lodjong) also places much more emphasis on developing understanding with others than with oneself.

It is about concretely lived compassion – and there primarily about compassion with ourselves and our weaknesses. This self-compassion is only briefly mentioned in the buddhist texts but – at least nowadays – it needs special attention. Here, too, psychotherapeutic support helps each one of us to really accept the one, now present feeling, to find the deeper lying fears and needs and to take good care of ourselves *before* we turn to others. Someone who helps others out of unresolved need will not really be able to be helpful, because she or he does not yet know the way to the detached being of deep acceptance. In this way, the practice of immeasurable compassion and boundless love also experiences its deepening through the typical individualization of the psychotherapeutic approach, which actually always turns first to the needs of the client her- or himself and only then extends this attention to the environment. Exercises in compassion, such as the Metta meditation, will only become truly authentic through real contact with one's own feelings of compassion, love and goodness, as experienced, for example, through the *Goodness exercise* (exercise N.3).

Particularly "risky" from the perspective of possible self-denial are the teachings on the bodhicitta mindset, which sometimes encourage an attitude of "giving up" oneself and one's needs for the benefit of others. This can be avoided by a healthy attitude of "us". "I" am a part of the "we". Thus, through the responsibility for the "we" I am also responsible for the "I", myself. A healthy path always leads from the *I* to the *you* and then into the *we* – and this *we* begins to expand and gradually include everyone I meet or think of. In this way we avoid the traps of the one-sided I-relationship, the others excluding you-relationship and the others excluding we-relationship where we only think of our own group. We step from the I via the you into the we and from there into an all including we – and back again to the I... without thinking of ourselves as the hub of the world.

This "I" is subjected to an exact analysis in the buddhist mind training (chapter G), whereby it becomes clear that there is no essential core in this I. I is through and through process, change, dynamic. A stable I cannot be found – but mental qualities can be found that give this process an increasing reliability, with a high resilience in challenging situations. This is the awakening of the inherent qualities of the mind, which are not born out of ego attachment, but are present in themselves as a natural expression of the mind. Buddhism calls it the "non-I" or "non-self", while psychology calls it a "healthy I" or the "True Self". Buddhist mind training and psychotherapy serve to find out of false self-images and to find one's way into the flow of a changing life, if possible, without blocking. Here, too, they reach out their hands, even if some dissolve the I delusion and others strengthen the I. It is a different I that is dissolved than the I that is strengthened – a mere confusion of language! How liberating it is for the buddhist practitioner to experience that it is only a matter of dissolving an illusion and that in doing this the I becomes stronger and more powerful. The I does not need to be denied but only seen for what it is. Even for people who are at home in the psychotherapeutic approach, it is brightening to understand that the qualities of the healthy, strong I actually do not belong to any I, but are the natural expression of a mind that is not caught in fixations – especially not in the fixation on a supposedly existing I separate from everything else. They actually originate from the non-self, i.e. the sphere of our being that "I" do not control consciously or unconsciously.

With the section on the Healing Buddha within ourselves (chapter H), we wanted to give a small taste of how comprehensively these awakened qualities can be activated inside us. When we open ourselves completely to the relaxed experience and a new view of ourselves and others, we leave the limiting view in which no buddha is visible far and wide, although awakening is the ever-present nature of our mind, which is immediately revealed when once – however short – no veils cover our true being. It remains to be seen how many psychotherapists can make use of this concrete visualization – the important thing is that we do not educate ourself on this view, but rather discover it, let it come gradually.

So, it is not about "positive thinking", but about discovering our divine spark, to put it in other words. And therein lies undoubtedly an incredible healing strength – it has helped people to survive displacement, torture and the worst disasters and even to find their way into compassion. The practice on the Medicine Buddha goes beyond limiting ideas; it goes beyond the belief that *I* cannot be healthy, that *I* cannot awaken. But we can; each one of us. This may sound like a credo, but everyone agrees on one thing: much of our mental suffering is nourished by a limiting view of ourselves. We need to believe in "ourselves" or, better yet, in what cannot be affected by any turbulence – let's call it the "non-self" or "true self". Awakening this is central to such practices with meditation deities like the Medicine Buddha.

To die in the trust in the true self, i.e. in the true nature of the mind, is a serene, peaceful death in complete harmony with oneself and everything. To prepare for it with a deep and at the same time comprehensive awareness training is the best preparation for dying (chapter I). And thus, these chapters on the connection between buddhist mind training and psychotherapy find their logical conclusion in the reference to the inevitable end of this life and the necessary preparation for the "great move", as some Tibetan texts call death. A lost is left behind here with which the ego has identified itself. What remains are the qualities that our stream of mind has released, whether through study, contemplation and meditation, or through constant therapeutic work with our own mind – or just through both.

Outlook on Part Two

In Part Two, which describes the inner work from a psychotherapeutic point of view in Essential Psychotherapy, we introduce central areas of this work and give you corresponding exercises, most of which can also be done alone. They are not only an excellent supplement to the classical buddhist mind training, but as an expression of the same inner attitude, they also lead naturally into the individual training of awareness and facilitate it.

The attitude of the therapist (chapter M) consists of accompanying the natural development process of the inherent qualities as a catalyst in an awareness that is as open and resonant as possible – in full confidence that health is already inherent in the client as potential and equal in this relationship to the resources and qualities of their counterpart. It is the same inner attitude: the view of the healthy and awakened.

This trust in the inherent qualities is transferred to our counterpart and strengthens his self-confidence. At the same time, the relationship with the therapist, just like the relationship with Dharma teachers, acts as a healing model or example for the client – it enables a new, healing experience and has a spiritual dimension, albeit often unspoken. The relationship is spiritual in the sense that it facilitates access to one's own true being and paves the way for awakening by providing deep experiential knowledge about the nature of being.

From a psychotherapeutic point of view, the necessary basis for turning to one's own problems with a fresh view and with the prospect of a solution is first of all to find and activate our resources (chapter N). This is exactly the concern of buddhist mind training. We need an inner safe place (exercise N.2) from which we can tackle the challenges; we need to be anchored in goodness, in fundamental goodwill (exercise N.3). Practitioners of buddhist mind training will immediately be reminded of the taking refuge and developing loving kindness (Metta) and the mind of awakening (bodhicitta) that are part of any meditation practice.

Extremely important as part of the awareness training is the strengthening of the inner observer, i.e. the ability to perceive inner processes. Some buddhist practitioners want to get rid of the observer all to quickly in order to experience nondual awareness. But the prerequisite for a repeated immersion in this nondual experience is the ability to perceive when we are in the grip, in an emotional reaction and the like. Without this ability, we cannot practice any of the five steps of working with emotions described in chapter A, and we cannot develop peace of mind or insight. This ability to accurately perceive one's own states of mind is the foundation for being able to use the inner pilot or inner master. It involves perceiving sensations, comparing their intensity and quality (exercise N.4) and recognizing their true, processual nature. Thoughtful reviews of the day (exercise N.5) as well as planning for the coming day are essential in order to take one's life into one's own hands – buddhists would say: to shape one's own action (karma). In order to be able to implement the impulses of shaping of the inner pilot, it is helpful to be able to consciously put aside any obstructive memories or triggering emotional reactions (exercise N.6). This increases the ability for self-control and the power of the will. Will, i.e. the ability to implement decisions, is central to the path of awakening – without it we drift through life like leaves in the wind of karma.

Despite a good will, we often fail to realize our intentions because of strong psychological patterns. To avoid being thrown off course by them, initial strategies and interventions (chapter O) are helpful. Their common goal is to expand our scope of action – in other words, to become a little more master of our own house. The exercises offered here correspond to steps one and two (pause and apply helpful methods) of the Five Steps in chapter A. It is about stimulating and using resources in order to gain space for deeper uncovering work on one's own patterns. Up to this point, the work is only stabilizing, as if in buddhist practice, we mainly practice the basic contemplations as well as refuge, love, compassion and peace of mind. Of course, all this already triggers processes of fear – and this is also desired, but unconscious emotional, biographical material is not purposefully brought to the surface.

The chapter on focusing (chapter P) introduces this phase of exploratory fathoming – it is about uncovering the causes for the jumping off of painful patterns. The counterpart to this in the buddhist mind training would be the attentive practice with unpleasant, painful sensations, whereby we open ourselves each time to the inner images and associations with which these sensations are accompanied, i.e. what triggers our narrow states of mind, how they arise, how they are overcome and how they are prevented.

This observation of the inner connections of our experience is described by the Buddha in the two teachings on the cultivation of awareness (satipaṭṭhāna) in the fourth section on the exploration of the regularities (dharmas):

> "If sensual desire is present in us (or ill-will, torpor, dullness, restlessness, concern, or doubt), we know that 'sensual desire is present' (or ill-will, torpor, dullness, restlessness, concern, or doubt), and if it is not present, we know that 'it is not present'. We also know how they arise, how they are overcome and how they are prevented."

The Buddha describes the same for the perception of our inner resources, also called "limbs of awakening". With them, it is a matter of noticing when the respective resource shows itself, how it is created and how it can be completed:

> "If the factor of awakening called awareness is present in us (or the other factors like investigation of dharmas, energy, joy, tranquillity, meditative contemplation, equanimity), we know 'it is present', and if it is not present, we know 'it is not present'. We also know how the factor of awakening called awareness (or investigation of dharmas, energy, joy, tranquillity, meditative contemplation, equanimity), which has not yet arisen, comes into being and is unfolded to perfection."

In order to be able to clearly observe and understand these inner processes, inner distance is required – in other words, exactly the opposite of identification. In meditation we learn not to identify with the ascending sensations and emotions. Psychotherapy has also developed methods to find out from identification and to disidentify consciously (chapter Q). It is about a sober, unidentified perception of situations and the corresponding experience.

We become aware of how some emotional patterns of inner identification occur in almost the same way and trigger almost automatic emotional reactions, as if they have a life of their own, which our inner pilot can hardly influence as long as we are identified with these patterns. We gain inner distance and the possibility to influence them by identifying them, naming them and giving them a place without letting them dominate us. These patterns of emotional experience can act as sub-personalities (chapter R) or they are an expression of our inner child (chapter S), i.e. of fears and needs that have been active in us since childhood, or they are structures and perspectives that we have inherited from our parents (chapter T). These terms are only aids to better understand the different patterns and structures and then to move on to the work of integration and dissolution.

In doing so, we will always work uncovering (chapter U) to gain deeper insight into our own psychodynamics. Many of us, even after years of meditative practice, come into contact with previous traumatic experiences (chapter V), which have an enormous power to distort our perception of situations and to switch off the inner pilot. They are worked on in a gentle work of oscillating between solidly anchored resources and carefully dosed awareness of the traumatic stress. This work needs the guidance of therapists; it is too risky on one's own. References to working with trauma are scattered thinly in buddhist literature; they are most likely to be found in descriptions of the lives of masters like Angulimala (disciple of the Buddha) or Milarepa. Their intensive practice in a protected setting, with deep roots in their resources, can be interpreted as a healing path to deal with their severe traumas.

Further revealing work takes place in dream analysis (chapter W), where our relationship to dreams must remain free of identification, just as in the Dharma. Dream analysis serves to trace our karmic imprints. Dreams are a wonderful illustrative material for how we function unconsciously, and they also clearly show how, thanks to our inner work, new, more healing perspectives and spontaneous reactions can arise in deeper layers of our being.

After the stabilizing, revealing and integrating work with our patterns, it is finally – just like on the buddhist path of education – about finding a constructive, alert action in the world. Suggestions for this can be found in chapter X in the work with the will and an exercise to develop a clear inner direction or vision.

All work is in the service of revealing our true or higher self (chapter Y) and this is again in the service of those who live directly with us, first and foremost our life partners. The short passage on couple therapy (chapter Z) shows how the difficulties that inevitably arise in living together can be approached creatively. Dharma practitioners can see this as an encouragement to bring personal contemplative practice into the couple relationship and to test and develop the fruits of their spiritual practice in the concrete interpersonal encounter.

From the explanations in this chapter, it will probably become clear once again how all these aspects of the inner path are connected and how the path from A to Z consists in developing a loving awareness. We can consider the different chapters of the book as variations of this basic theme – from a buddhist point of view one would say: the play of compassion and wisdom in inseparable unity.

PART TWO

Psychotherapy based on Buddhist mind training

Preparing the Ground

K. Introduction

In this part of the book, we will guide our readers through a cycle of teachings designed for training in Essential Psychotherapy (EPT). Many exercises are presented and marked accordingly as 'exercise'. Most of them can be carried out as self-study by interested readers, without a therapist. Other exercises and methods are specifically designed for psychotherapists and the psychotherapeutic setting. These are specially marked as 'method'.

In Essential Psychotherapy, in addition to the awareness training presented in Part One of the book, there are elements taken from various existing psychotherapeutic disciplines. Essential Psychotherapy is compatible with all existing psychotherapeutic approaches and values them all. What counts is that they do not in essence contradict the basic ideas of the buddhist transmission of awakening. It is founded on the basic assumption of the process nature of experience, together with an ethical orientation, i.e. an orientation towards basic values of buddhist practice, and towards the intended long-term healing effects.

In the following chapters you may find one or the other method or exercise that you are familiar with, for example from the Behavioural Psychotherapy of Watson and Grawe, Rogers' Conversational Psychotherapy, Focusing (Gendlin), Psychosynthesis (Assagioli), Somatic Experiencing (Levine), and Imagination Method (Phyllis Krystal). There may also be references to a psychoanalytic approach following Freud or Jung with corresponding psychoanalytic directions or some systemic psychotherapeutic approaches, for example according to Virginia Satir.

Our approach is characterized by method openness and method integration. It is therefore conceivable that in the future further psychotherapeutic methods, including previously unknown ones, will be included in EPT. The special integrative achievement of Essential Psychotherapy is the merging of buddhist mind training, accordingly a two-thousand-five-hundred- year-old wisdom tradition, with the insights and procedures of psychotherapeutic healing approaches as they have developed in our western culture since the beginning of the last century. Through this "flowing together", which is particularly expressed in the EPT therapist's attitude, many of the already known procedures have a different taste, often a different intensity and usually also, a higher effectiveness.

In addition, many well-known exercises in the EPT are enhanced, not only by the special approach of the therapist, but also by the inclusion of new modules, such as the mostly imaginative representation or symbolism of the buddha or an aspect of wisdom. And, of course, some training methods from buddhism are also brought directly into the therapy situation as interventions. Some methods and exercises have been newly developed in the course of our work over the last few years. Where we have included an exercise or method from another therapy school in the EPT and developed it further, this will be mentioned or pointed out in the text.

Since this book is intended to give an overall impression of the work with Essential Psychotherapy, the procedures are concise, clear and also presented in *essence*. In this way, the contents remain easily understandable for the reader. For more in-depth information, we refer to the extensive list of literature and to the possibility of engaging with Essential Psychotherapy, i.e. the experience or "taste" of EPT on a seminar or training course.

The insights gained from buddhist mind training lead us into a different – deeper – and above all a more comprehensive experience of reality. There is an experience of existence that is accessible to anyone who engages in this path of training (see Part One). For psychotherapeutic work this has a meaning: this extended view of reality must not be missing in any art of treating and preventing disease that wants to do justice to the human being as a whole. Essential Psychotherapy is thus the attempt to develop and apply an art of treating and preventing disease that does justice to the basic nature of being.

L. The Structure of the Psychotherapeutic Part

The structure of Part Two of this book can be understood by comparing it to an actual therapy situation. It is characterized during the first meetings by getting to know each other, developing trust, establishing a trusting working relationship, making a therapeutic decision and often by naming a first therapy assignment. The therapist usually takes the case, formulates an initial diagnosis and, under certain circumstances, draws up an initial therapy plan, possibly also an expert opinion on coverage of costs.

The client may have an unresolved problem from their professional or private life, or unresolved conflict, possibly with their partner, or a separation due to death or divorce. Often clients come with specific symptoms, sometimes referred by other practitioners. It could be a phobia, a fear of confined spaces (claustrophobia), fear of an exam, or even very general and unspecific fears. Some clients have difficulty controlling strong feelings such as anger or aggression and come to therapy because of this. Often there are issues that are in the affective and emotional arena, such as long- lasting depressed moods , for example a development of depression.

In these cases, when it seems obvious to the client what he or she is suffering from, an initial therapy prescription can quickly be issued, which is later reformulated at a different level of knowledge. Their aim is to solve the known problem or to alleviate or cure the symptoms. For the therapist, this can mean working first with what the client is aware of, i.e. a focus on problem solving and changing the symptoms. In addition to building a supportive, healing relationship between therapist and client (chapter M), the focus here is then on working to actualize or build up resources (chapter N) and using coping strategies and interventions (chapter O). In these approaches, the client's symptoms and problems, such as anxiety or a workplace conflict, are treated more directly and immediately.

Astrid Schillings is the author of chapter P on "Focusing-oriented therapy" after Eugene T. Gendlin. This method, which also involves a special inner attitude of the therapist, is strongly process-oriented and can be seen and used as a deepening for all procedures. Furthermore, it can have a revealing effect, as already mentioned in chapter J.

In chapter Q special methods of disidentification are presented. Through this kind of disidentification one can find one's way into something detached, free, not fixed, like free space or an open awareness, similar to what we also strive for in meditation.

With a specially depth-psychologically oriented approach, as described from chapter S onwards, symptoms such as anxiety or, for example, an eating disorder or a somatization disorder are more likely to be seen as an indication of another underlying theme. This symptom then often has a function in the client's entire inner psychological dynamics. Let's take as an illustration, a behaviour which can often be observed with a certain form of eating disorder:

Client S. lives alone and feels lonely in their apartment after a hard day at work. They then begins to eat without feeling hungry until they no longer feels the sadness of their loneliness. They is not aware of the causes of her behaviour and may develop obesity with their compensatory eating behaviour.

In the course of therapy, it becomes clear that some burdensome situations and the client's way of dealing with them occur again and again, repeat themselves and we can talk about a pattern. If this is the case, it is possible that certain experiences of the client, which may also have happened long ago, shape their current experience and are repeated again and again and are experienced by them in a new and troublesome way. Perhaps old feelings from childhood are repeated or "triggered" in the client's current life situations. We speak here of unconscious psychodynamics, which often has unprocessed fundamental conflicts as its root. These then control the client's experience and make him or her or their environment suffer.

Here is another example to illustrate this: client G. often experiences a feeling of repulsion or rejection in contact with other people. This offends him, makes him sad, sometimes desperate and then often makes him angry. He then tends to behave inappropriately, so that he has never stayed at a workplace for long. It was discovered that the client felt rejected by his father in childhood using uncovering methods, as presented in chapter U. This old unprocessed feeling was repeated in his current life situations, especially with male superiors. He would then react very emotionally, almost like the five-year-old boy who felt rejected. By using belated inner parenting (see chapter S, on inner child work) of this part of himself, the client found a needy inner child. He released this dynamic and became more capable of relationships, resilient and joyful in life.

This kind of in-depth treatment of mostly unconscious emotional patterns and basic inner psychological conflicts has been dealt with specifically in the chapters on sub-personality work (chapter R), work with the inner child (chapter S), work with parental images (chapter T) and methodology of revealing work (chapter U). We have highlighted chapter U, uncovering methods, from a systematic point of view, because the approaches presented here are more active and solution oriented. But of course, all the other procedures described, from mirroring the relationship in the therapy situation, to trauma treatment, also involve a process of uncovering, i.e. of bringing into consciousness, raising and holding unconscious content.

Dealing with clients who have experienced a trauma requires a special approach – to avoid re-traumatization – and is dealt with separately in chapter V.

Chapter W explains how to work with dreams in the EPT. Working with will power and visualisations (chapter X) and with the higher self (chapter Y) comes after the chapters that represent the processing of the inner psychological dynamics. This happens for the following reason: After working on unconscious dynamics (chapter P – W), which trigger pre-structuring fixations of our perceptions in the senses and in thinking, energy is released. This energy is used for a creative transformation. Generally, it is a prerequisite to be able to really decide and act out of a freer self, less controlled by unconscious fixations and identifications. Only then can one's own will, (as defined by Assagioli), be used to take life into one's own hands with these forces. This step of taking responsibility is of central importance. It is a prerequisite for being open to inner visions, that can show us our own calling or an inner mission. Only in this way a person can individually find and take the right place for themselves, according to of the individuation process of C. G. Jung.

If, on the other hand, one always has to react in the same way, because an unprocessed insult controls the experience with feelings of despair, sadness and anger, as with client G., there is little room for shaping one's own relationships. There is not really a choice: Do I let the feeling of the angry child in me take over or not?

It can be expressed like this in a simplified way: after working on unconscious patterns and releasing energies, a process or new formation takes place, which makes it increasingly possible to work and shape how one really wants it deep from inside. Life can be consciously steered in the direction that is considered meaningful. In this way, life can be increasingly aligned and oriented towards aspects and goals, such as an altruistic motivation of a Bodhisattva. The freedom and thus the creative momentum grow.

Chapter Z introduces work with couples in essential psychotherapy.

At the beginning or end of each chapter or exercise, we often refer to buddhist mind training to highlight similarities and differences. In addition, the exercises and methods are preceded by their respective indications, or the field of indication, and the original therapy schools from which the exercise originated are also named. If not otherwise mentioned, the exercise has been developed within the EPT.

In the appendix there is a toolbox of exercises (E), which are suitable for self-study for any reader and a toolbox of methods (M), which are more for therapists or professionals. These indexes (method cases) help to easily find an exercise. They are marked in the text and also in the method cases with a number, page number, priority indication and short description.

The exercises that are in the compendium and curriculum of Essential Psychotherapy, which in their original version come from other therapeutic or meditative traditions, can be recognized as such in the text. Since some of our instructors at the Institute of Essential Psychotherapy are also instructors in other therapeutic schools, there are also exercises that come from the compendiums or curricula of their respective training institutes, some of which are unpublished. Or they are published elsewhere in their original version. Some exercises in their original version are taken from the Phyllis Krystal Imagination System, which Friederike Erhardt teaches as a trainer at the Institute for EPT. Some exercises are part of the Compendium of Psychosynthesis Training in the original version. For this, Ulla Pfluger-Heist, Wolfgang Erhardt and Friederike Erhardt are the trainers. Furthermore, there are exercises from the compendiums of couple therapy training institutes. Here Irma Dockter and Elgin Schrewe-Krome are the trainers. For exercises that originate from Focusing, co-author Astrid Schillings (see chapter P) and Ulla Pfluger-Heist are the trainers. We would like to take this opportunity to thank our trainers for their extensive support and for their permission to use the teaching material in this book. Special thanks to our trainers for their review of the contents of Part Two of the book.

M. The Therapeutic Relationship

The attitude of the therapist

In Essential Psychotherapy, special emphasis is placed on anchoring the therapist in a path of awareness training (as described in Part One) along with the resulting attitude. If you look at the first part of the book, which presents the inner work based on buddhist mind training, it becomes clear how important it is to rest in open awareness, especially in a live therapy session when you are in contact with the client. Through their training, the EPT therapist accesses their own qualities, dwelling in open, awake, non-fixed awareness, the basic nature of our being. EPT therapists need training in continuous awareness in order to be able to align themselves again and again with this level of open presence in therapy sessions. All the exercises and methods explained in part one of the book are applied. From this lived experience (attitude) the therapist then accompanies the manifestation of this dimension of awareness (the buddha nature or ground of being) in the client.

The therapist can use different approaches. This is done by making the client aware of the dimension of "true self" or "buddha nature" as source of simply being. Perhaps they inwardly formulate the greeting: "I welcome the enlightened part in you" (like the "Namaste" in India) or visualizes a sphere of light in the heart area of the client. The therapist can visualize the client inwardly as their buddha nature might appear, for example by visualizing them as Medicine Buddha or Tārā. On the level of awareness potential or even the fundamental nature of being, client and therapist are not separated. We also call this alignment the building of a healing field. We have thus a development from the relationship to the relationship field and further to the healing field between therapist and client.

The EPT therapist rests in an attitude of open awareness, free from fixation and identification, awake and mindful, with an active empathy. They invite the "unknown" into the therapeutic process and support the client's trust that this source of existence is whole and indestructible. It is based on the knowledge that the process of becoming aware or conscious has a healing effect. This dynamic can also be seen as a flow or direction of flow: a flow for recovery, for healing. The healing process takes place on the basis that the mind in its depths is already healthy in itself! The flowing, therefore, in reality only allows that which has always been and is healthy anyway to "shine through". It is necessary not to hinder this dynamic. This can best be described as "stepping aside a little" so that what is, can show itself and be seen.

It is of central importance for the therapeutic process how the therapist is *present* in the therapy situation, with what quality of awareness, and inner orientation and attitude. *Whichever* psychotherapeutic methods are used (chapter N-Y) get their special effect through *how* they are applied. The appreciation of the process nature of all existence is expressed in an attitude of openness and awareness. When therapists are present with this greatest possible inner openness, aware of the ground of being, this alone has a healing effect on the client. This is an appreciation of existence in the sense of "seeing" and "being seen" on this level by the therapist and client. It enables both of them to allow this "level of the true nature of being" more and more.

In this context it is interesting to note that Tom Yeomans (an American psychosynthesis trainer) considers the injuries on the "soul level" as the deepest injuries in humans. They are caused by not seeing and not appreciating this deepest level of being. An experience which is unfortunately very common, since there are not many people who are aware of this level.

The effect of the therapeutic relationship

It is well known, and confirmed by recent results from therapy research, that a good relationship between therapist and client is crucial for the success of therapy. The relationship itself is considered to be one of the most important, or *the* central factor in the therapeutic situation. The relationship between therapist and client is particularly important because it is internalized as a new relationship experience. This changes the inner processing of earlier – often deficient – relationship experiences, for example with biological parents. These have had a significant impact on the client's experience, perception and ability to form relationships (chapter R, sub-personality work and chapter T, working with parental images). The therapist is a role model for the client through their way of being present and the way they shape the relationship. This relationship experience of the client is often internalized anew like a corrective.

Attuning Meditation (exercise M.1)

To illustrate this, let us consider the beginning of a therapy session in the EPT:

(1) Before or at the beginning of the therapy session, the therapist anchors themselves by accessing the basic nature of existence or the greatest possible vastness of awareness accessible to her or him. This can happen, for example, through an inner refuge or awareness of the basic nature of existence (see Part One of the book). Other inner exercises can also be applied, such as the alignment with the Higher Self (exercise Y.1) or the other exercises for working with the Higher Self (chapter Y) such as the Light Triangle (exercise Y.5) or the alignment with the Healing Buddha (chapter H).

(2) When the client is present in the therapy room, the therapist can inwardly invite the client's basic nature or simple being ("namaste" or by visualizing a sphere of light in the client's heart).

(3) If the client can engage in a finely tuned inner orientation and it fits the therapy situation, the therapist can guide a short meditation (see exercise E.1). Here is a short summary:

> Please direct your awareness to the sensations of the body...
> Then extend it to the sensory impressions of hearing, seeing, smelling and tasting...
> Then add the mental movements of thinking in words and pictures...
> When all senses are activated, explore inwardly: What is the experience like?

(4) After this tuning in, the therapy session can be continued with the question: "What do you want to work on?"

N. Activating Resources

Resource-oriented work is of central importance in the EPT because updating resources strengthens the client's self-esteem, self-confidence and social skills. In addition, if the client is able to activate their resources, he or she will be provided with the basis from which they can turn to stressful or painful experiences and memories. Recent findings from therapy research, and also especially from brain research, confirm this.

The EPT has access to an almost unlimited treasury of teachings and methods of meditation and awareness training (see Part One of the book), thanks to the still active and intact transmission lines of buddhist mind training based on 2500 years of experience and knowledge. To apply this treasury of wisdom, to live it out and thereby to experience suchness, is certainly the deepest resource there is. This strongest resource is activated and anchored in the client by staying in contact with this level of being, living it, perceiving and appreciating it. The therapist does this for themselves and for the client, who is usually not yet aware of this resource. It is one of the central themes of this book.

The central concern of buddhist mind training is indeed the activation of resources, or in other words, the bringing forth of inherent qualities. It is assumed that awakening as well as complete mental healing is already inherent in us as potential. The mind is seen as a wish-fulfilling jewel that only needs to be uncovered. As soon as the mind is freed a little from the emotional and cognitive veils, the inherent qualities reveal themselves and take the lead in the further healing process. The visualizations of the Tibetan tradition are a resource activation par excellence, where we cultivate a completely pure view of ourselves and all others as buddhas, embedded in the development of trust and compassion, and with the help of the mantras and visualizations it is as if we enter into a pure land where the process of awakening takes place. This is similar in its nature to the pendulum movement between resource and challenge in the therapeutic process: the emotional burdens arising in meditation are connected to the resource – the wisdom and compassion of that buddha aspect – and thus processed and integrated.

Let us now take a look at how the therapist helps the client to activate the resources they are aware of. The client is asked about their existing resources in the first interview: "What are your resources? Are there situations in which you feel really comfortable, where you feel really good? What gives you strength? Where can you recharge your batteries? Where have you felt really good in the past?" With the answers, the therapist and client create a list, for example: "When I am in nature, especially in the mountains" or: "My family gives me support and strength."

Often the first reorientation of the client already happens at this point. The fixation on what is burdensome is released. It can be contextualised or seen in a different light. Being able to "summon" a resource then becomes one of the prerequisites in the further course of therapy, in order to be able to turn to serious, stressful life circumstances or traumatization. The more serious the disorder or trauma of the client is, the more important a basis of security in the ability to summon resources becomes. This also applies to "swinging" between resource and stress, a method used in trauma treatment (see chapter W). In this approach, areas of the brain that are activated when impressions are stressful are coupled with areas of the brain that are activated when impressions are relaxing. This leads to a healing change in the perception of the situation experienced as stressful. It becomes clear how valuable and important it is to have reliable access to one's own resources and to be able to "call up" or "recall" these resources.

Let's move on to some exercises that are given a particular favour, or effectiveness, by the therapist's special attitude in the EPT. This can serve as an illustration of how, for example, normal tasks in the "Tea Ceremony" of Zen, become a path of awakening through the attitude of the one who carries it out. In this way, the therapeutic approach with this particular attitude also becomes a path of awakening. In what follows we present some exercises that are applied in their original form in behavioural psychotherapy, in conversational psychotherapy (according to Rogers), in psychosynthesis (according to Assagioli) or in other therapeutic schools.

Finding Resources (exercise N.1)

In the course of psychotherapeutic work, this exercise can also be used to desensitize fears or to work with traumatic experiences. Parts of this exercise were originally used in various strands of behaviour therapy, mostly in the form of 'the quiet image', in EGO-State Therapy according to Watkins and in psychosynthesis according to Assagioli. It is intended for the treatment of trauma, but also for all anxiety disorders or generally for strengthening the I, or in the treatment of depressive moods.

At the beginning of the exercise the therapist anchors himself/herself in an awareness of the greatest possible openness in the sense of mahāmudrā. Without having to mention it, they then visualize a sphere of light in the client's heart, which symbolizes and invites this very openness and all awakened qualities in the client. In addition, it is possible to imagine the inspiring, accompanying presence of an aspect of wisdom like the Medicine Buddha in the room. Alternatively, we can imagine all those present as Medicine Buddhas. The most important point is to get in touch with potential healing powers and to create a healing field of light, lightness and warmth. As companions, we experience a deep certainty that complete healing and awakening are possible. Thus, the therapist anchors himself/herself in an open, healing awareness and allows a healing field to develop. We always start the exercise instructions with the client from this attitude:

Before starting this exercise, please estimate your current inner tension on a scale of 1 to 10 (*see exercise N.4*).

Please adopt a comfortable sitting position and focus your awareness on the body sensations, perhaps on the sensations in your feet, then also on those parts of your body that are in contact with the chair and then on the sensations of your abdomen as it rises and falls with the flow of breath. It is helpful to close your eyes. However, you can open them again any time you need to. Let yourself be guided by the questions: "What is the experience like? How are the sensations experienced in the body?"

Then let these perceptions fade into the background and please think of life situations in which you felt quite comfortable, which were especially pleasant for you. This could have been a special event, or a special body sensation you once experienced, or a special encounter or memories of special places: the last mountain hike, the beach vacation, the splashing of the waves. Nobody wants anything from you...

Whatever it is, let it arise again now. We all have the ability to perceive something pleasant. If you have found such an experience, bring it to mind. How did the body feel, what did you see, hear, smell? Was there a taste? Let the experience be completely there once again, as it is now still perceptible and noticeable in your body through memory.

Where in the body can you feel it most at this moment? Let it be all there, and perhaps it is even possible to imagine that the subtle breath spreads this sensation throughout the body, into every cell, tissue and muscle. See how this sensation spreads further and further. Maybe other memories of similar pleasant physical sensations will appear. Maybe you can think of a word for what you are feeling or a symbol. Just stay in touch with it.

Then let this exercise slowly fade and come back to the present again, open your eyes and orientate yourself in the room. You can also now do a short second scaling of the inner tension and assess whether anything has changed. You may want to make some notes on this.

By measuring the tension on this scale, you may have been able to determine the percentage by which you have been able to relax through this exercise and most importantly – made yourself aware that it was you, yourself, who made this change.

In the debriefing session, the therapist is guided by the fact that the client is clearly aware that it is his or her own power and competence which creates this experience, and they have the ability to recall it again and again. This has a self-affirming effect. They are encouraged to practice this exercise daily on their own until the next therapy session. Practicing this exercise at least until they feel these pleasant, open body sensations. They can also remember the word, or name or symbol for this experience more often throughout the day, especially in situations that are not experienced as so pleasant.

The resource work of this exercise can be extended even further to experiences that go back a long way, perhaps even to the time of your own childhood. During the exercise, you are invited to look for situations where you felt quite comfortable in your childhood. For example, with suggestions like: "And now go back even further into your memories, perhaps to experiences in your childhood that you experienced as particularly pleasant."

The Safe Place (exercise N.2)

This exercise puts more emphasis on the aspect of "feeling safe". It can be used for all kinds of fears and especially for an external or internal need for protection. The therapist anchors himself/herself in an open, healing awareness and creates a healing field (see chapter M and exercise N.1). Then the exercise instruction begins:

Please go inwards with your awareness, directing it to the sensations in your body, especially to the sensations in your feet.

It helps to close your eyes, but you can open them again at any time you need to. Then you may go to the sensations in those parts of the body that are in contact with the chair, observe for a few moments the sensations in the abdomen as it rises and falls with the flow of breath. Let yourself be guided by questions like: "What is my experience? What is the experience of physical sensations and other sensory impressions?".

Then take your memory back a little and look for somewhere where you felt completely safe and secure.

Maybe it was a very specific place, maybe it was connected to a specific person. What did it feel like there? How did it feel in the body? What was it like to feel safe and secure? What is the taste of feeling safe and secure?

Then please go back a little further in your memory, perhaps to your childhood. Was there also a place, perhaps connected with a person, where you felt completely safe and secure? How did it feel? Let it come completely alive again in the memory and feel that in your body.

What is the "taste" of feeling completely safe and secure?

Let the feeling spread throughout the body and direct the sentence internally to the feeling "Show me a symbol for the feeling of safety."

It can be that a symbol or a sentence comes, it can be that nothing comes up. Both are fine. Just stay with the feeling of safety and with the physical sensations associated with it.

Stay there as long as it is right for you and then come back very slowly. Feel the sensations in your feet first, then open your eyes and orient yourself in the room.

You may want to take some notes.

In the debriefing phase, the client is given space to talk about her or his experiences. The therapist asks for the symbol or sentence. The symbol contains the whole experience and it's easy for the client to stay in contact with it mentally even after the exercise. The symbol can repeatedly serve as a mental "anchor". It makes sense for the client to practice it daily after the session. It is then filled with "the force of awareness" and turned into a healing force that can help the client in difficult, fear-inducing situations.

Developing Kindness (exercise N.3)

The Kindness exercise originates from psychosynthesis. It places more emphasis on a good relationship experience as a resource and is suggested for clients who need to feel more secure and accepted in their contact with other people. It can be used as a preparation for a meditation on loving kindness (metta) or compassion (karuna). In doing so, a real personal experience with feelings and sensations becomes the basis for further meditations on compassion.

The therapist anchors himself/herself in an open, healing awareness and allows a healing field to develop (see chapter M and exercise N.1). Afterwards the exercise instruction begins:

Make yourself comfortable in your chair and take your awareness inside, close your eyes and direct your awareness to the physical sensations, especially the sensations in your feet. Whenever you need to, you can of course open your eyes. Follow for a few moments the sensations in the abdomen, as it rises and falls with the flow of breath.

Let yourself be guided by the questions: "What is the experience like? What is the experience of the physical sensations or the experience of any other sensations like?"

Then try to recall an experience where you experienced something like kindness from another person from someone who really meant you well. Maybe there are several situations, then choose one and let the situation be completely alive again. How did you feel, which sensations were present in your body? What is the "taste" of experiencing kindness like? Let yourself feel it calmly in your whole body.

Then go back in your memory a little further, perhaps even to your childhood. Was there also an experience of kindness there? What did it feel like? What were the sensations in your body like? Just let it be there completely and expand out in your body. What is the taste of this experience like? What is the taste of experiencing kindness like? What does this do to you and your perception?

Then you come back into the now and think of a situation in which you were kind. How does it feel to be kind? What are the sensations in the body? Let it be completely there and let it expand. And what is its taste, what is the taste of kindness?

Then direct the sentence inwardly to your sensations: "Show me a symbol or give me a sentence for this feeling of kindness."

Sometimes there is a symbol, sometimes a sentence, sometimes not. Everything is right.

Then come back very slowly. Go back to the sensations in your body, in your feet, open your eyes and orientate yourself in the room.

Maybe you would like to make some notes, maybe you would like to paint a picture or just reflect a little bit more.

The client can describe the experience in the therapeutic debriefing. If they had a symbol or a sentence, it is good to stay in touch with it, that is, to think about it often deliberately. Once the symbol is called up, it is connected to the force of our awareness or "filled" and initiates healing developments. When practicing for oneself, the symbol is imagined at least until it has an effect on the sensory level of experience.

Strengthening the inner observer

Many of our exercises and interventions are intended to strengthen the inner observer. The inner observer is also referred to as the self (after C. G. Jung or R. Assagioli) or as the "adult me"; or informally as "the captain, the pilot, the conductor...".

In this kind of inner work, we aim to develop a high degree of awareness and mindfulness and at the same time strengthen the ability to make decisions (see chapter X, Will and Vision). In the following, we will now present some exercises that pursue this goal.

Scaling a Sensation (exercise N.4)

The exercise of classifying sensations on a scale from 0 to 10 is relatively simple. It is used to observe and measure experience, such as a pain in the foot. It was originally developed in behavioural psychotherapy. A "step back" is taken from direct perception, through the act of measuring and a cognitive process of comparing and evaluating is initiated. This is useful in some situations, as people sometimes feel at the mercy of a particular perception (such as pain or fear or strong emotions of sadness or anger). It is as if they are controlled by the emotion and are identified with it in their experience:

> Sit comfortably and take your awareness to a specific sensation, for example a pain somewhere in the body or a tension in an area of the body. Then measure this sensation with your subjective assessment on a scale from 0 to 10. Please let me know your rating.
> (In our example, the pain in the foot would have been scaled as 3.5. A different tension in the upper abdomen might have been 5 on the scale).

A simple additional structuring of the scale, for example:
0–5 = green area, 6–7 = orange area and 8–10 = red area, helps clients with the assessment. The client learns that, by the time they get into the red zone, they will use an intervention that has been practiced previously.

The scaling helps people to initially distance themselves and then disidentify with certain stimuli (pain, or strong affects such as anger). After scaling anger = scale 8, a client can then be asked to say the sentence: "I have anger, it is 8 on the scale. I have the anger, but I am also more than the anger, because after all, I can measure it." This simple sentence, which can also be spoken or thought several times, has the effect that the client can get "behind the wheel" again, i.e. with self-control or self-regulation. Furthermore, scaling a sensation before and after an intervention helps to perceive the change in sensation. If a client experiences that their perception of the sensation of pain as pain is reduced through an exercise on breath, mindfulness, and has scaled and measured it, then this enhances self-esteem and feelings of being at the mercy of the sensation of pain and feelings of powerlessness in the face of pain are reduced. This in turn usually leads to a rise in mood.

Reviewing the day mentally (exercise N.5)

Reviewing the day strengthens the ability to reflect and introspect and can be used as a foundation exercise for other exercises and methods. For example, by repeating the exercise, one can focus on moments of experiencing joy (which helps to reduce depression). The basic form of this exercise originates from psychosynthesis according to Assagioli. The therapist anchors himself/herself in an open, healing awareness and allows a healing field to develop (see chapter M and exercise N.1). Then the instruction for the exercise begins:

> Make yourself comfortable in your chair, close your eyes and focus your awareness on your physical sensations, especially in the feet. Then follow the sensations in the abdomen for a while. It rises as you breathe in and falls as you breathe out. Let yourself be guided by the questions: "What is this experience like? How are physical and other sensations experienced?"

Then let these perceptions fade into the background a bit and remember the moment of waking up in the morning and from there start to go through your day until you reach the present. Just as if you are watching a film, the film of your day: the first movements, getting up, making breakfast, going to work... Go through the whole morning, then lunch, afternoon and evening. Review the events of the day once again. Often you can structure the memories of the day a bit with reference to meals or specific activities, or meetings you had. It is important that the day is gone through without judgement, only observing, perceiving, just like a cameraman who makes a film without judgement or criticism.

Continue until you reach the present, then go back to the sensations in your body, open your eyes, and orient yourself in the room. The goal of this exercise is to look back over the day.

This strengthens the force of the inner observer and creates a conscious memory. This is an act of the will which selects something, (the memory of the day and then traces it further back) and remains with its attention on it. The inner observer can be used very specifically to observe a certain feeling such as joy, or a sub-personality (see chapter R) in the second cycle. An observation of moments when joy is felt could be beneficial for a client with depressive symptoms.

The review of the day can also be done from the present moment back to the start of the day (i.e. in reverse order to the exercise above). Likewise, keeping a diary has a highly therapeutic value, as it strengthens the ability to reflect and introspect. However, the prerequisite for this is that it is not written from a critic perspective. It should therefore be only observational, not evaluative.

Furthermore, it can be useful to write down a certain characteristic or behaviour as a daily or weekly log (a method that is very popular in behavioural therapy). For example, a mildly depressed client can simply always write down a green "J" with a scaled number like 5 in their diary or, in case of anger, a red "A", in order to increase the moments of joy they experience.

Discarding the memory of an unpleasant situation (exercise N.6)

This exercise serves to consciously and deliberately put aside contents of awareness, for example memories of very unpleasant stressful events that simply appear in the awareness via a chain of associations and are experienced as invasive, threatening or overwhelming, consciously building a "defence barrier" (for example, contents of situations that have been experienced as trauma, such as an accident or something similar). This is an ability that strengthens the observer, which has traditionally been referred to in psychotherapy as an ego-strengthening power, referred to also as 'willpower' (see chapter X).

The therapist anchors themselves in an open, healing awareness and allows a healing field to develop (see chapter M and exercise N.1). Then the instruction for the exercise begins:

> Sit comfortably on a chair, feel the backrest against your back and focus your awareness on the physical sensations, especially the sensations in the feet and legs, then on the parts of the body that are in contact with the chair, then to the sensations in the abdomen, which rises and falls with the flow of the breath. Rest there calmly for a few moments and count the breaths, number each breath while exhaling.
>
> Then think briefly about an unpleasant event, for example a minor car accident or an embarrassing experience. It is enough to do this in words. Everything associated with it is considered – remembered images, emotions and feelings, and the thoughts that go with them. Now put them in a good, safe place in your imagination. You can present the content in a beautiful box or package, in your imagination. Then close the box.
>
> Alternatively, you can put everything in a package, close it and tie it up and then put it, for example, in the cellar in a certain room with a lockable steel cabinet, like a safe. The steel cabinet or safe is then locked, the cellar is locked, and you are

the only person who has the key. Only you have access and can decide when you want to get it out again. Alternatively, the sealed package with the deliberately placed contents can be buried somewhere under a tree or placed in a chapel or temple in a cupboard or even in a safe place that symbolizes wisdom for you.

Make sure that the contents are properly stored there now. If you think of anything more, put it almost automatically immediately back into this package in the steel cabinet.

Then slowly finish the exercise and make yourself aware once again that you have the power one who can put something down. How does it feel to have this power? Then direct your awareness to the body sensations, especially those in your feet. Open your eyes, orient yourself here in the room.

This practice of consciously discarding difficult or stressful things is a power of the self and, as a capacity, a prerequisite for being able to turn to memories of stressful situations in a therapeutic setting.

O. Coping Strategies and Interventions for Mental Problems and Disorders

At the beginning of this chapter, we will introduce you to a certain approach to psychotherapeutic work (method O.1), which has proven quite useful in practice. It's simple and general structure is easy to learn and can be applied to a variety of different problems and symptoms. We simply call it 'the work in 7 steps' or the 'Seven Step Work'.

Seven Step Strategy (method O.1)

This strategy or method can be used for many symptoms, such as symptoms of anxiety and restlessness, or even where the client is overwhelmed with affect. For illustration purposes, the method is illustrated by the example of a reactive upsurge of anger:

The client *recognizes* (1) that they feel strong anger at this very moment, which they may also be familiar with from one or more past situations.

They *scale* (2) the anger on a scale from 1 to 10.

They *verbalize* (3) the feeling: "I accept, I feel anger, which is 8 on the scale".

They *intervene* (4): "I count my breaths while observing the rise and fall of the abdomen." Or the client realizes that the anger, because it is familiar to them, comes from events in their childhood, so it is the anger of the inner child, and they start an inner dialogue with the inner child (see chapter S): "I see your anger and I am there."

They now *scale* (5) a second time and if their intervention was successful, they state: "Now the anger is only at scale 5."
They *enhance* (6) this effect: "If I could reduce the anger by 30% in 3 minutes, how would I experience myself differently then? What could this quality of experience be called?"
They *disidentify* (7) in the next step: "I sometimes feel anger, but I am more than the anger." (The rage continues to decrease).

An overview of the strategy in 7 steps

Indication: Used in therapy with affect upsurges, in our example with strong anger – but it is applicable to any other emotions, such as fear, sadness, pain or generally for impulse control.

1. Recognition
2. First scaling
3. Accepting and verbalizing: e.g. "I accept I feel anger, scale 8".
4. Intervening:
   a. Mindfulness exercise, counting the breaths (chapter E)
   b. Inner child work (ch. S)
   c. Mahāmudrā (ch. E)
   d. Further therapeutic interventions, e.g. Focusing (ch. P)
   e. The Wise Friend (ch. X)
   f. Refuge (ch. C)
   g. May tree (ch. X)
5. Second scaling
6. Amplifying: how is the experience with the positive change?
7. Disidentification: e.g. "I am angry, but I am more than the anger."

When experiencing *fear*, the work would look like this:

The client *recognizes* (1) that they are afraid.
They *scale* (2) the fear as a 7 on the scale.
They *accept* (3): "I am currently afraid, scale 7."
They *intervene* (4) by focusing fully on watching the movement of the breath in the abdomen and counting a number with each exhalation, either aloud or internally.

They *scale* (5) again: "I am now just afraid scale 4."

They *strengthen* (6) the effect by more positive self-perception "If I could lower the fear in 3 minutes by 30%, how would I experience myself differently then?" Do I have a name for this quality of experience?

They *disidentify (7)*: "I sometimes experience fear as part of my overall experience, but I am also more than my experience of fear" – and thus further reduces the fear.

Desensitization in Sensu (method O.2)

The desensitization in sensu (in the senses) is used to treat anxiety symptoms or phobias. It originated in behavioural therapy and can be seen as a precursor of the work of alternating between stressful and relaxing experiences, as it is used today mainly in trauma treatment according to Levin. Desensitization *in sensu* means that the therapeutic work takes place in the senses, i.e. in the imagination and not *in vivo*, hence not in a real-life situation. Out of which it is possible that a client once familiar with the desensitization exercise, might also try out a confrontation in the actual real-life situation itself in small steps. This method combines anxiety-inducing stimuli and relaxing stimuli in the brain, which in the long term reduces the level of anxiety and results in a desensitization of the experience. It is used for a wide variety of anxieties, for example, fear of heights or claustrophobia, an anxiety when you are in confined spaces, such as in an elevator.

A prerequisite is that the client has mastered at least one procedure, such as calling up a resource (exercise N.1) or even a safe place or counting breaths from the mindfulness of breathing practice, and feels secure with this as a relaxation method. If this is not yet the case, these methods first need to be practiced several times during the therapy sessions. The therapeutic method of desensitization in sensu requires the presence of the therapist at least initially. The client's basic tension level is measured in advance. They are asked: "How tense do you experience yourself as, in this moment? If you rate this on a scale of one to ten (exercise N.4), what number would you use?" The therapist needs the estimation of the basic tension to be able to detect changes later. The client gains confidence through these self-measured changes. They know that the method can bring about positive change in them. Here is an overview of the steps of the work of desensitizing in sensu:

1. Scaling.
2. Remembering the situation causing the fear (not for trauma!).
3. Holding the tension and scaling while continuing to hold it (e.g. at 9 on the scale with body symptoms) for at least 60 seconds.
4. Prompting the client to change the image immediately and access a calming image.
5. Scaling how the tension has developed (perhaps at 5 on the scale).
6. Amplifying via a more positive self- perception.
7. Repeating the coupling of *fear-inducing memory* with the *calming image* or *resource image* no sooner than half an hour later and, if necessary, a few more times a week later.
8. Strengthening this through awareness of the more positive self-perception.

Case study for desensitization in case of fear of heights

The client, Ms. M., came to the practice because of massive fear of heights. She had developed an avoidance attitude and suffered greatly from the limitations in her life. Her fears and the associated limitations in life were particularly evident on bridges. She lived in Bonn and had to cross the Rhine at least twice a day for the trip to her workplace and back. This was only possible for her even on the bus or in the car with massive symptoms of anxiety.

Ms. M. had a basic tension of 2 on the scale of 1-10. By calling up her resource picture, a reminder of a very relaxed vacation situation, she could easily reduce her experienced tension to 0.5.

(Phase 1) Then, after receiving detailed information, Ms. M. decided to try the method of desensitization in sensu. She sat relaxed on the chair opposite the therapist.

Therapist: Now please remember the situation on the bridge over the Rhine that frightens you so much. *(Any memories could be called up here, which were all similarly filled with fear).*
The client tenses visibly.
Therapist: Please briefly measure your tension and communicate it.
Client: I am now at 9.5.
Therapist: Please still hold the picture and the tension, now hold the tension for about 30 seconds, now 10 seconds and now drop the picture and immediately think of your resource image.
The client visibly relaxes.
Therapist: If you measure your tension now, how high is it now?
Client: Significantly less, now I'm at 5.
Therapist: How does it feel to feel 40% less tension in your experience now? *The client feels and remains in her experience.*
Client: It is good, my tension decreases even further.
Therapist: Let it happen and stay with it for a while.
Therapist: Now please come back completely and open your eyes, orient yourself in the room, feel the sensations in your feet.

This procedure was repeated after half an hour (the client's basic tension was back to 2) and after a week, 2 more times. The client experienced the recall of the anxiety-triggering memory with less and less tension (the 4th time with tension 6), and after 2 more times during the therapy hours also with tension 5.5.

(Phase 2) Then the client was asked if she would like to do this desensitization exercise in sensu at home, just for herself. She tried it and after a few attempts, where she did not succeed so well at first, she was able to achieve a similarly low tension in calling up the fear-inducing memory as in the therapy situation.

(Phase 3) In the next phase the client was asked whether she could imagine this way of dealing with fear in a real-life situation, i.e. on the bridge in a car. She should drive over the bridge together with a trustworthy companion and carry out the desensitization after having allowed and measured her fears for the first time. The client chose a good friend with whom she felt safe. The friend drove the car, and the client reduced her anxiety on the bridge, moving from scale 7 to scale 3.5 (the therapist does not work in vivo, otherwise he would have been in the car during the bridge crossing). This desensitization in vivo with the friend in the car was effective and after some repetitions the measured tension of the client in this anxiety-inducing situation was only 5.5 on the scale. The procedure was then continued in the therapy situation, with the tension finally falling to 4.

Later on, the client practiced alone on the bridge, even when she took the bus to work, and later also when crossing the bridge on foot. The fear of crossing the bridge could be reduced to scale 3 with this method of coupling the experience of fear with a relaxation/resource experience. In the course of this work, the client had completely abandoned her avoidance behaviour and reduced her anxiety tension to a residual tension that she could easily bear.

For another client, the methodology of desensitization in sensu was strengthened by the addition of different resource image. During the desensitization work, he imagined himself in the open left hand of a large golden buddha statue (the hand was resting in the buddha's lap on his upturned heels, like statues of the historical buddha touching the earth). This increased his anxiety reduction and strengthened his feeling of security. Since he also had frequent fears and nightmares at night, he also used this image when falling asleep. According to his account, the fears and nightmares were significantly reduced. In some of the client's resources from the area of the Higher Self appear associatively when they call up their designated resource images (for example, the hiker in the mountains). This immediately offers further resources for the therapist, which can strengthen the healing process.

The As-if method in a professional role (exercise O.1)

This is another exercise for anxiety, which can be used as a further intervention in context of the seven steps (method O.1). In this intervention the client imagines as a resource, a situation in which a problem is solved or a pleasing situation.

Example: A client has a social phobia in upmarket restaurants. He notices that he feels insecure in them, maybe he feels observed or he is afraid of doing something wrong or attracting attention. He may feel slightly overwhelmed by this situation. He is asked to scale this fear in advance. (He measures fear scale 6)

Exploration: The therapist searches for a life experience of the clients, similar to the resource exercise, in which the client feels completely competent and secure. Perhaps this is at their workplace, or another social context. The therapist allows the client to re-live this situation from memory. The client should remember Their "professional role", for example how they feels at the workplace and act *as if* they are in that situation now. Then the client is asked to feel whether a safe or a relaxed feeling is also created in the body through this exercise. (See also exercise N.1; maybe also scale the change in sensation before and after).

Then, in connection with these pleasant sensations and the visualisation of the "professional role", the client is asked to go into the fear-inducing situation in the restaurant. The client then describes their experience – including whether they felt more secure and relaxed with the visualisation.

If this is the case, the client is encouraged to apply this in real life situations, i.e. in our example at the next visit to the restaurant, and to report back in the next therapy session.

The "As-if method" in connection with the "professional role" can be extended as desired. The idea of being a buddha or having a certain quality of a buddha, e.g. the healing buddha, with the appropriate visualisation, can be used by people who are familiar with this meditation practice. Or the idea that one is "Tārā" – a female buddha, the "conqueror of fear". Then, in our example, one would enter the restaurant in the imagination as "Medicine Buddha" or as "Tārā" (they have a certain form). In the meditative tradition of Vajrayāna, also known as Tibetan buddhism, much work has been done with these forces of imagination for thousands of years.

Advice to a Good Friend (method O.3)

Similar to a role play.

"Advice to a good friend" can help people who need to create distance, because they cannot see a solution to their problem because of their identification and strong emotional involvement. They are "operationally blind" and can find a certain perspective through this exercise. This usually leads to a more objective consideration and assessment of the facts or problems to be solved.

The therapist needs an empty chair to be placed somewhere in the room. Then the client is asked to imagine an acquaintance or good friend sitting on it who has the same problem as themself. Our client is then asked to switch to the consultant or coach role. This is similar to a classic role play, except that the client does not sit on the chair of a different person but imagines another person sitting on the empty chair with the client's own problem. Through this exercise the client is able to distance themself from the problem or stressful situation. They are then able to judge the situation objectively. This has the effect of enhancing self-esteem and also disidentifying and helps the client to solve the problem. It opens up approaches to solving the problem. Resources are activated. They usually find a solution for the problem with the distance of this exercise.

> Imagine that a friend of yours has exactly the same life situation or unsolved problems as you (in our example, she is always devalued by her boss). This friend appreciates you very much and asks you for advice.

She is sitting here now (a chair is provided for her in the therapy room and the friend or colleague is imagined). What would you tell or advise her?

"I would advise her to tell the supervisor about what it does to her when he treats her so disparagingly and whether he considers it beneficial to the work situation!"

There may be initial objective advice after an assessment. Then the therapist asks if the imagined friend (who sits there for the client) has heard this advice. The answer may then be: "Yes, but she doesn't dare...", and then the dialogue is continued, so that the client keeps going back and forth in the imagination between the identified part (in the example, the friend with the unsolved problem) and the objective advisor.

It also helps to point out to the client that we all have the skills to give good, factual advice on how to assess a situation. However, we are often a little "operationally blind" or completely entangled or identified with inner patterns or feelings. This exercise repeatedly leads the client to distancing from the problem or life situation, so that they can reflect on a meta level.

Below are some intervention methods for specific life situations. The procedure of "removal after separation" has become known to me from the work on mourning according to Büntig.

Detaching after a separation (method O.4)

The following procedure is designed to let go or detach from a person that the client has lost through separation or death. It helps mourning work to be initiated for effective processing. This method can be applied in written form, in which case the client writes a letter: for example, to the deceased person (the letter is not sent, of course, but is only for the client) or the client formulates sentences in his or her mind that help the letting go. The form of conversation is that of direct speech with the person from whom the client wants to detach.

The first part of the detaching sentence is given by the therapist and then completed by the client (examples of possible answers in brackets):

> I resent you for... (having left me).
> I remember fondly... (how we had dinner at the Italian restaurant).
> I forgive ... (how you insulted me).
> I'm sorry that... (I did not approach you earlier).
> I thank you... (for the beautiful moments together).
> I beg you... (let's stay friends)
> I wish you... (all the best for the future)
> (Continue spontaneously) ...

At this point, the clients own spontaneous sentences may also arise and be written down. Or maybe more feelings are articulated, such as: "*It makes me sad that we are no longer together*" (verbalization of the feeling).

Using key sentences (method O.5)

Working with key sentences is used in many therapeutic methods, such as the work on will power of psychosynthesis according to Roberto Assagioli. Resolutions are formulated in words, for example: "I will live smoke-free." The client memorizes this sentence over and over again; under certain circumstances they can use the "as if" place (exercise O.1). They then imagine in this example that they already live smoke-free. They are asked to tune in to how the body responds to the sentence: "How does it feel? Is there some area in the body where you sense it most strongly?" If asking for a symbol, one addresses the bodily sensations that have arisen internally with the sentence: "Show me a symbol." Then he or she repeatedly comes into contact with the key sentence or symbol and fills it with "the power of awareness".

In the therapeutic setting it is supportive if the client voices his key sentence out loud, guiding this themselves, together with the therapist several times at the same time.

The Inner Garden (exercise O.2)

This exercise serves to set the client apart from other people and their demands. It is often used as protection against subtle attacks such as appropriation or against another person's claim to dominance.

Make yourself comfortable on the chair, feeling the backrest against your back and direct your awareness to your physical sensations, especially to the sensations in the feet and legs, and in the lower body. Rest, observing your breathing for a while, and the rise and fall of the abdomen with the flow of breath.

Then let these perceptions fade into the background a bit and imagine: You are in a garden – your inner garden. You can either enter it consciously through a garden gate or you can imagine that you are in your inner garden immediately. Consciously perceive everything that is in it with your senses: the colours and shapes and sounds, the plants. Then direct your attention to the garden wall or fence. Consciously note how far your garden extends and perceive the safety of the garden fence or garden wall and what that means for you.

Note how high it is and give it a shape that feels right – with regard to its height, shape, and texture. Then again, see your garden as your private space, where only you can be alone and only you decide who can enter through the garden gate.

How does it feel? Give space to the experience and if it triggers pleasant sensations in you, then let them spread throughout your body. Feel the safety created by the garden wall or your boundaries.

Then make it clear to yourself that this image with the corresponding feelings and sensations is always available to you, especially in situations where other people or circumstances are experienced as being too close and possibly too intrusive.
Then come back. Feel the sensations in your body, open your eyes and orient yourself in the room.
You may want to take notes.

In the therapy situation, the therapist asks what the client has experienced and a debriefing, to help further processing, can take place. The client is encouraged to use this mental image creatively for themselves, without talking about it, with people who are difficult for them in everyday life. If someone attacks them verbally, the garden fence in imagination can also have a mirrored surface on the outside from which all aggression bounces off.

Verbal demarcation (method O.6)

Quite a simple method of "demarcation" from other people, which is of a more role-playing nature, is that of verbalizing being different. Let us take as an example: a client who is trying to demarcate herself from her mother. She would either hold the image of her mother in her imagination or imagine her actually in the room. The client is then asked to say the following sentences to her mother:

I am me and you are you.
I have my family, and you have your family.
I have my thoughts and opinions, and you have your thoughts and opinions.
I have my body with my sensations, and you have your body with your sensations.
I have my feelings, and you have your feelings.
I have my friends, and you have your friends.

I have my life, and you have your life.
I am me and you are you.

This verbal form of demarcation and referring to oneself can, of course, also be carried out only in single sentences which are then repeated several times or expressed only in thought form or in writing.

The Lying Eight (exercise O.3)

This symbolic exercise also works, in the broadest sense, for demarcation, especially from people who the client experiences as penetrating or overwhelming. It is a basic exercise, which we will return to in this book in later exercises. It originates from the Phyllis Krystal Imagination System.

Some spiritual practitioners have trouble with demarcation or allowing themselves to be demarcated. They seem to understand the statements of the mind training as an invitation to constantly open themselves to everything – to let everything into their own field of practice. But it is by no means wise to open up to all kinds of influences and disturbances just like that – this requires an enormous inner permeability. What this exercise is all about is feeling of one's own strength and independence in a clear, loving and not entangled way, very similar to the protective circles of Tibetan buddhism.

Sit comfortably and focus your awareness on the physical sensations, especially the sensations in the feet. Follow the breath for a few moments as abdomen rises and falls in its flow. Then let these perceptions fade into the background and imagine that you yourself are in a golden circle of light, the radius of your outstretched arms. You can try it out again with your eyes closed to get a feeling for how big the room actually is. This circle of light is on the floor. You sit in the middle of this golden circle and in front of you there is a second golden circle of light, which is also on the floor. The circles touch each other; they lie next to each other without overlapping. The circle of light in front of you is empty.

Now imagine that the person you want to do this exercise with is standing or sitting in the middle of the circle in front of you. Everyone has their own circle, which also symbolizes their own space. Both circles are the same size. A neon blue light starts to flow at the point where the two circles touch each other. It flows within the golden circle of light, first on your left side around the other person back to the point where the circles touch each other and then continues to flow to your left side. It then goes all the way around you and then continues to flow in such a way as to create a figure of eight. When you finish this exercise after two or three minutes, let the neon blue light flow around the other person one last time. You then end at the point where the two circles touch each other.

Then take your time to finish the exercise at your own speed. Come back slowly and orient yourself in the room again with your eyes open.

The therapist allows the client's experience to be shared in the therapeutic situation. This debriefing serves as a basis for processing and mistakes and difficulties can be addressed. For example, one should take care to ensure that the two circles are really imagined as the same size and that the person in the opposite circle stay where it is and does not enter the client's circle or overlap with it. For clients who are able to engage in this, Phyllis Krystal recommends that they begin the exercise with an alignment with the dimension of awareness of the Higher Self (see chapter Y).

Working with basic patterns and counter-patterns (method O.7)

This method can easily be combined with a ritual such as the exercise "weeding, sowing seeds" (exercise O.4). This work originally comes from psychosynthesis. First, the client explores a basic pattern. This is then contrasted with a healing counter-pattern. This is very similar to the buddhist exercises, where we contrast our neurotic ego-identification with the healthy self-esteem of being a buddha or wisdom aspect (yidam).

For example, client M. reported that in her experience there was only direct attention and praise from her parents when she had done something special. "You are really such a lovely daughter; you have already set the table so well and you are so good at everything you do..." The client could not remember that she had a feeling of being loved and accepted even once without having done something else, like looking after the younger sister. There were still many memories of situations where she was praised for her performance and only in those situations, she felt loved. So, she formulated one of her basic patterns:

"I always had to do something to be loved." The basic pattern here is: love in return for performance. Other basic patterns often encountered are: "Whenever I am well, something bad happens" or: "I must not be well if the others feel bad."

In the therapeutic work of this method (method O.7) a new pattern, a counter-pattern, one could say a healing counter-pattern, or a new key sentence (method O.3) is sought. The counter-patterns should be completely right for the client and do not have to be linguistically perfect, often they are very short sentences that seem most fitting to the client.

In our example with the client M. with her pattern "I always had to do something to be loved" this would be the counter-pattern: "I am loved for my own sake without having to do anything for it." Or: "I am lovable for my own sake."

In the second example: "Whenever I am well, something bad happens. ("Don't rejoice too soon, the hard part is still to come") the counter-pattern could be: "I am allowed to be really well without worries, I am allowed to be happy". It is important to start with oneself before we – often prematurely – make the wish that others or even all living beings are happy.

In the third example: "I must not feel good when others feel bad", the counter-pattern could be: "Even when others feel bad, I can enjoy life...". After all, how else could we be of assistance to them? We should really make sure that we are doing well, especially when others are not doing so well.

The counter-pattern core sentences are developed together with the clients. They are sometimes the contrary to or the opposite of the basic pattern in the verbal formulation. Like the core sentences, they should be formulated without negation. Once the basic and counter-patterns have been found, this work can easily be coupled with an imaginative exercise (exercise O.2), which is later concluded with a ritual. This exercise was originally created by Piero Ferrucci, a psychosynthesis therapist from Florence.

Weeding weeds, sowing seeds (exercise O.4)

This exercise can be used in a variety of ways to initiate voluntary change processes. It can also be used, for example, to break away from undesirable behaviour, such as smoking, and establish a new behavioural pattern, such as regular exercise, in its place. We will now illustrate the exercise by breaking away from a basic pattern.

Sit comfortably and go with the awareness inside, maybe close your eyes and stay with your body sensations and breathing for a few moments.

Then imagine that you have weeded the weeds that you now want to burn. Here in the room, you light a fire in your imagination.

You pile up wood and light the fire with some paper. You watch the fire burn strongly. Then you write your basic pattern on a piece of cardboard or paper and then throw it deliberately with all your willpower into the fire and watch it burn very carefully. Then the whole fire burns down.

Now remember that you have symbolically freed yourself from this old basic pattern that has influenced your life for so long and affirm and strengthen this freedom that it has in this moment.

Then something new will be planted in the place of the weeds (sowing seeds).

To do this, you now take your counter-pattern or the new key sentence.

Think of this key sentence several times very carefully and bring all your willpower into it. You can also say the new sentence out loud. This will now continue to shape your life...

This ritual burning in imagination should ideally be followed by a real fire on the same day. The client could burn a paper at home somewhere – preferably outside – on which the old basic pattern is written and then "water" their new counter- pattern regularly, like the seeds of a plant. To do this, they can decide to contact the new sentence often, to think about it often, or to speak or write it often, to fill it with the power of awareness and will.

This practice is found among the Tibetans, where harmful things were written down and handed over to the wisdom fire. Liberated from the negative, one then offers gifts (into the imagined or real fire) and directs the mind towards something deeply positive, such as the realization of inner qualities. One also waters the positive counter-pattern through daily practice.

The Beach Ball (exercise 0.5)

The exercise with the symbol of the beach ball also serves as a delimitation or setting boundaries. Its function is to protect against external threats of a physical or verbal nature. This exercise originally comes from the Phyllis Crystal Imagination System.

Sit comfortably in your chair and focus your awareness on the sensations in your body, especially the sensations in your feet.

For a few moments, follow the rise and fall of the abdomen as you breathe in and out.

Then let these perceptions fade into the background and imagine that you are sitting inside a big beach ball – a simple, colourful beach ball, like you often see on the beach.

However, this beach ball that surrounds you is much bigger.

It has the radius of your outstretched arms on all sides.

You sit in the middle of the beach ball.

Any negativity that comes towards you from the outside simply bounces off the surface of the beach ball and you can feel completely safe.

It is filled with golden light on the inside, and you can see right through it.

Stay with this image for a few moments, for as long as you need and then come back to the room.

Open your eyes and orientate yourself in the room.

Debriefing helps to integrate. The therapist can encourage the client to do this exercise in real life situations where they feel threatened from the outside.

As a "protective circle", an exercise of this kind is an integral part of many Tibetan practices. The light tent in which we sit is a protective space created by our clear inner Page 396 perspective and wisdom. No harmful, intrusive thoughts can enter this space of protective awareness – awareness recognizes them immediately and puts an end to them. The same applies to the following exercise of the light cylinder – the Tibetan tradition visualizes it as large as the entire mental space.

The Cylinder of Light (exercise O.6)

The following exercise offers a subtle protection. Especially for people who experience themselves as highly sensitive. The exercise makes it easier to stay with themselves and not to get lost in too many sensory impressions. It originally comes from the Phyllis Krystal Imagination System.

Sit comfortably in your chair and focus your awareness on the sensations in your body, especially the sensations in your feet. For a few moments, follow the rise and fall of the abdomen as you breathe in and out. Then let these perceptions fade into the background and imagine that you are in a golden circle of light. This circle is on the floor and has the radius of your outstretched arms.

Then imagine how this golden circle of light now becomes a cylinder of golden light. You pull the circle upwards. It can also be imagined like a curtain of golden light. This visualisation can go as far upwards as you want or need.

Then please imagine that everything around you in this light cylinder is filled with golden light. This golden light protects you from very subtle forces that sometimes exist between people (for example: influence or manipulation) and helps you to be more with yourself and to preserve your own "space".

This defined space of your light cylinder can be closed above your head by a cover of golden light, if the cylinder reaches that far. You are in the centre of your light cylinder and completely present to yourself.

Feel how it feels inside your light cylinder and then, if you like, come back to the room keeping the idea of your light cylinder. Open your eyes and orient yourself in the room.

A debriefing session is used for processing. The client can be encouraged to use this imagination in situations with other people, where they are worried that their inner space might be violated or where they have the impression that they are being taken over. The light cylinder is particularly suitable for highly sensitive people as a daily exercise.

The Shining Star (exercise O.7)

This exercise is an imagination method that reduces anxiety symptoms – it originates from the Phyllis Krystal Imagination System.

Sit comfortably in your chair and focus your awareness on the sensations in your body, especially the sensations in your feet. For a few moments, follow the rise and fall of the abdomen as you breathe in and out. Let these sensations fade into the background.

Now think of an event where you have experienced fear. It may have been a strong experience of fear or an easily manageable fear. Experience this situation again in your imagination and feel the corresponding sensations in your body.

Where in the body is it located as a feeling of tension? What does it remind you of? (For example, glowing coal, a drill, a fist).

Now imagine above your head in front of you a star of golden light, which is attached to a pulley. Pull it down and let it stop about 15 cm in front of your solar plexus.

Then please breathe out the symbol chosen for your fear (for example the glowing coal). In the middle of the light star there is something like a black hole. The exhaled fear symbol (glowing coal) is attracted by it like a magnet and disappears into it.

Then you absorb the golden light that emanates from the light star with your inbreath and fill the space where the anxiety sensations were in your body with it.

After some time (5 minutes at most), when the sensations of anxiety are no longer perceptible, push this light star back over your head to its starting position.
Then come back to the room again, open your eyes and orientate yourself in the room.

This exercise can be repeated with other anxiety inducing situations. Light breathing should not last longer than 5 minutes. In the debriefing session, it is useful for the therapist to get the client to share what has been experienced. The exercise resembles in some respects a Tibetan practice called the purification breath.

Here, one breathes out intensely dark light that dissolves in the vastness of existence and then breathes in five-coloured light like in a nourishing stream, which fills us with the blessing of fivefold timeless awareness (see introduction to chapter B) – also called the blessing of the "dakinis".

Pendulum for Decision Making (exercise O.8)

This exercise can be used for all kinds of difficulties in decision-making. It begins with an analytical part where the client is asked to collect all the arguments for and against a decision. For example: What are the arguments for renting this apartment, what are the arguments against it? What are the arguments for continuing the relationship with your wife, what are the arguments against it? The therapist names the questions. Then the client is asked to tell the therapist all the pros and cons and writes them down themself.
Then the second part of the exercise begins:

Sit comfortably in your chair and focus your awareness on the sensations in your body, especially the sensations in your feet. For a few moments, follow the rise and fall of the abdomen as you breathe in and out.

Then close your eyes and lift your hands with your forearms a little bit to the side so that they don't cross over, the palms of your hands open and pointing upwards. This results in something like a scale, where the hands with the forearms embody the scales.

Now you decide in which hand you want to put the pro-arguments and in which hand you want to put the contra-arguments. Then, I will read you the pro-arguments you have mentioned, and you will put each of them one by one into the corresponding hand (in our example the client has the decision about whether he wants to change his job as a question; he determines the right hand as pro-argument hand, the left hand as contra- argument hand).The therapist observes how the pro-arguments hand sinks further down with each argument read out.

Next, the therapist reads the contra-arguments to the patient one by one, and the client is asked to put these contra-arguments in his left hand during the exercise. The therapist observes how the left hand now moves down, and the right hand rises again.

After all arguments are read out, the client is asked to let the balance swing. The therapist observes, where the hands move to. Then the therapist asks, if the scale is now completely balanced. If the client says yes, the therapist asks the client for a percentage estimate. (In our example this was 65 percent pro and 35 percent contra).

The client is asked to open his eyes again and finish the exercise. This exercise makes it clear to the client in his internally which direction his decision is moving in. It beautifully illustrates the decision-making process.

A dharma variant of this exercise could be to question, in the same way, how weighty the arguments are in the face of the four traditional basic thoughts with which we can clarify our priorities. How weighty is the argument (1) in view of the precious opportunity of this life? (2)

In view of the fact of constant change and the possibility of death at any time? (3) In view of the long-term effects of our decision or action? (4) In view of true happiness and the realization of our deepest goals in life?

Transition to Focusing

Focusing is, from a Dharma perspective, a healing application of the fourfold cultivation of awareness (chapter E). It is a wonderful way to combine mindfulness of the body (physical formations) with the exploration of emotional states and moods (mental formations and mind). Without falling into analysis, Focusing explores the connections between something that moves us emotionally and physical experience. It then rests in the physical experience with the awareness and associatively allows further emotional issues to rise in consciousness. Thus, connections, deeper concerns and inner principles ("Dharmas") become obvious and, in addition, by staying awake and unwaveringly present to our experience, possible shifts reveal themselves. Through loving, accepting "awareness", there is increasing relaxation, until the central "shift" in experience takes place, where we see the world and especially the initial problems in a completely different light – deeply solved.

In Dharma, too, just like in Focusing, a process language has developed in which perceptions are not captured, but rather followed in their fluid, elusive nature, always open to the new – and always knowing that words can only be pointers and are never able to capture the actual experience. This is how the intuition develops for what is underneath or behind the words – a delicate experience that is all too easily hidden from grasping conceptual thinking and labels. Hence, language is suspended as subtle hints of the inexpressible are forever in process at the service of awareness.

P. Focusing – A Door into Essential Psychotherapy

by Astrid Schillings

Focusing is what Eugene Gendlin, philosopher and professor of psychology, calls the time spent with something that is not clear but can be felt concretely in the body. This "sensation" certainly has something to do with something in our lives – a question, a decision, a creative project or something difficult, perhaps even painful, sometimes it has to do with the meaning of our life or the lack of it. Thus, it is not the uncomfortable chair or tight-fitting shoe. It is an awareness that goes along with something that is physically palpable without us already knowing what it is. We only sense from within the experience that it relates somehow to a situation or an aspect of our life. Gendlin calls the physical sensing of "all this" with a situation, an idea, or a question about life *felt sense*. It is an artificial word that he developed especially for this purpose. Another description Gendlin has used for it is *Edge of Awareness*. Something that shows itself at the edge of awareness, and we can feel that there is more still...

A *Felt Sense* can come with regard to anything in our lives, from a simple matter to a deep question – we can turn to all of these and let the *Felt Sense* come to us. We pause for a moment and trace the resonance that arises in our bodily experience – for example, a response to a person who we don't even know how we knew. Maybe it feels very dominant in the body or quite subtle or even shifting. So, if we stay on the edge of our awareness with this physical sensation, it can open up and more will reveal itself. We realize that it may be "joyfully vast" or "tightly restrained" – and still we don't know where we know the person from, but our physical resonance lets us feel more and more what kind of encounter we have had with this person. Our bodily experience knows more than we are aware of at the moment. Everything we have experienced with this person is fully registered.

If we have patience and continue to stay with the unfolding *Felt Sense*, it may suddenly occur to us: "Oh, that's how we know each other!" Usually this realization – oh yes, that's it – is accompanied by a physical relief, a release of tension. It is a physical change that Gendlin calls *Felt Shift*. Probably, each one of us has experienced that at some point.

How was Focusing found?

As a philosopher, Eugene Gendlin investigated the question of how meaning arises from non-linguistic experience and how non-linguistic experience and meaning change.

He wanted to develop a new embodied experiential phenomenology. A subtle zigzagging movement between experience and language or image, it could even be between experience and a gesture or symbol – any representation on the edge of awareness.

Important for Gendlin is that we do not move from concept to concept, idea to idea or image to image, perhaps not realizing that our actual life is not changing, not really touched.

In the psychotherapy research of the 1950s/60s around Carl Rogers (one of the founders of humanistic psychology), how people change in therapy was investigated and what the conditions for this change were. This was also very interesting for Gendlin from a philosophical point of view and so he joined the Chicago group focused on Rogers. The researchers had recorded, classified and analysed hundreds of therapy sessions for their investigations. The results were surprising in several respects. People who changed in therapies often paused, as if they were stuttering a little – for example: "Yes, I was angry about... (pause)... Eh, eh... no not really angry, (pause)... Eh, rather excited, almost fluttery... (pause)... Yes, and... eh... there's also something worried in there... (pause)... OK yes, something worried..."

It was the ability to dwell in and with an unclear physical sensation and to keep this unclear, not so special sensation and to be able to relate to it. This is a special quality of attention, a way of being with oneself, which these people already brought into the therapy.

As the example shows, it was not the already known, pre-defined feelings such as sadness or anger that were addressed, nor did considerations and interpretations seem to be the decisive factor that brought about change. It was rather the pause, a break, an introspection into something that is physically felt but not or not yet clear. Gendlin wanted to make this essence of successful change processes communicable so that it would be accessible to all people. Thus, focusing was born as an invitation to experience a natural human process of change.

Focusing is therefore not an additional method, but an attitude in and towards life and a development-related awareness. For Eugene Gendlin Focusing is a philosophical practice for life and existence. A special application of this practice is the Focusing-oriented therapy. Both aspects are relevant for Essential Psychotherapy.

The self as a process

There were other surprising results in research: people in successful therapies increasingly experienced themselves as a *process*. They no longer perceived themselves as a fixed self that they identified with certain concepts and perceptions. Instead, their decisions and behaviours were rooted in their experience of the current situation. Their concepts and ideas about themselves were constantly changing or were even discarded in their immediate experience. This was a groundbreaking observation at the time. For it had been assumed that the self was fixed and would only change in a limited way through therapy.

Carl Rogers then formulated the concept of the *Fully Functioning Person*, a person who lives from the inner authority of their organismic experience, spontaneously and authentically, according to the current existential situation. But Gendlin went even further in his philosophically precise investigations.[67]

In his "Theory of Personality Change" (1964) he makes a radical paradigm shift from content to process. He describes the self and all life as a *permanent* (on-going) *interaction and ongoing interactional process:*

> "The self exists to the extent that the individual carries and continues the processes he feels through his own symbolizations (words, images, thoughts, gestures, signs) and through his behaviour or attention."

Gendlin does not assume a fixed self, but something that changes every moment and only exists in so far as it is alive in interaction. If this interdependency is interrupted, it does not unfold (at least in this way) or does not exist. It might be interesting to consider this description together with the process of the five skandhas described elsewhere in this book.

The inner relationship to experience – The client's client

To illustrate the dynamics of change, I (Astrid) would like to start with an example from therapeutic practice:

A thirty-two-year-old man presents himself for therapy. About a year ago, he hit a six-year-old girl in his car. After several operations the girl will probably be left with a limp. He had worked through the shock, and now he realized that he was not to blame, since the child had suddenly run into the street between parked cars. He could not see her. He knows that he has to accept the accident as something that

67 As a psychologist, later professor of psychology, he developed together with M. H. Klein, P. L. Mathieu, and D. J. Kiesler, the so-called "Experiencing Scale" (University of Wisconsin, 1970) to scientifically investigate the depth of experience and change in therapeutic processes.

just happened, and he gets support through his meditation group. Nevertheless, there is something of a shadow over him.

Client: I cannot understand it. I realize that it's not my fault, not even paying attention would have helped. The girl really ran into my car.
Therapist: You actually did everything right and yet it happened
Client: Yes, at first I thought I couldn't drive anymore. Then Somatic Experiencing helped me. I can do it again – and yet, somehow, I can't accept what happened. I did everything right.
Therapist: You did everything right and yet you couldn't control it.
Client (*with a thin voice*): I just wish it hadn't happened. But nobody has anything that can change it.
Therapist: I hear this simple wish: 'I wish it had not happened.'
Client: Yes, but it doesn't change anything.
Therapist: Even if it may sound absurd: how would it be, just as a little experiment, to trace this wish once, see how this simple wish feels in the body – maybe there is a resonance in the stomach or in the chest? (pause) ...you can also close your eyes if that helps.
Client takes his attention inside and closes his eyes.
Client: I don't really know; I don't feel anything.
Therapist: OK, and would it be possible to give this 'not feeling' in there some time? It must be unusual for you to feel there. All this with the wish. 'May something come.' Something like this can be very subtle, warm or expansive, constrained or heavy, there may be some resonance in there with all that... *Pause... dwelling...*
Client: There might be something, something quiet, something disbelieving... OK...?
Therapist: Is it possible to give the silent, almost disbelieving, time to be there?
Client: OK... *Pause... Dwelling... Client starts to nod very slowly.*
Therapist: Here comes a fine, slow nod.
Client: Yes, there is this sentence: 'I wish it hadn't happened. It should not have happened.'
Therapist: There is this sentence inside you: 'I wish it hadn't happened.'

Client: Yes. *The fine slow nodding continues.*

Therapist: Is it possible to stay with this 'I wish it hadn't happened', to keep it company?

Client: (*Nodding continues*) It's warm, trickling warm from the head through the throat into the heart.

Therapist: Ah, yes, it's warm, trickles warm from the head through the neck and into the heart.

Client: Yes, and somehow it continues. *Deep outbreath.*

Therapist: Somehow it goes further inside you.

The face relaxes; the nodding becomes smaller until it slowly stops completely.

Client: It feels good to feel this desire, ...it is a heart's desire.

Therapist: A heart's desire – and it feels good to feel it in there. How does it feel to take your time, so that the wish has room to be felt? *Deep breathing again.*

Client: (*The eyes open. Relieved breathing.)* Yes, the wish is there. And it feels healthy, somehow right ... (pause) ... I wish in my heart that it had not happened. That is the truth. Even if it did happen.

Therapist: 'This is the truth. Even if it did happen.' You feel a great relief there. Yes, it happened, and in your heart, you wish it hadn't happened.

This section shows some focusing elements. I will discuss them here in terms of the inner relationship to experience. First of all, there is *simple listening*, i.e. listening to what moves the client and repeating it back. Gendlin also calls this *hearing back*. If a person feels heard, they are, in most cases open to engage with more depth. They feel the space, and security, to listen to their inner experience. Gendlin also says: *The client of the client*, which means that the client begins to listen to her or his own experience, in the same way that a good therapist hopefully listens to their clients.

With this client I first of all repeated back everything that was clear to him. And then I also repeat what is on the edge of awareness, that is, what is implied: somehow a "being able to control the situation", if you had done everything right. And that is the moment when the client jumped to his wish that it should not have happened. But his reason and probably also his spiritual aspirations reject this wish as a "wish to escape".

In Focusing, people like to invite what has not been heard, what sounds unclear or inconspicuous. This was my therapeutic invitation: "How is it, in its entirety, with the desire to feel into it?"

When the client got involved and felt into his body experience, the felt sense unfolded. He kept it in awareness: this warmth trickling down the neck... the nodding, as a gesture, is part of the unfolding felt sense. Then in the further staying present, a felt shift happened, the process of life "carries on", as Gendlin says, or "continues". What was not allowed to be felt, this heart's desire, brings the change. The client listened to his wish for the first time. Now that the wish was allowed to come alive, he can acknowledge that it was there. Both the wish and what happened are part of this human situation. Nothing is rejected. Everything can be there.

The language of process

An important helpful aspect, the *process language* that is typical of focusing, is also apparent the above section. It may sound a little strange at first, but for many people it speaks directly to the physical sensation.

"I am experiencing *something* in me. I feel, I experience something inside me that feels warm, or there is something silent inside me." This language opens space, physically felt space. "There is something in me and I am more than this or that content." The language helps to dwell with this 'something' so that it can open up, and more can come...

Words describing physical sensations are used again and again to invite the feeling into the body experience like something "constrained", "expansive", "heavy", "tingling"... etc. Especially for people who are not used to feeling into their sensations, this helps them to find the level where they can sense in order to feel the *whole of the situation.* (More on this below). We can feel *what* it is, also *how* and *where* it can be felt.

So, for example, *how* is it pleasant, *how* is it unpleasant, *how* is it neutral..., *how* is it alive in the body...

We do not ask *why* something is. This usually invites a distance from experience and can lead to thinking. There are meditations in which it can be helpful to label experience in this way. In other situations, categorizing or minimising, for example: "This is sadness, anger, this is neutral, this is pleasant etc." But it can also block the path to immediate, fresh experience and thus hinder change. Focusing helps, no matter which view of life or spiritual orientation we have, to find among all our concepts a direct connection to experience. We become intimate with our life.

The slowing down, the pauses, the dwelling are actively invited in order to give the sensing time and to create the space in which the Felt Sense can unfold.

At the top of the segment, the client was invited to stay with his wish. At first, he did not feel anything. Then the invitation: "...would it be possible to give this 'non feeling' in there some time? Together with the wish, that maybe something will come. Something like this can be very subtle, warm or expansive, constrained or heavy, and there may be resonance in there with all that..." made it possible for him to find some feeling. Only by staying present can the small changes, the precise resonances be felt. These movements of life are easily overlooked in the speed and apparent clarity of conventional language. It needs this space, which the related awareness holds. In this space the fresh life comes by itself.

Related awareness

Gendlin speaks of "holding in awareness and letting (life) come" or of "being aware and letting it come". "Being aware" is therefore not static; awareness is interactive (I will go into the exact meaning of this later on). We keep something that wants to make itself known, in awareness, and in this way open up space for building a relationship with it. We refer to the feeling of the entire situation (mental state), the emerging Felt Sense.

> "The related awareness in Focusing gives space, keeps company. It has the quality of being with, allowing, marvelling, sharing interest, being committed to the process. Everything may be there. The related awareness does not identify itself and it does not disidentify itself. It makes space for more...".

Gendlin: "The body felt from the inside is at the same time a feeling of the environment." In his *philosophy of the implicit*, Gendlin develops an expanded understanding of the living body. When he talks about the body, he means far more than a kind of physiological machine:

> "Not only do we physically experience circumstances around us... our physical feeling body is actually part of a gigantic system, of the place here and other places, the time now and other times, of ourselves and other people – at the bottom of the whole universe. This feeling – of being physically alive in a vast system – is the body felt from within."[68]

Living bodies are part of and have never been separate from the environment, the situation. Even plants know directly about light, earth and water. They exist in and through interaction with the environment. So, there is not a plant in isolation, there is also the environment, and they interact. Plant, environment and interaction are not separate but continue to develop interactively. From the deep ground of the interaction between body and environment, the behaviour of animals, their five senses, their emotions and perception emerge as a continuing and increasingly complex movement of life. It is essential for Gendlin to refer to this: "Interaction First". For him therefore, interaction comes *before* perception. And it is the immediacy of this original interaction that is effective in all that lives.

68 Gendlin, 1978.

Mostly interaction is understood as a coming together of two factors. Gendlin "dynamizes" the understanding of interaction by saying: It is not that there is an ear and there is a sound that meet, and then there is "hearing". Rather, the hearing organ is created directly through interaction with a particular environment and in interaction with a particular organism. The human ear *implies* the hearing of certain sounds relevant to human life. Hearing organs of other living beings imply the hearing of other relevant sounds from their environment. Hearing is therefore not composed of different parts but is to be understood only as *a* process in which one implies the other and everything reacts to each other.

So, when we say "hearing" or "noise", this is already a human achievement in abstraction. In direct experience there is not here the ear and there the sound. This specific sound is experienced, the whirring of the engine, the chirping of the bird, the slamming of the door. It is a very specific interactive context that implies a certain complexity. Our bodily experience does not hear an abstract sound and then cognitively add that this was probably a slammed door. It becomes physical, not linguistic, knowledge.

As everything interacts with each other, everything is already changed at the moment of interaction. For example, when a person enters the room where I am working on something, at the moment of entering (i.e. interacting) both his body and my body are already changed. Everything is implicit in the situation, beginning with the breathing in, which implies the breathing out, up to this smile shared with a particular person in the situation. Everything we have experienced with each other so far interacts implicitly in this situation and continues our life. But it does not continue in the present arbitrarily, everything we have ever experienced together is experienced as a *dynamic, inter-effecting wholeness*. From there, further steps become possible.

The body senses the situation as a whole, not every detail separately. It does not put everything together through the senses and perception. By *situational body*, Gendlin means that the body experiences all the many implications of a situation, a question about life, an inexpressible feeling inside, it senses it as a whole.

The understanding of interaction as a process is thus *radically dynamized* in Gendlin's phenomenological studies of living. Nothing stands on its own, nothing is separate from any other, everything works with each other, but in a specific way. Gendlin speaks here of "intricacy", of complexity or multi-layeredness, not of a merged wholeness. In this way he abolishes dualities between the conscious and the unconscious, body experience and the soul, body and awareness, inside and outside, subject and object.

How does change come about?

Change needs a certain climate, an interactive atmosphere, in which there is a chance that we are able to physically sense and respond to situations. I would like to give the example of a story from the life of Buddha. This story has many versions. I have heard two of them at lectures and I am reproducing them from memory. The first version can be found in the Therīgāthā, the source of the second version is unfortunately not known to me.

> "A desperate woman comes to the Buddha. Her child has died, and she asks the Buddha to give her a medicine that will bring the child back to life. The Buddha says, 'If you can bring me three mustard seeds from a house where death has not yet occurred, I will give you this medicine'. The woman goes from house to house and people talk to her, want to help her, but in every house, in every family, someone has died. The woman returns to the Buddha. She understands that everyone dies."

I don't want to comment on the Buddha here but rather take a look at this story from a focusing point of view. It is very likely that this woman met other mothers whose child had died. This was not uncommon at the time. She probably experienced a lot of compassion, people who kept her company in her pain. She may have felt particularly understood at some point and something moved inside her. Something gave way in her. Yes, everyone dies. Everything is transitory. And she is not alone in this.

The Buddha did not give the woman in her pain a teaching on the Noble Truths or on other aspects of the path, but rather the possibility to live through her own personal process and to enter into a relationship with other people who could probably empathize because they knew such pain. All this helps the woman to feel her own situation. Through the experiences she shares with other people, she can change during her search and can experience how her personal situation expands and carries on as a whole.

> In the second version of the story, the woman comes to the Buddha and shows him her dead child that she is carrying in her arms. She asks the Buddha, "Don't I have a beautiful child? Do I not have a beautiful child?" It is said that the Buddha felt compassion in his heart and after a long silence answered: "Yes, you have a beautiful child."

In this version, the Buddha is side by side with the woman, where she is faltering in her pain. He stays there with her, is silent, is *there* in silence. From there he tells the woman, "Yes, you have a beautiful child." Nothing more. No verbal teaching, no saying that the child is dead after all. There is also no reporting that the woman says anything else. The content does not seem to change. The context, the interaction, changes the situation. The woman gets the chance to stay present in the "Yes, I have a beautiful child". Maybe she feels a physical resonance, maybe the felt meaning of her words "I have a beautiful child" change while consciously staying present, maybe the resting makes space for more...

How would it be for you to try this for yourself? And to rest present with these words yourself, with the words of the mother and the Buddha in this situation.

First, I invite you to feel for a moment into your bodily experience, how you are sitting, how are your feet and legs, sitting in an armchair or wherever, how it feels to breathe maybe... And then you linger in your chest cavity, where breathing is alive. And now I invite you to be with this sentence "Yes, I have a beautiful child". All this with the context of the whole situation, how does it feel? What is the resonance? If you allow yourself a break from reading...

You will have experienced a process of your own. It's not about whether thoughts came or not, a memory, words, pictures, physically felt sensations or a moment of change. I suggest that you honour what has come for a little while before you read on.

I would also like to say a few words about my process. The second version of the story did not leave my mind for several years because I did not really understand it. Only in a Focusing process, in which I myself kept all this in awareness with the described situation, could I feel how the meaning of the words, the sentences, slowly changed in interaction with my experience:

> If I allow the pause... I feel a vastness in my chest, a slightly sad, somehow melancholic vastness. And here comes the memory. How I was with the dead body of a loved one. Touching him, feeling the cold of his body in terror, holding his hand. The consternation in me, how beautiful he was there in this quiet being, deeply relaxed. How slowly out of all this an expansive love became palpable in me... This brought amazement and came completely unexpectedly...

If we dwell with something, keep it in the physically felt awareness, an unexpected door can open...

Change arises in interaction – Awareness as a process

Above I spoke about an environment, an interactional atmosphere, which is helpful for change. In both versions of the story of the Buddha and the woman with the dead child, interaction between people was implied. However, this is usually not explicitly emphasized as an effective factor in the telling of the story. It is only said that people could not give her mustard seeds because death was already in every family. The story also does not tell how the woman's relationship to her experience changes. Rather the result, her insight "Life is transitory" is reported, but not the process.

Interaction is an effective factor on several levels: as interaction *between* people, i.e. *inter-personal*, and as contact with one's own experience, i.e. *intra-personal.*

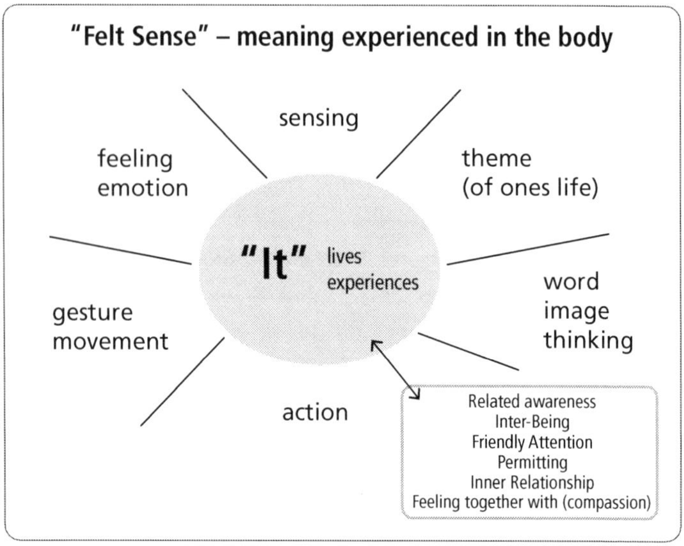

It is true for most sentient beings that the members of their own species are each other's most important environment. In psychotherapy, this "from person to person" as a *therapeutic environment* is worthy of special attention. Focusing orientation means in psychotherapy first and foremost that I, as a therapeutic companion, make sure that I am *there*, that I can be *there*. This seems to be something simple, but it is not self-evident.

How am I, the person who comes to me vulnerable or in trouble, other human beings, the environment? Have I been able to give this person space to really hear him or her? Focusing does not mean that I have to teach all patients focusing or how to find the Felt Sense fastest by following certain instructions. But Focusing can help me as a therapist to be *with* the client in a better way. The way I am *there* is an effective factor in the therapeutic situation, and it is immediately communicated, from body sense to body sense.

Is it possible that the therapist can be there without hiding behind a role? And be it the process expert? Or be able to pick out therapeutic steps from all the methodological tools they have? Is it possible to be there with a person without anything in between? For Gendlin, this question was decisive for every therapeutic encounter:

> "Can I accompany the person inside, who looks at me through these eyes, who is trying to find a way to live?"[69]

The therapist should therefore be in good contact with all the implications of this in their own life, if it is needed for the process.

> "Where the therapist cannot be intimately in tune with their own life, at least potentially, they will find it difficult to support the client to be intimate with his or her life. It therefore requires the continued openness of the therapist to get to know their own life and experience."[70]

As a therapist, I can let the client know in a way that is appropriate for them that I want to support them in coming into contact with what actually want to live. Where the life actually is. I can let her know that

---

69 Personal remark to the author, 2005

70 Personal remark to the author, 2003

we will work together to take care of what hurts or is afraid, what doesn't know what to do.

I offer them the chance to find out how this fear, this question, this (...) can move on, if they are willing with my support to get to know "these places within", so that they can open up. This is often understood surprisingly well. I ask the client to tell me immediately if they does not feel understood.

What I am interested in is that they can slowly gain confidence in their own life process, confidence that life lives itself out on its own and that they are ultimately not dependent on someone telling them how to live – whether in everyday life or in their search for spiritual meaning. All situations in life, every suggestion, every piece of advice, every teaching can be sensitively checked out in their own experience on the edge of awareness. This is what I work for as a therapist.

With the paradigm shift *from content to the process of the living body*, Gendlin opens up an expanded understanding of the unconscious and learning. He points out how, from a perspective of life, every disturbance, every disruption, something "psychopathological", is an interrupted movement of life. Something unable to be continued in a life situation, causes disability or freeze. The unconscious is therefore not understood by Gendlin as already existing content. Or a history of dysfunctional learning, not as something that needs to be restructured from the outside. Gendlin needs this twist, this shift of paradigm: How was life trying to live? Where did it want to go, and how was it interrupted? What was implied and then somehow could not happen? No theory, no model, no method, no diagnostic description is rejected with this.

Rather, Gendlin wants to uncover the source of change with his investigation of the nature of change.[71]

As therapists, we can rely on the fact that life knows how to live by itself. The living body sense interacts directly with everything... with culture, social forms, traditions, evolution, personal situations, language... also with the therapist's body sense/presence. And in this immediate, spontaneous interaction it always brings something new, implies more... Our life and experience lives from the deep foundation of the direct interaction of all existence (Interaction First) and always brings another new step. This life and movement of experience is always quicker than conscious perception... Here a concrete process:[72]

Process description (case study)

A 67-year-old woman, Marga S., retired executive, divorced and mother of two successful daughters, came down with moderate depression and anxiety. She had suffered a heart attack while riding her bicycle a year ago. After rehabilitation she suffered from neurological limitations such as orientation problems and memory gaps. She had practiced mindfulness meditation for 15 years before the accident.

---

71 Working materials from the *Focusing Institute Cologne, 2013.* Only if I do not forget that all diagnoses, concepts and theories do not describe the individual human being – because every human being is different – can I place all these diagnoses and concepts next to me via therapy, ready to hand at any time. Because every theory and every description of diagnosis emphasizes something that can help to understand experience and make implicit things clear. Perhaps it describes a way of being in the world that I never would have thought of myself. But it must not stand between the therapist and the client. This also applies to Focusing. But I can also take one or two books of wisdom or works of literature or art, basically everything that has ever helped people, into the therapy room so that it can be there when it is needed. Like for example just this fairy tale, which meets the Felt Sense, this therapeutic situation and helps to move the process. This is then not a cognitive-eclectic accumulation, but by running the process through the physical Felt Sense, I have all of this available as possible implication of my lived life.

72 Presentation World Congress for Psychotherapy, 2010.

Her meditation teacher showed compassionate empathy, which was good for the patient. He gently encouraged her to accept everything. The patient came when she felt so anxious and depressed that she Page realized she needed help.

So far, we have worked for about 20 hours. Feelings of fear, shame, desperation rose in her when she was disoriented in familiar places. She has found a deep feeling of loneliness and abandonment, and she can feel that there are two places in her: the "now" place where she feels alone in the acute disorientation and a place that feels "like earlier" through which she comes into contact with her small inner child who feels abandoned. Through the therapy sessions she can turn to this inner child.

Client: It works now and again to symbolically hold the little one *(her inner child)* when this feeling of abandonment appears. This is the one from back then. And somehow it works. If I don't know where I am now, I can ask people for help sooner.

Therapist: ... you can really feel it now, how both places are there. You can hold the child from when you were young, and you can now ask for help when you need it...

Client: Yes... *(I sense a slight hesitation)*

Therapist: ...and that is somehow not yet over... *(The somehow is an invitation to something vague, which I sense in the client's hesitation).*

Client: I don't know... *(small break)* Nevertheless, I am sometimes so completely confused, run here and there. I panic and can't calm down.

Therapist: There's something completely confused, even panicky, and you can't calm down then. *(I wait to see how she reacts. She will name what is important now and with what comes next, we can pause).*

Client: Yes, I am completely confused.

Therapist: There is something in you that feels completely confused. Is it good to keep this one company, this 'totally confused' one?

Client: Yes, maybe from here it is. I am just confused when I am alone and then I panic.

Therapist: So here there is space to keep this company, all this – being confused. *(Here probably means this (therapy) space, here with me. She feels safe enough here. The relationship-space creates some free space)*

Client: Yes. *Silence.*

Therapist: Take your time with it, I am also here... *(I want to let her know that she can take the time she needs to explore it with her attention. I let her know that I am there and that she doesn't need to do anything to keep our contact) Silence.*

Client: Somehow this is not just confused.

Therapist: There is more... *(I help her to make space for something that wants to come.) Pause.*

Client: Yes, there is something which is somehow odd.

Therapist: There's something strange. *(I supported her to stay with the funny thing there even before the confusion and panic arise that flood this unclear, fine being there in a way that she does not notice it.)*

Client: Yes, it's odd.

Therapist: Is it possible to stay with this strange, how it feels in the body? *Silence. She closes her eyes.*

Client: Yes, strange, strange ... like wrong.

Therapist: Like wrong...

Therapist: Can you let this strangely wrong feeling be there and feel the resonance it creates in the body?

Client: It feels like something pressing and hollow in my chest.

Therapist: Is it possible to let this like hollow impression be there? *I encourage her to keep this hollow-like impression in awareness. Process language helps the experience to feel recognized and to continue. We sit together in silence while she takes her time to listen into this hollow impression. I myself reconnect freshly with the ground under my feet, the air, the light in the room, feel the further existence, feel the ground within me. I feel that something wants to come out intensely in the patient and I want to support her to bear with not knowing what it is. From there I say:*

Therapist: I am here, let me know if you need anything. There seems to be a lot going on in there. *She is very quiet and nods slightly.*

Client: Yes... like a search... I feel that it is there.

Therapist: You feel that it is there... *I keep her company on the edge of awareness.*

Client: I do not want to live. *She gasps for breath. Her eyes open.* I do not want to live. I have experienced everything that I need to. I had two daughters, good work and experienced love with my friends and family. Why should I still be here now?

Therapist: This is what is coming now: Why should you still be here? *I am a bit cautious in repeating back and the phrase this is what's coming now is meant to help make room if needed.*

Client: I should not have been saved. *Tears slowly stream from her eyes, and a deep sigh rises.* It was done. *Silence.*

Therapist: Your life felt complete as it was, and you wished so much that you had not been saved. *I also give feedback on the intensity in the so much. The client starts to tremble, especially the chin and legs.*

Therapist: Is it possible to let the shaking go through? Can you feel the floor, the chair? *She nods and I notice that it works for her. The tremor is part of the discharge after some shocks or traumatic reactions.* Yes, you can let it be there, the tremor.

Client: Yes. Uhh ...

Therapist: Take your time ... *I say such short sentences again and again so that she feels how I am with her and that this tremor can have as much space as it needs and how it carries her process forward. I also make inviting noises like: Mm, Yes, yes, Ok, stay there, yes... Again, and again I say: Yes, yes, this could be it... In this way I can support her attention so that she can continue to keep her fresh experience in awareness. I also ask: Is the floor still there? The armchair? I support her in finding her base, her own ground. – Slowly the trembling subsides. – She becomes very still. Her arms start to move... subtle, slightly undulating movements... I feel the movements within me, feel the resonance within me, my arms move with me... It feels soft and wide. I accompany this for a while and answer it from my feeling of the whole.*

Therapist: It's almost like little waves that move... *After a few more moments the trembling stops and only her upper body swings slightly. With a gentle pulsating nod.*

Client: It is somehow the stream of life... just expansive... *We sit there, breathing, long silence...* Now I can live a new life. And I should not have been saved.

The client later recounts how confusing it was to relearn everything about life – what a table is and a bed. She had to get acquainted with her house all over again, to her friends. She had ignored this confusion, although she had been clear from the start with the knowledge: "My life was complete, and I shouldn't be here." But the people around her, who honestly meant well with her, were overwhelmed by this and could not hear her. So, she became confused and felt guilty of not being grateful for her rescue.

As a therapist I accompany the client to the edge of awareness, where what wants to be lived implicitly is still faltering... Her knowledge "I should not have been saved" could not move on, because in the interaction with her life, her friends, her meditation teacher it was and remained *blocked*. This caused confusion and panic in the patient. In this vulnerable state she was not able to trust her inner truth. But she took the step into therapy.

Every time the client felt understood in therapy, her experience was repeated back very precisely and given a symbol, it could open up and move on again, the meaning could transform (shift). This is experienced as a relief, usually a sigh of relief. The repeating back is therefore not simply a mirroring or reflection by the therapist. It requires a force of heart and awareness in the therapist, physically, to hold this unclear what is not known yet, to keep the client company from there and – if needed – to repeat her words again and again.

In the above process the change arises out of a mood of depression. The bodily experience of the client interacts directly with the associated awareness and brings about the shift: "Hollow like impression". Again, we remain in the awareness of sensing and thus create more space again and again. Nothing can be overlooked. We cannot *make* the next shift. It can only arise from life itself.

Open questions and intuitions

As the above process illustrates, in phases where the life process gets stuck, focusing offers the opportunity to work with open questions or impulses[73] and thus realign the client's attention. Examples of such intuitions are: "Maybe you can feel what it is that makes you so constrained and sad or so... is it something in your life?" or "When you are with it, what does it actually want or what is the essence here? "When you are ... where would it want to live, where is fresh air?"

Even the act of rejection or resistance can be openly addressed by the therapist: "There is something that... would rather not go there." Or: "There is something that feels defiant and we listen to it, get to know it. We listen to what defends itself and does not want to go there. We listen to how it is likely to feel and what it wants or doesn't want in that place. Anything is allowed to be present – even ambivalences. We can repeat these back as two aspects, for example: "Ah, there is something in you that actually wants to paint this picture, that feels like it has warmth and dynamism and there is another place (part) that prevents you from being creative.

This too is explored and brings about the next step.

Structure-bound experience

Focusing orientation during a therapy helps the therapist to be with the client with the therapeutic relationship through the development of his own felt sense. It is about the question: What exactly does this therapeutic relationship need? The client is neither interrupted nor

73 Focusing Institut Cologne, 2005.

simply mirrored. As a therapist I feel the felt sense of the present interaction and respond out of it in such a way that the interaction proceeds with a quality that goes beyond old patterns, i.e. the blocked life process of the client.

In "A Theory of Personality Change" (1964) Gendlin also describes the blocked life process as a *structure-bound process of experience* of the client. Structure-bound experience is no longer in contact with its many implicit meanings. It skips over the experiencing process, no longer participates in it. We have seen this in the process examples.

> "Structural bonds can arise, for example, when parents or other important people were unable to meet the needs of their children, even in the event of loss or trauma. Structural dependence means suffering; the experience is limited and rigid".

The therapist connects to the part of the experience that "works" and, beyond that, to what the client implicitly wants to experience. This is the edge of the physical sensing awareness. They focus not on the deficits, but on the deeper nature of change. In the structure-bound state the client needs the answer, the lived resonance of the therapist, in order to be able to interact once more with the blocked process. In this phase they will often feel more like themself in the presence of the therapist than when alone or in relationships where they are exposed to judgement or lack of empathy.

It becomes clear that the question of indication and contra-indication is only partially relevant in focusing oriented work, because – as shown – the familiar intimacy of the therapist with their own felt sense to the therapeutic relationship and the client's experience is fundamental. Interestingly, it is not possible to predict from the diagnosis whether focusing will be difficult for the client or not. Depending on the complexity of the structural dependence, e.g. if a feeling in the body is initially experienced as threatening, it may take a long time before the client can connect with the life process through focusing.

As humans we *are* life, and we keep it in awareness.

Whole Body Focusing

I (Astrid) don't want to end this presentation of the Focusing process without taking a look at Whole Body Focusing. In this development of Focusing, we work explicitly, i.e. consciously, with the deeper base of environment interaction between the body and its environment. We have seen that in classical focusing this interaction is always encouraged in the background, when we slow down, when we allow for pauses to feel the whole of a situation, even when creating open space. However, it is not explicitly named. Non-verbal experience (movement, gestures and posture) plays a special role in Whole body focusing. It expands the possible ways of connecting with what wants to be experienced.

In Whole Body Focusing I first allow myself to be grounded in presence – I allow my body experience to be consciously present, to feel how it connects with the ground, the earth, how gravity is at play, how it rises up in us, ... also the interplay with the environment, the light, the air, other life. Deeper reality is consciously invited, whereas in classical Focusing it is implicit. This means that different dimensions of experience can open up.

Out of grounding oneself in being present the next explicit step arises "Life lives by itself". And how that is, is immediately explored physically: "How does the foot want to place itself, how does the body want to sit, breathe, stand up, how does it want to eat, drink? What does it need to be present? Can I allow yawning, stretching, shaking?" The self-regulation of the organism is given space and time ... *body time, being time.*[74] It is explored anew through the relationship with grounded presence. Through this interaction the body also has the chance to regulate stress, shock and aspects of trauma. We enable a felt sense of our embodied existence as a whole to develop and if we allow this to happen again and again, our attitude towards life and who we think we are will change.[75]

74 Focusing Institute Cologne, 2011.

75 This has far-reaching implications for stress and illness management, burnout prevention and work organization.

Here a story comes to mind that is attributed to Master Bankei, an unorthodox Zen master in 17th century Japan: a priest approached him, boasting about the miraculous powers his master possessed. Then he challenged Bankei to show what he could do. Bankei replied, "When I am hungry, I eat, and when I am thirsty, I drink." With these simple words Bankei points to the real miracle. By exploring this life, which is alive on its own, in its direct simplicity, our everyday experience gains a sense of wonder and depth.

Another aspect of Whole Body Focusing which differs from classical Focusing is the ability to turn a specific place within us by asking: "Does anything need my attention? Maybe there is a question, a project or even something difficult in my life, where it is faltering, maybe a recurring feeling of abandonment, inhibition, pain? Of course, it could also be a new step in life that I don't quite dare to take yet." We invite the resonance in the body and sense: "How does it want to live from there... ah, yes, does it want to move like that, is that how it wants to?" Often our hands in particular know more quickly and more about what is missing, what is needed. So, we work directly with gestures and movements, with non-verbal experience and awareness. The quality of the movement coming from within changes from a regulation of the organism to a more meaningful movement. This transition can be different, sometimes flowing, sometimes difficult with long pauses.

There is yet another difference with Whole Body Focusing. We develop our own dynamics by keeping *both* the Felt Sense of the specific question or situation, as well as our reasoning for going into it and being present with it. Often, we also work standing and moving, which increases the possibilities for the body to find new shifts directly and non-verbally. On the one hand, this kind of explicit whole-body work is more demanding in the sense that as a therapist I am continuously anchoring myself in just being, on the other hand, it invites an effortlessness, a "by-it-selfness", precisely because of this. Ultimately, in this way, space is consciously created in felt sense for support through development, through all of life, through the ground in us. We do not have to work for this; we keep it in awareness and stay in "informed" not-knowing. Through this immediacy, the power of focusing increases.

> "At the end of a process of whole body focusing, we allow time for the new life movement to take root, to carry on. Often people experience how their thinking calms and they only want to dwell in presence. They feel as if they have arrived and are unconditionally present. This state is often compared to advanced meditation. By providing space and time, new life can take root and carry on interacting. This is often experienced as effortless and, In a way, natural. Therefore, it can easily happen that this vital, full just being is missed, because nothing new seems to be happening. However, it is essential to honour this time of living silence."[76]

Some elements of this potentiated dynamic were already brought to bear in the process example with Marga S., although it was not yet a complete whole-body focusing. But already by consciously basing myself as a therapist in the body/environment process and inviting wider existence, the quality of the therapeutic interaction changed. I can trust that my own grounded presence influences the client through body-to-body experience. It will help both me and the client to relate differently to what is difficult or painful. The direct emergence of self- regulation – in this case trembling – and body movements (nodding and arm movements) triggered the shift and opened the life stream.

It is the strength of focusing and especially of whole body focusing that it keeps this completely unmistakable piece of existential existence of this one person in this specific situation in awareness and at the same time opens the space of interaction with the potentiality of all living things. Is this the direction in which Bankei wanted to point when he said: "Trust the unborn, dwell in the unborn"?[77]

---

76 Focusing Institute Cologne, 2011.

77 Focusing Institute Cologne, 2015.

The essential ground of Focusing

In Essential Psychotherapy we use different approaches to developing awareness. The experience of wisdom – the emptiness of a solid self and the interdependence of all existence – is called on, as well as the experience of compassion. The variety of the doorways correspond to the variety and diversity of human life.

> "Focusing as a practice of life and therapy is based, as we have seen, on Gendlin's view of the living human body as a process of interactive awareness. It is about embodied awareness."[78]

Gendun Rinpoche has the following description:[79]

> "Fully aware of even the smallest details and without hindering the movements of the mind, we rest in the awareness that mind and phenomena are interdependent and inseparable."

He invites us:

> "...not to block thoughts or emotions to create an artificial emptiness"

And speaks of:

> "...the interdependence of mind and appearances."

Gendlin wants to open up the possibility of *creating open space*:[80] Our body-mind is neither identified, i.e. merged with the phenomena, nor artificially separated in an effort to disidentify. In its natural state, the body experience senses how it is more than any issue or problem.

In a disciplined, open-minded way, Gendlin's embodied phenomenological exploration of experience – i.e. focusing as a philosophical life practice – leads to insights and descriptions of reality that can also

78 Focusing Institute Cologne, 2010.

79 Gendun Rinpoche in "Heart Advice from a Mahamudra Master".

80 See the following exercise "Creating Open Space".

be relevant and helpful for buddhist therapists. In a conversation with meditators, Gendlin warns: "Do not just 'aware' things away...".

> "When meditators try to use spiritual practice to bypass an engagement with their structural experience, John Wellwood calls it spiritual bypassing. And there is the opposite tendency, which I would like to call psychological bypassing: It is when psychotherapy leaves out the ground of being, the ultimate questions of our lives. In contrast to Wellwood, I see that Focusing can open a door there as well[81] – one of the many doors of essential psychotherapy..."

I would like to end with a quote from one of the conversations that I have had with Eugene Gendlin over many years. He once said about spirituality:

> "I go for what is in the way, so that spirituality does not come from outside, ...that you have to believe something. If you have to believe something, you're already disconnected from the ground of being."

Creating Open Space – and developing it (exercise P.1)

We invite Open Space as the first practice of classical Focusing. We therefore call this practice "Creating Open Space" or in its extended form when we take a journey through the body "Unfolding Embodied Open Space". Gendlin has provided us with several possible ways of doing this. One of them here, along with a journey through the body.

81 Study materials of the Focusing Institute Cologne, 2012.

Outer Open space

I feel into my bodily experience: Is there a place that good for me? If I am accompanied, we can also feel a harmonious rapport. I feel the fit of the clothes, are they comfortable and loose enough? What is the temperature like... is it pleasant or not? What posture would I like to take now... sitting or lying down? I can move and change at any time.

Journey through the body

I let my kind attention rest in my feet, feel how they are. Feel the floor, how it bears the weight. I allow the lower legs, knees, thighs all the time and space they need to be felt in presence. They feel my attention, which doesn't want anything. It also gives space to my sitting posture; I feel my weight on the chair. In my own time I take the sensing awareness into the lower back... slowly up to the shoulder blades. Again, and again feeling how it is to be alive there. Maybe I can also feel the breathing in my back... Anything is allowed. I can't go wrong here. I linger in the shoulder blades, the shoulders. Sometimes noticing the small movements which help to feel the sensations. Bringing kindly awareness to the upper arms, elbows and hands. Everything is allowed to be as it is – even tension has its place. Then I slowly move into the neck and feel how things are there, again, small movements may help. No need to try hard to improve anything. Everything is allowed just to be in sensing awareness. The back of the head, the head, the face. Always allowing time to feel how it is alive. The neck. Then we let our attention rest in the chest and abdomen, where breathing moves. We take our time to arrive there.

Inner free space

I rest with awareness where the breathing is alive... in the stomach and chest... feel myself being present...

How is it right now? Is there something internal that is stopping me from feeling good? Something that is currently occupying my experience? This could also be something beautiful or joyful...

If something arises, I welcome it, I let it know that I am aware of its presence. "Oh, yes you..." – and I feel briefly how it expresses itself in the body... Maybe I give it a name...or maybe it already has one. I can then write it on an imaginary piece of paper, for example. Or find it a good place in the room outside to stay. If it is going to be placed in the room, I feel where it would be comfortable and what the right distance feels like.

Sometimes it can also be helpful to feel whether it has a shape or colour.

I take my time with... what's about to come. I know it is there and for this the moment something like a holiday from what might be problematic or difficult is allowed... like putting down luggage. I can feel in my body if something has changed... maybe it has become easier or more expansive or more alive.

I take my time.

I know what has arisen, and that I am prepared to come back to it when needed. I can repeat this several times until I feel that everything that is important in my life has been given a place. I allow myself a moment of time to feel my existence... to be present.

Nothing has to happen, nothing has to be done, I can't do anything wrong now... there is room for everything, everything has its time and place... By getting to know this inner landscape, open space is created: I am more than... all these individual themes and questions.

Now I can either devote myself to one of them in a Focusing session or finish the exercise of creating open space and thank everything that has come. I can still paint or write something down and return to those places in the body at a later time, for example in a later Focusing session. Alternatively, I can look after things in a different way and contact them when needed.

Developing open space is a process of getting to know and welcoming everything that is currently affecting me, anything that might be somehow preoccupying me – maybe even without me consciously noticing it. It is a kind of inner tidying up... Everything is allowed to be there and is given a place.

We are not yet working with what appears, we are not yet going into it. If the brief sensing of how it expresses itself in the body opens up a process, I just welcome it kindly. We can also imagine it as a meeting. I look around to see who has come, not engaging in conversation immediately, but greeting each and every guest, I give them a seat and am present now. In unfolding embodied open space, we allow a pause, a break. Gendlin writes about this:[82]

> "In allowing such a pause, the body aligns itself back with its original source. It stops being the problem... the body gives in, relaxes and feels expansive. How did the body originally come into existence? The individual person was not in charge of that process and could not decide or control this with the will. So, in this way, I can at least temporarily give up control over my life, so that my body can feel itself again in the natural interplay of forces in which it is created and maintained."

Developing open space is about *neither identifying nor disidentifying* oneself. Rather, we can experience how we are *more* than our contents – than the difficulties, emotions, issues, concerns. Just by finding some distance from a problem, we begin to experience it. In this way we can create a state of body-mind life that is as natural as possible. This is open space in which relationships can develop. By pausing to creating open space, we come into contact with the space of the body felt from within. In this state of physically felt space we are neither identified nor unidentified. If we turn to a topic from within this state, we can experience how the uncontrived bodily experience is not actually merged with our problems and this allows us to approach the questions and issues of life afresh, not narrowed down by identification.[83]

---

82 Gendlin, 1978.

83 Focusing Institute Cologne, 2012

Q. Deliberately induced Dis-identification

According to Roberto Assagioli, the founder of psychosynthesis:

> "We are dominated by everything with which we unconsciously identify."

This sentence could be written by a buddhist teacher, since the heart of buddhist mind training is to uncover and dissolve unconscious identifications wherever possible. When the Buddha teaches about seeing the body [simply] as a body, the sensations [simply] as sensations, the mental formations [simply] as mental formations – then he means exactly that: not identifying with the experience but looking directly in order to discover that there is no "I" in experience any ware which is the core of being. There is no centre. The exercises that follow are designed to help lead to further insight. To illustrate the process of conscious disidentification, let us first give an example of being unconsciously identified, in this case being identified with a strong feeling:

A client reports he had an aggressive emotional uprising, during which this he shouted at his wife very strongly. He insulted her and had violent aggressive fantasies, which he did not live out. During the exploration it becomes clear that the strength of his anger had slowly increased or built up. At first, he had been a bit annoyed by reactions from his customers (annoyance scale 3), then a road user had not given him right of way (annoyance scale 5) and finally he had to listen to patronizing comments from his wife at home (anger scale 6.5). Finally, in the face of his wife's harsh accusations (anger scale 9), he experienced an aggressive emotional upsurge. Quote: "My collar burst." He became loud, insulted his wife violently and was on the verge of becoming violent.

This example shows the unconscious identification of the client with anger (fury) as well as the strong effects on his perceptions, his physical symptoms and on his behaviour and activity, and out of this the effect on communication in the relationship. The effects of these various, unconscious identifications with strong feelings are well known.

Disidentifying with physical sensations, feelings and thoughts (exercise Q.1)

The following exercise enables you to consciously disidentify. It originates from psychosynthesis.

Sit comfortably on your chair and focus your awareness on your physical sensations, especially the sensations in your feet. Then move to the sensations in the abdomen, as is raised and lowered by the breathing. These sensations should then be allowed to fade into the background. You will now visualize some parts of your life experience: You start with the first part, with your body and physical sensations. Sometimes your body is healthy, sometimes it is sick, sometimes it is full of energy, sometimes it is tired. There are many small individual sensations in your body. Now please think the following sentence while remaining totally mindful:

"I have a body and physical sensations, but that is not all I am. I am more than my body and my physical sensations."

Then please go to another large part of your experience: your feelings. There are so many feelings – joy, anger and sadness, so many moods, so many emotional tones that make life worth living. It is often said that feelings are like the spice of life. It is a large area of our being. Now please think the following sentence While remaining totally mindful:

"I have feelings, but that is not all I am. I am more than my feelings."

Now please turn to another large area of your experience: the mind, thinking, contemplation, cognitions. There are so many different ideas, labels, words, concepts, hypotheses, opinions – often we are busy thinking all day long. Especially with us adults, thinking in language, thinking in phrases is a very large area. And yet it is not everything. Now please think the following sentence very carefully:

"I have my mind and thinking, but it is not everything that defines me. I am more than just thinking."

Perhaps now the question arises in you: What am I then, if I am neither the body with its sensations, nor the feelings, nor the thinking? Please continue to stay in what you are experiencing right now. Perhaps you can think of a word for this experience? You can let the exercise end here or let the Question resonate inside you: What is my experience?

Then finish the exercise. Maybe you want to make some notes. In a therapy setup, the therapist can ask the client about his or her experiences. The debriefing serves to process the experience. Through this exercise, some people gain deeper experiences of not being fixated or open into a greater inner expanse, which is also the aim of practicing meditation. Individual elements of this exercise can be prioritized for each respective client which are then highlighted. In our example of the client with the aggressive emotional experience rising, the sentence: "I have anger and rage, but I am more than this anger and rage" would be an efficient intervention – perhaps in conjunction with scaling (method O.1).

The therapist can also suggest this exercise on intentional disidentification to clients who are very identified with one side of their experience, for example thinking, and who may find it difficult to access other areas such as feelings. The therapist would try to introduce more balance between different aspects of the client and the same time, try to bring other areas, such as the client's feelings, more into awareness. The client would then be encouraged to ask themself often during the day what they are feeling or experiencing.

Alternatively, they could do a daily review (exercise N.5) of feelings more often.

The formulation "I am more than..." is in many respects simpler and more effective than the negation: "I am not... (my sensations etc.)". This 'more than' lets the questioner sense further, into new areas. It leads from the affirmation of the present experience into a further experience, until all realms of experience are included, and it becomes evident that this supposed I is an extremely dynamic all-encompassing event. "I am I – and this I is nowhere to be found" – it is the entire experience and not separated from it, open, flowing, in constant exchange.

The Suitcase (exercise Q.2)

This is another disidentification exercise which can be used effectively in group work, but also with individuals. It originates from psychosynthesis, where it belongs to the compendium of education. The group participants or clients should have some ability to introspect and have already done some self-exploration on the main identities they are aware of. The therapist can assist a client in an individual therapy setting in finding these main identities.

> Take a blank sheet of paper and divide it into eight equal parts. Think of names for eight of your conscious main identities or main identifications, such as: the yogi with the bodhisattva ideal, the professional at work, the father, the husband, the homeowner, the jack of all trades, the conscientious, the strong-willed, the good driver, the good thinker, the manager, the organizational talent, the jogger, and others. Then write on each of the slips of paper the name of one of your main identities or one of your predominant personality traits.

Then hold the eight slips of paper in your hand and turn your awareness more inwards, close your eyes and feel the sensations in your body. You cannot go wrong with this exercise. Follow the breath and the sensations in the abdomen, as they rise and fall with the flow of breath. Then let these sensations fade into the background a little.

We now begin with an imaginary journey: You have planned a big trip to a completely different and distant continent, a faraway country. You have planned well, organized well, packed well. You have packed eight suitcases for the trip. Now, in your imagination, the taxi stops in front of the door and the suitcases are loaded. You get in and the cab takes you to the airport. You are in the airport at your terminal at the counter and unfortunately there is an unpleasant surprise: You have too much luggage. Two suitcases have to remain behind. If you want to start the journey, you have to make a choice. Choose two of the eight slips of paper that you do not need to take and leave them behind. Put them in front of you. Decide well. Put these suitcases, these identities away very carefully with the internal thought: "I will leave this one here, I will let go of this one now".

Did you leave two pieces of luggage behind? Now you are on the plane. It is a long journey, a long way over the sea to a very distant continent. Then you arrive at the airport of your destination. You already see another airplane on the runway, with which you will continue your journey soon. This airplane is a little older, it has already clocked up many air miles. When changing planes, you will be told that this plane cannot carry that much weight. You will need to leave two suitcases behind to continue your journey on this aircraft. Take your time. Choose well which two suitcases, which two identities you want to leave at the airport. Consider what you can really leave behind, what you can really let go of. Now continue your journey with the remaining suitcases.

You are heading inland with this small airplane. You have a great view from up there. In the distance, in front of you, you see an immense mountain range. This plane manages to drop you off safely at a small airfield in the mountains. You feel the clear, cool mountain air on the airfield. A mountain guide is waiting for you. He has a donkey with him and knows the mountains very well. Unfortunately, he has to tell you that you cannot take four suitcases with you. One suitcase must remain. Two suitcases can be carried by the donkey, one by the guide, but one must remain. Choose well. If you want to continue the journey, you must put down and release another piece of paper with an identity. Place this identity in front of you fully conscious and aware. You can also say to yourself: "Yes, now I will let go of the suitcase with this identity.

You resume your journey. You have considerably less luggage than at the beginning of the trip, but still three suitcases. The donkey carries two and the mountain guide carries one. It is a straight path, which ascends quickly. All the time you have the vastness of the view of the mountains in front of you. There are snow-covered high peaks in front of you, and it is simply a magnificent view. On the way you see beautiful flowering plants. Maybe you also feel a thirst for adventure or a simple joy of being. The path gets narrower and steeper, and you stop at a hut. The mountain guide says: "The donkey can't go any further now, the path is too narrow. The donkey stays at this hut, and a suitcase must also stay there". The mountain guide can carry a suitcase, but you have to carry a suitcase yourself. Choose well, from which suitcase, which identity you can really separate from. Put that sheet aside very carefully. With all your awareness, really let go of the identity using the inner sentence: "Yes, I am leaving you behind now."

Now the two of you, the mountain guide and you, continue your hike. It goes further uphill. You have this wonderful mountain panorama. You also have to walk more carefully, because the path gets narrower and narrower. You can see that you will soon reach the snow line, with its permanent snow. It has a very special charm. It is very beautiful. But the mountain guide tells you: "I can't go with you anymore. If you want to continue, you have to go on alone. I will stay here with one suitcase, if you want to carry the last one". First of all, you rest on a green grassy area and enjoy this wonderful view, this wonderful panorama and the pleasant mountain air. You can look out into the wide-open country and the immense snowy heights. You can really take your time to consider whether you want to go further or stay there with the mountain guide. If you decide to go further, one suitcase must be left behind, because you can only carry one. You have to decide to really let go of one more identity. Do this very carefully. Take your time for your decision.

If you go further up, then you have to climb. Clarity and coldness surround you. This is a really high mountain range. You become aware that you are on a rocky staircase that leads far into the clouds. You follow this rocky staircase step by step. Suddenly you are standing in front of a steep rock in the middle of the clouds. It seems that the stairs end here. But then you notice that the rock has a hole – just big enough for you to squeeze through. Of course, there is no room for the last suitcase. If you want to go through it, it has to stay behind. You have to decide. If you decide to really let go of the last suitcase, the last remaining identity, then do so very carefully, very consciously.

And then crawl through the opening in the rock. Open yourself to the experience. Let it be there completely. You have time. Stay as long as it is right for you.

If you want to finish the exercise, come back, at your own pace, open your eyes, stretch, orientate yourself in the room. You may want to make notes.

In the therapeutic situation, the client can, if he/she wishes, tell the therapist about his/her experiences. The debriefing serves the purpose of processing. In a group situation, after writing down and absorbing experience, a one-to-one group exchange round is a good idea. After that, the whole group can exchange experiences.

This exercise is a bit of an opposite to the previous one, where the phrase "I am more than..." was used. Here it is about: Who am I when I let go of one identity after another? Who am I without that? What remains of me when I slip through the eye of a needle that no longer allows for identification? It leads to the discovery of being a fully viable, carefree, joyful nobody.

The next exercise takes a similar direction: discovering the unattached, unidentified being.

Guiding the client towards the True Self (exercise Q.3)

Do you remember the pendulum exercise on decision making (exercise O.8)? There we filled the client's hands with the pros and cons of a situation and let them balance themselves. In this exercise we go a step further and try to lead the client more into their true self, into something completely free and unattached. After balancing and after the decision-making process has been well developed, the therapist asks the client:

> Take a look inside and ask yourself, "Who is doing this exercise? Who is the one who can look at both hands and balance them? Who is the one who evaluates, classifies, weighs, observes?"

These questions can trigger a different direction of exploration in the client and allow them to experience a slightly less fixed way of being for a moment. When the client is in this detached state, the therapist encourages them to stay there as long as possible. Then the client is asked to talk about his or her experience. How it was for them, what they experienced?

Working with the inner dynamics of the Personality

R. Working with Sub-personalities (method R.1)

The origins of this psychotherapeutic work lie the psychosynthesis of Roberto Assagioli (1888 – 1974) and Jim Vargiu. Today they are often used in a somewhat modified form in many common psychotherapy practices, such as the Gestalt psychotherapy of Fritz Perls or the EGO-State therapy of Watkins. In the following presentation you will find a form of sub-personality work that has been developed in Essential Psychotherapy.

Sub-personalities are parts of the personality that have acquired a certain autonomy (within the personality). They can also be called aspects of personality or sub- or partial personalities, C. G. Jung called them complexes. These are parts of the personality, i.e. ego states, which, similar to a reflex, trigger a certain way of reacting in us. They are still quite close to consciousness, unlike deeply repressed or dissociated content. From a depth psychology point of view, it is called an unconscious dynamic that has a controlling or dominating effect. There are then linguistically formulated thoughts, or even pictures, or sensations and feelings, or all of them together. One may know about the presence of an inner critic within oneself. For example: Maybe anger arises about the fact that certain household chores, such as taking out the rubbish or cleaning out the fridge, are still not done. Or maybe there are internal reproaches: "Why did I make this stupid mistake again?" Something is not how this nagging part wound like or thinks it should be.

Another example would be a teacher who continues to 'teach' at private gatherings with their friends or family, who usually unconsciously, acts out their professional role in private life, i.e. they are identified with this sub-personality "teacher".

It is important not to see these sub-personalities as completely independent – as if they were permanent and unchangeable and could exist by themselves. These are processes that have a certain autonomy in our thought processes, reacting and perceiving and that are still relatively accessible to our consciousness. We call these structures with their dynamics 'sub-personalities' in order to be able to work with them better.

Sometimes this unconscious dynamic is directed toward oneself, the complaining subject of this example, and sometimes against other people they know, such as a spouse. Mostly this leads to suffering for us or for those around us and it binds energies that would otherwise be freely at our disposal. And of course, it is detrimental to be controlled by unconscious mechanisms.

In psychotherapeutic work with these personality parts, the sub-personality work, the sub-personality is treated like a role in a role play. In the example of the sub-personality 'nagger', an attempt is made to bring more mindfulness and awareness into this almost automatic dynamic. Perhaps the practitioner is motivated to no longer be controlled by this reflex mechanism. They take a similar attitude (or tendency) to awareness practice in meditation. In sub-personality work, this attitude is called the 'inner observer' or the 'self' in inner work. It is characterized by a less identified, and certainly not an unconsciously identified awareness.

In buddhist mind training, these sub-personalities would be considered a group of habitual patterns. This refers to ingrained, almost automatic emotional reaction patterns and attitudes that together make up a role or sub-personality and which are not normally reflected on. Part of the path of awakening is to step out of these unconscious emotional reactions and to dissolve them completely in order to gain greater inner freedom. For this, the patterns must first be seen through consciously and seen as compulsive. It actually helps to name them – don't worry, they don't become more real or powerful but are consciously perceived and can be put in their place at a later stage. These are the first steps towards their disempowerment and finally integration into a more comprehensive awareness of hidden needs, fears and capacities. Identifying sub-personalities helps to find humorous ways of dealing with them and so break out of the identification with these patterns.

Self-exploration: Who am I, how am I, what am I? (exercise R.1)

The following core questions serve the purpose of self-exploration and can help as a preparatory exercise in finding sub-personalities:

Who am I?
How am I?
What am I?

Take some time to write down what comes to your mind in relation to these questions. *"Who am I?"* may make you think of the roles you play in everyday life, such as husband or wife, son or daughter, customer, employee, employer, etc. – and the question *"How am I?"* may bring more awareness of your personal qualities. The question *"What am I?"* could lead to answers like: "I am a human being, a citizen of the earth, etc.".

Among the answers that have to do with roles and characteristics, we can find references to sub-personalities that we might want to change – for example, the inner perfectionist, for whom everything has to be 200 percent, thus creating so much tension internally that even the internal organs are affected and the tissues changes.

The House of sub-personalities (exercise R.2)

This imaginative exercise comes from psychosynthesis and helps to discover one's own sub-personalities. Discovering these is of great benefit to everyone, because it helps to understand one's own reactions better and to make inner conflicts between different parts of our personality clearer. In discovering sub-personalities, we experience a multitude of inner patterns, which now become nameable and whose influence on our feelings and actions becomes obvious and therefore controllable. We are blocked less often and can activate the patterns more and more only when it make sense to do so. We can then allocate them their proper place amidst the concert of inner voices.

Sit comfortably and take your attention slowly inwards. You can't get this exercise wrong. It is a little journey that you undertake in your imagination, in your fantasy.

With a long out breath, calmly imagine that all unwanted fixations leave with your breath. Then make sure that your feet are in good contact with the ground and take some time to feel the sensations in your feet and body. If it is possible, keep your eyes closed. But you can also open them again any time you need to.

Now imagine that you are somewhere in a beautiful, pleasant, landscape. It is warm, it is a beautiful summer day, and you are in a meadow. Let this vision become completely alive in your senses: You feel the grass under your feet and smell the flowers and perceive the colours very intensely. The sun's rays are warming rays, maybe you can hear the birds singing. You perceive your body sensations very intensely – the freshness of the air, the smells. You are completely awake in your senses, maybe there is a breeze or a light pleasant wind as you start to move around the meadow in your imagination. After you have completely settled into your experience there in the meadow, look up and begin to explore the surroundings, first through your eyes. You will notice a house at some distance. Take a look at how the house looks from a distance. Your interest has been aroused. You feel that there is something special in this house. Now walk towards the house, maybe you will feel the strength of your body, your muscles.

You are curious about what you might find in this house. As you get closer and closer, it becomes very clear that your sub-personalities live in the house. You may even hear individual voices coming from inside. You go on and notice how the front door opens very slowly and how two or three sub-personalities come out and talk to each other in a lively way. You are fully awake and as a silent observer you perceive what is going on, who is coming out, what the sub-personalities look like, what they are wearing and what they are saying.

Then a sub-personality approaches you and speaks to you. Just talk to it. Get to know it better. What do you want to say to it, how do you feel about it and how does it feel about you? You can also ask it what it wants. See if getting to know it better will make you feel lighter, to find out if something in you feels any different. Pay attention to your physical sensations during this internal conversation. If you like, you can also slip into the sub-personality for a short time and feel how things feel from this perspective. If it is possible for you, try to find out what this sub-personality needs. Then let the conversation slowly come to an end.

The sub-personality rejoins the other sub-personalities and goes back into the house with them. You see the meadow with the warming sunrays and your body sensations again. Then you slowly come back to the starting point of your journey and feel your body. Come back completely to your own rhythm, open your eyes and orientate yourself in the room.

Take your time to arrive and time to process. You might want to write down something of what you have experienced.

In this imaginal exercise some parts of the classical sub-personality work (method R.1), as it is used in the psychotherapeutic two-person-setting with chairs, are addressed or integrated. In the first phase of inner work (exploration) the client explores this sub-personality, for example the inner nagger: "Get to know it better...."

This is followed by further phases of accepting, separating and coordinating and integrating, accompanied by the questions: "What does it want? What does it need? "

You can use the exercise of the mental daily review (exercise R.3) or the keeping of daily and/or weekly notes or writing a diary, for a longer exploration of one or more sub-personalities.

When starting with the chair work (method R.1) in the framework of sub-personality work in psychotherapeutic practice, the client can talk about some situations where they discovered this side of themself, where it was active.

Let's stay with the example of the inner nagger, complaining about the housework not being done yet. An empty chair is placed near the client. The client decides where and at what distance the chair is to be placed. The place on the empty chair henceforth represents the place of the sub-personality (in this case the client's inner nagger).

Then the client is asked to place the above-mentioned situations where the sub-personality was active on this chair now in the imagination and fill the space energetically with it. The idea is to create a dialogue between the ego state of the sub-personality and the observer state of the client. We then talk about the observer's place and the place of the sub-personality ("nagger"). The client begins to say something, interacting in a role-play with the sub-personality, such as: "Don't always nag so much...".

Then the client changes chairs and sits down on the nagger's seat, i.e. on the other chair, and answers from there. They sense what it feels like from this perspective in the body – is different from when they were in the observer's chair? They identify internally with the sub-personality of the nagger, which is very familiar to them, and answers as it: "You need the pressure and my criticism, otherwise you wouldn't get anything done."

This creates a dialogue between the driver and the observer, and it often takes a long time to change positions – in our example between the sub-personality "nagger" and the "observer" position. It is not easy to keep the individual personality parts, the different ego states or identities apart and in so doing create order. It is subtle work. In the first phase, the task of distinguishing is often still taken on by the therapist until the client is so familiar with the sub-personality work that they increasingly manages to find their way into the disidentified state of the observer on their own.

When changing positions from the observer's seat to the nagging seat, for example, it is important to always feel the body very carefully and to sense if anything has changed. If the client feels a lot of force in the nagging seat, it helps to let the client feel this force completely and to bring it into the experience: "Yes, how does it feel to feel this force? Give it room, so that it spreads throughout the whole body."

The 5 phases of working with sub-personalities (with elements of EPT)

The dialogue with the sub-personality has the following phases: recognition, acceptance and separation, coordination, integration and synthesis.

1. *Recognition:* Training in mindfulness and awareness. Possible exercises: Daily review, meditation. This is a phase of observation.
2. *Acceptance* and *Separation:* What do you want? What do you need? Establish a dialogue.
3. *Coordination:* Use the organizing capacity of the observer; establish a contract with the sub-personality.
4. *Integration:* What do you need? Gradual growing together through more and more subtle awareness,
5. *Synthesis:* Dissolution. Possible exercises: Summit hike with sub-personality, the potential of the sub-personality is freed up, creative transformation of the energy caught up in the sub-personality.

In all the phases, the therapist tries to perceive where the client is at the moment and knows what is at stake. The therapist's interventions can help to guide the process. The questions "What do you want, sub-personality? What do you need, sub-personality?" are used in all these phases of the process.

The goal of the process is to disidentify with the sub-personalities, to free the energy caught up in them and make them accessible to the self. In this way, the energy and force that may be caught up in a sub-personality become accessible to awareness for decision making.

In psychotherapeutic work with chairs, one can add another chair and place it, for example, as the seat representing wisdom, next to the other chairs. This chair can represent the Buddha or another wisdom symbol such as the cosmic parents or a wise friend. Placing this chair helps us to remain aware of this level of existence, the wisdom level or buddha nature and to create a healing field. One can also include this wisdom seat for the buddha in the dialogue, working with questions or requests. It is also possible that the client sits on the seat that represents the wisdom aspect and influences the dialogue from there. Here a beneficial effect is created by having a representation of the wisdom level.

Once sub-personality work creates awareness of unconscious fixations, the energies bound in the structures created by them are released through their dissolution. If the practitioner is familiar with this kind of inner work and knows their sub-personalities, they can influence the reactive patterns as soon as they appear, even before they fully unfold. This could mean, for example, when the nagger appears, it is noticed in the moment when the perception begins to change. The dynamics that would otherwise automatically follow might then be interrupted by a thought like: "Hello nagger, I see you, as you are appearing – what do you want, what do you need?"

In psychotherapeutic work, the therapist sometimes stops at acceptance and separation of the sub-personality from the observer, at the end of the therapy session. The client may choose to observe the sub-personality regularly by means of a daily review (exercise R.3) or by asking the sub-personality what it wants and what it needs, when it appears.

When all five phases are worked through in complete sub-personality work, there is usually a reconciliatory, integrating experience. An inner contract between the client and his or her sub-personality could come out of it, for example: "Nagger, don't always put me under such pressure and I will give you more recognition." Or a synthesis could be achieved. This is the case when energies of the higher self, come into play or there is a greater inner openness, in the sense of recognising the basic nature of existence, and the forces of the sub-personality can be directed by the higher self. Sometimes a sub-personality dissolves or the positive potential of the sub-personality is released. The autonomy of the sub-personality changes through continued sub-personality work. It is directed more towards the decision-making faculties of the self and to awareness. The person can then consciously use the sub-personality.

Sub-personalities often arise in childhood, according to Ken Wilber's model of developmental psychology, at the earliest from the age of eight. They can also arise in adulthood. They often appear in quarrelling couples. When the client notices the sub-personality nagger, he or she may react with a feeling and a tendency to retreat in shame or get caught up in self-deprecating reproaches. Sometimes this goes quite deep. Then old feelings from childhood, feelings from earlier ego states, for example those of the inner child (see chapter S) are awakened. In this example it would be a confrontational appearance of the sub-personality Nagger with an ashamed inner child. So: self-deprecation by the nagging sub-personality ("How could I have done that wrong!?") accompanied by the emotional reaction of the part of the inner child with shame and the sense of feeling small and wrong, – a total failure.

The causes, or triggering situations, are mostly actual experiences we had as a child with adult caregivers, usually parents, grandparents or older siblings. The inner processing of these actual experiences led to an internalization with a tendency to unconscious reproduction. In our example, it could have been the nagging of the biological mother that was the root of the inner nagger.

Daily review of a sub-personality (exercise R.3)

This exercise serves to deepen the awareness of a sub-personality.

Please proceed in the same way as you would with the mental day review (exercise N.5). Then go through the day again for a second time and make sure that the sub-personality you have chosen, in our case the nagger, was active during the day. Ask yourself:

- Under what external and internal circumstances did it come on stage?
- Which qualities or traits of the sub-personalities helped or hindered you?
- Were the impulses of the sub-personality in accordance with what you wanted or were you dominated or controlled by them?
- Have you tried to maintain influence or reconcile it with your goals in life?

If necessary, take notes from the exercise and repeat it often.

Even without using the concept of sub-personalities, it is interesting to become aware in more detail of the emergence of certain emotional patterns and their effects on our thinking, speaking and acting. Over the course of months and years, we gradually focus our awareness on the various emotions, patterns and sub-personalities that determine our lives and examine how they recur in different forms and change our perception. In contrast to classic meditation, we are interested in the content and ask about the needs that are expressed? – and about the actual basic concern. We then focus our attention on these needs in order to find new solutions.

Climbing a mountain with a sub-personality (exercise R.4)

This exercise has an exploring, integrating and synthesizing effect and originally comes from psychosynthesis.

Slowly take your attention inwards. You cannot get this exercise wrong. Feel the sensations in your feet and in your body. You can imagine exhaling all unwanted concerns with a long outbreath.

It is best to do the exercise with your eyes closed. If you feel uncomfortable, you can open your eyes again at any time. Choose a sub-personality with whom you will now make this inner journey, preferably one that is already somewhat familiar to you.

Imagine you are a meadow in a beautiful landscape. It is a summer morning, and the sun is shining. You notice the sensations in all your senses intensely: the grass under your feet, the colours of the flowers in the meadow. Maybe you hear the birds singing. Maybe you feel a breeze on your skin.

You are fully awake and feel well prepared for this inner journey. In the distance you see a mountain, not too high, but a proper mountain that rises up clearly above the meadow.

Now you and your sub-personality begin to follow a path that leads you up the mountain. The path climbs slowly. You consciously notice the landscape you are walking up through, the meadows, then a stream, you are walk through a forest. And you notice how the interaction with the sub-personality unfolds. Is there a conversation or do you walk in silence? You climb the mountain further and further. Now you have to use a little more effort. The higher you climb, the further you can see over the landscape, and perhaps it is similar in your inner landscape, as if space is freed up internally, just as the view can stretch into the distance. Perhaps you also feel more clarity in the air as you continue to climb.

Pay attention to the connection with your sub-personality, notice if anything changes. Then you reach the plateau of the summit and enjoy having reached your goal.

You stand up there, with your sub-personality and watch the sun's rays falling on the ground, creating something like a field or sphere of light. Now stand with your sub-personality in this sphere of light and notice what happens. Just let it happen and stay aware. Does it do anything to you or the sub-personality? Notice the sensations in your body. Perhaps you stay in this sphere of light for some time, then step out and return to where your journey started.

Take your time to come back to the room inwardly. Feel your body, your breath. In your own time, open your eyes and orient yourself in the room.

You might want to write something down or you take your time to let the impressions fade away.

In the context of a therapy situation, the therapist asks the client to describe their experience: "What did you experience?" Or: "Would you like to tell me something about your experience?"

Case study on sub-personality work

The 47-year-old client Mrs. A came to the practice and was diagnosed with exhaustion syndrome. The symptoms she complained of were restlessness, sleep disorders, various fears, feelings of being overwhelmed and aggressive emotional outbursts. The sub-personality work, which we are reproducing here in extracts, was started in the tenth session of the therapy.

Therapist: What do you want to work on?

Client: I always have these self-deprecating thoughts, when I make a little mistake, and I am full of self-reproach. 'My God, you are stupid, you can't even do that. You really are a loser.'

Therapist: Ah, yes. You have mentioned these self-deprecating thoughts and self-reproach before. Would you like to work on this a little more deeply in the session today?

Client: Yes.

Therapist: You have already described these self-deprecating thoughts to me several times. Do they appear especially when you make a mistake?

Client: Yes, exactly, but often just on their own, for example, sometimes right after waking up, or if I can't sleep at night and lie awake.

Therapist: I suggest using an efficient therapeutic approach: the sub-personality work. We will look at these pejorative, self-judgemental thoughts as if they have a certain autonomy, because when they appear out of nowhere, they are difficult to control.

Client: Yes, I can't control them at all, it's like a reflexive reaction and it is annoying.

Therapist: In this work we will treat these judgemental and self-deprecating thoughts as a sub-personality with a certain autonomy. A bit like a role-play, as you are well aware.

Client: Yes, I know.

Therapist: Then I'll take this chair. *(Therapist fetches an empty chair and places it near the client.)* This chair now represents this side of you. Is the position *(pointing to the chair)* good like this or should it be a little further away?

Client: Yes, a little further away is better.

Therapist: *(Therapist puts the chair half a meter away. The chair is on the client's right side two meters away)* Is this a good distance?

Client: Yes, it is good like that.

Therapist: *(Therapist stands behind this chair)* What shall we call it? How about judge?

Client: Yes, judge is good.

Therapist: *(Touches the chair now with both hands and says carefully:)* This is now Mrs. A's judge. Please turn your chair a little bit, so that you are sitting directly opposite the judge. *(Client turns the chair, is now opposite the 'judge's' chair)* Now we will try a dialogue between you. You sit in the seat of the observer or the seat of the self as well as the seat of the judge. The dialogue is through direct speech, and you change places frequently, sometimes talking from the "self-seat" and sometimes from the "judge-seat". How do you feel on your seat? How does your body feel, what are the sensations?

Client: I am a bit tense, my hands are a bit cold, but otherwise I am okay.

Therapist: Is there something you want to tell the judge?

Client: You are right – but always wearing me down like that is not okay.

Therapist: Then please change to the "judge's seat". *(Client gets up and sits down on the other chair.)* First at all, properly arrive there. How does it feel? Feel into your body. Do you see Mrs. A sitting there on the other chair?

Client: Yes, I see, I feel okay.

Therapist: Does your body feel the same as it felt over there on the other chair?

Client: Even better, somehow, I have more strength.

Therapist: Ah, there is more power, let yourself feel the power completely.

Client: Yes, that is good, feels good.

Therapist: Now I will briefly repeat what you just said. *(Therapist repeats the last sentence from the self-place:)* "You are right – but always wearing me down like this is not okay." Do you want to answer her?

Client: You do so much wrong and then you always have to fix everything. You are simply much too unfocused. My God, pull yourself together a bit.

Therapist: Is that all the judge has to say right now?

Client: Yes.

Therapist: Then please switch back to the other chair, to the self-seat. *(Client gets up and sits down on the other chair, the self-seat. Therapist summarises what the judge said:)* "You do so much wrong and then you have to fix everything. You are too unfocused. Pull yourself together." How do you feel in the self-seat?

Client: Not as good, just as I often feel, kind of down and small, really stupid. The judge is also so overpowering; my hands are getting colder *(suspected anxiety symptoms).*

Therapist: If the judge is so overpowering, you can also add another chair representing strong or wise friends to support you. For example, a good strong person from your childhood, or even Mother Mary as a Christian symbol, or Buddha or another figure you trust could sit there.

Client: Yes, the Buddha *(client has been practicing buddhist meditation for several years)*, that is good. *(Therapist gets another chair and puts it close to the client's left side.)*

Therapist: Is this the right place?

Client: Yes, it's good there, he can sit very close to me.

Therapist *(holds the chair briefly with both hands)*: This is now the Buddha's seat.

Client: That feels good, I can relax immediately, my hands are getting warm again.

Therapist: Do you want to answer the judge now?

Client: I don't like that at all, it doesn't help at all, judge. You make me feel so bad here and then I feel really stupid. I want you to stop it.

Therapist: How do you feel now?

Client: A bit better, it just doesn't work, I often lie awake at night and then I always have this wearing me down. You should just stop it, just leave me alone give up all these accusations. I am old enough myself. I know that I am not perfect, but people sometimes make mistakes. That has to be accepted, even by you, judge.

Therapist: How do you feel now? Feel calmly into your body.

Client: Now my strength is slowly coming back. My cold hands are completely gone too; I no longer feel that powerless. And you *(turned to the judge)*, you will now simply leave me alone, especially at night. Constructive criticism is okay, but not in that way.

Therapist: Why don't you ask the judge: "What do you want, judge?"

Client: Well, what do you want, judge?

Therapist: Now please go back to the judge's seat. *(Client gets up and sits down on the other chair, therapist repeats the sentence:)* "What do you want judge?"

Client: I want you to be good at everything so that you are respected by people. So that you have a good life. *(Client changes the chair and sits down on the self-place.)*

Therapist *(repeats the sentence):* "I want you to be good, so that people respect you, so that you have a good life."

Client: Yes, judge, that's okay, I can acknowledge that, but not like that, I often can't sleep, and I lie awake and feel really bad and then the next day I'm tired and more mistakes happen. Something has to change, you can give me constructive advice, but this is wearing me down and has to stop.

Therapist: How do you feel now, what does the body say?

Client: Strength, feel good, a bit like being the master in the house again.

Therapist: Okay, please keep in touch with it. Let yourself feel it all over again, all the strength, how it feels to be the master of the house again.

Client *(becomes calm and says after some moments):* I feel much better this way; I have my strength again. Here too *(pointing to the heart area)* it feels much freer and more open.

Therapist: Very nice, would you like to stay with it for a moment?

Client: Yes. *(Client remains in feeling and sensing for two minutes.)*

Therapist: Can you please ask the judge: "What do you need, judge?"

Client: Yes, so: What do you need, judge?

Therapist: Now please change to the judge's seat again. *(Client stands up and sits in the judge's seat.)* How does it feel now? Still the same as before?

Client: No, different, not as strong and powerful as before.

Therapist: Ah, yes. *(And repeats the last sentence:)* "What do you need, judge?"

Client: I only mean well, so that you have an easier life.

Therapist *(repeats the sentence):* "What do you need, judge?"

Client: I need you to see that I mean you well.

Therapist: Yes, if that's all that comes from the judge's seat, then please change. *(Client switches to the self-place.)* Just calmly arrive on the self-seat. Feel and notice the body. *(Client seems relaxed. The therapist repeats:)* "I only mean you well, I need you to see that."

Client: Yes, judge, I can see that *(client visibly relaxes more and is moved, has tears in her eyes).* I can't say anything more right now, but I'm fine. I can tell the judge that I can see that he means me well. *(Is further touched, sobs.)*

Therapist: Yes, tell him again.

Client: Yes, judge, I can see that you really mean me well. *(Client becomes very quiet, something seems to be going on inside her.)*

Therapist: If you like, stay still with what you are feeling now.

Client: I feel somehow completely flooded.

Therapist: Stay with it. *(Then after a while:)* Does it still have a momentum in you now? Does something still have to happen?

Client: Not really, that's fine. But what about the buddha seat? *(Points to the chair.)*

Therapist: Yes, would you like to sit on the buddha seat?

Client: Yes, if I am allowed to.

Therapist: Yes, then sit down on the chair that represents buddha's seat. *(Client stands up and sits in the buddha seat.)* And sitting in that chair and perceiving, what is it like there? Take your time. *(Client remains seated with closed eyes for a long time.)*

Client: My experience here is very deep and open.

Therapist: Yes, would you like to stay there a little longer?

Client: Yes.

Therapist *(after a while)*: You can now sit back on the self-seat again. Stand up slowly and carefully and take everything you experience in the buddha seat with you into the self-seat. *(Energetic work. Client stands up very slowly and slowly changes places back to the self-seat.)* And did you manage to take anything with you?

Client: Yes. *(Client is obviously in an open, relaxed and detached state and seems very calm.)*

Therapist: Is it okay for you if we end this sequence now?

Client: Yes, it's fine.

Therapist: Then I'll put the chairs away now and you take your judge and the buddha with you when you leave. *(Therapist shakes the chairs once, symbolically to "free them from their representative meaning again" and puts them back in their original place in the room.)*

The client and therapist then agreed that if there was any more self-deprecation and self-reproach, she would enter into a brief inner dialogue with the judge sub-personality and report back in therapy on how it was developing. In addition, the client and therapist agreed that she would regularly conduct a mental daily review on the sub-personality (exercise R.3). In the further course of therapy over the next six months, sleep disorders disappeared except for some residual symptoms. The client was able to recover very slowly and to take better care of herself. Above all, the massive self-depreciation improved. After a year of regular inner work with client's judgements her the massive feelings of guilt and the resulting feelings of depression had decreased significantly and were no longer an issue. There was also an improvement with regard to the aggressive emotional outbursts, but several other therapy methods were used in therapy.

S. Working with the Inner Child (method S.1)

Psychotherapeutic inner child work is an efficient method that is used today in many psychotherapeutic disciplines. It works with active imagination. I (Wolfgang) became familiar with work on the inner child through training in psychosynthesis.

Let us follow a simple subdivision of personality parts into child ego, adult ego and parent ego. Often identities swap around without people being aware of it. It is commonly observed in life, especially in intimate relationships, that one partner takes the parent ego part and the other partner, the child ego part. One of the goals of working with the inner child, is that unconscious inner dynamics are stopped from controlling a person's behaviour, thoughts or feelings. Take an example of a loving husband, who, when certain childhood experiences are triggered, together with corresponding feelings of despair, by certain behaviours of his wife, becomes a quick-tempered, angry and aggressive opponent who shouts down his wife. With this example then, apart from the goal of affect control and the investigation of the difficult childhood experiences that caused it, a further goal would be the client's own internal parenting of the needy child part. Thus, unmet needs or unprocessed offenses can be healed and matured through self-parenting. In other words, we give the unsatisfied parts what they needed in childhood. In this way the path to healing is prepared. Often there are not enough satisfied needs within any given relationship; needs for security and reliability, or for protection, the need for someone to be there, to be held, the need to be seen, the need to be loved, to be accepted along with the feelings one had as a child.

So, many of our basic needs, which we had as children and often still have as adults, can be listed. If these needs remain unsatisfied (as could have been the case for a client in their childhood), then there is a tendency for the client to repeat old patterns, or ways of processing, and these become the basic way of functioning of the unconscious dynamics, determining the way he or she forms relationships with him- or herself and with other people.

The Inner Child in the Buddhist view

When looking at the dynamics that take place between spiritual teachers and their students, it becomes clear how much the needs and fears of the inner child play a role in many cases. It is a re-staging of the search for the ideal father and the ideal mother with all the projections that go with that. The fears of not being accepted, not being seen, not being heard, not being loved are as much a part of it, as the wish to please the teacher, to make them happy, to avoid conflicts or even to replace their absent partner. We also often unconsciously expect our teachers to behave like our parents, for better or worse. As a consequence, there are the perfect conditions for disappointment in our unconscious projections. So, it is really worth doing the work with the inner child (chapter S), as well as the work with the internal parent figures (chapter T) that we carry within us.

This cleaning-up work will help us to build reasonably healthy relationships with our teachers, without expecting them to meet the needs that could not be met in our family – and also without burdening the relationship too much with the fears that accompany our biographical wounds. Although the practice of guru yoga actually also allows for subsequent parenting, the visualization of the guru usually lacks a direct reference to concrete life experiences. In fact, the practice of yidam, i.e. meditation on ourselves and others as buddhas, would actually make it possible to build a wholesome new self-image in which old patterns of parent-child interaction no longer apply. However, experience shows that meditations rarely – there are certainly exceptions – deal deeply enough with these emotional burdens. Therefore, the more Dharma practitioners can be encouraged to do this work; the faster the inner path will go. Above the door of a Tibetan school, we read:

When a child is criticized, it learns to judge.
When a child is attacked, it learns to fight.
When a child is mocked, it learns to be shy.
When a child is shamed, it learns to feel guilty.
When a child is understood and tolerated, it learns
to be patient.
When a child is encouraged, it learns to trust itself.
When a child is praised, it learns to appreciate itself.
When a child is treated justly, it learns to be just.
When a child is safe, it learns to trust.
When a child is recognized, it learns to like itself.
When a child is accepted in friendship, it learns
to find love in the world.

Giving to the Inner Child what it needs (exercise S.1)

Let us get a taste of this work with the Inner Child through an exercise. For this exercise the therapist anchors himself/herself in the greatest possible natural openness, visualizes a light sphere in the client's heart and allows a healing field to develop through taking up this inner attitude and alignment (see chapter M and exercise N.1). Then the exercise instructions begin:

Please take your attention inwards; it helps to close your eyes. You can of course open them again any time you need to.

Direct your awareness to the sensations of the body, calmly, first to the sensations in the feet, then to those parts of the body that are in contact with the chair: the thighs, the buttocks, the back, the forearms. Follow your breath for a few moments, perhaps you can observe how the abdomen rises when you breathe in and falls when you breathe out. Stay there quietly for a few moments. Let yourself be guided by the questions: "What is the experience of physical sensations or other sensory impressions like?"

Now let anything that represents healing for you be present. You can also imagine a symbol of wisdom and love in the room, close to you, like a buddha or another expression of awakening, or imagine being surrounded by a field of light.

When you feel ready for the next phase of the exercise, imagine that behind a door is your inner child waiting to come to you. Try to remember what you looked like as a child and imagine that this child is now standing at the door. And when you are ready, ask it to come in. It opens the door and stands in front of or next to you. First, take your time to look at the child. How does the child stand? What posture? What is the facial expression? What clothes do they wear in this inner scene? Are you ready to look them in the eyes? What does this trigger in you? Do the sensations in your body change? Be very attentive to how the child expresses themself in the inner scene and what it triggers in you, even if other inner images appear...

Then start a dialogue with your inner child. Ask it what it wants. Maybe it wants to play with you or show you something. You can take some time to explore what your inner child wants. The answers can show themselves in different ways – in pictures or feelings or thoughts. You don't have to react immediately; it is important that you are ready to listen.

Then it goes a little deeper and you ask the child: "What do you really need?"

Allow yourself time to see if you are ready to give your inner child some of what it needs. You can also tell it in the same way whether you want to give it what it needs or maybe just some of it or maybe nothing at all. It must be authentic and possible to implement in life.

If you don't feel strong enough yourself, you can also ask your wisdom symbol (the Buddha, or others) to help you. An example of such an offer could be to give the child two minutes of undivided attention or time to play every day.

Be attentive to the child's reactions: what does it look like now? Does it say something or has the facial expression changed? And how does your body feel?

Then you gradually come to the end of the exercise. It may be that you are saying goodbye to your inner child or that it stays. Feel the sensations of your body again. Open your eyes and orient yourself in the room.

Take your time to follow up on this exercise or write something down.

The therapist could suggest looking at some childhood memories or bringing them to the therapy sessions to look at together. Photos can refresh the memories and often help to imagine the inner child. It is not advised to use this method, when, for example, it is known from medical history that there was a severe trauma in the client's childhood. In this case, this procedure would not be advisable due to the risk of re-traumatization. Similarly, if the client completely refuses to deal with their childhood.

The child self is very caught up with feelings and emotional experience. Which means its identity, including unconscious identifications are mainly held in the body and bodily sensations and feelings, but hardly at all in logical abstract thinking. The older the child becomes, the more the identification can also move on to ideas about itself.

The healthy inner child – and everyone has such experiences within themselves – is one of our deep resources. In many adults, inner children are activated by sport and through movement, where responses are often very simple.

Most people have experienced insults, emotional hurt, rejection and losses all the way until they reach adulthood, which still bind energy like scarred wounds, which have never quite healed. Often there is the danger that they will break open again. The following case study serves as an illustration.

Case study no. 1 on working with the Inner Child

Client R., a 38-year-old man, tells me (Wolfgang) in a therapy session that he had felt completely rejected in an everyday situation, and he had experienced this many times before, together with strong feelings of sadness, followed by strong self-doubt. He tells me that the shop assistant in his regular bakery, from whom he looks forward to picking up his bread and who always says goodbye with a nice smile, didn't smile today and was somehow so different, so reserved, and seemed a bit irritated.

Through inner work it became clear that this situation had caused old childhood feelings to resurface. He remembered situations in which he was not seen and felt rejected by his mother. The strength of his feelings of rejection was caused by the opening of the old wound. He was unable to feel grown up in that situation ("It's a pity that the saleswoman isn't smiling, or friendly today, maybe she is having a bad day"), instead he experienced the old sensation of feeling rejected. Life situations have a certain range of emotional involvement for us as adults. If this is clearly exceeded, as was the case here with client R., old emotional patterns are usually activated or updated.

In this example we would assume a slight feeling of distress (on a scale of 0 to 10 it would consistently be between 1 and 4). In his self-assessment, client R. had rated the feelings of grief and rejection at 8.5. Inner Child Work is a sensible and efficient way of dealing with this situation arising from of the client's condition. In this session, as well as in future sessions, client R. learned how to approach his hurt inner child in the way he needed it as a child from his parents. He learned to parent his inner child. The dialogue with the inner child is directed to helping the child feel noticed and taken seriously, for example in its pain or whatever the actual injury is. This requires a counterpart. Client R. got into dialogue with his inner child with the words: "Yes, I can see how bad this is for you and that you feel rejected and how sad you are about it." Already in this first session, client R. was able to observe a decrease in grief on the scale to 3.5, through using this imagined inner childcare method. He decided to have a regular dialogue with the inner child, especially in or after situations in life in which he felt strongly rejected.

The dialogue between the adult self and the inner child is individually directed to the needs of the child. Sentences such as: "I see how you are; I see your grief or your fear, I see your feeling and I am there" have proven to be quite effective, but it is above all about how seriously meant each very individual dialogue is. Sometimes only the inner image is worked on, without using language. In this situation, the child of the imagination may be the first person to be taken out of the remembered situations, especially if they are threatening, and brought to the present, into the therapy room. It can be helpful to name the inner child's feelings and to reflect them back.

Sometimes the client experiences themself as not having enough strength in their self/adult role. Then we can add a wise, strong friend, like a buddha, which can be used as a strong resource. The buddha can be imagined next to or behind the client, or he can be given a place as an inner figure in the client's imagination. It is then possible in the inner dialogue to move back and forth from the buddha-seat to the inner child, to alternate.

Also, in a situation where an actual memory of the child is being used, in this key situation, after the child has been removed from the situation in imagination and brought into the present, a wisdom symbol such as the Buddha, can be given a place in the original memory, so that the original situation also gets healing. Sometimes clients also feel responsible for the parents or other people involved and it's easier to let go of the situation, if the buddha remains present for the child within the stressful memory. In addition, this symbolizes the level of wisdom, which has a healing effect in itself.

Breathing from the heart (Tonglen) with the Inner Child (exercise S.2)

Another efficient exercise in the work with the inner child is the heart-breath (see chapter F), the practice of sharing and receiving with the inner child.

Sit comfortably on your chair and focus your awareness on your physical sensations. If you like, you can start with the sensations in the feet.

Then imagine that you exhale all unwanted concerns with one exhalation, then follow the flow of your breath for a few moments and the abdomen which rises with and falls with each breath.

Imagine that there is a sphere of light in your heart or even above your head. If you wish, you can also imagine the Buddha or an aspect or quality of the buddhas or another symbol of wisdom in this sphere of light. It could be a wise friend, traditionally the root lama. But it is also sufficient to imagine this sphere of light, which symbolizes the basic nature of existence.

Then call your inner child. Maybe it stands in front of you or sits on your lap...

Imagine that as you breathe out, bright, radiant light flows from the light sphere in your heart to the inner child. A light which contains everything the child needs: healing, love, acceptance, security and protection.

With the inbreath in you can imagine that everything that is burdensome for the child flows in the form of dark light into the light sphere in your heart. As it touches the light sphere, it automatically completely dissolves.

And as you breathe out, again a bright, white, radiant light flows back towards the child. You might want to stay longer in this sharing of light when breathing out, and might even add wishes, such as "May you be happy and free from suffering. May you experience the safety you need...".

Then let the activity of taking in everything burdensome fade into the background and allow the bright light to flow intensely to the child for a few breaths.

Finally concentrate for a bit on the light sphere – the buddha in the heart – and bring the exercise to a close.

Slowly return to natural breathing, open your eyes and orientate yourself in the room. It is good to feel the effects of this exercise for a few moments. Maybe you wish to write something down.

This breathing from the heart can also be used when it is difficult to work with concrete childhood memories or when a dialogue with the inner child is not easy.

The Tree (exercise S.3)

This exercise originates from the Phyllis Crystal Imagination System and can be very nourishing. It is resource-oriented and often allows one to slowly turn to one's inner child using of the security of the connection with wisdom figures.

Turn your attention inside. Notice the breath, as the abdomen rises and falls with the flow of breath. Let a tree appear to your inner eye. Just notice at which tree appears without forcing it. If there are several trees, then choose one.

Then go to the tree and greet it. You can hug it or touch the bark. Try to feel it and make sure by shaking it that it is stable and can withstand your weight.

Turn around in your imagination, so that the tree is now behind your back, at the same time actually moving your back forward about 6 inches from the back of the chair. Then you let your back fall against the back of the chair with the idea that the tree is supporting you. Feel the support in your back, the stability it gives you. The that up the identity of the tree. This could be a bit unfamiliar, but it may be that you manage to become the tree. Turn your attention to the roots, the part of the tree that is usually not visible. In this exercise the roots of the tree are rooted in cosmic mother earth, a part of your higher self. From this source of nourishment, ask inwardly for all that you need, especially what you might have needed from your bodily mother as a child and have not received in a sufficient manner, such as love, safety or to be seen.

As you exhale, you can imagine that you are letting go of all the things that stop you from taking in all the healing nourishment of the cosmic mother, such as negative memories, frustrations, pain.

Stay with this image for a few breaths. Then, go up to the top of the tree to the branches, twigs and leaves that stretch out towards the sun, the cosmic father, who is the other part of your higher self. Now, from this nourishment source, ask for everything you need, especially what you did not receive as a child from your physical father, such as protection, love, recognition, praise.

Again, with the inhalation, from the cosmic father sun, you take in everything you need, and with the exhalation you can let go of everything that hinders or blocks, such as thoughts like: "I am not worthy of...". Then direct your attention simultaneously to both streams – to what you are taking in from the roots and from the branches and twigs. You may feel the two energy streams mixing, spreading throughout your body and balancing you internally.

Then ask your cosmic parents to appear as people next to you: the cosmic mother earth will appear on your left and the cosmic father sun on your right. At first this can be quite vague and shadowy. Their characteristics are that they are very tall and very loving. If you like, you can put your hands in your lap open upwards and imagine that you are hand in hand with the cosmic parents, perhaps even that the cosmic parents are hugging you or simply holding you, just like parents hold their children.

Feel the contact, perhaps it will trigger a feeling of connectedness, solidarity and safety. Stay in this contact as long as you need to.

Then ask your inner child to appear and pass on to it the love, security and safety that you yourself have just received from the cosmic parents, so that it receives what it needs now.

Then let the exercise slowly fade away and bring your awareness back to the physical sensations, the breathing. Open your eyes and orient yourself in the room. Take your time to let the exercise have its effect, you may want to write something down.

This exercise is usually experienced as nourishing. If it is not possible for the client to offer parenting to the inner child themself then it is more likely to succeed in giving the inner child what it needs from the cosmic parents or the wisdom figures.

The House of our Childhood with a person as a resource (exercise S.4)

This exercise originally comes from Psychosynthesis. It is used for exploration and healing. An imaginative parenting takes place going back to an original situation, i.e. in the parental home.

Set yourself up well, so that you are sitting comfortably, then direct your awareness to your physical sensations and close your eyes. Now go back in your life a little. Think of the first house or apartment you can remember from your childhood. Take your time until the first memories appear and then walk through this apartment in your imagination. Go into the hallway and then into the individual rooms.

What is the smell like? What kind of furniture, pictures, carpets are there? Where did you spend most time? What was the atmosphere like in this apartment, in your first home? Did it feel more light or dark? Did you like to be there, or did you prefer to be outside of the house? What were your favourite places?

Go through each room: the living room, your parents' bedroom, the kitchen, the bathroom. Was there a separate children's room? Experience this atmosphere once again very intensively.

Once you have gone all the way through the apartment, see if you can see your mother, or if she is not there, see if someone else is there, maybe your father or grandparents.

What is your mother (or the other person) doing right now? Check inside yourself, is there something you need from your mother right now? And if there is, imagine that you get exactly what you need (for example, that she has time and plays with you).

Fulfill the needs of the child completely in your imagination and feel in your body how it feels when you get what you need.

If that feels good, then give this sensation space and allow it to spread throughout your body with the subtle breath. You can then also imagine a wisdom figure, such as the buddha in the home, having a healing effect on the whole situation.

Then let the exercise fade away very slowly, take the time you need to come back to the present. When you are ready, open your eyes and orient yourself in the room. Maybe you need a little more time to let the exercise die away or write something down.

This exercise leads back into and reactivates old memories and sensations and feelings. This is useful for inner child work. But if the client's childhood was very stressful, this exercise should be used with caution.

Case study no. 2 on working with the Inner Child

The client Mr G. came to therapy with various fears. He described these fears as particularly intense in the context of his new relationship. He had restlessness, fear of failure and feelings of inferiority, sexual dysfunction and above all self-deprecation in relation to his partner.

Therapist: Please remember a situation where this inner restlessness and uncertainty happened in the recent past.

Client: Yes, I can see the situation. It was the other evening. We had a nice dinner and then we had a drink at her place. It seemed to boil down to the fact that we would make love, but then I didn't feel good at all, I felt small and overwhelmed, I was also suddenly tense.

Therapist: When you tell me this, can you feel some of these sensations right now, in this very moment?

Client: Yes, I have raised my shoulders a little bit and I am breathing a little more shallowly.

Therapist: Is this felt most strongly in the shoulders?

Client: Yes, but even more in the heart area, it is as if there was a hole there.

Therapist: Please, even if it is unpleasant, keep your attention there for a moment.

Client: Yes.

Therapist: And then, in your thoughts, direct a sentence to the sensation in the heart area. "Show me a situation where you originally developed this sensation?" and pay attention to images that arise.

Client: Yes, now I see a situation from my childhood with my mother.

Therapist: Ah, yes and what is going on there?

Client: I am crying, maybe I am seven. My mother scolds me because I got only an F in the maths test. She says that Micha (the client's older brother) always had A's. And that I was a disgrace to the family. Such a shame.

Therapist: How does the boy feel in this situation?

Client: I would have loved to sink into the ground. And it was so bad, because I was afraid that my mom didn't love me anymore.

Therapist: Please take this boy, your inner child in imagination out of this situation and bring him here to this room into the present. And put a symbol or representative of wisdom, like the Buddha, in the situation with your mother, in your imagination.

Client: Yes, I've done that, it feels good, it relaxes me, somehow it also relieves me.

Therapist: And then please look at the seven-year-old boy in front of you. Can you see him?

Client: Yes, he is there, here very close to my left leg.

Therapist: See what he needs. You can ask him.

Client: He is afraid, so afraid that his mother doesn't like him anymore, that he doesn't want to exist.

Therapist: Can you be a good mother and father (parenting) for the boy and take good care of him?

Client: Yes, I can tell him that I see that he is very afraid and that I am here now.

Therapist: Yes, do that, very nice. How does he react?

Client: He becomes calmer.

Therapist: Ah, he becomes calmer.

Client: Yes, he relaxes a little and leans more against my leg.

Therapist: If it is congruent for you, then you could stroke his back.

Client: Yes, that feels good, now he is lying with his upper body completely against me and over my leg, so that I can stroke him even more on his head and back.

Therapist: Fine, yes, just keep it up. Maybe you can also tell him that you are really there for him now and that it is not so bad if you get an F in math, that you still love him.

Client: Yes, I did.

Therapist: How did he react?

Client: He looked up in amazement.

Therapist: Maybe you should repeat that it's not so bad to get an F and that he doesn't have to be like his brother and that you are there now and won't leave.

Client: It is good for him.

Therapist: How can you tell?

Client: The boy has now placed himself very close to me and in my body the heart area feels very warm and open.

Therapist: Very nice, see if there is anything else that needs to happen or if that is enough for the moment.

Client: I will stay like this for a moment.

Therapist: Does the boy need anything in your life, in your day-to-day life, maybe in situations with your partner?

Client: Yes, he said that he wants me to be there. Then, I told him that I would simply contact him every day and see how he was doing.

Therapist: Fine, and maybe even when the fear comes out strongly, as in the situation with your partner that you described to me at the beginning of the session.

Client: Yes, right, if I think about it then, but that would be good.

Therapist: Apparently there is something going on in these situations with your partner that trigger these old feelings towards your mother and an old fear of rejection by mother.

Client: Yes.

In the following therapy sessions, the client reports his regular internal attention to the boy (the inner child part) and that this always does him good. He also reports that he generally feels a little more secure in many life situations where he had previously felt insecure. After four more sessions he reports another, similar situation with his partner. They were at her place again in the evening after a visit to a restaurant and he again felt the expectation that it should get a little more intimate after a glass of wine.

Therapist: How did it develop then?

Client: I felt how I started to tense up inside again, was really under stress. Fearing inadequacy.

Therapist: Yes, and how did this situation develop?

Client: I then turned inwardly to the boy for some time, as I had done many times before. I brought him to me and told him that I could see his fear and that I was there, stroking his back.

Therapist: And did it help?

Client: Yes, little by little I got less tense, the fear of failure simply reduced.

Therapist: Ah, that's good.

Client: Yes, at some point I didn't even think about it anymore and it was just very relaxed and nice between us.

Therapist: Nice, very nice.

In the following months, the client regularly again and again got into good caring parenting contact with his inner child and his anxiety symptoms were significantly reduced. The relationship with the partner also became more relaxed and freer of fear. The problem of the mother projection combined with the anxiety triggering situations of childhood, had been updated and dissolved. The effect on the client's sexual function, which he had at the start of the therapy, disappeared except for minimal residual symptoms.

T. Working with Parental Images (method T.1)

Let's consider the personality traits child ego, adult ego and parent ego. In this chapter we will deal with the structures of the internalized parents, i.e. the parental images, i.e. mother-image and father-image. They are also called parent-imago or parent-introjects, mother-introject, father-introject. These are inner processes based on earlier relationship experiences with the biological parents or with other significant people we had close connection with, such as with the grandmother or with the grandfather, sometimes it is also older siblings who took over educational tasks. The messages and relationship patterns of the parents were internalized. These parental images are made up of imprints of previous actual relationships, how the parents related to the child and its siblings and how father and mother dealt with each other and with themselves.

In this way, parental messages continue to have an influence as internalized parents. They influence perception and also the way we communicate and our relationships with other people. The more unconscious these structures are, the greater their effects and the less control the self has over them. The child ego part and the parent ego part are often in internal opposition or contain a certain contrary, oppositional dynamic, just as parents and child did not always agree in the past. The inner observer, the adult ego, or 'the Self,' is in demand with its disidentified perspective (not identified with child ego parts or parent ego parts) and attitude towards self-regulation as an organizing influence.

In the therapy process an inner reworking takes place. It is about working the parental force into the psyche in a new and different way. This is of course a longer and more differentiated process of emotional expression, detachment, gradual understanding, forgiveness and reconciliation. Similar to sub-personality work (see chapter R), it is about steps of recognition, acceptance, coordination, integration and synthesis, i.e. a real reworking of the inner relations between forces, the psychic dynamics. As an effect, this is then expressed on the interaction level of the client in their relationships. On the one hand, a new understanding of the external parents as fallible people, as they were or are, and an equalising out of relationship with them is created. On the other hand, unconscious father and mother transmissions to other people will occur less often. The whole impulsively spontaneous emotional experience changes. Feeling unconsciously like a child is transformed into being a real adult with the corresponding feelings of an adult man or woman. Let us illustrate this with a case.

Case study on working with parental images

Mr. S., forty-eight, came to the practice because of aggressive emotional outbursts against son and wife and depressive states. He also became violent in isolated instances during the emotional breakdowns and was afraid of losing his wife and becoming a bad role model for his son, who was also prone to violence against classmates at school. Mr. S. had grown up in a parental home where there was violence between father and mother, but also against him and his two siblings. He describes his father as loving, but also unpredictable when he had his anger attacks. He describes the mother as controlling, addicted and latently aggressive. She would often have provoked the father, and the father would then strike out indiscriminately in anger. In these situations, everyone had been at the father's mercy, and he had been very afraid for himself, his mother and his younger siblings. He experienced this as a child as quite terrible.

After a phase of getting to know each other and building up a relationship of trust, self-regulation methods such as scaling anger, inner verbalizing and intervening by counting breaths and other de-escalating measures such as pulling out the inner red card and going into another room were practiced more intensively. During this time, he had become confident in calling on his resources. From the fifteenth hour of therapy onwards, the therapist and client tried to focus more on the internalized images of the father. For this purpose, the client regularly conducted the daily review (exercise N.5) of his everyday angry states and the fantasies and actions associated with them. At the same time, he became more and more confident in the regular work with his desperate inner child part. According to him, the outbursts of the emotion had already decreased significantly by that time. Then in the twenty-second session, the client reported a relapse, he had once again beaten his wife in a longstanding argument, which he now felt very sorry for. A sequence from the therapeutic work of this hour follows:

Therapist: Let us turn to this outburst of the emotion once again.

Client: Yes.

Therapist: Can we engage in an inner process? It is similar to the procedures you have already experienced here.

Client: Yes, we can do that.

Therapist: I would like to ask you to sit down comfortably and to close your eyes. *Client closes his eyes.* Take your attention inside. Notice the breath, as the abdomen rises and falls with the flow of breath. Take your attention to the sensations in your body. *Client relaxes.* Now bring this scene you just described, where you hit your wife, back to mind. See if this image now triggers a resonance in the sensations of your body.

Client: Yes, I feel a little bit of anger and my hand forms a fist and I could scream. I feel it most strongly in my throat, which is as if it is tight.

Therapist: Then please stay with this sensation in your throat and direct your thoughts to this sensation. "Show me a situation from the past where you were created, sensation!" And then pay attention to images from memory that arise. Please let me know when an image appears without stopping the inner process.

Client: Yes, I have done it. Yes, there are images, even many images from memory, all from childhood.

Therapist: Just go to the oldest picture, where you were youngest, or whatever comes up, and share it with me, keeping focused internally.

Client: Oh, this is terrible, I feel so alone *(client starts to cry).*

Therapist: What is going on?

Client: Daddy and mummy are fighting (*client experiences the situation as if he was a child*) and they also beat each other. Dad wants to leave, but mom does not let him. She holds him down, then daddy hits mommy very hard. I am afraid for mummy and get between them.

Therapist: Get the child out of this situation in your imagination now, and bring the child in your imagination here, in this room, here to you, to the present moment.

Client: But he is afraid for his mommy and the other smaller siblings and for his daddy. He cannot leave.

Therapist: Ah, yes. Instead of the child coming here, try to put a symbol of wisdom, like Mary or Buddha, in the bad situation. See if that is possible.

Client: Yes, I did it, that's good, now it will be easier. Now the boy can come here.

Therapist: Well, then please see what the boy needs.

Client: He is recovering now, his desperation lessens, he is relaxing, also my heart area feels easier again.

Therapist: Stick with it, feel what he needs and try to give it to him.

Client: Yes, I will do that. He has now pressed himself against me. But the hand of the father also appears, as a fist.

Therapist: Ah, yes. Do you know that?

Client: Yes, I know it well, there is something brutal about it. It is a big, strong, hairy hand, a giant fist. (*The father boxed for many years in his youth).*

Therapist: Ah, yes, he used to box as a sport.

Client: Yes, everyone is afraid of the fist, he is a thug. *(Client becomes thoughtful, his voice changes a little, it is no longer the desperate*

voice and mood of the child.)
Therapist: Yes, what is happening right now?
Client: I realize my father is really a thug *(Client is visibly affected)*.
I don't want to be like that, I really don't want to be like my father, I know that very well.
Therapist: Yes, you know that very well.

So much for the sequence of dialogue from this session. It had a great effect in the therapy process. The client reported that this "I don't want to be like this" never left him from that moment on. There were still the odd emotional outbursts, when the child's old feelings of despair were triggered, but the intensity had changed. He would then take care of the desperate inner child and the "I don't want to be like this, I don't want to be like my father" would then help him a lot. He would be himself again more quickly *(thus more mature in feeling and action)*.

According to his reports, the aggressive fantasies he experienced would also be much less threatening for his relatives. So, he had no more killing fantasies and there had been no physical violence against his wife or son since then.

During this session, but also during the whole therapeutic process, the client was able to disidentify more and more from this part of the father image (the thug) with observable positive effects on the relationship with wife and son.

Exploration of parental images (exercise T.1)

The exercise mainly serves the exploration of mother-image and father-image (parent-imago) and originates from psychosynthesis.

Sit comfortably on your chair and direct your awareness to your physical sensations, the sensations in the feet. Follow the breath, as the abdomen rises and falls with the flow of breath. It helps to close your eyes, but of course you can open them at any time you want.

Imagine father and mother standing before your minds' eye in front of you. They can be the parents from your childhood. Who is on the right, who is on the left?

How does your body respond, do you notice changes? Also try to feel the space, or look into the space, that is between your parents and around you. Is it light or dark?

Do you feel that your parents are more together or are they each on their own?

Then let one parent come forward. You can take the father or the mother, whichever comes spontaneously. Halve the distance and sense, if it triggers something inside you. Then you can reduce the distance by half again. Pay attention to your sensations.

Now reset this parent to the original distance. Then double the distance from there and then double it again and always feel how it feels in the body. Then find the right distance which feels best for you and leave this parent there.

Now bring the other parent forward and perform the same exercise with them: first halve the distance and then halve it again, followed by the original position. Now the distance is doubled and then doubled again. Then fathom the correct distance to this parent and leave it there.

Please remember this placement of the new correct distance.

How does the space between the parents feel now? Different than before?

Then the parents' places are changed. If the father was on the right, then he is placed to the left and the mother to the right. Then you feel again how this feels now.

Now put the parents back into the position you just found to be the most comfortable, remember this position and stay like this for a few more moments.

In this exercise it becomes clear how strongly the parent images still have an effect. Especially the body sensations give information about how strong the effect of the parental images is and whether it is even possible for the client to change them.

Experiencing one's parents in their own healing environment (exercise T.2)

The following exercise follows on seamlessly from the previous one. It can be done without any feedback from the practitioner or accompanied by continuous exchange with the therapist, who accompanies this process sensitively. It is helpful to deal first with one parent and then with the other, i.e. to take either the mother or the father first.

Create a healing field around your mother (or father) as you already know it (see exercise N.1). You can visualize the presence of awakened companions or simply create a light field. In this healing field, all the supporting forces and helpers that your mother (or father) would have needed in the past and might still need today are revealed. Allow a new picture of life to emerge in your imagination, in which the traumatization your mother (or father) experienced in the past, such as in war, never happened and instead ideal conditions for the development of their inner potential were present.

Perhaps now, in your mind's eye, scenes from your mother's (or father's) childhood with their parents answering and fulfilling all their needs arise. Take your time to let these images arise, where everything your mother (or father) would have needed is there.

(Additional exercise:) If you wish, this can be followed by another inner journey, in which you can imagine that you, too, come into contact with a grandfather, who is present and heartfelt and who is with you in a loving way, and that you have an emotionally strong grandmother at your side, who is deeply responsive to your needs. Take your time with this phase of the exercise as well.

Give a small sign with your hand, when the exercise feels complete. Then finish the exercise by gradually increasing the attention to sensations in your body, feet, and breathing movements and let the exercise slowly fade away.

Open your eyes and orient yourself in the room. Let the exercise linger a little longer.

Maybe you would like to take some notes. If you wish, you can also express the impressions you have experienced and anchor them through contact with the therapist.

In order to become more aware of the effect of these personality traits, it can be useful to regularly review the father-image or the mother-image for a period of time (exercise N.5).

Another simple exercise (Z.2) is to write down on one page all the characteristics and behaviours of the father that you observe in yourself. On the other side all characteristics and behaviours of the mother, which one observes in oneself, are listed.

Let us continue to want to detach ourselves more and more from these unconscious structures, or even better, to subordinate them from the unconsciousness to the self's conscious control.

Writing a letter to our father or mother (exercise T.3)

This exercise helps detach from our external parents. At the same time, it is also a processing of the internalized parental images in the sense of a raising of awareness and integration.

This letter could begin with the sentence: "I still want to tell you....". This letter is only for the client; it is not really sent. Topics of this letter could be acknowledging the achievements of the parents and expressing gratitude, naming what went wrong or what you still resent the parents for, what you have forgiven and anything else that is important to you.

The letter is written by the client at home and then read to the therapist in the therapy situation. It often triggers strong feelings in the patient. It makes sense to give space to these feelings and to encourage the patient to allow this emotional process to take place, because often many strong, unexperienced feelings are still repressed in relation to parents. But it is necessary to feel these in order to become independent from our internal parents.

Detaching from a person (exercise T.4)

A particularly effective exercise for creating independence from parents is the disidentification ritual suggested by Phyllis Krystal. It is performed with the client by a psychotherapist experienced in this method and it is important that the client feels safe with the therapist. In the preparation phase of the actual ritual, it is necessary to go through the horizontal figure of eight (see exercise O.3) for two minutes every morning and evening for about three weeks with the person (for example, the mother) with whom the disidentification ritual is to be performed.

First phase:

Focus your awareness on the physical sensations. Follow the breath, as the abdomen rises and falls with the flow of breath. Then let these perceptions fade into the background and begin to imagine that there is a circle of golden light on the floor around you. You sit in the middle of this golden circle of light. It has the radius of your outstretched arms. Then please imagine that there is a second golden circle of light in front of you, the same size as the one you are in. You put in this circle, the person you want to work with, in our example your mother. The circles are adjacent to each other, but do not overlap. Then imagine that a neon blue light flows within the golden circles, creating a figure of the eight.

Second phase, the actual ritual of detachment:

This phase is performed within a therapy situation. Since experience has shown that these rituals last longer than one hour, the appointment should be scheduled in such a way that there are no time constraints. It is best to be prepared for up to two to three hours. During the ritual, the client is asked to follow only the therapist's questions and instructions, which all relate to the ritual, and not to address any other issues. The client is asked to sit down comfortably (preferably on a chair, not on the floor) so that they are able to sit in such a way for up to 2 hours. Eyes should be closed during the ritual, because the client will have many inner images and should act from within these different internal scenarios, i.e. in their imagination, following the guidance given.

Please take a seat and make yourself comfortable. Close your eyes and focus your awareness first on the physical sensations, especially the sensations in your feet. Then follow the breath, as the abdomen rises and falls with the flow of air. Now let the sensations fade into the background and start the visualization you are familiar with:

Imagine a horizontal figure of eight with the two circles of light, with you in one circle and the person who you are performing the ritual with, in the other circle. In this exercise you can imagine that you are looking at the scene from above, as if you were sitting on a high-chair or looking from the side, so that you can see the space between the bodies clearly. Now ask your higher self to show the bonds between your body and your mother's body, especially the parts of your body where the endings are attached. Also try to perceive any tension, pain or other sensations in your body that may come up during this exploration. Please tell me about these symbolic ties when you have recognized them (for example:

"There is something like a rope between my hand and my mother's hand. Sometimes the bonds also go into the body, anchoring the rope.")

Now ask your higher self internally, which bond you should free yourself from first? How is it symbolized in the internal scenario; what does it consist of? Then ask to be shown appropriate ways of releasing this bond and ask that the appropriate tools be made available to you. Please tell me how this first bond with your mother is to be released or cut. Please remove this bond in the manner shown to you and place the severed bond in your own circle. It will be destroyed later on.

Next please check if any part of the body freed from this constraint needs healing. If it does, ask for healing energy in your hands, and then place your right (or main) hand on that part of your body and your left hand behind it, so that the part to be healed is right in between. Check if healing is really starting.

Then, please find out if any part of your mother's body needs healing as well. If this is the case, please ask the higher self to give your hands healing energy and putting the palms of your hands together, pass this healing energy on to your mother.

Afterwards, following your higher self's instructions, release all further bonds/blockages one after the other until all bonds are removed from both bodies and healing begins. Please let me know when you are done with this.

Then destroy the bond you have placed in your circle. Asking your higher self again how to do this. (For example, they could be thrown into a furnace.)

Now explain to your mother in your own words that this ritual has created freedom for both of you. Then thank your mother for giving you a human body and for everything you learned from her. Ask her to forgive you for all the suffering you have caused her. Ask your higher self for forgiveness for all the wrong that your mother has done to you. Forward the forgiveness you have received to your mother. Then ask your mother to leave your inner being. Send her away with your blessing. Then clear the circle where your mother was, following the higher self's instructions.

The clothes you wear in the internal scenario symbolize behaviours that you have adopted as a result of the old dependency and now need to be destroyed. Take off these clothes in your imagination. They will be destroyed later.

Then a ritual bath is performed for cleansing. Let your higher self show you a body of water (for example, a lake), where you can take the cleansing bath. Let yourself be shown something (for example a piece of soap) with which you can wash away these subtle dependencies in your imagination.

When all the old behaviours are dissolved, express the newly gained joy, maybe it feels very light or joyful. Maybe you feel the urge to jump, or dance, or fly or whatever your joy wants to do to express itself. Then, following the instructions of the higher self, destroy the old, discarded clothes that symbolized the old behaviours.

Then you find new clothes in the internal scenario on the branches of a tree. You can ask your higher self to find the appropriate tree that gives you protection. Then you put on the newly found clothes.

The tree is a symbol of protection. Place your hands on the bark and greet it in your imagination. Then turn so that it is behind you, lean a little forward from the back of the chair and then let yourself slide back onto the tree trunk. Imagine you are this tree with its roots reaching deep into the cosmic mother earth. Now, in your imagination, breathe in everything from cosmic mother earth that you might have needed from your biological mother and did not receive in sufficient measure (such as, for example, love, being accepted, being seen, support and protection). Breathe out any anger or resentment or disappointment you might still feel in relation to your biological mother.

Then you climb the tree in your imagination, stretch out towards the sun, towards the cosmic father. Next breathe in everything that you did not receive in sufficient measure from your biological father (such as love, being seen, praise, recognition, understanding, being there).

Then breathe in through both energy sources and feel how these forces flow through you. Stay with it for a while and then inwardly thank your cosmic parents, who together form your higher self.

Now let these perceptions and images fade into the background and focus your awareness on physical sensations, especially in the feet and legs. Maybe there is the need to move a little, or stretch, as if you just woke up. Then come back to the present moment completely (day and time can be named). Open your eyes and orient yourself in the room.

Since this ritual may have been very intense for the client, the therapist gives the client plenty of space and time to return. It is recommended not to talk about the ritual for the first three days afterwards and to write a letter to the person with whom one has performed it. In this letter, the mutual freedom gained can be expressed once again. It is only for the writer and will not be sent.

U. Working with Investigative Methods

The basis for investigative work is a good relationship of trust between the therapist and the client. If the therapist has an unarticulated working hypothesis that unresolved basic conflicts, usually old unresolved emotional patterns from childhood, are activated or triggered by a presented topic, they can suggest some inner work on this topic, for example what is suggested below, to the client. An indicator for the therapist could be the clients significantly excessive emotional involvement (there are of course differences in basic emotional involvement) in a life situation where you would not normally expect such strong emotional involvement. Old emotional patterns are probably being triggered. Method U.1 serves to uncover the old triggering situations. This method should not be used in cases of severe traumatization, to avoid destabilising or retraumatising the client. The clearly excessive emotional involvement comes about because old feelings from earlier life situations, mostly from childhood, are actualised and are added to the normal, more appropriate emotional involvement.

Investigative work in conjunction with Inner Child Work (method U.1)

This method is not suitable for practice alone! It requires the guidance of a competent therapist.

Client W. reports, for example, that he had an experience the other day that left him feeling bad all day long. Every morning, he was greeted by the shop assistant in the bakery with a friendly smile and she always said goodbye. They often exchanged other pleasantries.

That morning there was neither a smile nor a friendly word. The client felt strongly rejected and took offence. The therapist asks the client if he would be willing to engage in inner experiential work. If he says yes, the therapist explains to him that he cannot do anything wrong during the exercise and that he can open his eyes and finish the inner work any time he needs to.

Please sit comfortably and direct your awareness inwards, perhaps first to the sensations in your body, especially to the sensations in your feet. Then follow the breath, as the abdomen rises and falls with the flow of air. Then let these perceptions fade into the background and think again about the situation you just described to me (in our example the client in the bakery with the saleswoman).

Let it arise again in front of your inner eye (1).

See if there is a resonance (2) in your body. (Client says: "Yes, the chest gets very tight.")

Then I ask you to mark this place or area in your body where you feel the sensation with an imaginary circle of chalk (3).

Afterwards please direct a sentence there in your thoughts, that is, you now silently speak to (4) this feeling: "Show me a situation from the past in which you originally came into being, where your roots are."

If a remembered image (5) appears through the chain of associations, we would ask the client to communicate this without interrupting the inner work. (In our example, the client has remembered a scene where, as a three-year-old boy, he felt unseen and rejected by his mother and in addition she was in hospital for two weeks and the boy could not contact her.)

If the client's recollection is not so clear, the therapist can help with the following questions: "What is going on? Show me more! Do you see the child? How old is the child?" In threatening situations for the child or in situations of great stress, the client is asked to take the inner child out of this key situation and bring it into the present moment to this place, into the therapy room and see what it needs from the client. Here, in the current situation, a subsequent parenting process begins (6).

You can then imagine a symbol of a wisdom figure (7) in the remembered situation (for example, the historical Buddha, or the Medicine Buddha, or the cosmic parents, or the wise friend, Christ, Mary). This makes it easier for the client to leave this situation as it is (sometimes the client has feelings of responsibility or worries about what will happen to the mother or the siblings). Then dialogue is conducted silently with the inner child, very closely focused on the needs of the child. Ask or feel what the child needs (in our example, the client's inner child needed to be seen and understood with feelings of rejection and to have the assurance that the mother will return). If the client feels overwhelmed alone in the inner dialogue with the child, he can also imagine having a strong, wise friend like the buddha in the space behind him. (The dialogue with the inner child could be conducted in this way, "I see your fear and your sorrow, I am here ..." as described in chapter S) Sometimes the inner children need protection and security during the imagined physical contact.

The client is also repeatedly asked to make sure that the child has heard the support ("Did it hear you? How can you tell?") (8). The noticing often happens when a physical sensation changes for the client or when the image of the inner child changes. Then the therapist (who usually feels the changed sensation within him or herself) encourages the client: "Yes, that's it, stay with it...."

What does the child need from you now, or is there something else it needs, perhaps in your life, in your everyday life? (9). Are you ready to give it something of what it needs?

If the dialogue is completed, the client will be asked to come back. While coming back, in a good connection with their inner child, they can be asked to think again about the original situation (10) (in our example the situation in the bakery) and to check if it still feels like it did initially, or if it feels different now. (In our case study the client now felt safe, no more feeling of rejection or being offended. He could now quickly explain to himself that the changed behaviour of the saleswoman had nothing to do with him, maybe she just had a bad day.)

Then the client is asked to slowly come out of the inner work at their own speed, to direct awareness more towards the sensations in the feet, to open their eyes and to orientate themselves in the room.

In case that the question "Show me a situation from the past..." does not bring up an image from memory (11), the therapist can simply continue working with a focusing process on feelings (see section P). They can also ask the client to verbalize and accept their feelings (see method O.1). Then calmly enter into an inner dialogue with this sensation and silently voice the sentence: "I accept that you are there, tightness in the chest, because you are there right now, and therefore you are real, and I accept you."

To illustrate this, the structure of the procedure is set out once again:

1. Bringing the current situation mind
2. Feeling a resonance in the body
3. Marking the sensory area internally
4. Silently entering an inner dialogue with the sensation
5. Remembering an image of the original triggering situation
6. Subsequent parenting
7. Bringing a symbol of wisdom into the original situation
8. Making sure that the inner child is engaged in the process
9. Continue the work with the needs of the inner child
10. Verifying the effectiveness of the intervention
11. Alternative procedure, if no image appears from memory or in case of resistances. The therapist respects this and continues with stage 11.

The Corridor (exercise U.1)

The following exercise works under the assumption that the client is familiar with the tree exercise (S.3). It originates from the Phyllis Crystal imagination system. The corridor exercise is a very effective exercise for finding the cause of a current problem. It can help clarify the following questions: “Why do I keep having this particular fear? Why do I keep behaving in a certain way? Why do I have such low self-esteem?”

Take a comfortable seat and close your eyes. Focus your awareness on the sensations of the body, especially the sensations in the feet. Then follow the flow of breath in the abdomen, which rises and falls as you breathe in and out.

Then let these perceptions fade into the background and ask your higher self to show you a tree. Do the tree exercise (S.3) in a short form and let your cosmic parents appear. Ask the cosmic parents to accompany you during the rest of the exercise.

Then imagine that you are in a long corridor with many doors with different things written on them. On the doors that you see in the corridor, there will be signs with your problems or issues written on them. For example: Anger, lack of self-esteem, insecurity or fear.

As you now walk down the corridor in the inner landscape, read the inscriptions on the doors. Continue walking until you find the door with your issue. Then examine the door. What material is it made of and how can it be opened (for example, with a key, a knob, a bolt, or any other way of opening it)?

After you have ascertained this, open the door and enter the space behind it, together with your cosmic parents. Look around you, what do you see? Ask your cosmic parents to see and experience what is important here. Then ask the cosmic parents to take corrective and healing action or to explain how the old pattern can heal.

Once you have gained enough insight, leave the room together with your cosmic parents and close the door behind you.

Then, in the inner landscape, go back to the tree together with the cosmic parents and lean with your back against the trunk. As you inhale, take in the energy of the tree through your spine and as you exhale, let go of anything that might prevent you from taking in the energy of the tree.

Then ask the cosmic parents to embrace you. Thank them inwardly for their help and support and finish the exercise with the knowledge that you can contact the cosmic parents again at any time. Now come back.

Open your eyes and orient yourself in the room.

If the client wishes, there can be a debriefing. Here the client can tell the therapist in detail about the experience without entering into it too much again (with perspective).

The Inner House of our whole Personality (exercise U.2)

The following exercise is mainly exploratory in nature. It is best suited for people who already understand themselves a bit and are also familiar with inner work involving sub-personalities, the inner child and the parental figures.

Make yourself comfortable on the chair and focus your awareness on the sensations of the body, especially the sensations in the feet and then for a few moments on the sensations of the abdomen, which rises and falls as you breathe in and out. It is beneficial to close your eyes. Then please let these perceptions fade into the background. You now begin in your imagination with a short inner journey. You can't do this wrong, just let the inner images unfold and of course you can always open your eyes and re-orient yourself in the room.

Imagine you are in a meadow somewhere. You see the lush green of the meadow and there is a blue sky above you and it is warm; the sun is shining. There are flowers in the meadow, they are blooming, and you feel good. You see a small path that heads a little upward. This path leads to a house with a wall and an entrance gate.

You decide to go to this house. It is not very far, and you follow the path. The path then becomes a small road that leads directly to the house. This house holds a fascination for you and now it's only a few meters away. The house is quite big. You see that it has several floors.

Now you are at the garden gate and enter the garden surrounding the house. Determined, you continue on to the entrance of the house. There may be a few steps to the threshold. You have a feeling that this house will bring you some insights and you are curious what you will find there.

Open the front door and enter the house. You will notice some doors that have inscriptions and lead you into very special rooms. On the first door it says, "Inner Child" and you go into this room. You are fully awake and look around. Can you see your inner child? What does it look like, what is there in this room? Then there is an adjoining room, the teenager's room. What does it look like in there? Who do you meet? Just notice everything, including the mood that is there and how your body reacts.

Now leave the room and close the door behind you. Stay in the hallway for a few moments and connect with your body sensations. Then when you are ready, continue on your journey of exploration. You will see another door marked with "sub-personalities". When you enter this room, you will meet your sub-personalities. Who will you meet there? How does it feel in this room, what are sensations in your body react? After you have noted everything very attentively, you leave this room and close the door behind you.

You are back in the hallway and feel your breath flow, the sensations in your body. Then, when you are ready, you go to the last room on the first floor of the house. Here a door has the inscription: parent-figures. What is there to discover here? How does it feel? What do you see here? How does your body react? Be wide awake and notice everything that this room triggers in you. Then leave this room as well and close the door.

Now go up to the second floor. To do this, you need to go to the stairs and up them. In the hallway on the upper floor there are also doors with inscriptions. You go to the first door. There is the inscription of your role as a man or as a woman. You open the door and enter this room. What do you find here? What does it look like? How does it feel? How does your body react? Then there are three side rooms.

One is the room of relationships. What do you find here? How does it feel? What is there to discover? From there, another room opens up. It is the space of your sexuality. What do you find here? How does your body react in this space? How does it feel?

There may be another room, which goes off from this room. If so, this could be the room of parenthood. What role you have taken as a mother or father. What is there to find here? Then leave this room and this entire floor.

Now go further up to the second floor. To do this, you need to climb another, somewhat narrower and steeper staircase. There is only one door up there. And already in advance you become aware that it will be a very special place that you now visit. This room bears the inscription 'wisdom' and a particularly vibrant and peaceful atmosphere sets in up there. You open the door and allow yourself to become completely involved in the experience of this room. How does it feel there? What do you perceive? What does it look like here? How does your body react? What kind of sensations do you have? You can stay here a little longer if it is comfortable for you. You might even settle down for a short meditation.

Maybe there is a wise friend, or it's just the space, or the light, or something indefinable. You are fully awake to your perceptions. Maybe there is a question that can be solved in this space of wisdom?

Then you start to slowly say goodbye to this room and its elements. And as you leave this room as well, and make your way back down, visualize everything you encountered in this house and what you want to take with you.

Then leave the house, go down the stairs to the front door and open it. Let the impressions as you leave the house become quite conscious. Take a look at the garden that surrounds the house.

Maybe you walk a few more steps in the garden and notice it. What is there? Plants, flowers, the smells and other sensory impressions. Then move towards the garden gate and leave the property through the gate and go to the meadow, to the starting point of your journey.

Come back completely at your own speed. Open your eyes and orient yourself in the room. – You may want to make a few notes.

It helps the inner processing when the therapist lets the client tell them about the inner journey into the house of their personality. Questions such as: "What meaning do these experiences have for personal growth, for relationships, sexuality or for spiritual growth?" also promote processing. In this exercise it is also possible to visit only single rooms (like the relationship room) and not the whole house.

V. Working with Traumatic Experiences

Traumatic experiences, be they shock traumas or developmental traumas, require special attention in order to avoid unwanted re-traumatization, and therefore also a special form of psychotherapeutic treatment.

These experiences (for example: a traffic accident) are characterized in their emergence by the fact that the organism blocks out certain stimuli or perceptions for survival, because they would lead to an overload of the mental capacity. In the experience, this appears in such a way that the person affected simply no longer notices anything about the experience in the key situation. It's as if they are unconscious and have no conscious memory of what has happened in the past. Let us illustrate this with testimony of a patient:

> "I saw that fully braking would no longer be sufficient to avoid a collision with the vehicle that had suddenly moved from the right lane into my left lane, and I swerved onto the unplanted central strip with the guard rail in the middle of the lane. I heard a shrill noise as my car scraped along the central guardrail. From then on, I don't remember anything until I found myself on the hard shoulder on the right with the damaged car, but unharmed myself. I must have passed 2 vehicles on the left and then braked on the right hard shoulder. One of the vehicles also stopped and the driver confirmed this sequence of events to me. Just as I could not remember what I had experienced immediately afterwards, this experience remained inaccessible for 21 years."

This shock trauma remained unconscious. If there is no processing, these traumas usually remain unconscious. This usually has the price that certain other experiences associated with it can also no longer be remembered. Sometimes a symptom, such as a feeling of tension in the body or an unexplainable fear, appears seemingly independently. These symptoms then appear as if representing the unremembered shock trauma. In the rarest of cases, the people affected establish a connection between the experiences, often far in the past, and the symptoms of their physical or psychological condition, which they just cannot explain and because of which they not infrequently come to therapy. Rarely if this is the case, but otherwise quite often, there is also the symptomatology of dissociation. Here, an unconscious dynamic in the client controls awareness in order to prevent the contents of the traumatic experience from coming back into consciousness. The associative stream of perceptions is interrupted, and the client continues to perceive, think and talk about less stressful contents. This is a dynamic that most people who are not specially trained do not necessarily notice in everyday life.

The diagnosis of traumatic experience and trauma treatment have gained more emphasis in recent years. There are special therapeutic approaches – some known as trauma therapies – that are predominantly concerned with trauma treatment or trauma processing. Here, "Somatic Experience of Peter Levin", NARM – the "Neuroaffective Relationship Model" for trauma healing of Heller and the "EGO-State-Therapy" of Watkins are worth mentioning. Trauma processing also plays a major role in Erikson's hypnotherapy techniques.

Special treatment of traumatized clients or people diagnosed with Post Traumatic Stress Disorder is practiced in most mainstream psychotherapy schools today.

In what follows we would like to present some methods that are used in Essential Psychotherapy. They have proven to be efficient with the special approach of EPT and resource orientation.

Alternating between resource and trauma (method V.1)

This way of working with traumatic experiences in clients requires some preconditions:

1. The client should be well oriented and able to (re-)orient themselves quickly.
2. They should have a resource (exercise N.1) available and feel confident in using it.
3. The therapist should be aware of and familiar with, trauma treatment.

At the beginning of the treatment the client is given overview (1) of the course of the inner work. They are asked again and decide (2) whether they want to work on the traumatic experience now. They then make contact (3) with their resource (exercise N.1) and remains in the experience (4) of security or strength until it is also felt physically (for example in the sensation of strength in the arms).

They stay in contact with the sensation and say where (5) they want to have the resource image or resources imaginatively in the room. (An example of a resource: a special experience during a mountain hike – name of the resource: "the mountain hiker". In the example, our client wants to have their resource the mountain hiker standing close to their right side. Another resource from the realm of the Higher Self – see chapter Y – is the buddha for our client. This is imaginatively placed in the space above the client and gives a sense of vastness and openness, especially noticeable in the chest/heart space.) Then the client is asked to remember the traumatic experience/or to get in contact with it (6) (this can happen either verbally or as an image).

In our example, the client could now remember violent experiences in his parental home. He is asked to bring the offended, hurt or traumatized part, (in our example this is now a shocked child) into the present, that is here into the therapy room, to this moment (7).

For the triggering situation, another resource (in our example again the resource is the Buddha), can be imaginatively placed in the parental home (8) and left there to represent the client. It remains there in place of the affected child and allows healing to occur. The shocked child remains with the client. The buddha is asked to care for the child along with the resources. (The child may now be imaginatively on the client's lap or standing close to him.) His grievance is felt, for example, in the sensation of tightness in the chest (fear/shock) and in pain from the father's beatings.

Then it's as if a pendulum is swung between the open feeling – buddha resource – and the tight feeling or between the feeling of powerlessness (forehead headache) and the feeling of the resource – mountain hiker – strength in the arms. The client is asked and supported to go back and forth internally between the offended and hurt feeling and the feeling of the resources – this is how the alternating happens (9). If this is not possible for the client on the sensory level (because it is perhaps experienced as too threatening), it can also be done imaginatively at first. (The affected child in the scenario on the lap and the mountain hiker to the right of him. Or for even more distance, seeing everything on two separate screen windows).

When this has happened a few times, and in our example the child is still being cared for. It will be asked from the self-place what it needs, if it is strong enough (10) (method S.1). This attention sets further healing processes in motion and is continued as long as the client needs it. In the process, a resource can be asked about it again and again or the client switches to a resource place.

At the end of the therapeutic work of this session, the therapist asks the client how they will continue to deal with the affected part in their everyday life (11) in the future. Agreements can be made such as: "Whenever you report a certain fear, I will be there for you, or I will report to you once a day until the next therapy session and then I will be there for you" (see chapter S, on working with the inner child).

So, in the course of this method a smooth shift into working with the inner child (method S.1) has happened.

Case example for trauma processing

A 38-year-old patient had witnessed many incidents of violence between parents and towards himself, during his childhood. There was also prolonged neglect. At the beginning of the treatment, he had a high level of permanent physical tension and often strong fears of loss arose. Furthermore, he complained of a continuous pain in his upper abdomen – probably due to the high internal tension. He had controlled his strong aggressive impulses for many years through intensive martial arts training. He was regularly attacked by nightmares.

In the course of therapy, a solid, trusting relationship had developed. The client had a good command of calling on resources and had generally stabilized well. The nightmares had become rare. The upper abdominal tension had almost completely disappeared, and the fear of loss had also decreased significantly. His external life was stable. In the 35th therapy session, the client had decided to turn to the memory of a traumatically experienced incident for processing.

Therapist: Is it right for you now to turn to the stressful memories of your childhood?

Client: Yes, today I feel strong enough to do that.

Therapist: Then first take your awareness to your physical sensations. Perhaps first mainly to the sensations in your feet and legs, so that you feel well grounded, and then for a few moments follow the sensations in the abdomen, which rises and falls as you breathe in and out.

Client is inwardly completely with the sensations and relaxes.

Therapist: Then please direct your awareness to the resource.

Client: Yes, I am visualizing myself in the lap of the Buddha.

Therapist: Fine, what sensations does that trigger in you?

Client: I feel quite safe, the chest/heart space expands, my breathing becomes calmer, there is the feeling that nothing can happen to me.

Therapist: Just let the sensations be all there and expand them throughout the body. Is it felt most strongly in the chest/heart space?

Client: Yes.

Therapist: Then please think of the memory from childhood.

Client: Yes, that's there right away. My parents are there yelling at each other. Dad is hitting mum, and I am scared for her.

Therapist: Can you feel the fear in the body now?

Client: Yes, I feel very strange, I also feel the fear strongly now and I am very rigid, especially in my arms and legs and I hold my breath.

Therapist: Can you go back to the sensations in the heart space?

Client: I'll try, yes, that relaxes me, I can take a breath again.

Therapist: Please stay there with the awareness. Completely feel the relaxation and security again. You are completely in the lap of the Buddha.

Client: Yes, that feels good. Nothing can happen to me here.

Therapist: Stay with it, nothing can happen to you here, here – in or with the resource – you are completely safe.

Client: Yes, I can be there.

(Therapist leaves the client for quite a while until the client has visibly relaxed again in experiencing the resource.)

Therapist: Can you now move again toward the other sensation of rigidity in the arms and legs?

Client: Yes, I'll try.

Therapist: What are you experiencing now?

Client: I still feel so helpless and small, but not quite as rigid anymore. Breathing is shallow, but it's okay.

Therapist: Yes, maybe you can stay with these sensations for a little while longer.

Client: Yes, now I am getting quite sad too. *(Client begins to sob.)*

Therapist: Yes, there is sadness.

Client: Yes.

The therapist holds the client as he cries, as he experiences pain and grief.

Therapist: Then switch back to the sensation of expansiveness in the heart space.

Client: Yes, that goes well *(Client sobs with relief.)*

Therapist: How does it feel there now?

Client: Good and safe, also somehow even lighter than before.

Therapist: Stay there a little longer.

Client: Yes, I am relaxing more again, also my heart is lighter.

Therapist: Can you look from where you are now, from the sensation in the heart space to the sensation in the arms, just look?

Therapist: And if you now feel there from the safety of the sensation in the heart… i.e. without moving completely away from the heart sensation.

Client: Yes, that works, it also amazes me, it's as if it flows from the heart with the exhalation to the arms and then also to the legs.

Therapist: Fine, stay with it, let it happen.

Client: Yes, first it was only on the surface of the arms, on the top of the skin and now it is all encompassing, now the arms can be felt fully, warm and pulsating.

Therapist: Ah, yes, please stay with it. And the legs?

Client: They are a bit more thawed out now. They are slowly getting warm again and I can feel them again.

Therapist: Then just stay with the process as it develops.

(Client remains inwardly with his changing sensations for a while.)

Client: Yes, now I can also feel my legs completely again. The ankles still hurt.

Therapist: Ah, yes, the ankles still hurt. What is that about?

(Client remains inwardly in his experience for a while).

Client: I see an infant being held by the ankles with the head down.

Therapist: Yes, do you want to follow this even further?

(This is where a shift into inner child work happens.)

Client: Yes.

Therapist: Go ahead and ask internally, what's going on? Show me more.

Client *(is in his inner experience)*: There is this infant. I just see that he is quite in need of protection.

Therapist: Yes, follow your inner process. Just be there for the infant as you feel it.

Client: Yes, I take him in my arms and cradle him.

Therapist: Yes, please stay with it. Bring the infant gently into the present, into this safe situation.

Client: Yes, I am bringing him here, he comes with me into the lap of the Buddha.

(Client remains silent in his inner experience).

Therapist *(after a while):* Where are you now in your inner experience?

Client: I am holding the infant very close to me and gently rocking it. It has now curled up completely and fallen asleep.

Therapist: How does it feel for you?

Client: Good, I am now completely relaxed and calm, it also feels comfortable and safe.

Therapist: Fine, stay with it a little longer. *(The client remains visibly relaxed for a while.)* Just enter very gently into the infant, so that you inwardly change into the position of the infant in your imagination.

Client: Yes, that is very deep, deeply relaxed.

Therapist: Does it feel safe?

Client: Yes, quite good and quite certainly.

Therapist: Ah, yes, then stay there for a few moments and then switch back to the position of the adult.

Client: Yes, it's close together.

Therapist: Is there anything else that needs to happen or is it just fine?

Client: It's good, I feel very deeply complete within myself.

Therapist: Ah, yes, stay there a little longer and then come out of these inner scenarios and experiences again when it's right for you.

Client: Yes. (*He opens his eyes after a while.*) Thank you.

Therapist: With pleasure.

After applying the method of alternating between resource and trauma (method V.1), it shifted to inner child work in the process of this case study (method S.1). (The moment when the inner image of the infant appeared, and the client was asked if he wanted to work on it further).

Detaching with the help of a symbol (method V.2)

Another method of trauma treatment originated with Phyllis Krystal. In this exercise, the work with the higher self and being guided and anchored in the higher self (see chapter Y) is used as a resource and a symbol for the trauma is used. Thus, the trauma is worked with covertly – without the client fully remembering the key incidents and associated feelings.

Please sit comfortably in your chair and focus your awareness for a few moments on the sensations in your body, especially in your feet and legs. Then for a few moments, follow the sensations in the abdomen, which rises and falls as you breathe. Then, as a preparatory exercise, begin with the maypole (exercise Y.4) or with an alignment with the higher self that you are very familiar with (see chapter Y) Then ask your higher self for guidance for this exercise. You communicate internally in your imagination that you are looking for a symbol for the trauma you have experienced. To do this, you use a method of distracting your mind and thinking. The symbol should come from another part of you, not controlled by your thinking side. You can distract yourself by watching an exciting movie or a radio play or other strong sensory stimuli where you are with your waking consciousness. The therapist can also guide the client through another exercise, such as the tree exercise.

In your left hand (or not your main hand) you have a crayon and a sheet of paper or plasticine. Now ask your higher self to guide your hand in drawing to get a symbol for the trauma. This will then find itself. The client should not control the hand, so that it draws or forms from the plasticine as if by itself. During this time, the client's waking consciousness is completely with the television or the listening or internal forms of the exercise that the therapist is doing with them. It is not with what is happening with the left hand.

The client then continues to work with the symbol found in this way for about four to six weeks on their own, performing the horizontal figure of eight (see chapter O) with the symbol in the opposite circle at least twice a day (preferably for two minutes in the morning after waking up and two minutes in the evening before going to sleep, because then one is close to the unconscious). Often this symbol drawn on paper, is difficult to visualize, because it is abstract. In this case it is recommended that the client places it on the floor in front of them and traces the figure of eight in front of them on the floor in imagination. The client could also draw the figure of eight on a large sheet of paper, paste the drawn symbol into one circle, and visualize himself in the other circle.

After this time of preparation, in another therapy session, the circles are separated according to the instructions and guidance of the higher self.

The session begins after a relaxing preliminary exercise and alignment with the higher self with the visualization of the horizontal figure of eight – client in one circle, the symbol in the other circle. Then the symbol is destroyed in imagination according to the instructions of the higher self (for example, it could be burned in a blast furnace in imagination, or whatever arises in the inner scenario as a course of action). Once this imagined symbol is destroyed, also erase the now empty circle of light in an appropriate way (for example, it could be wiped off a blackboard like chalk, or it could also be cleaned away or erased).

Then later after the session, but on the same day, the sheet of paper with the painted symbol is destroyed or the formed symbol is changed or destroyed.

If this exercise was intense for the client, it is good to follow up with the tree exercise (exercise S.2) for stabilization or as a nurturing exercise.

Let us stay with our case study of the client with the car accident. He had auditory memories of the accident once again in the phase of the exercise where it was necessary to find a symbol – he was guided by the therapist during this time with his waking consciousness through Phyllis Krystal's tree exercise. He heard a very loud shrill noise – the sounds of the de-scraping of the central guardrail during the accident – and then he persisted in drawing the symbol through the therapist's cue. The sounds disappeared. After the ritual was completely finished, the symbol destroyed, the circles separated, the client's symptoms disappeared, such as the tinnitus that the client had since the accident.

W. Working with Dreams (method W.1)

Work with dreams in EPT is partly psychoanalytical and partly uses Gendlin's focusing dream questions. Sigmund Freud, the founder of psychoanalysis, said: "... the interpretation of dreams is the via regia (Lat. *royal road,* or *supreme path)* to knowledge of the unconscious in the life of the soul." This indicates the opportunities presented by working with dreams in understanding and healing the client.

Dream-Work from a Buddhist perspective

It is interesting that in buddhist mind training this particular royal road is not included initially in personal practice. Dreams are seen as mirrors of our karma, i.e., our emotional patterns, habits and tendencies but the practitioner is advised not to explore more deeply the contents of their dreams. The reason is that it is primarily a matter of seeing through the dream-like nature of the experience during the day – and here nocturnal dreams serve for at this point, only as an example of how much one can take an imagined reality as real, complete with all its emotions and even physical reactions, although it is only a dream. So, it is recommended immediately upon awakening to radically drop any identification with the dream and not to pay any further attention to it. We are also warned against drawing conclusions from dream experience for the shaping of everyday life, because all too often one is mistaken in the interpretation of one's own dreams and projects one's own fears and expectations into them.

But this does not mean that this analytical royal road is excluded. In dream analysis we try to avoid any hasty conclusions of dream interpretation and gently reveal one layer of emotional meaning after another – in order to avoid exactly what the buddhist masters warn against: drawing hasty conclusions from dream experience. The work consists precisely in understanding our karmic mirror and thereby gaining insight into what we have to work on during the day.

In buddhist training, inner work with dreams does take place at a later stage: dream yoga is part of the path of liberation. The point is to first find our way fully into lucid dreaming, that is, to become aware in the dream that I am dreaming. We then use this awareness to shape the dream entirely as we wish. This includes not only changing the story, but also multiplying or dissolving appearances as they arise in the dream, drinking fire, breathing under water, walking through walls – in other words, doing all the things that are only possible because they are not real. It is also practiced in order to go on dream journeys to other realms or outside the body.

At this point it becomes really interesting, because in the dream one begins to practice the Dharma, that is, to meditate, to bring about the welfare of others, and to perform the same practices as during the day. This involves seeing through the nature of the experience and practicing Mahāmudrā in the dream, that is, entering into nondual awareness. This exhausts the karmic impulses that lead to normal dream experience, for they are no longer attended to, no one attends to them, they receive no nourishment, and they dissolve. Thus, the dream phase can be used at night for the continuation of the awareness practice. The content of the dreams is no longer taken care of. It is only about being aware of the nature of the mental movements. But this is quite a long way down the path. As long as we are still struggling with stronger emotional patterns, it can be quite useful to subject significant dreams to a dream analysis with the help of an experienced therapist. There are many good reasons and excellent methods for this.

Dream analysis in six phases

The following is an interpretation model for specific dream elements and dream levels in six phases. We follow the methodology of free association (phase 2). In phase 4 (see below) the dreamer identifies with individual dream elements. This approach was originally developed by E. Gendlin.

In working with dreams, the therapist takes the same attitude (see chapter L) at the beginning of the therapy session and during the session, as with all other procedures in EPT. That is, they are centred internally, they rest in the timeless open awareness or are in contact with wisdom figures, like the Medicine Buddha and there is the creation of a healing field (see chapter M and exercise N.1).

The practical guide to dream interpretation presented below, distinguishes between different phases and levels of processing and thus lends itself to a structured approach. However, it is not necessary to apply it phase by phase, elements can be picked out depending on the individual's process. The prerequisite is that the client has decided to make a dream and dream work the subject of the session:

1. The client is asked to *remember* and *recount* the dream as fully as possible (if they have written it down, they should not read it). The therapist writes down the dream completely.
2. The client is now asked to *associate freely* with the dream content: "What comes to your mind about the dream or about certain parts of the dream?" Sometimes the chains of associations lead to experiences in the client's distant past that seem to have nothing to do with the dream itself. The therapist follows this at first. Further work is then done with this situation under certain circumstances. For example: the client has retrieved a memory of an unmet need from childhood via a chain of associations, at this point we could continue with inner child work (see chapter S). Here the dream is an entry point, almost like a fantasy, which in the process of the therapy situation leads clients and therapists to important, sometimes still unprocessed experiences.

3. The content of the dream is examined to see if there are real people as dream elements with whom the client has a relationship. The people are seen as real objects or relational people of the client. The therapist then asks about the relationship (level of relationship or interaction in the client's reality). Does the dream provide clues to the quality of interactions along with emotional components to these people the client is in relationship to? This also applies to dream objects. Psychoanalytically, this is considered an interpretation at the object level.
4. Intra- or inner-psychic levels or also interpretation on the subject level: the dream is understood as the dreamer's inner arena. All people or objects manifesting in the content of the dream can represent different sides of the dreamer. The client should briefly identify with these individual dream elements during the course of the session. Important dream elements (for example: significant people or objects) are determined and picked out. The client determines the order of the dream elements they want to start further inner work with. They would then be asked, for example, with a dream in which they dreamed of a ticket collector: "Please, even if it is unfamiliar to you, identify yourself just for a moment with this dream element ticket collector. Please be the ticket collector from the dream completely, right now. How does it feel? If it stood for a side of you, which side would it stand for?" The client may answer this question by saying that this dream element "ticket collector" could stand for their aggression. The therapist then asks the client to drop the identification. "Now please let go of the dream element. Go back to feeling the sensations in your body, especially in your feet." Then the process continues with the next dream element. The therapist proceeds again with the same questions. One by one, different elements of the of the client personality are mentioned. The therapist can now relate them to each other analogously through the structure of the story in the dream.
5. At this stage, the therapist asks the client to close their eyes once again and continue dreaming the dream as a daydream. "Please

close your eyes and pick up dreaming the dream as a daydream. Abandon yourself to the images and try not to control the process." This continuing to dream in the therapy situation is usually started at the end of the narrated dream. However, it can also begin at another important point. Dreaming on often indicates the process direction of a certain dynamic. In dreams with stressful themes, especially nightmares, continuing to dream can take away the heaviness.
6. At this stage, the therapist can ask the client questions about the dream. For example, a question such as, "If the dream had meaning for your personal development, what might it be?" Or "If it had meaning for your sexuality or for your spiritual development, what might it have?" By unlocking the interpretive schemas, good insight into the client's repressed emotions and attachment patterns can be gained.

The dream can also tell the therapist something about further resources and possible development space for the client. Our subconscious sides are often more advanced than we are! The therapist can use the power of the observer in the dream and the awareness itself as resources. This can be done as an intervention to strengthen this resource in the client, or to point out in the first place that this ground of being always exists and of course was present in the dream.

Then the therapist can then summarize and interpret the dream dynamics – the highlighted personality elements and the attachment patterns, analogous to the dream events in their relationship with each other (the new story). In addition, they can encourage the client to create a dream diary or to keep paper and pencil by the bed and write down dreams immediately after waking up.

This approach has proven itself in practice. However, it can be supplemented by further categories, for example, of Jungian dream interpretation, or transference. For more in-depth information, please refer to the further reading section.

Case study on dream work

The following case study is of a fifty-nine-year-old client.

Therapist: Would you like to describe your dream?

Client: I am definitely on a train, in a compartment, and not a passenger compartment, but a kind of service compartment. It is bigger, too. It is more of a lounge, but it is also a railway carriage. There are a total of three or four ticket collectors. I have something to do with them.

What comes to mind now: there is also something to do with ticket inspectors, I'm doing something with them, I'm discussing things with them and then – I don't remember whether it was directly in the dream or right after I woke up – I thought, "Wow, what's that? You were in the ticket inspectors' compartment. You took the train, but you were in a completely different compartment." It was only then that I realized that. And then there was something else where I was sitting in a real compartment. But I can't remember if it was before or after the compartment with the conductors and inspectors. I remember that I reprimanded one or the other of them for not behaving properly. I don't know exactly what happened, but I told them: "I don't think that is the way you behave here."

And then afterwards the surprise that I was in this compartment, although I was actually just taking the train. That was the main thing.

(The narrative of the dream ends here.)

Client: And then there was – this is perhaps related to a real situation: we returned from Switzerland on a City Nightliner. It was not a nice experience because it was a pretty dirty and run-down train – not very appealing. And the situation on the train was not very appealing either. These were not nice, clean ICE compartments. So, that can be related to this actual occurrence.

Therapist: You are starting to get some ideas. You can close your eyes, if you like, for a few moments and visualize the dream again. So, all these dream images with the train and the compartment, which is a bit like a service compartment and a bit like a lounge, with the three or four ticket collectors who are perhaps inspectors. And there is discussion, and you are upset, "Well, that's not the way to do it." You rebuked them – Don't think too much, follow whatever arises freely, your spontaneous associations – please share these thoughts with me.

(Client was encouraged to stay more in the primary process – in the association process – and not to go into reflecting the – secondary process.)

Client: What comes back, is the question: which train am I actually on? Or which train do I want to be on? Both, at the same time. And also, the surprise: if I was actually on a train, I would be dependent on the ticket inspectors. Without a ticket, they could fine me. But here it was the other way around: they have nothing to say to me at all. It is me who has something to say to them. That astonished me.

Therapist: Can you think of anything else to say about this?

Client: It was shortly after the discussion that I noticed: wow, they are really a bit scared. I said something, but I can't remember the exact content. It was a kind of role reversal. I still remember that. This kind of surprised me.

Therapist: Can you bring these dream ticket collectors to mind again?

Client: Two or three were very pale figures and one was a red-haired, shaggy-haired ticket collector who was quite aggressive. I told her that her behaviour was not okay. The others observed, but did not intervene.

Therapist: Then please let this shaggy, red-haired ticket collector be there once again as a dream phenomenon and see what else occurs to you, what associations there are. Just open yourself to the inner stream of associations. Sometimes you then find other concerns. What comes to your mind about this dream image?

Client: I only know that in real life I met such a woman on the train. She reminded me of my sister-in-law. She was also very chubby – like my sister-in-law, and also very insensitive, rude and impertinent to the fellow passengers.

Therapist: What about this sister-in-law, what is the relationship like with her?

Client: There was this know-it-all part that came through strongly with the ticket collector.

Therapist: And the sister-in-law?

Client: She has a lot of that too. At least that's how I feel about her.

(Questions about the level of interaction in reality)

Therapist: How is your relationship with her?

Client: Not very good.

Therapist: That's the wife of?

Client: My older brother's wife.

Therapist: Just see what spontaneously, associatively comes to your mind.

Client: Just this arrogant, matronly quality

Therapist: Can you think of anything else?

Client: A lot comes to mind about my sister-in-law.

Therapist: What comes to mind about her?

Client: A lot of prejudices.

Therapist: A lot of prejudices? *(Long pause.)* What's going right now internally?

Client: I don't really want to have that much to do with her.

Therapist: You don't want to have that much to do with her. *(Long pause.)* Does she remind you of anything else? *(Long pause.)*

(The therapist suspects that the client has remembered something but does not want to communicate it. An inner process is taking place in the client.)

Client: No, not really.

(Change to the intra-psychic level:)

Therapist: Please take on the role, for a moment of the red-haired ticket collector in the dream. How does that feel? If this dream phenomenon stood for a part of you, which part could it stand for?

Client: Perhaps hasty judgement (1).

Therapist: Rash judgement, Ah, yes. Let's go back to the overall dream image. There was also astonishment that you criticized the ticket collector because she had behaved so badly.

Client: The surprise was that they were all so unsettled and also a bit afraid: "What is he doing to us now?"

Therapist: Please see if you can associate something with that, if you have any ideas about being surprised that they get scared.

Client: I didn't intend that at all.

Therapist: Yes, being surprised that they got scared, although you didn't actually intend it.

Client: There is something liberating about it somehow.

Therapist: Something liberating (2). Are there any other associations?

Client: Yes, the association was that I do have more strength of my own, I am more powerful than I thought.

Therapist: Ah, yes. I do have more strength than I thought. I am more powerful than I thought after all. If you identify with that dream element for a moment: What does that feel like? And if that also stood for a part of you, what part might that stand for?

Client: Yes, that would stand for something powerful, for something striving forward (3).

Therapist: Aha, that would stand for something powerful and forward striving. Let's go back to the dream images. There's this service compartment. It is almost a bit like a ticket hall. Sometimes there are significant objects that catch your eye, that you remember particularly.

Client: There was a box. It did not have any...

Therapist: There was a box. Take a look. Let the box from the dream be there again and see if associations come up.

Client: What comes to me is from school days, from high school days.

Therapist: Yes, stay with that.

Client: There was a freight station near us. There were people who were employed by the railways. And when I think of this box, this compartment, that was also something old, not modern. That's what comes to my mind – they also worked on these old wagons. I have never been inside them; I only saw them from the outside.

Therapist: Stick with that, with the high school years and the freight yard. What's the next association, what's going on there?

Client: There was a gas station where we assembled our cars, a VW bus or others.

Therapist: How old were you then?

Client: Between 15 and 16, and with cars from 18.

Therapist: Just stay with it. Let the associations come. Take your time. How did you feel then?

Client: I can think of two situations *(laughs)*. One was with this VW bus. There is a road near Paderborn that winds around quite a bit. We just sped through it in the VW bus. The guy behind us took a picture and we said we'd see if we could lift the tire off the curb on the bends. Of course, we did not intend it to happen, but we drove in such a way that it could have. The photo then shows how the rear wheels are like this *(showing a big slant with the hands)* on this VW bus. Then I thought, "Well, you really lifted it off the curb." The others always said, "You are lifting the tires off the curb." I always said, "Why, it's not that bad." I had never seen where the tires actually were. But then I saw it on the photo.

Therapist: That was a lively time full of adventures.

Client: Yes.

Therapist: You were doing quite well then. Is that fair to say?

Client: Yes.

Therapist: Yes, that's when you almost lifted the tires off the curbs....

Client *(grins)*: But I was in full control of the driving. At least that was my sense. When I saw the photo, I wasn't so sure anymore.

Therapist: Yes, that was the one situation now. Feel into it again. Which part of you could that represent?

Client: The lively one (4).

Therapist: The vital one, yes. You said you can think of two situations with the box. Can you remember a second one?

Client: It reminds me of the situation at the train station. The second one was a few years later, and at the same time it came to my mind as an image. At the station, there is a bridge with an overpass over the railroad tracks. I remembered driving there in a very fat Maserati, which I had borrowed for a short time from people with whom I had hitchhiked. They were tennis pros that I had taken home with me. They had a big car, but not much other money. So, I said they could stay at my place, they didn't have to go to a hotel. I had to get money from the bank, and they lent me the car to go to town. Then I remembered a friend who had said, "If I had a car like that, I'd drive through Paderborn very slowly." So, I drove this car very slowly through Paderborn.

Therapist: You enjoyed that?

Client: Yes, I enjoyed that.

Therapist: If you identify again with the dream image and feeling, what part of you might it represent?

Client: There was a great sense of independence (5) in it. And of course, something to perform.

Therapist: At that age at eighteen, that has been something very special: Independence and something to perform. Can you think of anything else about that?

Client: No.

Therapist: Then let us look at the overall dream again. There is this compartment that is like a lounge. Are there any associations there?

Client: No.

Therapist: Is there anything else in the overall dream that caught your eye? Sometimes it's objects. Or something that kind of jumps out at you now?

Client: No, no more objects. Only this surprise is quite clear.

Therapist: You were actually surprised about your strength and the effect of your power?

Could that also have a message or meaning for your personal growth and for your life now?

Client: It could.

Therapist: It could. So, it might also be that you are be surprised by your power and your effect?

Client: Yes.

Therapist: Let me summarize again. We have four elements: (1) the part that's quick to judge, represented by the redhead, then, (2) the power and liberation felt in rebuking, (3) the lively part, and (4) the independent and showing off part, which had more to do with the being eighteen years old. And also, there is the surprise about the power and effect your words and actions have.

Maybe sometimes you would also like to lift the tires off the curb... *(statement with interpretative character).*

Client (agreeing): Hmm...

Therapist: See if something else comes up, if there is still an impulse, if there are still associations or if you want to leave it there.

Client: I think it can stay like that.

Therapist: If you were to continue dreaming the dream now as a day-dream, how would it continue? Please close your eyes and let the inner images take over while you continue dreaming. And please tell me what you see.

Client: This is not easy for me.

Therapist: It stops, where you are surprised about the effect of your words. You could continue to dream; the images can continue to run like in a film without any control.

Client: There is no image in that sense, at most a feeling. But I don't quite trust that yet – a bit like a space for further development.

Therapist: Let it be there for a bit; give it space to show and express itself.

Client: There are a lot of different things coming up now.

Therapist: What is coming up?

Client: New orientation, which I am a bit afraid of because it means uncertainty.

Therapist: You are somewhere on a journey in the train compartment and the train. It is going somewhere.

Client: yes, basically there is the question: which train do I want to get on now?

Therapist: Which train do I want to board? Which one do I want to take, which one do I want to be on? Can you think of anything to say about that?

Client: There is this contradiction. On the one hand, the completely unreasonable, like with the VW bus, and the so-called reasonable and feasible.

Therapist: And that creates a relationship. You interact with each other. You were interacting with the redhead in your dream. If you continue to dream like that, – do you have an idea where the train is going? Where could it take you?

Client: That's not quite so clear. But what definitely comes is: more water, the sea. And that, of course, stands for a ship.

Therapist: Ah, yes, that stands for a ship. Let yourself be led there.

Client: I think that has a lot to do with community.

Therapist: It has something to do with community. *(Therapist senses that something feels very wide and open.)* There is also something vast about it.

Client: Yes.

Therapist: Could this have something to do with your spiritual development?

Client: This ship has had a very decisive influence on my spiritual development. Or the experience on the ship.

Therapist: What experience on the ship? (*Therapist notices hesitation in the client.*) Or do you not like to talk about it?

Client: I can't really describe it that way now.

Therapist: Yes, that is where it took you, that is where the train went. Do you want to stay with it for a moment, or should we leave it like that?

Client: We can leave it like that.

Therapist: Then please drop the images. Would you like to say something about what happened?

Client: Yes, it's interesting and also amazing. I would have had no idea of any of that. Thank you.

Therapist: You are on the train and in the end, it leads you to the point that it also has something to do with your spiritual path. And there are controversies on the train. The ticket collectors, after all, have something to do with authority. You manage to put an arrogant, quick to judge authority in its place. You yourself are amazed that you can do this. You feel your power in doing so and there is a bit of: I create space for myself here, I make myself heard there, I can show myself wholly. Can it stay like that?

Client: Yes, thank you.

Summarizing interpretation:

1. The dream leads associatively to the real experiences of disgust and indignation with the dirty compartment of the Swiss train – furthermore to the time as a young lively man with the daredevil driving with the VW bus.
2. Then, on the interaction level, it leads to difficult, perhaps conflictual relationship experiences with the sister-in-law.
3. On the intra-psychic level, the following interpretations are possible: There is this astonishment ("Wow, you are in the ticket collectors' compartment" a process of awareness) and then the rebuke or rejection – an act of will – towards one or more ticket collectors ("No, I don't want it that way"). Thus, free space can emerge through disidentification from the controlling part – perhaps a sub-personality such as the inner judge symbolized by the ticket controllers but especially by the ticket collector. ("It has something liberating") This releases energies, correspondingly energies flow in. It creates the opportunity for something else to come out. These quite lively parts show up (symbolized by the box, which leads to memories of the time of the young man with the group experiences with the VW bus). An independent side shows itself, symbolized by the Maserati driving.

Let us summarize again: the disidentification from the condemning and controlling side allows a sense of power and aliveness to emerge and a striving for independence and autonomy to show itself.

In general, the big issue remains: the possibility of deciding (in the dream when dreaming on, as an opportunity to decide between two trains). Only the decision made (act of will, an act of personal strength) enables a process of opening oneself (there is something vast), and expanding oneself and thus, accessing existential and spiritual (symbolized by the memories of the experiences on the ship) levels and experiences.

X. Working with the Will and with Envisioning

After *working through unconscious dynamics and disidentifying from controlling patterns*, space, power and free energy emerge for creative work. If the client knows some of the unconscious dynamics that influence or even control their perception, emotional experience and relationship forming, and is aware of these forces, perhaps can even control them more internally, then the capacity to make decisions, set directions, shaping and the use of will power can gain additional meaning and present further possibilities.

According to Assagioli, *we are dominated by everything with which we are unconsciously identified.* This means we can find our *creative power*, our ability to form, when the greatest unconscious identifications (see chapter Q – W) are resolved.

Getting to know the taste of a decision (exercise X.1)

Let us start with a simple exercise to discover the force of the ego, the *will*:

> Please turn your attention inwards. Start by directing it to the physical sensations, especially the feet. Then rest for a while with the movement of abdomen as you breath in and out.
>
> Then let the awareness of sensations fade into the background and remember back to earlier in your life. Think of a situation in which you decided, perhaps a big decision, where there may have been pros and cons, and you had to decide. Let

this situation arise again in your inner eye. If there are several situations, please select one.

How did you feel after you made the decision? Did it have an effect on the sensations in your body? How did it feel to decide, what is the taste?

Feel free to give it some space, especially if it was a pleasant experience for you. Let it spread out in your body. Can you perceive a body part where the decision was felt most strongly?

Then continue to stay in contact with this part of the body and with the taste of having decided.

Then let this exercise fade out and give yourself some more time to reflect or contemplate. You may also want to take some notes.

This exercise can also be coupled with a small preliminary exercise (for example, a situation in which you did not take a decision, although you ought to have taken one). Then the difference becomes even more palpable.

Through this exercise you can experience how it is possible to feel when you use the power of decision making more often. This is a very strengthening exercise that can lead to freer, less identified states, which of course can also be used as a resource.

We may also know this from awareness meditation. There is an impulse to follow a certain phenomenon in perception (for example, to think of an unsolved problem) and with purpose we direct the perception quickly to the actual meditation object or follow the stream of further sensory impressions and stay in the process. The same inner forces are at play here.

Alternatively, you can focus your mind specifically to the wholesome and avoid the unwholesome, and have to take a decision in a moment, by means of the mental power of awareness and your will and internally align yourself with a choice. For example: being aware of the Bodhisattva motivation or the qualities you want to develop.

Goal Setting (exercise X.2)

The following exercise originates from psychosynthesis and can be applied very well in the implementation of decisions.

Take your awareness to your physical sensations, especially the feet. It helps to close your eyes, but you can always open them if you need to.

Then let your awareness rest for a few moments on the sensations in the abdomen, as it rises and falls with the rhythm of the breath.

Let these perceptions fade into the background and think about some important goals in your life. It can be something very immediate, like painting the fence, or something big, like learning and practicing a new profession. The goal should be important to you. If you have several goals, please choose one, a real goal with an importance for you.

While you are thinking about the goal, you can also formulate a sentence inwardly: "Yes, I will qualify as a natural medicine practitioner" and tune into your physical sensations. Perhaps there are places where you can feel this. Then direct the inner sentence there: "I want a symbol. Show me a symbol for this goal." (In this particular example a symbol of healing might emerge).

Now imagine that you are on a long road that is quite straight, long and unobstructed. You see this road rising slightly in the distance, going up a small hill. At the top of the hill at the end of the long road is your symbol. You can still make it out in the distance.

You set out step by step, your destination before your eyes.

You go forward with determination. You are in touch with your whole body as you walk. With every step you feel your foot as you put it down. You feel the strength in your muscles, in your legs, in your whole body. You keep walking toward your goal.

As you progress, you notice beings or circumstances or situations along the way that try to distract you, that try to take you away from your goal.

These beings will do anything to distract you, but you know deep inside that they will not succeed. You have the deep certainty that you will not let anything stop you from achieving your goal.

The beings can't really block your path. They may want to lure you or make you feel guilty or give you an excuse for not walking on. But you know deep down that they cannot keep you from your destination. Just go and look at these beings or these circumstances, examine, analyse how they are trying to dissuade you from your goal and then go back to the road, to your path to the destination.

Gradually, you may start to run up the hill and it may not be that far until you reach your destination. You may already be able to see your symbol clearly. Then you reach your destination. Take time to fully taste this experience. How does it feel? How does the body feel? You may even feel like spontaneously expressing your feelings in the inner images.

Stay up there for a moment more, contemplate the path you have travelled and see the obstacles that appeared and that you have overcome.

Stay with your experience for a few more moments, then focus again on the sensations in your body and feet. Come back completely at your own pace.

Let the exercise fade some more and open your eyes, orient yourself in the room. If you like, you can take some notes.

The therapist has the client tell them what was experienced in the debriefing session. The way the obstacles appear provides insight into what is preventing the client from realizing their resolve and can be given special attention in the therapy situation.

Envisioning: "Where do I want to be in 5 years?" (exercise X.3)

This exercise works more with the creative power of our mind:

In the first phase of the exercise, we let the client determine a time frame for their vision (between 3 – 8 years, here 5 years). Then we have them go through all the different areas of their life. The client says where they want to be then (for example, having a condominium, being physically healthy, being in a relationship and having two children, etc.). It helps to tell the client that it is an exercise using will power and imagination in relation to what their life could be like in five years if everything turned out the way they want, within reason of course. We go through all the different areas of life. How are things in relationship, physically, sports, hobbies, health, psyche, friends and social network, work, travel, place of residence and how are family, projects, material goals, spiritual goals, etc.? In this *collection phase* the therapist makes very exact notes, preferably verbatim. Once this phase is completed, the client is guided inwards.

> Please make yourself comfortable, take your awareness to your physical sensations, follow the flow of breath through the abdominal a few moments. Then let this fade into the background. I will now read to you everything you just said about your vision, slowly and mindfully, speaking for you in the first person.
>
> When asked, where do I want to be in five years, you gave the following answers: "I will still live in my house with my wife...."

After the therapist has read out everything carefully and has also pointed out to the client that more goals can now be added, if any had been forgotten, while centring, the client is given the instruction to let everything *sink in*, to internalize it even more and to dwell with it for a few moments. Then the therapist asks the client to repeat the following sentence internally: "Now repeat the sentence internally:

show me a symbol, an image for my vision of the year." The therapist allows the client some time to do this and also points out that some people do not see symbols or images, if this is the case it could come in words.

Then follows the *as if* step. The client should now act inwardly *as if* the vision had been fulfilled. "Now pretend that your vision has been fulfilled. How does that feel?" Then, if it feels good, the experience is given some space, so that it can also be felt throughout the body, in every cell. "If it feels good, then give space to the sensations until it is felt everywhere." After a while, where the client stays with the experience of their fulfilled vision, the *grounding phase* comes. Now, from the *as-if-place*, look back to the present time: "And from this fulfilled vision, please look back to today to ... (name the date) – What is my next step (in this direction)? Sometimes you have already taken it, sometimes you still have to take it. – Stay with this for a moment and then slowly end the exercise. Focus on the body sensations and open the eyes to orient yourself spatially."

The client can be given time to take notes. In the debriefing, the therapist asks the client if he saw a symbol and what it looked like and then also if he found a next step and what it looks like.

The symbol carries the entire vision in this exercise. It is like the seed of a tree. It is useful to think of this symbol often, consciously bring it to mind often, especially in the first few days after doing the exercise. It is a bit like *watering a young plant*. Then, after a few months, the exercise can be refreshed again. Especially the next steps change according to experience.

With this exercise creative energy is used to stay in contact with the vision. It significantly increases the chance that everything will manifest in that way.

For many clients it is important to experience that it is not only about revising, processing and working through triggering experiences and unconscious dynamics, but that one's own mind can also be directed and that this has power and gives strength and strengthens one's own resources. The energy stuck in unconscious fixations and perceptual pre-structuring is freed up and is available to the ego and free will. It can be directed into healing. There is more space or free will for creativity.

Y. Working with the Higher Self

We could have combined this chapter with chapter M on "Resources" because work with the Higher Self is a very nurturing, resource-oriented or resource-based work. It is presented here as a separate chapter, to give it special attention,

The term *Higher Self* was introduced into psychology by C. G. Jung. Today it is used in many psychotherapeutic approaches, including psychosynthesis and Phyllis Krystal's imagination work. The Higher Self, in the broadest sense, refers to the *soul level* or spiritual level of the human being. This level would perhaps be referred to in Christian terminology as the Christ-power, that is, the Son of God; in Hinduism it would be Brahman and Atman; in buddhism it would be the Buddha or buddhahood. From our perspective, it is a subtle level of our awareness that allows us to sense, or experience, awakened, timeless awareness. The level of the Higher Self is often addressed in imaginative exercises through visualizing light.

As stated in the first part of the book, most of the Vajrayāna exercises (see ch. H) would naturally fit in this chapter on working with the Higher Self. We have limited ourselves here to supplementing what we have said earlier, with some exercises that come mainly from Assagioli's spiritual psychosynthesis and the Phyllis Krystal Imagination System.

Alignment with the Higher Self (exercise Y.1)

The following exercise was originally used in psychosynthesis, where it is still performed by client and therapist together at the beginning of a psychotherapy session. However, this exercise exists in very similar forms in various spiritual traditions. Through it each person tries to get in touch with more subtle forms of awareness and to include this level for the whole of psychotherapy session or even for the entire process of therapy. This often gives the session a slightly different *flavour*, it has a different *tone* or *quality*, often it also has different *intensity*. Many clients experience themselves as more supported, held or guided.

> Sit comfortably in your chair and focus your awareness on the sensations of the body. Then, follow the breathing and the movements of abdomen, as it rises and falls with each breath.
>
> Then imagine above your head a bright source of light, like a sun or a star, very bright, without the heat of the sun, just the brightness and the radiance. Stay with this imagination of the light source above your head for a while (maybe two minutes).
>
> While doing this, you can also formulate a question, for example asking the theme of the session to present itself, if it is not already known, or that what needs healing will present itself and that healing will happen. Then slowly let the show fade and reorient yourself in the room.

After this inner alignment, the therapist might begin the session by asking, "What do you want to work on?"

The Wise Friend (exercise Y.2)

This exercise also originates from Assagioli's psychosynthesis and also from David Bach. It emphasizes the relational aspect of working with the higher self and is therefore also well suited to enhancing a sustaining and nurturing relational experience and to connect with one's own spiritual resources. Unresolved life issues can also find new answers through this exercise.

Sit comfortably in your chair and close your eyes, focus your awareness on the sensations in the body, especially the sensations in the feet.

Follow the flow of your breath in the abdomen, as it rises and falls. Then let these perceptions fade into the background and become aware that you are ready for a little inner journey.

You are in a valley on a meadow. You perceive the lush green of this meadow and the many colourful flowers. It is a pleasantly warm summer morning; the blue sky and the sun are shining above you. In front of you, not too far away, you see a mountain that somehow attracts you, so you decide to follow a path that leads to this mountain.

You follow the path and perceive everything intensely with your senses: the strength in your body, your muscles as you walk, the gurgling sound of a nearby stream, the pure, clear mountain air, and how you enjoy the movement and your sensory impressions.

Perhaps you also feel the anticipation of a special experience during this mountain climb. You come through a forest and notice the changes in the environment quite intensely, the air, the smell of freshly chopped wood and the atmosphere here in this forest.

Slowly, the path climbs a little more and maybe you go a little slower, paying attention to the flow of your breath. The path climbs higher and higher until you have a wide view of the valley below through the trees.

Finally, the path leaves the forest and climbs even more steeply uphill. At times you have to scramble over larger stones or small rocks. You keep climbing up furnishing a little more effort. But your body strength is stable, you are in good shape and, so you are sure to reach your destination. You climb slowly and steadily, getting higher and higher.

Now you are going through the haze of a cloud. The moisture on your skin is refreshing and invigorating. Again and again, you see the dark blue of the sky above you. You breathe in the pure clear mountain air quite intensely. Now, only a few meters are left to reach the summit. You need to climb a bit and use the help of your hands.

As you reach the plateau at the summit, you stop and carefully take everything in – together with the feeling of having reached the destination. You look at the wonderful panorama, which extends far into the country and across other mountain ranges. Enjoy the vastness of the view.

Then, very slowly, look up into the sun. There you will see a face – the face of a wise friend. Invite the friend to come down and stand next to you. Feel the presence of this humorous, very wise and very lovable person who is completely there for you.

This being wishes you very well and is full of compassion and kindness. Step closer and feel the presence of wisdom and love. Look into the wise friend's eyes and talk to them. Perhaps there are questions about certain problems, or you have a request or simply some wishes that the friend can witness in deep wisdom.

Take your time to connect and for the conversation to unfold. Then listen to the answers. These answers can be very varied, they often appear in images and ideas, sometimes in words, sometimes in silence. Listen very attentively in silence.

After a while, please say goodbye to the wise friend for the time being. Then return.

Finish the exercise completely in your own time, let it fade away.

Then open your eyes and orient yourself in the room.

If you wish, take a few notes.

In the therapeutic setting, a debriefing will help with processing the impressions. If an inner guidance was received or some answers to questions, reflect together: what does this mean for the client? How might it influence everyday life? The client is encouraged to get in touch with this wise friend again and again, also independently of the therapy situation.

Temple of Silence (exercise Y.3)

This exercise also originates from psychosynthesis. It facilitates access to deep experiences of how things are and gives spiritual resources.

Sit comfortably in your chair and close your eyes. Focus your awareness on the physical sensations, especially the sensations in the feet. Then follow the breathing for a few moments, the movement of abdomen as it rises and falls with the flow of the breath. Then let these perceptions fade into the background and begin an inner journey to the Temple of Silence.

You are in a beautiful meadow. Around you are many different flowers and plants, a small stream, the air is pleasantly warm, the sun shines, the sky is blue, and the air is clear. You feel that this is a special day, and that you will experience something exceptional.

Your gaze wanders over the landscape and you see a temple on a hill. A very special aura emanates from this temple. It is the Temple of Silence, and they say no one has ever spoken there. You decide to go to the temple, finding a path that leads up the hill.

You feel your muscles as you walk and the strength of your body, also the power of your decision to follow that path and go to the temple of silence. Now you have already walked a large part of the path, and, looking around, you can see the peaceful meadows below you. The path becomes steeper, and you have to exert a little more effort.

Then it is only a few steps until you reach the plateau of the hill on which the temple stands. Finally, you have arrived. Take your time to enjoy this moment: the temple with its very special aura in front of you and the vastness of the view from up there.

You decide to enter the temple. You climb some stairs until you see a heavy wooden door. You touch the massive handle, push it down and open the door. Instantly, a very special atmosphere envelops you, a silence of great weight and intensity. You enter and close the door behind you. Give yourself the time to get used to the intensity of this silence and to look around in the hall.

As you do so, the silence and stillness in the temple grows stronger and stronger, and you notice in the centre, on the floor of the room, a circle of light, like a cone of light. You walk there very mindfully. Then stand in this bright circle of light and let yourself be completely touched and filled by this light.

Perhaps you experience it as strengthening or healing; perhaps you become more and more luminous in the process. Maybe you will become more and more a part of this special luminous silence. Let yourself be completely filled by light and stillness and stay in your experience as long as you feel it to be pleasant and right.

Then walk very mindfully back to the door and step out into the beautiful summer morning. Maybe you hear birds singing, maybe you see trees and plants or simply the vastness of the meadows and the landscape. You may experience nature a little more intensely than before. You carry the experience of silence within you, and also the calm, deep peace that has spread within. You become aware that the temple of silence is within you.

Then return entirely at your own speed. Take the time you need. Then open your eyes and orient yourself in the room.

Perhaps you want to take some notes.

In the therapeutic context, the client can talk about his or her experience. The debriefing serves to process and integrate what has been experienced. The client can be encouraged to keep in touch with the experience even after the therapy session.

The Maypole (exercise Y.4)

Phyllis Krystal's maypole exercise is very nourishing and can particularly strengthen and activate the client's spiritual resources.

Sit comfortably in your chair and first focus your awareness on the sensations in your body, especially in the feet. Then follow the breathing for a while, the movement of the abdomen as you breathe in and out. Then let these perceptions fade into the background and begin imagining:

In the centre of the room, imagine a large, tall maypole, like the maypoles you know that are often seen in marketplaces in May – perhaps with a log of wood that is well anchored in the ground and is very tall. At the top is a golden ball of light or even an embodiment of the higher self for you (perhaps your personal teacher or the Buddha or Christ). Trust your inner images completely.

From the top of the maypole, which symbolizes the higher self in this exercise, different coloured ribbons hang down. In the inner landscape, walk towards this maypole and with both hands grasp a ribbon that flows towards you. With this ribbon loosely in your hands, go back to your place in the inner landscape.

Now place your hands on your thighs with the backs of your hands open, like two bowls and be aware that your ribbon, which is connected to the top of the maypole, is inside the bowls. You can use this ribbon like a telephone wire to your higher self. Perhaps there are topics or questions that are particularly bothering you right now, or there is something that does not allow you to really settle down right now. You can hand this over to your higher self, as if the topic were flowing upwards through the ribbon to the higher self and you can let go of it.

Then ask your higher self for all the relaxation you need right now. Ask for relaxation on all levels, first on the physical, then on the psychological, and then on the spiritual level. For example, you can imagine your forehead expanding. Imagine that all the relaxing energy you need is now flowing into you through this ribbon as you breathe in. And when breathing out, all the tension can leave you.

Now, ask for healing. Imagine how healing energy flows into you through the ribbon as you breathe in. This can happen again on a physical, psychological or spiritual level – for example to a precise pain in the body or a trauma of the inner child or to certain unwholesome thought patterns. As you exhale, let go of all unwanted fixations.

Then, ask for cleansing energy, and imagine taking it in as you inhale. For example, a clear mountain stream might flow through you and take away everything with it that is harmful to you. You can also imagine all illnesses or unwanted fixations flowing out of you as you exhale.

Then, ask for strengthening energy, perhaps that you have more energy and strength. Imagine taking it in as you breathe. You can also ask for a very specific capacity, such as for example the growth of joy and mindfulness. Ask for the strengthening of all healing elements within you.

Then, ask your higher self for unprejudiced and unconditional acceptance and love. Gently open yourself to this energy. Take as much as you need. As a support you can imagine a flower in your heart, which opens wider and wider with the energy of the higher self. And the energy can continue to flow from there into every cell of the body, so that little by little you are completely filled with it.

Once you are completely filled, let people in your life who are close to your heart, appear in front of you. Place your hands together, with palms touching, and imagine that the energy of the higher self is completely effortlessly flowing to these people.

Groups of people can also come to mind who need the energy of the higher self, such as people in nursing homes or on clinics or refugees. Large groups of people who need the energy of the higher self may come to mind, such as people in war zones or those living in poverty and disease, experiencing famine and thirst, like in Africa and elsewhere.

Afterwards, place your hands on your thighs again and ask once more for the unconditional love and acceptance of the higher self for yourself.

Then leave this exercise very slowly, open your eyes and orient yourself in the room. Perhaps you need to stretch. Do whatever you need to return.

In the therapy situation, a short debriefing can serve as further processing or even better understanding of the exercise.

The Triangle of Light (exercise Y.5)

The triangle of light also comes from the imagination system of Phyllis Krystal. She recommends placing this exercise at the beginning of a therapeutic session to establish guidance by the higher self or by the buddha, or from the basic nature of existence. The exercise is intended to create a field of awareness and compassion and to establish access to inner resources.

Please sit comfortably on a chair and direct your awareness to the sensations in your body, especially your feet and legs. Then, for a while, follow the sensations in abdomen, as it rises and falls with the breath. Close your eyes and let other perceptions fade into the background.

Imagine on the floor around you a circle of golden light. It has the radius of your outstretched arms. You are sitting in the middle of the golden circle of light.

Then imagine in front of you another golden circle of light, in the middle of which is another person, in this case the therapist. The circles are next to each other; they touch but do not overlap.

Now, please imagine that there is a golden ray of light on the ground connecting you and the other person. This golden ray of light forms the baseline of a triangle of light: please imagine a golden light ray flowing from this baseline on the ground up through the other person's spine and head, emerging from the top. Another golden light ray is flowing up through your own spine and head, also emerging from its top.

The two light rays (from the spine of the person in front and from your own) meet at the apex of the triangle of light, connecting both of us to the common higher self. It is possible for the higher self to manifest as a symbol or figure.

Now both – the therapist also imaging this and the client – ask the higher self for guidance for this session. Then both breathe in the love of the higher self with that quality of complete acceptance. As they exhale, therapist and client can imagine breathing out all that separates from receiving the acceptance and love of the higher self.

The Hourglass (exercise Y.6)

According to Phyllis Krystal, the sandglass is used specifically to dissolve external and internal limitations.

Sit comfortably in your chair and focus your awareness on the sensations in your body, especially in your feet. Then follow the sensations in the abdomen, as it rises and falls with the breathing.

Then let these perceptions fade into the background and imagine a golden circle on the floor around you with the radius of your outstretched arms. Pull the circle of golden light up into the air so that it becomes a golden cone. Its tip has an opening located only a few centimetres above your head.

Now, above that, visualize a second cone upside down, with its tip on that of the lower cone, creating a sandglass. Everything is made of golden light. The opening between the cones symbolizes your higher self in this exercise. The upper part of this hourglass is wide open to the sky. You are in the lower part of this golden sandglass.

Now ask your higher self to give you all that you need, even that of which you may have no knowledge. If you have a particular wish, you can ask for its fulfilment. However, do not be too concrete in your expectations.

Inwardly declare to your higher self that you trust and accept and thereby embrace what is happening, even if it is not quite what you had in mind.

Then give thanks and come back, open your eyes and orient yourself in the room.

In the therapeutic situation, a short debriefing helps better processing. To be effective, the client should repeat this exercise on their own at home for some time.

Z. Couples Therapy

Essential Psychotherapy does not primarily focus on couples' therapy. But when working with individual clients, some understanding of the theory and dynamics of relationships, and a generational, systemic perspective are important. Thus, participants in the three-year advanced training in EPT are given a sense of what it's like to work as a couple therapist. Those who wish to know more can then deepen their understanding by looking into the literature on the subject and by participating in one of the wide range of trainings offered by various schools in couples' therapy.

In a therapy for couples the therapist usually has two people as clients. But nevertheless, one applies first of all the same attitude and methodology as in an individual therapy session. So, the therapist will anchor themself in an awareness of the greatest possible openness. Then they can inwardly, as in the individual sessions, welcome and be aware of the clients on the level of their basic nature. In some circumstances, if desired by the couple, there may be a small attuning, inner alignment or meditation.

In the couples' therapy setting, the therapist is especially challenged to maintain *neutrality* towards both clients. This means that – again and again – both are seen together as a couple, and also one maintains this neutrality individually. The challenge is not to be drawn into siding with one of the clients.

There are some symbolic concepts that help the therapist to keep the neutrality. For example, one imagine at the beginning of the therapy session the couple in a common field of light or in a common sphere of light. This symbolizes the field, or atmosphere of the couple's field.

Then, usually, an objective is discussed for the course of couples' therapy. For example: the couple may want to address certain unresolved issues. They might be in a specific area of communication, or family planning, or sexuality, or the relationship is in crisis and the issue is gaining perspective and whether and how to move forward with the relationship.

The therapist can explore this in addition to asking about what issues important issues are. The next exercise can help.

Journey into the past with our experiences as a partner (exercise Z.1)

The exercise, originally from Gestalt therapy, serves to explore *being a partner*. It can be done with the partners in a relationship individually or together, as a couple exercise, or in groups.

Make yourself comfortable on your seat and give attention to the sensations in the body. Then, direct your awareness more specifically to the sensations in your feet and legs. Now, become aware of the sensations in the abdomen as it rises and falls with the flow of your breath. You can close your eyes while doing this and open them again whenever you need to.

Look at yourself, take your attention inside, and ask yourself: How do I experience myself today, in this present life, as part of a relationship, as one of the two partners?

In case you are separated or have no partner at the moment, then look at yourself as a single person. You can be totally honest with yourself – you alone feel how it really is.

Do you feel basically comfortable in your relationship?

Do you feel secure, constricted?

Can you express important parts of yourself?

Are you in good communication with your partner?

Can you give within your relationship? Can you take?

Can you separate yourself and say "I"? Can you merge wonderfully?

How do you cope with everyday life? Can you cooperate? Can you ask for things?

Can you insist on solidarity? Can you be in solidarity yourself?

Do you tackle life together with your partner?

Do you experience something beautiful together?

Do you have common interests? Friends in common?

And how do you experience your sexuality in this partnership?

Now we leave the present and travel back five years. How old were you five years ago and what were your circumstances then? Did you have the same partner or a different one or none at all? Was it good or was it difficult for you?

Let go of this point in time as well and take a leap back, another ten years. How old were you then and what was your life like? Who was important to you in terms of a relationship? Or maybe no one? How comfortable and secure or insecure and lost did you feel?

If this inner journey into the past also brings up memories of a crisis in your relationship, please ask yourself the same questions.

And now you take a big leap back into puberty, whenever that was. How old were you? Perhaps there was a new interest in relationships, in the opposite or the same sex, in eroticism, in the awakening body that wanted to express love and was perhaps nevertheless afraid of it? Did you feel lonely or misunderstood? Or were you part of a circle of friends – if so, what was your role? What were your first experiences of kissing and anything else exciting?

There could certainly be many more questions about that time, but please come right back to the present now. Today, here, as a partner.

Then, a big question: How do you feel as a woman? How do you feel as a man? How do you get on? How do you feel?

Feel the sensations in your body as you sit in the chair. Perhaps there is a need to move, to relax or stretch. Then please come out all together and orient yourself in the room.

You may write down anything you experienced or even draw a picture about it.

After this inner journey, the therapist can deepen certain topics in the debriefing.

An exploration of what the client's parents were like can also help. What was your father like in his role as husband and partner and how was your mother in her role as wife and partner? An *additional exercise* (exercise Z.2) on the roles and behaviours of parents in the relationship is: both partners in the relationship write down for themselves what they have probably adopted as behaviours from their father or from their mother. It is quite easy to make two lists – one for the behaviours taken on from the father, one for the mother.

Notes for couples living together (methods Z.1 and Z.2)

One approach, which comes from behavioural therapy, aims to an effect on the relationship and the behaviour of the partners in the relationship, by means of agreed interventions. Rules are then drawn up for dealing with each other, and both relationship partners agree to abide by them, possibly even in writing, like a small internal contract. Only a few individual interventions are mentioned here, with reference being made to further reading for more in-depth information.

Arguing on top of a table (method Z.1): For couples who want to argue less or differently the therapist arranges with the couple to climb onto a stable table, if they have an argument, and to continue arguing there. Alternatively, if the couple is arguing, they can go to the smallest room in the house, such as the guest bathroom, and continue their argument there. These interventions usually result in the absurdity of the situation causing the couple to disidentify and end the argument or take it in a different direction.

Pulling out the yellow or red card (method Z.2): Also, the couple can show each other through a prearranged sign, that they need to deal with each other differently, with for example making a sign or using cards, as in a football (soccer) match If an argument starts to escalate, one partner can symbolically pull out the yellow card, which means something like: we must be especially careful now. If a situation is on the verge of escalating in a way that is not desired (clients can each assess their concern or other feelings on a scale of 1–10), a red card can be pulled out symbolically and in the imagination. This then means immediate spatial separation of the partners in the relationship. One person simply says: "yellow card" or "red card".

Further suggestions: Regular couple conversations about themselves as a couple can be arranged, such as a one-hour conversation once a week, possibly with rules as suggested above.

Some further questions for the partners to explore by themselves: How do I react and what do I react to? Do I respond well to my partner's good suggestions? Do I succeed in not acting out emotionally when my partner gets emotional? Is my partner's well-being really more important to me than my own? How can I overcome my own discomfort?

The five steps of Karma Chakme (see chapter A) can also be applied in the relationship to deal with stressful emotions:

1. Pause – instead of getting carried away, pause, stabilize awareness.
2. Apply remedies – using helpful methods such as therapeutic interventions, stabilizing oneself through mindfulness of breathing, taking refuge, saying an inner prayer, directing the mind to something beneficial.
3. Transform the view – welcoming the unpleasant, feeling as one's own buddha nature.
4. See the nature of emotions – realize their insubstantial, intangible nature; see through fear as centreless.
5. Take the emotion as a path – for example, stimulating fear and seeing through it again and again.

Three central aspects characterize a secure attached relationship:

1. Accessibility: you give me your attention and are emotionally

open to what I say.
2. Receptivity: you accept my needs and fears; you provide comfort and care.
3. Engagement: you are emotionally present, responsive, and engage with me.

Therapy sessions with couples

Depending on the couple and the dynamics of the couple's communication, certain rules can be set for the session. The couple can both be asked to let the other partner speak. A talking stone (a small stone or other object that is always held by the person who is talking and then passed around) can help here. If one partner gives long monologues, it may also be useful to introduce a speaking time limit. Both partners should agree to this, and both should set the time together (for example, a maximum of 5 minutes). The therapist will then act as a moderator to ensure that this speaking time is adhered to.

Furthermore, it can be useful to ask both partners to refrain from blaming and reproaching each other in their communication, but to use I-messages instead. This means, for example, "I experience that, I get too little attention from you" instead of "You notice me too little".

For couples' sessions:

There is an approach, in couples therapy, that predominantly reflects the couple's communication patterns, which is talk therapy oriented. Here, the therapist reflects in the therapy session the effect that the behaviour, gestures and especially what is said by one partner has on the other.

For example: Did you hear what your husband just said? What effect does it have on you? What is it like for you when your husband says that? What does it do to your body? Are you aware of how what you just said triggers your husband? What is your perception of what it triggers in your partner?

Moreover, the emotional content of what has been said is brought to awareness. How do you feel while saying this? How does your body feel? What does it do to you?

Other questions from the therapist: Where do you want to be by the end of this couple's session? What do you need for yourself? What do you need from your partner?

Of course, all the approaches learned from individual therapy are also used here.

Another depth-psychologically oriented approach looks more at the inner-psychic dynamics of each relationship and the effect on the dynamics of the communication between them and how they form relationships. It tries to uncover these and make them manageable.

Representing the inner dynamics in the couple by six chairs (method Z.3)

This method is good for illustrating the influences that are acted out, by the child ego, adult ego and parent ego within the relationship. There is an assumption that certain patterns of communication and behaviour are unconsciously repeated in the dynamics between the couple. That is, perhaps one partner feels and behaves like a child towards their mother in a particular situation and the other partner feels and behaves like a parent to a child. This approach originally comes from the systemically oriented family therapy of Virginia Satir.

To set up, the therapist puts six chairs in three rows one behind the other in the room. Two chairs are placed next to each other in each row. The first row are seats for the child ego aspect. The second row are for the adult ego, which is characterized by being disidentified from the child ego and the parent ego. The third row are the seats for the parent ego. The left row is for one partner in the relationship, in our example for Mrs. M., the right row is for the other relationship partner, in our example for Mr. M.

In this method, the chairs represent these individual aspects of personality, and the couple is asked in the process to share and reflect on a life situation and to sit on the appropriate chair which represents the dynamics to illustrate this.

Example: Mr. M. comes home from work exhausted and sees that certain chores, jobs that his wife normally does are not yet done. He is irritated, gets angry and starts to attack Mrs. M. "Am I supposed to do everything? How can you be so inconsiderate? You have enough time to do them." He gets angrier and angrier and remains in a reproachful, accusatory mood. Mrs. M. gets a little scared and has a guilty conscience. She feels small and becomes quite silent. The therapist asks the clients where they see themselves in this situation in terms of the ego parts. The client Mr. M. assesses himself in the parent ego position. Mrs. M. assesses herself in the child ego position.

The therapist asks Mr. M. and Mrs. M. to sit down on the corresponding chairs. Mr. M. sits down on the parent ego chair in the front right, Mrs. M. sits down on the child ego chair in the back left. The therapist asks if there was any more that happened in the couple's real-life example. The couple answers in the negative. It remained as a disagreement all evening. Then the therapist asks how there could be a resolution. How would it be if one or both of the partners were in the adult ego place. Mrs. M. says: "Then I would have said to my husband. 'Yes, you are right. I will do the housework in a minute; I haven't got around to it yet. You seem to have had a hard day at work and need some time to calm down, but if you are exhausted and irritated, there is no reason to take it out on me".

Mrs. M. sits down on the adult ego chair on the left in the centre. Mr. M. is asked what this does to him and how he would respond in the adult ego chair. "Yes, you are also right, I am sorry, I need to relax first". Mr. M. also sits down on the adult ego chair on the right in the centre.

The couple is asked about other real-life examples that seem to follow a certain pre-established pattern. They describe a certain situation where they as a couple got into an escalating argument very quickly.

Mr. M. came home exhausted and later than normal after a long day at work (he has a part-time job in addition to his full-time job and has been renovating the house for over 3 years). After a short greeting, Mrs. M. begins: "We wanted to go to the hardware store, you always come home so late, where have you been for so long? You must have gotten stuck again. You have time for the others, but never for me. The first thing you need to do is hang up the curtains I washed today. You know I can't do that with my back pain. Hurry up, or there will be no more shopping today."

Mr. M. feels unseen, misunderstood and put under pressure. He gets angry and yells, "That's enough, you're not thinking straight, you stupid bitch."

The question is, where the couple assesses itself, which aspect were they operating from in this example. Mrs. M. sees herself in the accusing, reproachful parent ego and sits down in the parent ego chair on the left front. Mr. M. sees himself in the angry, hurt child ego and sits down in the child ego chair at the back right.

When asked by the therapist how this situation continued, the spouses describe Mr. M. becoming increasingly angry (*in his experience he remains a desperate inner child*) and insulting Mrs. M. even more violently. This led to Mrs. M. becoming afraid and beginning to cry. According to her self-assessment, Mrs. M. also slid into the child ego part. She then sits down on the child ego chair at the back left.

This situation was particularly difficult for the couple in real life, as this type of situation had also led to physical violence by Mr. M. several times, which was the deciding factor for starting couples' therapy.

The therapist asks the spouses what a resolution on the adult ego level might look like. Mr. M. says: "I have to take care of myself now and calm down. I would now pull out the red card and go into the next room and count 20 breaths until I have calmed down again. Then when I am back in the green, on the anger scale, I would go back over to my wife and apologize for my freak out."

The therapist continues the situation and asks Mr. M. to sit in the adult chair in the middle on the right. Mrs. M. says, "Yes, I shouldn't provoke him like that. If it is already escalated, then it is really best we pull out the red card and go to different rooms. When you went over to the adult chair (*addressed to her husband*) my anxiety directly decreased, and I could think again. I would forgive you for that, also realize that I handled you badly when I pressured you. I will make sure that in the first half hour when you come from work, I will give you space, so that you can relax." Mrs. M. is back in the adult ego according to her own assessment and sits down on the adult chair in the centre left.

The couple M. thanks the therapist and they get given some more ideas about how to apply this method when the therapist is not there.

This method creates awareness of when the client is identified with one of the main unconscious aspects, the child ego or the parent ego, or with various sub-personalities, and what dynamics there are in the relationship.

To put it simply: where is the client identified with an unconscious aspect, and therefore does not behave the way they want? When do partners react like a father or mother, and do they actually want to react that way? How are *the buttons* pressed in the dynamics between the couple, with certain communication habits *triggered* by giving energy to unprocessed basic conflicts, which then escalate further with a momentum of their own, like in a film.

This exercise can be extended, if desired, by placing another chair for the inner source of wisdom. On the additional chair, which would be positioned to one side, the buddha, Mary, a wise friend or cosmic parents could be imagined.

Addressing the inner source of wisdom is possible at any point in couple therapy. All the methods that are a used in individual therapy can also be applied here. The Maypole exercise (exercise Y.4) and the Triangle of Light (exercise Y.5) are particularly well suited to couple therapy. The attitude of having inner guidance by a higher consciousness, which is practiced in these exercises, is also well suited to the couple relationship. Especially in crisis situations. It is possible for one partner to internally entrust themselves, with all their responses and feelings to the source of wisdom, for example the buddha. Their partner and the relationship in all its aspects, can also be internally entrusted. This usually results in an inner release or letting go of unconscious fixations or identifications, so that a new openness to the ongoing process of the relationship becomes possible.

One exercise (exercise Z.3) from the Phyllis Krystal imagination method is the figure 8 with pairs. We have already introduced the figure 8 exercise (exercise O.3) in chapter O. Here it is used in couple therapy. The figure 8 exercise is explained to the partners, and they then imagine, in the couple therapy, in the presence of the therapist as follows: each partner imagines her- or himself in a golden circle of light and her or his partner in the opposite golden circle of light. A flowing bright blue light is visualized, forming the figure 8 (which is also the symbol of infinity). This exercise, which the couple can also use in other life situations without the therapist, has a dissolving effect on the unconscious entanglements of the couple's dynamics.

Means of reconciliation

Harm in relationships is unavoidable. Unfortunately, the injured person almost always accuses the other person of intent or at least gross insensitivity. Yet most hurts are not deliberate or intentional. Nevertheless, they weigh on the relationship and cannot be released. Often there are arguments about who has hurt whom, and this leads to a dispute with accusations and justifications. In order to resolve the conflict, it is therefore crucial to make clear that an injury has occurred, even if it was not intended. Acknowledging the other person's injury is therefore of central importance in resolving conflict. Then, in the next step, it is important to take responsibility for it. After the injury has been clearly named without reproach, it can be resolved with a small ritual.

Reconciliation Ritual (method Z.4)

The following method belongs to the compendium of advanced training in EPT and is taught by Mrs. Elgin Schrewe-Krome; it is quoted here from Hans Jellouschek.

Partner 1: I hear and acknowledge that I have hurt you in the past (with this behaviour or statement), even if I was not aware of it at the time. I am sorry and regret it.

Partner 2: I see and hear that you acknowledge that you have hurt me in the past and that you are sorry. I accept that and it is okay with me now. I am ready to let go of my injury. I will not refer to it anymore in future arguments.
Let us make a new beginning free from this burden.

It often becomes clear during the couple therapy, that it would help further couple therapy work for one or both of them to work on their internal psychic dynamics separately in one-to-one therapy. This is addressed by the therapist and appropriate recommendations are made. The large area of sexuality and sex therapy in couple therapy is only noted here, and reference is made to relevant further reading (see the bibliography, page 521).

Final Words

This book provides an initial insight into buddhist mind training and its implementation in Essential Psychotherapy, a psychotherapy with a background in buddhist mind training. The compilation allows the reader to develop an initial understanding of this new, continuously evolving approach. However, it only presents a part of this special combination of inner work and therapy. To become really acquainted with it on the experiential level requires deeper mind training under the guidance of a competent teacher and direct learning and working within the framework of Essential Psychotherapy. Reading alone cannot replace this. But perhaps an interest in mind training and Essential Psychotherapy has arisen in you, dear readers.

With best wishes,
Tilmann Borghardt and Wolfgang Erhardt

Appendix

Bibliography

Some of the consulted literature for the original work exists only in German. We indicated the English publications, whenever we could locate them, and hope that they inspire you.

Abrams, J. (Ed.) (1990): *Reclaiming the Inner Child*, Jeremy P. Tarcher Inc., Los Angeles

Assagioli, R. (2022): *Creating Harmony in Life: a Psychosynthesis approach*, Youcanprint

Assagioli, R. (1999): *The Act of Will: A Guide to Self-actualisation and Self-realisation*, Psychosynthesis Research Foundation

Assagioli, R. (1993): *Psychosynthesis: A Manual of Principles and Techniques*, Penguin Random House

Assagioli, R. (2007): *Transpersonal Development: The Dimension Beyond Psychosynthesis*, Inner Way Productions

Berzin, A. (2000): *Relating to Spiritual Teachers - Building a Healthy Relationship*, Snow Lions Publications, Boulder

Birnbaum, R. (2003): *The Healing Buddha*, Shambala

Borghardt, T.; von Allmen, F. und Flückiger, U. (2015): *Mahamudra & Vipassana: Gewahr Sein – Unterweisungen zur Einsichtsmeditation und Retreat-Praxis* (Mahamudra & Vipassana: Mind-fulness – Teachings on Insight Meditation and Retreat Practice), Norbu Verlag, Lenzkirch

Cöllen, M. (2009): *Das Verzeihen in der Liebe* (Forgiveness in Love), Kreuz Verlag, Freiburg

Chopich, E. u. Paul, M. (1990): *Healing Your Aloneness: Finding Love and Wholeness Through Your Inner Child*, Harper One

Devereux, G. (1967): *From Anxiety to Method in the Behavioural Sciences*, Mouton, Paris

De Wit, H. (2003): *The Lotus and the Rose: Buddhism in Dialogue with Psychology, Religion and Ethics, Religion and Ethics*, Agora

Dörner, K. und Plog, U. u.a. (2015): *Irren ist menschlich* (To err is human), Psychiatrie Verlag, Rehburg-Loccum

Erhardt, W. (2009 – 2015): *Arbeitsmaterialien* (Working materials), Institut für Essentielle Psycho-therapie, Hennef

Erhardt, W. (2001 – 2008): *Materialsammlung* (Collection of materials), zum Thema Buddhismus und Psychotherapie, Teil 1+2 auf der Webseite www.essentielle-psychotherapie.com/en, Downloadbereich, Hennef

Erhardt, W. (2002): *Impulsreferat zur Psychosynthese* (Keynote speech on psychosynthesis), auf der Webseite www.essentielle-psychotherapie.com/en, Downloadbereich, Hennef

Erhardt, W. (2010): *Pathologie des Transpersonalen* (Pathology of the Transpersonal), on the website www.essentielle-psychotherapie.com/en

Ferrucci, P. (2009): *What We May Be – Techniques for Psychological and Spiritual Growth through Psychosynthesis*, Penguin Random House

Ferrucci, P. (2009): *Inevitable Grace Breakthroughs in the Lives of Great Men and Women: Guides to Your Self-Realization*, Penguin Random House

Ferrucci, P. (2016): *The Power of Kindness – The Unexpected Benefits of Leading a Compassionate Life*, Penguin Random House

Freud, S. (1999): *The Standard Edition of the Complete Psychological Works of Sigmund Freud*, translated by James Strachery, Vintage

Freud, S. (2006): *The Interpretation of Dreams*, Avon

Fromm, E. (1999): *Gesamtausgabe (Complete edition)*, DTV, München

Fromm, E. (1974): *Zen Buddhism and Psychoanalysis*, Souvenir Press

Galland, C. (2007): *Longing for Darkness: Tara and the Black Madonna*, Penguin Publishing Group

Gampopa, D. (2014): *The Jewel Ornament of Liberation,* translated into English by Khenpo Konchog Gyaltsen Rinpoche (several other English translations exist as well), in German: *Der kostbare Schmuck der Befreiung*, translated by Borghardt, T., Norbu Verlag in der Ekayana gGmbH, Lenzkirch

Gebser, J. (1995): *Einbruch der Zeit* (Breakdown Of Time), Novalis-Verlag, Schaffhausen

Gendlin, E.T. (1984): *The client's client*, in Levant, R.L. & Shlien, J.M.(Eds): *Client-centered therapy and the person-centered approach*, Praeger, New York

Gendlin, E.T. (1964): *A Theory of Personality Change*, University of Chicago, Worchel, P. & Byrne, D. (Eds), John Wiley & Sons, New York

Gendlin, E.T. (1997): *A process model*, The Focusing Institute, New York

Gendlin, E.T. (1982): *Focusing*, Bantam

Gendlin, E.T. (1990): *The small steps of the therapy process*, in Lietaer, G, Rombauts, J & Van Baalen, R. (Eds): *Client-centreed and experiential psychotherapy in the nineties*, Leuven University Press

Gendlin, E.T. (1998): *Focusing-Oriented Psychotherapy*, Guilford Publications

Gendlin, E.T. (2004): *Let Your Body Interpret Your Dreams*, Chiron Publications

Gendun Rinpoche (2010): *Heart Advice from a Mahamudra Master*, Norbu Verlag, Lenzkirch

Gendun Rinpoche (2012): *Emotions – The Great Peacock*, Dzambala Editions, in German: *„Der große Pfau, Die Umwandlung der Emotionen im tibetischen Buddhismus"*, Norbu Verlag in der Ekayana gGmbH, Lenzkirch

Gendun Rinpoche (1991): *Wir haben vergessen, dass wir Buddhas sind* (We forgot that we are Buddhas), Kagyü-Dharma-Verlag, Mechernich

Goleman, D. (2003): *Destructive Emotions: A Scientific Dialogue with the Dalai Lama*, Bantam Books

Goleman, D. (1997): *Healing Emotions: Conversations with the Dalai Lama on Mindfulness*, Emotions, and Health, Shambhala.

Goleman, D. (2006): *Social Intelligence: The New Science of Human Relationships*, Bantam Books

Grawe, K. (2004): *Psychological Therapy*, Hogrefe & Huber Publishers

Grof, S. u. C. (1989): *Spiritual Emergency: When Personal Transformation Becomes a Crisis*, Tarcher

Heidenreich, T. & Michalak, J. Ed. (2004): *Achtsamkeit und Akzeptanz in der Psychotherapie* (Mindfulness and acceptance in psychotherapy), DGVT-Verlag, Tübingen

Heller, L und Lapierre, A. (2012): *Healing Developmental Trauma: How Early Trauma Affects Self-Regulation, Self-Image, and the Capacity for Relationship*, North Atlantic Books

Hellinger, B. (1998): *Love's Hidden Symmetry: What Makes Love Work in Relationships*, Zeig Tucker & Theisen Inc.

Jellouschek, H. (2015): *Achtsamkeit in der Partnerschaft* (Mindfulness in relationships), Kreuz Verlag, Freiburg

Jellouschek, H. (2014): *Die Paartherapie – eine praktische Orientierungshilfe* (Couples therapy – a practical guide), Kreuz Verlag, Freiburg

Jellouschek, H. (1999): *Warum hast du mir das angetan?* (Why did you do this to me?), Piper-Verlag, München

Jellouschek, H. (1992): *Die Kunst als Paar zu leben* (The art of living as a couple), Kreuz Verlag, Stuttgart

Johnson, S. (2013): *Love Sense: The Revolutionary New Science of Romantic Relationships*, Btb. Verlag, Little Brown Spark

Jung, C. G. (1989): *Collected Works*

Karmapa Rangjung Dorje (2009): *Luminous Heart – The Third Karmapa on Consciousness, Wisdom, and Buddha Nature*, translated by: Brunnhölzl, K., Snow Lion

Karmapa Rangjung Dorje (2014): *The Mahamudra Prayer of the Definite Meaning*, Ekayana media library, in German: *„Das Mahamudra-Wunschgebet des Wahren Sinnes"*, translated and annotated by Tilmann (Lhündrup) Borghardt, Norbu Verlag, in der Ekayana gGmbH, Lenzkirch

Karmapa Wangchug Dorje (2017): *Mahamudra – The Ocean of True Meaning*, translated by Havlat H., BoD – Books on Demand, Norderstedt

Kornfield, J. (2009): The Wise Heart: A Guide to the Universal Teachings of Buddhist Psycholo-gy, Bantam

Kongtrul, Jamgon (2014): *Mahamudra – The Torch of True Meaning*, Ktd Publications, in German: *„Das Licht des Wahren Sinnes"*, translated by Borghardt T., Norbu Verlag in der Ekayana gGmbH

Kabat-Zinn, J. (2006): *Coming to Our Senses: Healing Ourselves and the World Through Mindfulness*, Hyperion

Krystal, P. (2001): *Cutting the Ties of Karma: Understanding the Patchwork of Your Past Lives*, Red Wheel/Weiser

Krystal, P. (1995): *Reconnecting the Love Energy: Don't By-Pass Your Heart*, Red Wheel/Weiser

Krystal, P. (1995): *Taming Our Monkey Mind: Insight, Detachment, Identity*, Red Wheel/Weiser

Krystal, P. (2013): *Phyllis Krystal Method, Workbook*, Phyllis Krystal Foundation

Kurz, R.(2007): *Body-Centered Psychotherapy: The Hakomi Method*, LifeRhythm

Lacan, J. (1975): Schriften 1 (Writings 1), Suhrkamp Taschenbuch Verlag, Frankfurt a.M.

Levine, P. (1997): *Waking the Tiger – Healing Trauma*, North Atlantic Books, Berkeley

Lodjong Text Collection, Lodjong –Sammelband, transl. Borghardt, T. (2009) *„Der große Weg des Erwachens – Grundlagentexte des Mahayana-Geistestrainings"*, Norbu Verlag, Lenzkirch

Lorenzer, A. (1973): *Über den Gegenstand der Psychoanalyse* (On the subject of psychoanalysis), Suhrkamp Verlag, Frankfurt a.M.

Lowen, A. u. L.(1994): *Bioenergetics: The Revolutionary Therapy That Uses the Language of the Body to Heal the Problems of the Mind*, Penguin

Lowen, A. (1995): *Joy: The Surrender to the Body and to Life*, Penguin

Merleau-Ponty, M. (2013): *Phenomenology of Perception*, Taylor & Francis

Mahler, M., Pine, F. & Bergman, A. (1980): *Psychological Birth of the Human Infant, Symbiosis and Individuation*, Basic Books

Moeller, M. (1999): *Die Wahrheit beginnt zu zweit* (Truth begins with two), Rowohlt, Reinbek b. Hamburg

Naranjo, C (1977): *On the Psychology of Meditation*, Penguin Books

Neumann, E.(1964): *Depth Psychology and a New Ethic*, Shambhala

Neumann, E. (2014): *The Origins and History of Consciousness*, Princeton University Press

Pfluger-Heist, U. (2007): *In der Seele liegt die Kraft* (The strength lies in the soul), Nawo Verlag, Rümlang

Pfluger-Heist, U. (2009): *Mal sehen, was das Leben noch zu bieten hat* (Let's see what life has to offer), Herder-Verlag Freiburg

Podvoll, E. (2003): *Recovering Sanity: A Compassionate Approach to Understanding and Treating Psychosis*, Shambala

Reddemann, L. & Wetzel, S. (2011): *Der Weg entsteht unter deinen Füßen* (The path emerges beneath your feet), Kreuz Verlag, Freiburg

Reich, W. (1973): *Charakter Analysis*, WRM Press

Rogers, C. und Stevens, B. (2021): *Person to Person: The Problem of Being Human*, Legare Street Press

Rogers, C. R. (2021): *Client Centered Therapy*, Robinson

Rothschild, B. (2002): *Der Körper erinnert sich* (The body remembers), Synthesis-Verlag, Essen

Sachse, R. (2010): *Persönlichkeitsstörungen verstehen*, (Understanding personality disorders), Psychiatrie Verlag, Köln

Santonelli, S. (2000): *Zerbrochen und doch ganz nah* (Broken yet whole), Arbor Verlag, Freiamt

Schillings, A. (2014): *Dwelling in the process of Embodied Awareness*, in *Focusing-Oriented Psychotherapy*, (Ed) Madison, G., Jessica Kingsley Publishers, London & Philadelphia

Schillings, A. (2007): *Stille und Gewahrsein von Mensch zu Mensch* (Silence and awareness from person to person), published in the magazine *Transpersonale Psychologie und Psychotherapie*, no 1/2007, Verlag Via Nova, Petersburg

Schillings, A. (1998 – 2015): *Arbeitsmaterialien* (Working materials), Focusing-Institut Köln

Schillings, A. (2009): *Sein, Gewahrsein, Sinnfinden* (Being, awareness, finding meaning) published in the magazine *Gesprächspsychotherapie und Personenzentrierte Beratung*, no 3/2009, Köln

Schillings, A. (2005): *Mitgefühl mit uns selbst* (Compassion with ourselves), Stadtraum Zeitschrift, Köln

Schillings, A., Hinterthür, P. (1989): *Qi Gong – Der fliegende Kranich* (Qi Gong – the flying crane), Windpferdverlag

Schmidbauer, W. (1988): *Liebeserklärung an die Psychoanalyse* (Declaration of love for psychoanalysis), Rowohlt Verlag, Reinbek b. Hamburg

Schmidbauer, W. (2010): *Paartherapie: Konflikte verstehen, Lösungen finden* (Couples therapy: Understanding conflicts, finding solutions), Gütersloher Verlagshaus

Schnarch, D. (2009): *Passionate Marriage – Keeping Love and Intimacy Alive in Committed Relationships*, W. W. Norton & Company

Sloterdijk, P. (Ed.) (1993): *Mystische Zeugnisse aller Zeiten und Völker* (Mystical testimonies from all ages and peoples), Diederichs, München

Steurich, M. (1999): *Tibetisches Heilyoga* (Tibetan Healing Yoga), Kum Nye, Herder-Verlag, Freiburg

Tarthang, Tulku (1990): *Knowledge of Time & Space: An Inquiry into Knowledge, Self & Reality*, Dharma Publishing, Cazadero

Tarthang Tulku (1981): *Hidden Mind of Freedom*, Dharma Publishing, Cazadero

Tarthang Tulku (1977): *Gesture of Balance: A Guide to Self-Healing & Meditation*, Dharma Publishing, Cazadero

Weber, G. (1995): *Zweierlei Glück* (Two kinds of happiness), Carl-Auer-Systeme Verlag, Heidelberg

Weber, S. M. (1991): *Return to Freud: Jacques Lacan's Dislocation of Psychoanalysis*, Cambridge University Press

World Health Organization (1992): *The ICD-10 Classification of Mental and Behavioural Disorders: Clinical Descriptions and Diagnostic Guidelines*

Wellwood, J. (2002): *Toward a Psychology of Awakening: Buddhism, Psychotherapy, and the Path of Personal and Spiritual Transformation*, Shambala

Whitmore, D. (1988): *Kreativitätsspiele mit Kindern* (Creativity games with children), Kösel, München

Wilber, K. (2001): *No Boundary: Eastern and Western Approaches to Personal Growth*, Shambala

Wilber, K. (1990): *The Atman Project: A Transpersonal View of Human Development*, Quest Books U.S.

Wilber, K. (1987): *Transformations of Consciousness: Conventional and Contemplative Perspectives on Development*, Shambala Publications

Wilber, K., Ecker, B., Anthony, D. (Ed.) (1986): *Spiritual Choices: The Problem of Recognizing Authentic Paths to Inner Transformation*, Paragon House Publishers

Winnicott, D. W. (1975): *Through Paediatrics to Psychoanalysis: Collected Papers,* Routledge

Yeomans, T (1998): *Seelenwunde und Psychotherapie* (Emotional wounds and psychotherapy) published in the magazine *Transpersonale Psychologie und Psychotherapie*, 4th year, no 1

Zimmermann, M., Spitz, C., Schmidt, S.(Ed.) (2012): *Achtsamkeit* (Mindfulness), Verlag Hans Huber, Bern

Zimmer, H., Campbell, J. (2026): *Philosophies of India*, Princeton University Press

Zundel, E. u.R. (1988): *Leitfiguren der Psychotherapie* (Leading figures in psychotherapy), Kösel Verlag, München

List of proposed methods

No	Method	Indication	Description	Page
O.1	Seven steps	Anxiety, affect breakthroughs, pain	Scale, verbalize, intervene	337
O.2	Sensory desensitization	Anxiety	Combines anxiety-inducing stimuli and relaxing stimuli	339
O.3	Advice to a good friend	Problems, stressful situations	Assuming an advisory position	344
O.4	Detachment after separa-tion	Loss of a person through death or separation	Complete detach-ment sentences	345
O.5	Working with key sentences	Difficulties of implementation	Developing and anchoring resolutions	346
O.6	Linguistic demarcation	Feeling appropriat-ed, proximity-dis-tance issues	Naming the difference	348
O.7	Working with basic and oppositional patterns	Dissolving old be-haviour patterns	Working out basic oppositional pat-terns	351
R.1	Working with sub-personal-ities	Working on inner-psychic dynamics	Working with chairs and imagery	403
S.1	Inner Child work	Basic conflicts, heal traumas	Inner dialogue with child ego	421
T.1	Working with Parent Images	Becoming Aware of Internalized Parent Images	Disidentifying Par-ent Images	437
U.1	Uncovering work in con-nection with Inner Child	Uncovering basic conflicts, traumas	Uncovering by means of inner dialogue	451
V.1	Swinging between resource and trauma	Trauma resolution	Coupling griev-ance and resource	463

No	Method	Indication	Description	Page
V.2	Detachment with a symbol	Trauma, basic conflicts	Indirect method for dream resolution	469
W.1	Working with dreams	Interpreting dreams	Multilayered work with dreams	473
Z.1	Couples therapy in case of quarrels	Quarrels in couples	Getting on a table or into a small room	510
Z.2	Yellow / Red card	De-escalate	Symbols for intervention in quarrels	510
Z.3	Representation of the inner-psychic couple dynamics	Inner patterns work in the couple	Chair work child, adult, parent ego	513
Z.4	Reconciliation ritual	Quarrel and grievance	Acknowledgement and forgiveness	518

List of proposed exercises

No	Exercise	Indication	Description	Page
M.1	Attuning meditation	Inner alignment	Expanding awareness	321
N.1	Finding resource	Trauma, fear, self-strengthening	Recalling positive memory	325
N.2	The Safe Place	Fear, need for protection	Establishing safety	327
N.3	Kindness exercise	Relational fears	Remembering safety in relationship	329
N.4	Scaling a sensation	Pain, fear, all feelings	Assessing the strength of a sensation	331
N.5	Review of the day	Anxiety, depression, behaviour in general	Self-reflection and self-regulation	332

No	Exercise	Indication	Description	Page
N.6	Discarding the unpleasant	Trauma, anxiety, self-strengthening	Controlling content	334
O.1	As-if in a professional role	Social anxiety	Imagining in safe role	343
O.2	Inner Garden	Fear, demarcation	Imagining the inner space	347
O.3	The Lying Eight	Demarcation, staying with oneself	Imagining a symbol	349
O.4	Weeding weeds, sowing seeds	Detaching from old behaviours	Ritual destruction of patterns	352
O.5	Beach Ball	Protection	Symbolic protection exercise	354
O.6	Light Cylinder	Fear of being appropriated	Protective exercise against subtle assaults	355
O.7	Shining Star	Anxiety	Symbolic exercise for anxiety reduction	356
O.8	Pendulum for decision making	Decision difficulties	Exercise for decision making	357
P.1	Free Space	Solving fears and problems	Setting problems down imaginatively	388
Q.1	Disidentification	Being identified with fears, feelings, thoughts	Linguistic inner disidentification	394
Q.2	Suitcase	Being identified with roles	Imagination exercise for disidentification	396
Q.3	Leading into the true self	Being identified	Disidentifying object, observer	400
R.1	Who, how, what am I?	Self-exploration	Reflective exercise for self-exploration	405
R.2	House of sub-personalities	Inner discovery of the sub-personality	Imaginative journey to discover the sub-personality	405

No	Exercise	Indication	Description	Page
R.3	Daily review of sub-personality	Releasing inner dynamics	Sub-personality is observed regularly	412
R.4	Climbing a mountain with sub-personality	Exploration and integration of sub-personality	Imaginative journey with a sub-personality	412
S.1	Inner Child	Working on basic patterns and conflicts	Inner work with image and feeling from childhood	423
S.2	Breathing from the heart with the inner child	Healing of emotional patterns	Heart-breath with inner child	428
S.3	The Tree	Needy inner child, self-strengthening	Imagination of tree, cosmic parents	429
S.4	House of childhood	Exploration and healing	Return to early childhood	431
T.1	Working with parental images	Exploration of internalized parental images	Imagining father and mother	441
T.2	Own parents in a healing field	Healing parental images	Imagining a healing story	443
T.3	Letter to father or mother	Resolving unresolved feelings about parents	Writing and reading the letter aloud	444
T.4	Disidentification ritual	Releasing unwanted connections to parents	Symbolic ritual for detaching	445
U.1	Corridor	Uncovering old basic patterns	Symbolic finding of emotional patterns	455
U.2	The Inner House	Uncovering, exploring personality parts	Imaginative exercise, personality parts	456
X.1	Tasting a decision	Difficulties in decision making, self-strengthening	Remembering a will decision	487

No	Exercise	Indication	Description	Page
X.2	Goal setting exercise	Difficulties in implementing goals	Imagination exercise for goal implementation	489
X.3	Vision exercise	Shaping life consciously	Life vision exercise	491
Y.1	Alignment with the Higher Self	Access to spiritual level	Imagination of light above the head	495
Y.2	The Wise Friend	Contact with a personified spiritual dimension	Imaginative jour-ney to a wise friend	496
Y.3	Temple of Silence	Access to deep levels of existence	Imagination journey into deep inner experience	499
Y.4	Maypole	Nourishing spiritual practice	Symbolic work with the Higher Self	501
Y.5	Triangle of Light	Inner alignment to higher self in twos	Symbolic higher self-work for a situation of two	503
Y.6	Hourglass	Releasing outer and inner limitations	Symbolic work with the Higher Self	504
Z.1	Journey as partner	Exploration of expe-riences as partner	Returning to expe-riences as partner	508
Z.2	List of char-acteristics inherited from parents	Exploration of inter-nalized behaviours	List characteris-tics of father and mother	510
Z.3	Figure 8 with couples	Proximity/Distance problems of a couple	Symbolic solving of subconscious dynamics	517

Epilogue: How Essential Psychotherapy came into being

by Wolfgang Erhardt

The exchanges between psychotherapists and buddhist teachers took place over eight years, each year for 5–7 days in France and Germany. The desire arose to make the results of our exchanges available to those interested in a training course that contains all the essentials for following or accompanying a therapeutic path that integrates harmoniously into a path of awakening. Thus, after twenty years of collaboration in working groups on this subject, Essential Psychotherapy (EPT) was born.

History: Before 1985 I had practiced Zazen regularly for several years under the guidance of Prof. Kiichi Nagaya Roshi. When he could no longer come to Europe at the age of 95, I intensified old contacts with teachers of Tibetan buddhism: with Tenga Rinpoche, with the Dalai Lama and especially with Gendun Rinpoche, my main teacher.

Vision: Then, when I was writing my thesis in psychology, I was very inspired by the idea that there could be a psychotherapy based on the Dharma, that is, based on a wisdom teaching. I thought that this was really necessary. Psychotherapeutic approaches seemed to me to be missing out exactly that which I experienced as so healing and helpful on the buddhist path of developing awareness. In this vision of a unified approach, I felt a strong connection to a Tibetan meditation teacher, the 16th Karmapa Rangjung Rigpe Dorje, and experienced it as an inspired and at the same time very inspiring inner mission.

First steps: After graduation, I made my first experiences with psychotherapeutic work in the context of advanced training courses. Soon we started regular working group meetings on the topic of Dharma and Psychotherapy. Jamgon Kongtrul Rinpoche, a Tibetan meditation teacher of the Karma Kagyu tradition, had led a congress on this topic in New York in 1987. One of his students, Dorothea Nett, asked me and other psychologists and psychotherapists practicing meditation whether we were interested in forming such a working group. Maybe it would be possible, inspired by the development in the USA with Jamgon Kongtrul Rinpoche, or by the *Mind and Life* conferences of the Dalai Lama, to organize something similar here in Germany or Europe. So, for some years we met regularly every six weeks for a day of exchange with the Working Group "Buddhadharma and Psychotherapy".

Years later: During one of my visits to Le Bost in Auvergne, the retreat monastery of my meditation teacher Gendun Rinpoche, I told my friend Tilmann Borghardt, MD, also known as Lama Lhündrup (his Tibetan name as meditation teacher) about these exchanges and about the congresses on the subject that were taking place and especially about this vision of a buddhist psychotherapy or better: a psychotherapy based on the buddhist training of the mind. I was able to arouse his interest. Although he was very busy at that time as a teacher in the perennial retreats in the monastery of Le Bost in Auvergne, France, he got involved in the idea of organizing conferences of meditation teachers and psychotherapists together with me and Lama Irene Frei (Dordje Drölma).

Expert conferences: In 2000 an intensive and qualified exchange with a high proportion of self-experience on the subject of buddhism and psychotherapy started. We, Tilmann, Irene and I, hosted, organized and prepared each year a 5-to-7-day symposium with meditation teachers from different buddhist schools and with qualified psychotherapists representing different psychotherapeutic directions who were familiar with regular meditation practice. In the first years these conferences were held alternately in the Auvergne, France, and near Bonn in Germany.

The working group meetings in the years from 1988 to 1998, these eight symposia from 2001 to 2008, and the many experiences of integrating this approach in my own psychotherapeutic work with clients were the soil from which Essential Psychotherapy grew. In the professional meetings it became clear over and over again how well the two fields complement each other – the classical path of meditation as practiced in the buddhist tradition and the insights and methods from psychotherapy. It all proved very meaningful and inspiring. It became clear that by bringing these approaches together with a certain integration of methods, a higher efficiency can be achieved in psychotherapeutic work as well as in Dharma practice, the path of awareness development. Since this could not be found anywhere else at that time, we decided, especially Tilmann Borghardt and I, to offer this together as an advanced training in a new psychotherapeutic approach called from the on "Essential Psychotherapy". It was developed for the classical setting in psychotherapy of a therapist with a client, a therapy situation in pairs, and it is predominantly applied there.

Advanced training in EPT

From that time on, Tilmann Borghardt and I worked together with some other instructors in the "Institute for Essential Psychotherapy", where three-year advanced training courses in Essential Psychotherapy have been offered since 2009. Many participants (we are at our 20th training cycle) have already become acquainted with Essential Psychotherapy in the frame of a three-year part-time training and apply it in practice.

To respond to the lively demand among experienced psychotherapists, we additionally offer condensed cycles of 1.5 years advanced training especially for them. In France, the fourth advanced training in Essential Psychotherapy is currently starting. In addition, there are postgraduate trainings, guided supervision groups lectures and short retreats in the context of EPT in Germany.

The time for a three-year training is limited: 432 hours of block training plus 48 hours of peer group work and 36 hours of individual sessions with the therapists. We had to make a choice for the training plan, which buddhist and therapeutic topics we would deal with and which methods we would practice. In this choice, we were guided by the question: what is essential and therefore should be taught, and what is secondary and therefore can be left out for now? The present book follows the same criteria and deals with more or less the same topics as the advanced training, without of course being able to go into the same breadth and differentiation.

Institute for Essential Psychotherapy
Owner and management: Wolfgang Erhardt, certified psychologist
Adress: Eichkuhle 22, 53773 Hennef, Germany
Tel.: + 49 (0) 2242/9175738 , Fax: + 49 (0) 2242/915285
Website: www.essentielle-psychotherapie.com/en/
E-Mail: info@essentielle-psychotherapie.de

Expressions of gratitude

I do not want to close this book without expressing my unlimited gratitude for the great support I have received in compiling and writing this book. My special thanks go to my friend, dharma brother and co-author Tilmann Borghardt. Without the countless exchanges on the content and our common desire to create this psychotherapy based in buddhist mind training in the form of Essential Psychotherapy, this book would also not have been conceivable.

My gratitude also goes to my friend Astrid Schillings, a colleague and contributor to this book. Her profound understanding of the human psyche has enriched our training cycles and this presentation. A big "thank you" goes to my friend and colleague Ulla Pfluger-Heist, as well as to my friend, colleague and dharma sister Elgin Schrewe-Krome, who reviewed the content of this book and offered many good suggestions while we were writing it. Thanks for the linguistic review of the text go to Doris Gottschalk and Nina Friesen.

A very big "thank you" for her support, tolerance and understanding goes to my former wife Friederike, who supported me throughout those busy times writing the book. And deep thanks also to all EPT trainees and clients, who make it possible for us to work in profoundly healing ways and to apply and develop Essential Psychotherapy.

May the readers feel some of the inspiration of our teacher Gendun Rinpoche, the blessings of the buddhas, the encouragement of the Mahāmudrā transmission lineage, and the healing power of the Medicine Buddha – all of which inspire and sustain us in EPT and in writing this book.

Thank you

Wolfgang Erhardt

"Essential Psychotherapy" is also available in German and French

T. Borghardt, W. Erhardt

Buddhistische Psychologie

Grundlagen und Praxis

Der Buddhismus betrachtet die Natur des Geistes als grundlegend gesund. Eine wunderbare Prämisse für eine vertrauensvolle, ressourcenorientierte Arbeit mit Geist und Psyche.

Hardcover | 608 Seiten | € 35,00
ISBN: 978-3-442-34176-4
Arkana Verlag | www.penguin.de/verlage/arkana

T. Borghardt, W. Erhardt

La Psychothérapie essentielle

Bases et applications

L'entrainement bouddhiste de l'esprit a pour but d'épanouir pleinement en chacune et chacun le potentiel d'éveil. Ce processus consiste à se défaire des schémas émotionnels et cognitifs et de déployer les qualités telles que l'amour, la compassion, l'ouverture et la sagesse.

Hardcover | 575 pages | € 46,00
ISBN: 978-3-944885-28-5
Norbu Verlag | www.norbu-verlag.de

Recommendation

Gendun Rinpoche

Heart Advice from a Mahamudra Master

This book contains the teachings of a Tibetan lama who spent three decades in meditation retreat in Tibet and India and then 22 years teaching Buddhism in Europe. It summarizes teachings that he considered vital for treading the Buddhist path to liberation, which he gave again and again to his Western students. His advice on Buddhist practice is simple and yet profound; it extends from the basics all the way up to the highest teaching of Mahamudra.

Softcover | 294 pages | € 16,00
ISBN: 978-3-940269-04-1
Get a copy on: www.norbu-verlag.de
Or order via e-mail: info@norbu-verlag.de

You can find further books and practice texts (mostly in German) on our website:

www.norbu-verlag.de

Norbu Verlag in der Ekayana gGmbH,
Raitenbucher Str. 17, 79853 Lenzkirch, Germany, info@norbu-verlag.de

Made in the USA
Monee, IL
12 November 2026

37e26798-a6ab-416f-a05b-ee26d1556471R01